Freedom and Entertainment

Rating the Movies in an Age of New Media

Here is a story that Jack Valenti has long tried to keep secret. *Freedom and Entertainment* is the first book to offer a behind-the-scenes account of the motion picture rating system and the Motion Picture Association of America under Valenti's leadership. The book is based on the private papers and oral history of Richard D. Heffner, who headed the Classification and Rating Administration for two decades, from 1974 to 1994, and was once called "the least-known most powerful person in Hollywood." The story chronicles the often tense working relationship between Heffner and Valenti and the sometimes bruising encounters Heffner had with Hollywood heavyweights such as Clint Eastwood, Oliver Stone, Michael Douglas, George C. Scott, Lew Wasserman, Arthur Krim, Jerry Weintraub, and many others.

Stephen Vaughn has taught the history of communication at the University of Wisconsin–Madison since 1981. He has been a past Vilas Associate Scholar at Wisconsin and is the recipient of two Fulbright awards. His previous books include *Ronald Reagan in Hollywood: Movies and Politics*, *The Vital Past: Writings on the Uses of History*, and *Holding Fast the Inner Lines: Democracy, Nationalism and the Committee on Public Information*.

Freedom and Entertainment

Rating the Movies in an Age of New Media

STEPHEN VAUGHN
University of Wisconsin

CAMBRIDGE
UNIVERSITY PRESS

CAMBRIDGE UNIVERSITY PRESS
Cambridge, New York, Melbourne, Madrid, Cape Town, Singapore, São Paulo

Cambridge University Press
40 West 20th Street, New York, NY 10011-4211, USA

www.cambridge.org
Information on this title: www.cambridge.org/9780521852586

First published 2006

Printed in the United States of America

A catalog record for this publication is available from the British Library.

Library of Congress Cataloging in Publication Data

Vaughn, Stephen, 1947–
Freedom and entertainment : rating the movies in an age of new
media / Stephen Vaughn.
  p. cm.
Includes bibliographical references and index.
ISBN 0-521-85258-7 (hardback) – ISBN 0-521-67654-1 (pbk.)
1. Motion pictures – Ratings – United States.   2. Sex in motion pictures.
3. Violence in motion pictures.   I. Title.
PN1993.5.U6V38   2006
384'.84–dc22   2005001236

ISBN-13   978-0-521-85258-6 hardback
ISBN-10   0-521-85258-7 hardback

ISBN-13   978-0-521-67654-0 paperback
ISBN-10   0-521-67654-1 paperback

In Memory of
Louise Mullen (1924–2004)
and for E. Eugene Mullen

Contents

Acknowledgments

In the course of writing this book, I have been helped and encouraged by many people, and I wish to thank them for their support. *Freedom and Entertainment* deals with the years since 1968, but in many respects the context for the book depends on research about the history of cinema and motion picture censorship that for me began more than two decades ago and that initially focused on the first half of the twentieth century. Some of that work culminated in a 1990 article appearing in the *Journal of American History* and subsequently in my book *Ronald Reagan in Hollywood: Movies and Politics* (1994), and there I have attempted to thank many people who contributed so generously to my understanding of movies and their place in American culture.

For several years, though, efforts to study the years after 1968 were frustrated by the lack of primary sources. Then, in 1999, I had the good fortune to meet Richard D. Heffner, who had recently retired from the Classification and Rating Administration that he had headed between 1974 and 1994. I am indebted to Professor Heffner, who on several occasions was willing to discuss his work with the rating system. More important, Heffner's oral history and related documents, which are now open to researchers at Columbia University, provided one of the most important sources for this book. In fact, without this collection, *Freedom and Entertainment* would not have been possible. All students of American cinema during the latter part of the twentieth century should find Heffner's papers of great value. I also wish to thank Mary Marshall Clark, director of the Columbia Oral History Collection in Butler Library, Columbia University, and her staff, for their help in using this collection.

I appreciate the insights of friends and colleagues who either read and commented on all or parts of this book, or who shared their knowledge about topics related to it. I am in the debt of several people who shared their knowledge about social science research on mass media. Joanne Cantor read the entire manuscript and made several suggestions for improvement. She was helpful in pointing to important research that has been done on media effects. Jack McLeod also read chapters that dealt with media effects and was helpful in explaining the political context of these studies and the strengths and weaknesses of different methodological approaches used by researchers. I profited from discussions with Robert Hawkins about catharsis theory and about such studies as the Surgeon General's Report of 1972 and the National Institute of Mental Health's report on *Television and Behavior* ten years later. Sharon Dunwoody read and commented on two chapters that dealt with media effects, and Doug McLeod was helpful in suggesting research that has been done on the significance of color in mass communication.

Friends and colleagues also shared their expertise on other topics. Paul Boyer, who read the entire work, drew on his vast knowledge of American intellectual life to make valuable suggestions about censorship, religion, and political culture. Bruce Evensen, at DePaul University, read most of the chapters and was helpful with context by sharing his great knowledge about film history and religion in the United States. Michele Hilmes read the entire manuscript and made many helpful recommendations, especially relating to broadcasting and regulation. I benefited from talking with Donald Downs and Robert Drechsel about the legal framework of censorship, and with James L. Baughman about television. Greg Downey and Jeremi Suri read sections that dealt with new media technologies and shared their knowledge on this subject. Along the way, Deborah Blum, Lewis Friedland, Jack Mitchell, and Hemant Shah made helpful comments. I wish to thank, too, Sharon Blum, Chin-I Wang, and Rob Rabe for their contributions to this work.

The impact of new communication technologies on cinema and American history is a central theme in this book. I am especially grateful to the staff of the University of Wisconsin Library Systems for their support helping to publish on-line my annotated bibliography *New Communication Technologies: Their History and Social Influence* (2003), which provides a context for *Freedom and Entertainment*. Director Kenneth Frazier was particularly helpful, as were Sue Dentinger, Donald Johnson, Nolan Pope, and Peter Gorman.

I wish to thank other archivists and librarians who have been helpful in my research. These people include: James Danky, Harry Miller, and Peter Gottlieb at the Wisconsin Historical Society; Maxine Fleckner-Ducey at the Wisconsin Center for Film and Theater Research; Angela N. Stockwell, secretary to Senator Margaret Chase Smith, at the Margaret Chase Smith Library in Skowhegan, Maine; Mary K. Knill, Archivist at the Lyndon Baines Johnson Library in Austin, Texas; Glenn Mason (director), Karen Deseve, and Laura Arksey at the Research Library and Archives, Cheney Cowles Museum, Eastern Washington State Historical Society in Spokane, Washington; Shawn C. Wilson, User Services Coordinator, Kinsey Institute Library and Archives at Indiana University, Bloomington; James D'Arc and Russ Taylor, Department of Archives and Manuscripts, Harold B. Lee Library, Brigham Young University in Provo, Utah; Kristen Wilhelm, Archivist at the National Archives and Records Administration I, Washington, D.C.; Mary Ronon, Fred Romanski, Steve Tilly, Elizabeth Lockwood, and David Painter at the National Archives and Records Administration II at College Park, Maryland; and Anne Coco at the Margaret Herrick Library, Beverly Hills, California.

My thanks go to the people at the University of Wisconsin who helped with the preparation of this manuscript. These include Lynn Schroeder, Nancy Massey, Janet Buechner, and Corinne Ahrens. The Graduate School at the University of Wisconsin–Madison helped move this work toward publication with a subvention grant to Cambridge University Press.

At Cambridge University Press, I benefited greatly from the assistance of several people. Senior Editor Lewis Bateman was a constant source of good advice. I am also indebted to Ciara McLaughlin, Helen Wheeler, and Barbara Folsom for their editorial assistance.

Finally, as always, I owe a special thank you to two people. Once more Robert Ferrell has been unfailing in his willingness to discuss this manuscript at almost every stage of its preparation. My wife, Beverly, has been my most demanding and supportive critic. She was also my best editor, taking time out from her work at the *Modern Language Journal* to edit carefully the entire manuscript. The wise counsel of these two people improved this work in many ways.

Abbreviations

AAAPSS	*Annals of the American Academy of Political and Social Science*
AAP	American Academy of Pediatrics
AC	*American Cinematographer*
AJOG	*American Journal of Obstetrics and Gynecology*
AMA	American Medical Association
APA	American Psychological Association
CARA	Classification and Rating Administration (originally Code and Rating Administration)
COHC-BL	Columbia Oral History Collection, Butler Library, Columbia University, New York
CST	*Chicago Sun-Times*
CT	*Chicago Tribune*
Final Report	United States Attorney General's Commission on Pornography, *Final Report of the Attorney General's Commission on Pornography* (Nashville, TN: Rutledge Hill Press, 1986)
IFIDA	International Film Importers and Distributors Association
IJCP	*International Journal of Criminology and Penology*
JAH	*Journal of American History*
JBEM	*Journal of Broadcasting and Electronic Media*
JMCQ	*Journalism and Mass Communication Quarterly*
KIA-IUB	Kinsey Institute Archives, Indiana University, Bloomington

LAT	*Los Angeles Times*
MCSP-NISM	Margaret Chase Smith Papers, Margaret Chase Smith Library, The Northwood Institute, Skowhegan, ME
Meese Commission Hearings, 1985–1986	*Hearings before the Attorney General's Commission on Pornography, 1985–1986,* Records of the Attorney General's Commission on Pornography, RG 60 (Justice Dept. Records), NARA 2, College Park, MD
MGM	Metro-Goldwyn-Mayer
MHL	Margaret Herrick Library, Beverly Hills, CA
Minneapolis Hearings, 1983	"Public Hearings on Ordinances to Add Pornography as Discrimination against Women," Session I, Minneapolis, MN, Dec. 12, 1983, Box 69, Records of the Attorney General's Commission on Pornography, RG 60 (Justice Dept. Records), NARA 2, College Park, MD
MPAA	Motion Picture Association of America (before 1945, MPPDA)
MPPDA	Motion Picture Producers and Distributors of America (after 1945, MPAA)
MPTRR-LC	Motion Picture and Television Reading Room, Library of Congress, Washington, DC
NARA 1	National Archives and Records Administration I, Washington, DC
NARA 2	National Archives and Records Administration II, College Park, MD
NATO	National Association of Theatre Owners
NATOR-BYU	Records of the National Association of Theatre Owners, Special Collections and Manuscripts, Harold B. Lee Library, Brigham Young University, Provo, UT
1970 Report	*Report of the Commission on Obscenity and Pornography* (Washington, DC: U.S. Government Printing Office, 1970) (also cited as *RCOP*)
NYT	*New York Times*
OHC-LBJ	Oral History Collection, Lyndon Baines Johnson Library, Austin, TX
OTA	Office of Technology Assessment

PCA	Production Code Administration
POQ	*Public Opinion Quarterly*
PT	*Poetics Today: International Journal for Theory and Analysis of Literature and Communication*
RAGCP-NARA 2	Records of Attorney General's Commission on Pornography, RG 60, National Archives 2, College Park, MD
RCOP	*Report of the Commission on Obscenity and Pornography* (Washington, DC: U.S. Government Printing Office, 1970)
RDH-COHC-BL	Richard D. Heffner Papers, Columbia Oral History Collection, Butler Library, Columbia University, New York
RDHPP	Private Papers of Richard D. Heffner, Heffner residence, New York
RKO	Radio-Keith-Orpheum
TRCOP	*Technical Report of the Commission on Obscenity and Pornography* (Washington, DC: U.S. Government Printing Office, 1970)
TRSGSACTSB	*A Technical Report to the Surgeon General's Scientific Advisory Committee on Television and Social Behavior*
TSBRP	*Television and Social Behavior: Reports and Papers*
UA	United Artists
USCC	United States Catholic Conference
U.S. House Hearings, 1977	"Movie Ratings and the Independent Producer," *Hearings before Subcommittee on Special Small Business Problems, Committee on Small Business,* U.S. House of Representatives, 95th Cong., 1st sess., March 24, April 14, May 12, June 15, July 21, 1977 (Washington, DC: Government Printing Office, 1977)
U.S. Senate Hearings [TV], 1954–1955	"Juvenile Delinquency (Television Programs)," *Hearings, Subcommittee to Investigate Juvenile Delinquency, Committee on the Judiciary,* U.S. Senate, 84th Cong., 1st sess., S. Res. 62 (Washington, DC: Government Printing Office, 1955)

U.S. Senate Hearings [Motion Pictures], 1955	"Juvenile Delinquency (Motion Pictures)," *Hearings, Subcommittee to Investigate Juvenile Delinquency, Committee on the Judiciary*, U.S. Senate, 84th Cong., 1st sess., S. Res. 62 (Washington, DC: Government Printing Office, 1955)
U.S. Senate Hearings, 1968	"The Committee on Film Classification," *Hearings before the Committee on Commerce*, U.S. Senate, S. Res. 9, June 11, 1968 (Washington, DC: Government Printing Office, 1968)
U.S. Senate Hearings, 1981–1982	"Copyright Infringements (Audio and Video Recorders)," *Hearings before the Committee on the Judiciary*, U.S. Senate, 97th Cong., 1st and 2nd sessions on S. 1758, Nov. 30, 1981 and April 21, 1982 (Washington, DC: Government Printing Office, 1982)
U.S. Senate Hearings, 1985	"Role of the Feature Film Industry in a National Effort to Diminish Drug Use among Young People," *Hearings before Permanent Subcommittee on Investigations, Committee on Governmental Affairs*, U.S. Senate, 99th Cong., 1st sess., Oct. 24, 1985 (Washington, DC: Government Printing Office, 1985)
U.S. Senate Hearings, 1997	"Television Ratings System," *Hearings before Committee on Commerce, Science, and Transportation*, U.S. Senate, 105th Cong., 1st sess., Feb. 27, 1997 (Washington, DC: Government Printing Office, 1997)
USSCCP-NARA 1	U.S. Senate Committee on Commerce Papers, S. 90A-E6, RG 46, National Archives I, Washington, DC
VCQ	*Visual Communication Quarterly*
WP	*Washington Post*
WSJ	*Wall Street Journal*

Introduction

During the 1960s a sea change occurred in the content of American movies and in the viewing public's tolerance for that new content. Preceding this transformation were the largely black-and-white films of the 1950s from which censors struggled to excise erotic imagery and amoral treatments of sexuality. The film industry's Production Code of 1930 still strongly influenced the tone of most movies. In the heyday of Will H. Hays and Joseph I. Breen, retribution against movie characters who violated the Code's morality was a staple of censorship. In the courts, obscenity cases involving films such as *Lady Chatterley's Lover*, banned by the New York censorship board in 1957, focused on portrayals of immorality but did not usually deal with nudity or profanity.

On the other side of the 1960s lay the more technically sophisticated films of the 1970s, which were often remarkably creative and entertaining and now showed graphically what once had only been suggested. Nudity, explicit sexual behavior, profane language, gratuitous violence, and themes of promiscuity, homosexuality, abortion, drug use, and other topics once forbidden by the Production Code as well as by state and local censors became commonplace. Punishment of movie characters who transgressed the Code's morality was no longer required. The nonmoralistic depictions of sexuality that moved prosecutors to action during the 1950s now rarely received a second look.

This book is about cinema and efforts to regulate it after 1968, a year that marks a sharp divide in the history of movie entertainment. In 1968, Hollywood adopted a new system that replaced the Production Code. A major goal of both the Production Code and the 1968 rating system was to prevent government censorship. But the two systems differed markedly. The 1930 Code attempted to bind motion pictures to Judeo-Christian morality and used prior censorship to obtain that end. Under this scheme, censors, who had a strongly conservative agenda, changed movie scripts long before they reached the production stage. The 1930 Code held motion pictures "directly responsible for spiritual and moral progress, for higher types of social life, and for much correct thinking." The agency that enforced this censorship, the Production Code Administration (PCA), prohibited treatment of certain topics or, if they were discussed, insisted that they were to be treated in a way that conformed with the Code. Filmmakers who chose to go outside the boundaries of the Code during the 1930s and 1940s were usually confronted by boycotts orchestrated by the Roman Catholic Legion of Decency and a legal system sympathetic to the prosecution of obscenity.[1]

Under the rating system created in 1968, filmmakers gained the freedom to show almost anything. The new plan abandoned prior censorship and claimed to make no effort to alter what adults (usually defined as those over seventeen) could see. Its goal was to give parents information to help them decide whether a movie was appropriate for their children by simply classifying films G through X. A G movie was suitable for all ages. Initially, an M indicated a film for "mature audiences." That symbol was changed to GP in 1972, and then to PG for "parental guidance" suggested. The R restricted admission for those under sixteen (later seventeen) unless accompanied by a parent or adult guardian. X signaled films that contained sex, violence, profanity, and other themes deemed inappropriate to anyone under sixteen (later seventeen). The X rating was the only label not copyrighted by the Motion Picture Association of America (MPAA) and the only one that could be self-applied by moviemakers. Over the years, Hollywood fine-tuned this scheme, adding such ratings as PG-13 in 1984 and NC-17 in 1990.[2] "The genius of the rating system," explained Richard D. Heffner, one of its long-time leaders, "is that nothing is approved or disapproved, just classified."[3]

If the Production Code represented a triumph for people who wanted cinema to be bound to morality, the voluntary system of self-regulation that Hollywood adopted in 1968 signaled a victory for the advocates of

---

[1] Quotation ("responsible"), from "Preamble," Motion Picture Production Code, 1930, reprinted in Vizzard, *See No Evil*, 366.

[2] Randall, "Classification by the Motion Picture Industry," *TRCOP*, 5: 223; and Cook, *Lost Illusions*, 70–71.

[3] Quotation ("genius"), Richard D. Heffner, Testimony, *U.S. House Hearings*, July 21, 1977, 202.

artistic freedom. Pressure to change content did not disappear, to be sure, but quarrels over alleged censorship were of a different order and usually of an economic nature. Disputes over what rating a movie should receive could be heated, but generally they were not about the filmmaker being denied the right to speak or show the truth as he or she saw it. Rather, the issue turned on how advertisers might react and on which rating would make the most money. An X-rated (or later NC-17) picture could generally be expected to play in many fewer theaters and to make less money than an R- or PG-rated film. The difference between an R and PG, or between a PG and a G could mean many millions of dollars at the box office.

Of course, much entertainment fell outside the scope of this rating system. In this work, I have used "cinema" in a broad sense to include not only mainstream films that come from Hollywood and elsewhere, but also many other varieties of moviemaking, both professional and amateur. During the 1970s, for example, a large number of pornographic films were made, most of which were never submitted to the rating administration. In addition, many types of out-of-the-mainstream productions – amateur, experimental, and avant-garde motion pictures – grew in number. These kinds of movies increased markedly with the arrival of new technologies during the 1950s and 1960s. Subsequently, as technology became more sophisticated, the volume of moving pictures that fell outside Hollywood's system of self-regulation grew exponentially. It is also difficult to separate cinema from other media. Earlier in the twentieth century, newspapers, fan magazines, and radio provided outlets for advertising and news about movie stars. By the 1950s, motion pictures began to appear with regularity on television, although not first-run features. By the 1970s and 1980s, as the use of cable, satellite TV, and video recorders grew, watching uncensored movies at home on television became more common than seeing them in theaters. With the widespread arrival of personal computers during the 1980s and the expansion of the Internet during the 1990s, the variety of moving images that people could watch expanded yet again.

Technology is central to this story. I have assumed in this book that communication technologies are keys to understanding historical change. Each innovation brings subtle, or often not so subtle, alterations in people's activities, their interactions, and the way in which they organize and perhaps even think. The innovations do not necessarily determine the course of history, but they multiply the possibilities for change. New communication technologies empower those who possess them and often threaten those who do not control them. Such has been the case with the technologies that have made motion pictures possible. This book argues that the breakdown of censorship provided under the Production Code resulted in no small measure from changes in the technology of communication, and that since 1968 new technologies have continued to frustrate efforts to regulate cinema and other forms of mass media.

Twice during the past century the arrival of new technologies helped to precipitate crises that forced Hollywood to adopt systems of self-regulation. The first of these crises was caused by the arrival of cinema itself and by such major innovations as the adoption of sound in motion pictures. The result was the Production Code of 1930, which lasted until the mid-1960s. The second crisis emerged from changes that occurred after World War II and culminated in the 1968 rating system.

Early in the twentieth century, critics found many things troubling about cinema. The movie theater rapidly became a popular and controversial institution in most American communities. It was thought to be an unhealthy place for youth – its wooden construction a fire hazard, its darkened recesses a magnet for prostitutes and nefarious activities, its location often in lower-class neighborhoods frequented by criminals and other unwholesome characters. There was also the advertising, first in garish color posters, then on billboards, in newspapers and fan magazines, and then on radio and television. From the critics' point of view, the ads all too often overemphasized sex and violence. Then there were the people who made the movies: the actors and producers. By World War I, if not before, actors such as Charlie Chaplin, Mary Pickford, and Roscoe "Fatty" Arbuckle had gained wide popularity and were better known in many circles, especially those frequented by young people, than were political leaders and some of the nation's most important historical figures. The fact that many of the actors and movie producers were Jewish lent criticism of cinema an anti-Semitic undertone. The rise of movie celebrities, it should be remembered, took place in cultures, both in the United States and elsewhere, that often harbored deep-seated prejudices against actors.[4]

Certainly the content of movies troubled censors. Throughout the twentieth century, moving pictures had been at the heart of America's so-called cultural wars. The technology of motion pictures made it possible to take controversial stories that dealt with sex, crime, authority, and much more – themes once confined to a reading public or to relatively few theatergoers in large cities – and project larger-than-life-sized images of these scenarios and the personalities who dramatized them onto large

[4] See Barish, *Antitheatrical Prejudice*.

screens in almost every locality. Cinema was a form of communication accessible to the literate and illiterate alike. It is difficult to find a controversial theme that moviemakers failed to exploit during the early years of cinema – nudity, adultery, divorce, incest, abortion, drug addiction, alcoholism, labor unrest, communism. Many of the controversies over content continued into the post-1968 era. Movie depictions of women, gender relationships, homosexuality, pornography, violence, substance abuse, religion, and history were among the topics that continued to spark intense debate.

By the 1920s, many cities and seven states had established censorship boards. Several other states considered similar legislation, as did the federal government. Hollywood responded to the threat of outside censorship by creating the Motion Pictures Producers and Distributors of America (MPPDA) in 1921 (renamed the Motion Picture Association of America, or MPAA, in 1945) and hired Will Hays, then the United States postmaster general in President Warren Harding's cabinet, to be its president. After several false starts, the Hays Office, as the MPPDA became known, adopted the Production Code in 1930 and then, four years later, created the PCA, with the Catholic layman Joseph Breen at its head, to provide and enforce prior censorship. The Roman Catholic Church also organized the Legion of Decency in 1934, and during the Great Depression the threat of boycotts by Catholics carried weight in Hollywood. Movie censorship was perhaps most effective during the 1930s, a time when the movie industry was vulnerable economically and the technology of cinema was costly and cumbersome. Most movies were filmed on studio sets; the equipment for recording sound alone weighed several tons.

The Code's power began to erode after World War II and ultimately collapsed. Historians offer several explanations for this development. The return of prosperity acted as a solvent to censorship. New leaders arrived in Hollywood. Eric A. Johnston, a former president of the United States Chamber of Commerce, replaced Hays as president of the MPAA in 1945. He wanted to use cinema to spread capitalism but was less interested in issues involving morality than Hays had been. Breen retired in 1954 and was replaced by Geoffrey Shurlock, who did not share his predecessor's commitment to the Code's morality. Even the Legion of Decency became more flexible. The American legal system also changed. In 1948, the U.S. Supreme Court required the large studios to sell their theater chains (*United States v. Paramount Pictures*). In *Joseph Burstyn, Inc. v. Wilson* in 1952, the Court finally gave motion pictures protection under the First Amendment. In *Roth v. United States* (1957), the Court made it much more difficult to prosecute obscenity. By the late 1960s, most of the legal barriers that had supported censors had fallen.[5]

Less appreciated among the reasons for the breakdown of Hollywood's system of self-imposed regulation was a revolution in communications that occurred between 1945 and 1968. By the late 1950s, television had become a strong competitor of motion pictures, but it was only one (admittedly a spectacular one) among many developments that changed the media environment in which cinema existed. Magnetic tape altered first audio and then video recording. More portable and affordable cameras gave many more people the opportunity to make movies. During the 1950s, use of 8-mm and 16-mm cameras became widespread. By the late 1960s, one person could film and record sound with equipment that weighed only about sixty-five pounds. Moviemakers moved away from studios and more often shot on location. The increasing use of color, improvements in the ability to duplicate images and other materials, and the arrival of offset printing, which made it possible for many more people to publish, were among the other innovations that helped to undermine the work of censors. By the mid-1960s, the Production Code operated in a world in which mass media were strikingly different from what they had been only thirty years earlier. Small wonder that the Code passed into history.[6]

The 1968 rating system emerged in the aftermath of the Code's demise and has survived into the twenty-first century. It became a model for classification systems adopted by television and such other entertainment industries as video games. Yet, since 1968, new waves of technological change have severely challenged this rating system – first in the form of a home entertainment revolution brought about by cable, satellites, and video recorders, and then by other changes that have included personal computers and the Internet. During the last two decades of the twentieth century, the spread of digital communication brought major transformations in

---

[5] These reasons are given for the decline of the Production Code in such histories of motion picture censorship as those by Black, *Catholic Crusade against the Movies, 1940–1975*; De Grazia and Newman, *Banned Films*; Jowett, *Film: The Democratic Art*; Leff and Simmons, *The Dame in the Kimono*; Miller, *Censored Hollywood*; Skinner, *The Cross and the Cinema*; Vaughn, *Ronald Reagan in Hollywood*; and Walsh, *Sin and Censorship*.

[6] I have examined these changes in greater detail in "Cinema, New Technologies and Censorship, 1945–1968," a paper presented to Society for the History of Technology Conference, Atlanta, Oct. 17, 2003; and in a companion volume to this book, "Morality and Entertainment: Cinema, Censorship, and Technology, 1907–1968" (unpublished ms). For additional context on new media and their possible influences, see Vaughn, ed., *New Communication Technologies: Their History and Social Influence: An Annotated Bibliography* (2003). This online work is at http://newcomm.library.wisc.edu.

many areas of life. Taken together, these changes called into question the relevance of a rating system created in a time when most people had to go to a theater to see a first-run, uncut motion picture. As we begin the twenty-first century, it is therefore again an appropriate time to rethink the system of self-regulation used by the entertainment industries.

In addition to the backgrounds of new technologies and cultural warfare, I have tried to place cinema into other contexts in this book. Behind the controversies about censorship and ratings there have usually been assumptions about the power of cinema and other mass media, such as television, to influence the way people think and act. These assumptions have been a common denominator in reactions to cinema and related media from their inceptions. Early in the century, many American critics feared that movies could undermine morality and even civilization itself.[7] European critics commonly assumed that Hollywood films could dissolve age-old traditions. The Soviet dictator Joseph Stalin is reputed to have said, "If I could control the medium of the American motion picture, I would need nothing else in order to convert the entire world to Communism."[8] That grandiose assumption was shared by an American actor who one day would become president of the United States. Hollywood was nothing less than "a grand worldwide propaganda base," said Ronald Reagan in 1965, speaking about the movie industry's role in the Cold War. Whoever controlled it had access to "a weekly audience of about 500,000,000 souls."[9] Pope John Paul II made a similar assumption about cinema's power in 1987 when he told entertainment executives in Los Angeles that "Humanity is profoundly influenced by what you do." Indeed, "your smallest decisions can have global impact," he said. The "world is at your mercy."[10] Or, consider this reflection in 1992 about the impact of cinema on our understanding of history and current events from Richard Heffner, who for two decades headed the movie ratings administration. It mattered little if the storyteller was truthful or irresponsible, Heffner wrote after watching Oliver Stone's depiction of the

---

[7] I have written about these critics in Vaughn, "Morality and Entertainment: The Origins of the Motion Picture Production Code," 39–65; and in "Morality and Entertainment: Cinema, Censorship and New Technology, 1907–1968" (unpublished ms).

[8] Joseph Stalin quoted ("control") in Smith, *Shadow in the Cave,* 187. See also Trumpbour, *Selling Hollywood to the World,* 18.

[9] Quotations ("grand," "souls"), Reagan, *Where's the Rest of Me?* 162.

[10] Quotations ("Humanity," "mercy"), from transcript of Pope John Paul II's address to communication industry executives, Los Angeles, Sept. 15, 1987, in *NYT,* Sept. 16, 1987, A24.

assassination of John F. Kennedy in *JFK* (1991). This new kind of history threatened "a media way of life in which first print and then its linear off-shoots, like television news, presented the world and interpreted it for us without peer or challenge." Using "surround-sound and big-screen visuals, and particularly through 'faction' (their deplorable mix of fact and fiction), . . . celluloid/video Pied Pipers will become our nation's leading storytellers," Heffner predicted. "They will set our national agenda, interpret our national past, determine our national future. . . ."[11]

Although there has been no shortage of assertions about the influence of cinema and related media, since 1968 a rapidly growing body of research on media effects has sprung up that has tried to move beyond mere speculation and draw conclusions based on credible evidence. I have tried to situate cinema in the context of this research. Social science research has been especially interested in examining the possible effects of explicit sexuality and violence in the mass media, and this book attempts to introduce the reader to the main currents of this work. Moreover, historians and others during the past two decades have done much to explain how motion pictures and television programs have interpreted history, religion, and the First Amendment. I have also drawn on that literature.

How the public regards this research has been influenced in no small way by the "unseen power" of public relations and advertising. Indeed, public relations and advertising have had an underappreciated yet influential impact on many controversies involving cinema and television. During the twentieth century, the entertainment industries created powerful publicity networks that extended into virtually every community and enlisted a wide array of media. It is significant that the three men who led Hollywood throughout most of the twentieth century – Will Hays (1921–45), Eric Johnston (1945–63), and Jack Valenti (1966–2004) – were all grounded in the worlds of business, public relations, advertising, and politics.[12]

Hays did much to set the movie industry's publicity juggernaut in motion. The MPPDA was created in the wake of the "Fatty" Arbuckle scandal in September 1921, when a young actress died in the actor's San Francisco hotel room after a weekend of drinking bootleg liquor. As MPPDA president, Hays was nothing if not a public relations man who

---

[11] Quotations ("media," "future"), Heffner, "Last Gasp of the Gutenbergs," *LAT,* Feb. 19, 1992, B11.

[12] Quotation ("unseen"), taken from Cutlip, *The Unseen Power.* In September 2004, Dan Glickman, a former Democratic congressman from Kansas and Secretary of Agriculture under President William J. Clinton, succeeded Valenti as president of the Motion Picture Association of America.

led a PR offensive designed to put the best face possible on Hollywood. He promoted the positive qualities of cinema and enlisted journalists, clergy, parents, teachers, and other opinion makers in local communities to endorse good movies. He claimed that by the time he retired from the MPPDA in 1945, there was a network of 600 thousand volunteers promoting movies. As much as anyone, Hays brought motion pictures into mainstream respectability.

Hays learned how to use publicity to discredit criticism aimed at Hollywood, even when it came from such credible sources as university scholars. Ever since the appearance of the Payne Fund Studies in 1933, the entertainment industry has contended that research – especially social science research – is inadequate to the task of evaluating what impact movies and other forms of mass entertainment may have. The Payne Fund Studies were the first and most thorough examination of the influence of motion pictures on American youth, and they argued that cinema had a major, and sometimes negative, influence on society. Part of Hays's counterattack strategy was to publicize the views of experts who held contrary opinions. Some experts, such as the philosopher Mortimer Adler, whose book *Art and Prudence* (1937) indicted the social science research used in the Payne Fund Studies, found their way onto Hays's payroll. Since Hays's time, the injection of entertainment industry money and publicity into questions related to research about cinema (and later television) has made it difficult for journalists and the public to gain a disinterested perspective on the possible effects of modern mass media and entertainment on society.

Hays's successors, Johnston and Valenti, also became adept at using public relations and advertising. Johnston continued to build and refine Hollywood's publicity machinery in an increasingly sophisticated media environment. By the 1960s, much had changed. Although some critics continued to denounce "passion pits," otherwise known as drive-in theaters, and "art" houses, Johnston could argue before his death in 1963 that the motion picture theater had become an institution as important to communities as the supermarket, public library, or post office. The entertainment industries devoted unprecedented amounts of money to advertising. Small wonder that, while prejudice still lingered against actors in some quarters, by the time Valenti arrived on the scene in 1966, movie stars had long since become icons for most Americans, and a strong relationship had developed between the corridors of power in Washington, D.C., and Hollywood.

I have long been a motion picture enthusiast and remain so. I have, though, devoted a good deal of attention in this study to critics of cinema. Part of the reason for this emphasis is that the critics have often been vocal in attempting to define cinema's place in our culture and help to throw into relief the ways in which cinema has seemed to threaten the values and power structures of society. Moreover, the critics have sometimes had insightful things to say, and they frequently have left behind a large historical record. It is the availability of that historical record, the primary sources vital to the work of historians, which has also helped to define this book. To a significant degree, *Freedom and Entertainment* examines controversies involving motion pictures through the correspondence and recollections of the man who headed the Classification and Rating Administration from 1974 to 1994. To date, Richard Heffner's papers and oral history at Columbia University remain the only major archival source available for scholars wishing to study the behind-the-scenes operation of the rating system and the workings of the Motion Picture Association of America under the leadership of Jack Valenti. (It is unfortunate that a far richer archival record exists for the first half of the twentieth century than for the last fifty years.) I found Heffner an interesting person. He began as a historian, worked in public television, and initially believed in TV as a forum for democracy. He was a Jeffersonian liberal with a strong faith in reason and the marketplace of free ideas, as the name of his long-running television program, "The Open Mind," suggests. Yet Heffner came to feel that these worthwhile values were too little respected in the world of moviemaking. He was also often at odds with Valenti, and his papers reflect that tension. If the view of Valenti found in Heffner's records is skewed, then one of the best correctives would be for the MPAA to open its historical files for scholars to study.

The historical perspective gained from the study of such documents is especially important because cinema and other new media confront citizens with a dilemma. These technologies have brought forth radically new ideas and ways of communicating during the past century and have given voice to many new people. As we look to the future, we see that the trend is toward accelerating innovation. On the whole, there have been and will be many advantages to these developments. Yet they are not without a price. A growing body of research suggests that some of the material conveyed by these new media – extreme violence and explicit sexuality – may under certain conditions have harmful effects on some people.

No easy or perfect solutions exist. A rating system based on voluntarism and true concern for the public well-being can continue to be valuable. Unfortunately, in the present movie and TV systems, self-interest too often dominates; producers of entertainment have the upper hand. Would it be desirable to return to the principles of the old Production Code? Would such a code even be possible in the twenty-first century? It is doubtful. The prior censorship practiced under the Production Code would be virtually impossible today if for no other reason than that the technology of making and distributing movies is vastly different from what existed during the 1930s and 1940s. Moreover, this kind of censorship lacks broad public support. Would government agencies be more effective as censors? Certainly throughout the twentieth century the threat of government intervention (often coupled with economic boycotts) was one of the most effective means of convincing entertainment makers to police themselves. It was a powerful factor in the adoption of both the 1930 Code and the 1968 rating system and in the creation of a television classification scheme in 1997. Government censorship is not impossible to establish, but it is highly undesirable. Given the partisan, intolerant nature of politics, it would surely cripple the free flow of ideas that has made possible one of the most creative societies in history. Disturbing, too, is the double-edged nature of modern technology. Though new technologies have expanded creativity in cinema and elsewhere, they have also made possible surveillance that is unprecedented in its invasiveness. Powerful pressures already exist to make these technologies even more sophisticated and pervasive. Such developments have great potential for undermining fundamental American freedoms. Wisdom dictates that government intervention should be avoided except in only the most limited areas (e.g., child pornography).[13]

Perhaps at no time in our history has there been a greater need for educating our citizenry about the issues involving cinema and other new communication technologies – what might be called "media literacy." This notion may seem a slender thread on which to depend, but if we value freedom, it offers one of our best hopes for meeting the challenges posed by a media environment that continues to change rapidly. The person "of knowledge increaseth [in] strength," it has been said, and "a wise man is strong."[14]

---

[13] There is a growing literature on surveillance technologies and privacy. Recent works include Norris and Armstrong, *Maximum Surveillance Society,* and Rosen, *The Unwanted Gaze.*

[14] Quotation ("increaseth"), Proverbs, 24:5.

I

New Leaders and a New System

When the Motion Picture Association of America revised the Production Code for the final time in 1966, it also adopted a "Suggested for Mature Audiences" (SMA) label that it applied to Warner Bros.'s movie *Who's Afraid of Virginia Woolf?* and to such other films as Ely Landau's *The Pawnbroker* (1965) and Paramount's *Alfie* (1966) as a way of exempting them from the Code. The classification came with the caveat that no one under eighteen could be admitted without a parent or guardian. The press scoffed at this hypocrisy. "Everything expressly prohibited in the Production Code apparently is to be approved, one way or another," said a writer for the *Motion Picture Herald*.[1]

After the SMA, the number of violent and sexually provocative films, such as Arthur Penn's *Bonnie and Clyde* (1967), Robert Aldrich's *The Dirty Dozen* (1967), and Mike Nichols's *The Graduate* (1967) increased, a trend that the industry's own data in 1967 and 1968 substantiated.[2] At the same time, the level of real violence in American society escalated. While some people argued that the movies only mirrored the problems of society, other critics held cinema partially responsible for those problems, and the public's desire to have the government do something about violence and permissiveness in entertainment gathered momentum. As

---

[1] *Motion Picture Herald,* quoted ("expressly") in Leff and Simmons, *The Dame in the Kimono,* 265; see also 264.

[2] For example, the Advertising Code Office reported a rise in material it rejected. See Randall, "Classification by the Motion Picture Industry," 222. See also Vizzard, *See No Evil,* 335; "Revised Code-Approved Pix up First 6 Months of 68," *Variety,* July 2, 1968; "'Mature' Films % Jump in 1968," *Hollywood Reporter,* July 2, 1968; and MPAA, *Year in Review* (June 1968), 1.

Senator Margaret Chase Smith (R-ME) pushed for a movie classification system at the national level and federal agencies started to investigate the connection between violence and mass media, local communities also began to take action. In Dallas, a film classification board, the first of its kind in the United States, attempted to use viewer age as the criterion for rating the appropriateness of films. Even though the movie industry successfully challenged this plan before the United States Supreme Court in *Interstate Circuit, Inc., v. Dallas* (1968), the Court did not declare classification invalid, and many people believed the case encouraged other cities to create their own classification boards. Indeed, MPAA president Jack Valenti thought that as many as forty local regulatory boards were ready to move into action by 1968.[3]

The debate over classification – labeling films according to their appropriateness for children – divided the movie industry during the 1960s. Like Eric Johnston, Valenti opposed classification, at least initially. Having noticed that theater owners in Europe would often refuse to book films for the weekend if they were rated for adults only by European boards, Valenti and most leaders of the major studios resisted any plan that would limit movie attendance. If the European pattern were followed in America, it would be difficult for adult-only films to turn a profit. Valenti, who preferred no restrictions on film entertainment, argued that classification amounted to censorship, could lead to government involvement, and would usurp parental authority. Moreover, a classification system was already available to the public, he contended, referring to the little-known publication entitled *The Green Sheet*, issued by the movie industry since 1933, which went to schools, churches, libraries, exhibitors, and newspapers, and provided age-appropriate ratings for films. As state legislatures considered passing legislation to require the classification of films, the MPAA increased circulation of *The Green Sheet*, doubling circulation in 1964 to 60,000. Between 1964 and 1966, *The Green Sheet* rated 600 films.[4]

Few people wanted government regulation of the entertainment industry. There were powerful advocates for voluntary classification. Major religious, educational, and civic organizations – the Catholic Legion of Decency (after November 1965, called the National Catholic Office of

---

[3] See Arar, "Movie-Ratings Boss Says System Works," *Cleveland Plain Dealer*, Nov. 25, 1993, L3. See also *Interstate Circuit, Inc., v. Dallas*, 390 U.S. 676 (1968); and Randall, "Classification by the Motion Picture Industry," 222.

[4] See Schumach, *Face on the Cutting Room Floor*, 260; and Randall, *Censorship of the Movies*, 181–83.

Motion Pictures, or NCOMP), the Protestant Broadcasting and Film Commission of the National Council of Churches, the American Jewish Committee, the American Library Association, the General Federation of Women's Clubs – favored a system self-imposed by the industry. They argued that it would aid parents, guarantee higher-quality films, and head off government regulation.[5]

Widespread support for classification existed within the movie business. The Production Code Administration's Geoffrey Shurlock called for federal licensing of theaters in order to enforce the industry's "adults only" rating, and such outspoken actors as Gregory Peck urged a system modeled on the British system that still regularly censored pictures. Theater chains and local exhibitors began putting their own ratings on movies. After the *Dallas* decision, theater owners in Florida went so far as to ask the state legislature to provide guidelines.[6]

Valenti feared that even if state and local censorship did not destroy the national distribution system, it would at the very least damage it. Being a political realist, he recognized that classification might be the best hope for avoiding government regulation. Members of the National Association of Theatre Owners (NATO), the country's largest exhibitor organization, also saw a ratings system as a way to prevent this kind of interference. After consulting with the MPAA's production companies and with NATO president Julian Rifkin, Valenti proposed a rating system in May 1968, and on November 1 the industry adopted it, thus making the United States one of the last major Western nations to embrace a plan for classifying films. Unlike classification in most other countries, however, the American plan was controlled completely by the film industry.[7]

The essence of the new system was "voluntarism," according to Valenti, who defined this term as follows: "a voluntary willingness by film creators and managers to temper freedom with responsibility, a voluntary willingness by the public to be discerning movie-goers and by parents to know what's playing in the theaters in order to guide the attendance of their children."[8] The system depended on "self-restraint" and

[5] Schumach, *Face on the Cutting Room Floor*, 256–7.

[6] Randall, "Classification by the Motion Picture Industry," 222.

[7] Ibid. See also Schumach, *Face on the Cutting Room Floor*, 275–8; and "Directors Approve Voluntary Classification at Scottsdale Meeting," *National Association of Theatre Owners, Inc., Newsletter* 3 (June 1968): 1–2, copy in Folder 8, Box 1, Mss 1446, NATOR-BYU.

[8] Valenti quoted ("voluntarism," "children") in "Motion Pictures Association of America: 1968 – A Year of New Developments," *1969 Film Daily Year Book of Motion Pictures*, 617.

"self-discipline," and it would not tolerate "license," according to the MPAA. Its core values were "freedom of choice," the right of the creative person "to achieve artistic excellence," and a recognition of the "importance of the role of the parent as the guide of the family's conduct."[9]

Although Valenti had initially opposed classification, he now took credit for the rating system's creation and called labeling movies G through X a "revolutionary plan" that would be the "redemption of our public responsibility." Once he accepted the need for voluntary classification, he became its impassioned champion. Its first goal, he said, was "to free the film maker, to loosen the artistic fetters around his creative ankles."[10] Valenti described the system as "a fragile enterprise," but it proved durable and lasted (at this writing) more than thirty-six years – a length of time comparable to the life of the Production Code. The ratings, according to Valenti, were aimed at only one segment of the population – parents. "If you don't have children this rating system has no meaning for you," he told a Senate investigating committee in 1985.[11]

Valenti and Richard Heffner became the two people most closely identified with the rating system during the first quarter-century of its existence. The tensions that developed between the two men reveal a good deal about how the ratings operated and what the system's shortcomings were. Publicly, Valenti's name became synonymous with the ratings. He wanted it that way. He was essentially a lobbyist who worked hardest to defend the interests of the large movie and television companies that made up the MPAA. He was skilled at political maneuvering and understood the power of personality – both his own and that of others – and also knew how to marshal the vast publicity potential of mass media. The ratings, though, were done by a board separate from the MPAA. The man who chaired that board for two decades, and who was once called the "least-known most powerful person in Hollywood," was Richard Heffner, who became head of the ratings administration in 1974.[12] Heffner entered Hollywood by way of the university and public television. Describing himself

---

[9] Quotations ("self-restraint," "conduct"), "The Motion Picture Code and Rating Program: A System of Self-Regulation," in ibid., 626.

[10] Quotations ("revolutionary," "responsibility"), Jack Valenti, Statement, *U.S. Senate Hearings*, Oct. 24, 1985, 91. Valenti quoted ("free") in *WP*, Oct. 5, 1968, 29, clipping [W.P.], in MCSP-NISM.

[11] Quotations ("fragile," "meaning"), Jack Valenti, Testimony, *U.S. Senate Hearings*, Oct. 24, 1985, 67.

[12] Unnamed source quoted ("least-known") in S. Mitchell, "The X Rating Gets Its Day in Court," *LAT*, June 21, 1990, F1.

as a Jeffersonian liberal, he believed in freedom of expression and considered the ratings system to be the best method of maximizing creativity in
movies. But he also had a strong sense of the limits of freedom and believed
that if the entertainment industry carried freedom of expression too far,
an outraged public might call for the reimposition of harsh censorship.

JACK VALENTI

Like his predecessors, Will H. Hays and Eric A. Johnston, Valenti came
from the worlds of business and politics. In Houston he had run an advertising and public relations firm. He had been well connected politically,
becoming part of Lyndon B. Johnson's inner circle and serving as the
president's special assistant between 1963 and 1966.

The grandson of Sicilian immigrants, Valenti had grown up in the Bible
Belt of southeastern Texas. His father clerked in the county tax office in
Houston. As a youth, Valenti earned $11 a week as an usher in a theater
that catered to Mexican Americans. His pay rose to $75 a month when
he became an office boy for the Humble Oil and Refining Company.
The company soon transferred him to the advertising department and
he enrolled in night school at the University of Houston. During World
War II, he flew more than fifty low-level bombing missions in a B-25 over
southern Germany and Italy.[13]

After the war, Valenti was a man on the way up. He received a master's
degree from the Harvard Business School in 1948 and returned to Humble
Oil to head advertising and promotion. In 1952, he joined with a former
University of Houston classmate, Weldon Weekley, to form Weekley and
Valenti, an advertising firm that had among its wealthy and powerful clien-
tele Continental Oil Company and several political candidates. Valenti
did not possess "resolute and fierce ideologies," and "was attracted to
men rather than . . . issues."[14] He campaigned for Dwight Eisenhower in
1952 and later conducted the advertising for Texas Democratic Congressman Albert Thomas. By 1956, he was Houston's Outstanding Man of the
Year. The following year, when Johnson, then the Senate majority leader,
came to Houston, Valenti was invited to meet him. Johnson's "animal
magnetism" captured him immediately. The encounter "lay somewhere

---

[13] Valenti won the Distinguished Flying Cross and an Air Medal with four clusters. Roberts,
LBJ's Inner Circle, 84–85; Canby, "Czar of the Movie Business," *NYT Magazine*, April
23, 1967, 47; and Valenti, Testimony, *U.S. Senate Hearings*, Oct. 24, 1985, 72.

[14] Quotations ("resolute," "attracted"), *Oral History Interview with Jack Valenti: I*,
June 14, 1969, 2–3, OHC-LBJ.

between the fascination of watching a great athlete in motion and the half-fear, half-admiration of seeing a panther on a cliffside, silken, silent, ready to spring," Valenti recalled. "From that day forward I was a Lyndon Johnson man." He called Johnson the "Great Persuader" in the weekly column he wrote for the *Houston Post*. He sought to gain the Democratic presidential nomination for Johnson in 1960, although he had little contact with the majority leader. "I literally was on the darker edges of the last ring of the peripheral circle," he recalled. But when Johnson became the vice presidential nominee, he asked Valenti to handle the ticket's campaign advertising in Texas. The Democrats carried the state by slightly more than 46,000 votes. A much closer relationship with Johnson began to develop during the fall of 1961, after Valenti started dating the vice president's secretary, Mary Margaret Wiley, whom he married the following June.[15] Valenti was in the fateful motorcade in Dallas on November 22, 1963, and after John F. Kennedy's assassination was with Johnson as he took the presidential oath of office on the plane back to Washington. For several weeks after the assassination, Valenti lived in the White House and was Johnson's constant companion, speech editor, letter writer, troubleshooter, and appointments secretary. He was, *Time* magazine said, "the little man who's always there."[16]

Swarthy and handsome, gregarious and smartly dressed, the five-foot, seven-inch Valenti moved crisply through corridors, with an easy smile and a natural bent for self-dramatization. "With his sharp suits, ingratiating manner and river boat gambler's drawl," wrote one observer, Valenti could easily be "mistaken by many for a glib, opportunistic Texas 'operator'" who inspired little confidence among Great Society liberals. Vincent Canby commented that there remained "about Valenti-in-action a good deal of the Houston huckster, tempered by the Valenti-the-small-town-boy-who-made-good-and-enjoys-every-minute-of-it."[17] To some, he bore a remarkable physical likeness to Alabama governor George Wallace; to others he "looked rather like an aging cheerleader" who had a habit of "turning his glowing dark eyes this way and that like luminous lamps."

[15] Quotation ("literally"), ibid., 4; see also 21–25. Quotations ("animal," "man"), Valenti, *A Very Human President*, 15; see also ibid., 16–17, 21. Valenti quoted ("Great Persuader") in Roberts, *LBJ's Inner Circle*, 85.

[16] Quotation ("little"), "The Little Man Who's Always There," *Time* 83 (April 3, 1964), 25. For Valenti's early months in the White House, see *Oral History Interview of Jack Valenti: II*, Oct. 18, 1969, OHC-LBJ.

[17] Quotations ("sharp," "operator"), Roberts, *LBJ's Inner Circle*, 86. Quotation ("Valenti-in-action"), Canby, "Czar of the Movie Business," 49.

FIGURE 1. President Lyndon B. Johnson reviewing draft of speech, with Jack Valenti, others in background.

He liked to quote Shakespeare, Voltaire, and Francis Bacon, but even those closest to him found his passion for purple prose cloying.[18] His speech before the Advertising Federation of America in 1965 in which he said that he slept better each night, "a little more confidently, because Lyndon Johnson is my President," drew snickers worldwide and gained him a reputation as a sycophant.[19]

Detractors called Valenti a "born hero-worshiper," and said that his influence with Johnson depended on his unqualified devotion to the president, who at six feet, four inches towered over him (Fig. 1). Reporters who covered the White House were not quite sure what to make of Valenti. In the eyes of many, he seemed to reside somewhere between being a "glorified valet" and the president's chief-of-staff. Some considered him

[18] Quotation ("cheerleader"), Anderson, *President's Men*, 316. Quotation ("lamps"), Vizzard, *See No Evil*, 319; see also 329; Valenti, "Voltaire's Timeless Eminence," *Saturday Review* 50 (March 11, 1967), 27, 138–9; Valenti, "Francis Bacon – The Glory and the Shame," ibid., 51 (Feb. 17, 1968), 22–23; and Roberts, *LBJ's Inner Circle*, 87.

[19] Quotation ("confidently"), "Of Extra Glands, Giant Agony and the Grey Stone Mountain," *Time* 86 (July 9, 1965), 20. Valenti modeled this speech after Winston Churchill's address to the French people after the fall of France in 1940. The prose was "a little bit overblown," he later said. But "that's the way I speak." Quotation ("overblown"), *Oral History Interview of Jack Valenti: V*, July 12, 1972, 22, OHC-LBJ; see also ibid., 20–23.

a "whipping boy," the first to feel the president's legendary wrath. It was, a former White House aide remembered, "painful to watch."[20] Johnson once made Valenti the butt of a joke by calling him "a valuable hunk of humanity. He can do anything for you and do it fast."[21]

Others who saw Valenti in action made a different assessment. Historian Eric Goldman, who worked in the Johnson White House, said that much of Valenti's time "went to important tasks, which he executed with a shrewdly underplayed savvy." Speech writer Harry McPherson said that Valenti was a "tremendously active member" of the President's staff, and a "hell of a lot more important" than detractors realized. Edwin Weisl, Jr. considered him "broad-minded" and one of the few people in the White House who had the courage to tell Johnson about possible mistakes. He recalled Valenti once quoting the historian Macaulay to the president to warn him against close advisers who would isolate him from the truth. The experience Valenti gained in the White House and the contacts he made while there played no small part in his being selected to head the MPAA.[22]

While working in the Johnson administration, Valenti came to know Lew Wasserman, perhaps the most powerful man in Hollywood. "The name 'Lew R. Wasserman' on a movie marquee would mean nothing to moviegoers," Murray Schumach wrote in the *New York Times* in 1962. "But in Hollywood – and in the nation's entertainment industry – he is regarded with a mixture of admiration, fear and animosity that suggests Richelieu during the reign of King Louis XIII." As Valenti put it in 1995, "What you have to understand is if Hollywood is Mount Olympus, Lew Wasserman is Zeus."[23]

---

[20] Quotation ("born"), Anderson, "Born Hero-Worshiper Who Serves His Hero," *NYT Magazine*, Feb. 20, 1966, 28; see also 29. Quotation ("valet"), Dallek, *Flawed Giant*, 68. Quotation ("whipping"), "Presidency: Revolving Door at 1600," *Newsweek*, May 9, 1966, 26. James Jones quoted ("painful") in Bruck, "The Personal Touch," *The New Yorker*, Aug. 13, 2001, 46.

[21] Quotation ("hunk"), Wicker, "Johnson's Men: 'Valuable Hunks of Humanity,'" *NYT Magazine*, May 3, 1964, 11.

[22] Quotation ("savvy"), Goldman, *Tragedy of Lyndon Johnson*, 116. Quotations ("active," "important"), see *Oral History Interview of Harry McPherson: II*, Dec. 19, 1968, 25, OHC-LBJ (Online: http://www.lbjlib.utexas.edu/johnson/archives.hom/ oralhistory.hom/) See also *Oral History Interview of Edwin L. Weisl, Jr.: II*, May 23, 1969, 19, OHC-LBJ. See also the positive assessment of Valenti by his assistant in the White House: *Oral History Interview of Charles M. Maguire*, July 8, July 29, and Aug. 19, 1969, OHC-LBJ.

[23] Murray Schumach quoted ("name," "Louis XIII") in McDougal, *The Last Mogul*, 295. Valenti quoted ("Zeus") in Kandell, "Lew Wasserman, 89, Is Dead, Last of the Hollywood Moguls," *NYT*, June 4, 2002, A19.

Wasserman, who came from a Cleveland, Ohio, family of Orthodox Jews, had started, like Valenti, as a theater usher. Although he never attended college, his intelligence and ambition so impressed Jules C. Stein, the founder of the talent agency Music Corporation of America (MCA), that Stein hired the twenty-three-year-old in late 1936. Wasserman rose rapidly to become president of MCA and soon turned the firm into the most influential agency in Hollywood. Wasserman's clients included some of the industry's biggest stars, including the future president of the United States, Ronald Reagan. Wasserman inspired both fear and loyalty. He kept a low profile but was an intimidating presence with a legendary temper and a reputation for both creativity and ruthlessness. Studio executives were reported to have vomited or collapsed in the middle of one of his tantrums. He played "his cards close to the vest," rarely wrote memos, and preferred to operate over the phone lest he be sued and his files subpoenaed. He was a "lean, taciturn man," Valenti observed, who "had that quickness of thought and that curious anticipatory instinct that is the baggage of the great political and industrial captains. He spoke quietly and seldom, but when he did speak, everyone in the movie world listened." His word was his bond, and this trait earned him respect as a negotiator.[24]

During the early 1960s, Wasserman became a motion picture producer and turned toward more active involvement with politics. It has been said that perhaps more than any other person in modern-day Hollywood, he created the expectation that motion picture executives would cultivate politicians and then exploit those friendships for their own ends. Although a registered Democrat, Wasserman supported Eisenhower in 1952, but he returned to the party in 1960 to back Kennedy. In 1962, he moved from the talent business into production when MCA acquired Decca Records, Inc., the parent company of Universal Pictures. The Kennedy Justice Department, citing antitrust abuses, forced MCA to divest itself of its talent agency. Although this turn of events was a blow to Wasserman, it made him realize the need for political allies. As a producer, he became a more visible and active fund-raiser intent on forging alliances with powerful politicians. Despite his differences with the Justice Department, Wasserman worked to raise money for President Kennedy and by 1963 had shown that he knew how to tap large sums in Southern California. With

[24] Valenti quoted ("cards") in Brownstein, *The Power and the Glitter,* 222. Quotations ("lean," "listened"), Valenti, *A Very Human President,* 254. See also Kandell, "Lew Wasserman, 89, Is Dead," A1, A19; McDougal, *Last Mogul,* 378.

regard to politics, he helped to steer Hollywood into a new period of activism.[25]

Another person important in helping to make Hollywood politically influential was Arthur Krim. Krim, who shared Wasserman's Jewish background and his shrewdness, came from more privileged surroundings. His father had owned a successful chain of cafeterias. Krim graduated Phi Beta Kappa from Columbia College and was at the head of his class at Columbia Law School. In 1932, he joined the New York law firm of the well-known trial attorney Louis Nizer (Nizer later became the MPAA's general counsel), which would also include Robert S. Benjamin. During the early 1950s, Krim and Benjamin acquired United Artists and turned the struggling studio into a profitable, innovative enterprise. Both Krim and Benjamin were Franklin D. Roosevelt liberals who backed Adlai Stevenson in 1956. After Kennedy's election in 1960, Krim became an enthusiastic fund-raiser for the president, arranging the 1962 birthday celebration in Madison Square Garden where Marilyn Monroe sang. Krim helped to set up the President Club which bypassed local Democratic organizations and raised money directly for the Kennedy campaign.[26]

After Kennedy's death, Wasserman and Krim became important figures in the Johnson administration. They were extraordinary fund-raisers – Wasserman even personally contributed $28,000 to the president's campaign in 1964. But they also assumed other roles. Immediately after the election, Valenti recommended Wasserman for a cabinet post. Johnson (so Valenti maintained) offered to make Wasserman secretary of commerce, but Wasserman declined. Valenti continued to cultivate Wasserman, who supplied the White House with political intelligence as he represented the movie industry's interests to the administration. The two men corresponded often, and Wasserman offered Valenti the use of his Palm Springs home in July and again in November 1964. Krim became even more closely involved with the president. He was Johnson's close friend and adviser on domestic politics and foreign policy. The president trusted Krim's judgment perhaps more than anyone else's during the latter half of his term, Valenti believed (Fig. 2).[27]

---

[25] See Brownstein, *Power and the Glitter,* 180; see also 179–88, 192–3, 197; and McDougal, *Last Mogul,* 299–302.

[26] See Brownstein, *Power and the Glitter,* 188–92.

[27] Valenti had recommended Wasserman to become secretary of health, education, and welfare. Valenti, *A Very Human President,* 212–13; see also ibid., 367–8n; Brownstein, *Power and the Glitter,* 195, 198–200; and McDougal, *Last Mogul,* 319–20. Although Valenti said that Johnson offered Wasserman a cabinet position, others close

FIGURE 2. *Left to right:* Lynda Bird Johnson, Arthur Krim, Mathilde Krim, Lew Wasserman, President Lyndon B. Johnson, Edie Wasserman.

Valenti considered Wasserman and Krim the most influential men in Hollywood, so when they sought to convince him to become president of the MPAA and the Association of Motion Picture and Television Producers, he listened. Since Eric Johnston's death in 1963, the presidency of the MPAA had been vacant, and several names had surfaced as possible replacements. Krim's former law partner, Louis Nizer, was thought to be the frontrunner. But he was sixty-four. Theodore Sorenson and Pierre Salinger from the Kennedy administration, and even Adlai Stevenson were mentioned. Wasserman and Edwin Weisl, Sr., who was an executive at Paramount Pictures in addition to being Johnson's attorney and longtime friend, approached Valenti in 1966. Weisl's influence and success at Paramount no doubt helped to sway Valenti. For these Hollywood power brokers, Valenti had several assets: he was young, personable, and politically astute – and he had the president's ear. Wasserman also sensed that

to the president doubted that Johnson would have submitted his name for confirmation. See Bruck, *When Hollywood Had a King*, 229–31. Wasserman denied that he had ever turned down an offer to work for the government under President Johnson. See *Oral History Interview of Lew Wasserman: I*, Dec. 21, 1973, 13–14, OHC-LBJ (Online: http://www.lbjlib.utexas.edu/johnson/archives.hom/oralhistory.hom/). See also *Oral History Interview of Jack Valenti: IV*, March, 3, 1971, 3, OHC-LBJ.

he could depend on Valenti's loyalty. That quality was particularly important because, as Wasserman acknowledged, the studio chiefs made up a corporate inner circle, not unlike a "university or social club" infused with "the fraternity spirit." Soon after Valenti assumed the MPAA presidency, he made Wasserman chairman of the Association of Motion Picture and Television Producers, an arm of the MPAA that handled labor relations. Wasserman held the post until 1974. Over the years Valenti gained the reputation for rarely opposing Wasserman's wishes.[28]

Valenti told Johnson of his decision to leave in April 1966. The president was not happy with this move. He told Wasserman, Krim, and Weisl, Sr., that he doubted that Valenti "could cut it" in Hollywood, and he suggested another person in his administration. Johnson was not eager to lose Valenti, and knowing his assistant's interest in world affairs, floated the possibility that he might be able to offer Valenti the post of ambassador to Italy. Part of the appeal of Wasserman's offer had been that he told Valenti that the MPAA position would allow him to pursue his interest in international politics. But the real reason he decided to go to Hollywood, Valenti told Johnson, was that he needed to make more money.[29]

When Valenti agreed in April 1966 to become president of the MPAA, its member companies included Universal Pictures, Columbia Pictures, United Artists, Warner Bros. Pictures (later Warner Bros.–Seven Arts), 20th Century Fox, Paramount Pictures, Metro-Goldwyn-Mayer, and Allied Artists Pictures. Over the years such companies as Walt Disney Productions and Orion Pictures would become members of the MPAA. These major studios, along with other companies, were also members of the Association (after 1982, Alliance) of Motion Picture and Television Producers. Valenti was president of this organization, too, with Wasserman as its chairman of the board. As president of the MPAA, Valenti's position meant he was a lobbyist for the entertainment industry and a spokesperson for those who dominated the MPAA – the big Hollywood studios. It is in this context that his rhetoric in the following

---

[28] Quotations ("club," "fraternity"), *Oral History Interview of Lew Wasserman: I*, Dec. 21, 1973, 5, OHC-LBJ. Edwin Weisl, Sr., had been chair of the executive committee in Paramount Picture's board of directors. See Valenti, *A Very Human President*, 253, 254, 276; Brownstein, *Power and the Glitter*, 195, 217; and McDougal, *Last Mogul*, 318, 376.

[29] Quotation ("cut"), *Oral History Interview of Lew Wasserman: I*, Dec. 21, 1973, 33, OHC-LBJ. See also McDougal, *Last Mogul*, 376. After George Reedy's resignation, had Johnson offered to make Valenti press secretary, Valenti probably would have accepted the appointment. Johnson named Bill Moyers to that post instead. *Oral History Interview of Jack Valenti: V*, July 12, 1972, 31, OHC-LBJ.

years about freedom, artistic creativity, and the public interest should be set. Given this context, it is hardly surprising that when disagreements developed between the major companies and the ratings board, Valenti usually supported the studios.[30]

As a lobbyist, Valenti was extraordinarily successful. He resisted sharing power, especially with anyone he might be unable to control. His flamboyance and flair for dramatization and hyperbole, his enthusiasm and energy, and his willingness to flatter others effusively all went over well in Hollywood and in Washington, two places where fantasy and politics intermingle. Even his critics admired the force of his personality, which bulldozed others into accepting his point of view. He cultivated presidents, members of Congress, and other powerful leaders. With each new administration, Valenti took the lead in getting motion pictures to the president. When he testified on Capitol Hill, it "was the best show in town!" recalled a former chair of the Federal Communications Commission. He was "theatrical, . . . a showman." When he walked through the halls of Congress, a friend reminisced, he exuded confidence like "a strutting peacock!" Valenti developed friendships with Warren Beatty, Angie Dickinson, and other movie stars, and he used them to promote legislation and fund-raising. He was "a true political operative," said the former head of Paramount Pictures, Frank Yablans. "He understood better than anyone else the power of celebrity, the power of Hollywood in the political world."[31] Valenti perhaps explained the connection between the political and entertainment worlds best when he said: "The fact, too long in the closet, is that politicians and Hollywood are sprung from the same DNA. They both deal in illusions whose machinations are oftentimes unseen by and unknown to the public."[32]

Like any good corporate public relations or advertising practitioner, Valenti wanted to control and manipulate information. He worked to create an image of himself as a Hollywood czar. He managed to limit what was known about the internal workings of the MPAA. Valenti felt

[30] Other member companies of the MPAA in 1966 included Bray Studios, Inc.; Cosmopolitan Corp.; Motion Pictures Associates, Inc.; Edward Small Productions, Inc.; Hal Roach Studios, Inc.; Terrytoons, Inc.; Walter Wanger; Warner Bros. Distributing Corp.; Afton Productions, Inc.; Perlsea Co.; The Mirisch Corp. of Delaware; Marten Productions (M.G.M.); and Charles F. Simonelli (Technicolor of America). *1966 Film Daily Yearbook* (New York: N.p., 1966), 382. See also MPAA, *Year in Review* (June 1968); and Valenti, Statement, *U.S. Senate Hearings*, Oct. 24, 1985, 88.

[31] Richard D. Heffner, interview with author, Aug. 13, 1999. Quotations, Bruck, "The Personal Touch," 51 ("best," "showman," Charles Ferris quoted), 56 ("peacock," unnamed friend quoted), 50 ("true," "world," Frank Yablans quoted).

[32] Quotation ("DNA"), Valenti, "It's Lights, Camera, Politics," *LAT*, Sept. 6, 1996, 9.

that "his power came not from dialogue with the public, but from *telling* the public something, *conning* it, not from trying to *inform* it," Heffner said. It became "the tradition of the MPAA, through the years, to try to do things sub rosa, not openly."[33] Historians, at least to date, have little material from Valenti's office about him or the MPAA that has not first been processed through the organization's publicity mill.

Although Valenti was a Catholic, and at some level his outlook was undoubtedly influenced by the Church, he was also a man of his times. Publicly, he was the artist's champion. "I am opposed to my priest telling me what movies I ought to see," he told Congress in 1977. "I am against prescribing or proscribing. I am a flat-out first amendment man, whether it involves my church, or anything else." The Church could monitor movies and offer recommendations, but Valenti rejected many of the opinions of Catholic leaders because they were "funded by and founded on church dogma and canon law," rather than on "the current mores of society."[34] In the controversy between those people who demanded morality in entertainment and artists who called for more freedom, Valenti sided with the latter. There was "no way to have a flourishing creativity," he said, "if you are going to put fetters on the creative man." No one has sufficient wisdom to tell the artist where to "draw the line."[35]

If the MPAA's leader gave moralists pause, people of a more secular orientation who were seeking principled leadership against excessive violence, sex, and profanity, also found him a disappointment. Heffner considered Valenti essentially amoral, even as he acknowledged the man's political skills and Catholic background. "Words were not designed to communicate ideas," Heffner said of Valenti, "they were designed to convince people; not to tell you the truth – Not 'Can I tell you something about what happened to me yesterday, so you know what happened to me yesterday?' But 'Can I tell you something about what happened to me yesterday, painted in such a way that you will today give me what I want from you?'"[36] Valenti once told Heffner that he considered the ratings system to be the "MPAA's best public-relations gimmick." Valenti

---

[33] Quotations ("power," "openly"), *Reminiscences of Richard D. Heffner* (hereafter cited as Heffner, *Reminiscences*), vol. 1, p. 81, Box 5, RDH-COHC-BL.

[34] Quotations ("opposed," "society"), Valenti, testimony, *U.S. House Hearings*, March 24, 1977, 15.

[35] Quotations ("no," "line"), statement by Jack Valenti before the National Commission on the Causes and Prevention of Violence, Dec. 19, 1968, reprinted in Prince, ed., *Screening Violence*, 63.

[36] Quotation ("words," "you"), Heffner, *Reminiscences*, vol. 1, p. 159, Box 5, RDH-COHC-BL.

was "always desperately involved in double-talk" when it came to the movie ratings, Heffner said. Valenti's defense of the major studios some-times seemed to Heffner to take on the character of "a Machiavellian conspiracy" against the rating board and the public interest.[37]

CARA

The organization created to rate films was initially called the Code and Rating Administration (CARA) and was established by NATO, the MPAA, and the International Film Importers and Distributors Association (IFIDA).[38] These groups appointed Valenti to administer CARA, although CARA was not formally part of the MPAA. Valenti worked hard, though, to have his name associated with the rating system, and many people automatically assumed that the ratings came from the MPAA. Valenti liked to describe himself as a "shield between the industry and the pub-lic and everybody else against the rating system." He appointed CARA's chair who, in turn, chose the members of the rating board. But the rating administration did not depend on the MPAA or other groups for money, although the MPAA often billed it for advice, legal services, and similar activities. Instead, CARA derived its operating income from movie com-panies that paid a fee per film, based on a sliding scale, to have their pictures rated.[39]

The system was voluntary, except for MPAA companies that formally agreed to have CARA rate all of their motion pictures. Any filmmaker, though, could submit a movie to CARA, although those who were not MPAA members were not required to do so, nor were they required to accept a rating once it had been issued. In 1985, Valenti stated that of the seven thousand movies that had been rated up to that time, only a little

---

37 Quotation ("gimmick"), "RDH Pre-Oral History Memo to Chuck Champlin for the Year 1985" (hereafter cited as Heffner, "Pre-Oral History Memorandum," followed by the year), p. 48, Box 2, RDH-COHC-BL. Quotation ("double-talk"), Heffner, "Pre-Oral History Memorandum for 1981," p. 2, Box 1, RDH-COHC-BL. Quotation ("conspir-acy"), Heffner, *Reminiscences*, vol. 1, p. 90; see also ibid., 34–5, Box 5, RDH-COHC-BL.
38 The IFIDA represented more than forty companies, most of which were located in New York City. See *Film Daily Yearbook*, 1969, 366.
39 Quotation ("shield"), Valenti, testimony, *U.S. Senate Hearings*, Oct. 24, 1985, 74; also 75. See also Heffner, interview with author, Aug. 13, 1999; and Heffner, *Reminiscences*, vol. 1, p. 86, Box 5, RDH-COHC-BL. Filmmakers paid CARA a fee that ranged from $150 to $3,000 to have their movies rated. The size of the fee depended on the cost of the picture and the distributor's gross domestic rentals from the previous year. See Randall, "Classification by the Motion Picture Industry," 224; and Valenti, testimony, *U.S. House Hearings*, March 24, 1977, 12–13.

more than one-third (37 percent) had been distributed by MPAA studios or their subsidiaries. The other films were made by companies that were not MPAA members.[40]

It should be noted that CARA had an opportunity to rate only a small fraction of the motion pictures produced annually throughout the world. At the end of the 1960s, the MPAA's member studios made only about 5 percent of the movies produced each year worldwide, and the United States had become a growing market for foreign-made movies.[41] An increasing number of pictures were also made within the United States by moviemakers who decided to keep their work outside CARA's purview. During the 1970s and 1980s, changes in moviemaking technology – especially those involving videotaping – led to the production of thousands of motion pictures, many pornographic.

CARA also generally rated fewer movies each year than did its counterpart agencies in such countries as Great Britain and Canada. Heffner speculated that the Canadians reviewed perhaps 2,000 to 2,200 films each year – many from India that were marketed to Canada's Indian population. During its first thirty years (1969–1999), CARA classified on average about 500 movies per year. During Heffner's tenure (1974–1994), CARA rated on average slightly more than 450 pictures per year, from a low of 318 in 1982 to a high of 635 in 1994.[42]

A majority vote by rating board members determined CARA's classification for a film. A dissatisfied filmmaker – once he or she had accepted CARA's rating – could challenge the classification before the system's Appeals Board. Requiring the moviemaker first to accept the rating before an appeal could be made gave CARA some leverage. Studios that feared bad publicity from a tentative X rating, for example, often chose quietly to make changes in order to obtain a less restrictive classification rather than challenge the rating board. Valenti chaired the Appeals Board, which was originally made up of two dozen members from the MPAA, NATO, the Producers Guild of America, and the IFIDA.[43] Until the early 1990s, the

[40] Heffner, interview (phone) with author, Aug. 27, 2002; and "The Motion Picture Code and Rating Program: A System of Self-Regulation," *Film Daily Yearbook, 1969, 626.* See also Valenti, statement, *U.S. Senate Hearings,* Oct 24, 1985, 92.

[41] MPAA, *A Year in Review* (June 1968), 17–18.

[42] Canadian figures from Heffner, interview with author, Aug. 13, 1999. Figures on films classified taken from CARA's *Annual Report,* 1969–99, RDHPP.

[43] Heffner, interview (phone) with author, Aug. 27, 2002. See also Heffner, *Reminiscences* (editing copy), vol. 8, pp. 1480–1, Box 5, RDH-COHC-BL; and Randall, "Classification by the Motion Picture Industry," 226; Cook, *Lost Illusions,* 271; and Farber, *Movie Rating Game,* 73–82.

appeals were held in New York. To hold them in California, Valenti told Heffner, would allow the studio heads to dominate the process. Later, though, Valenti allowed appeals to be heard in Hollywood. At first a majority vote was needed to win an appeal (although an X rating could be changed with just a one-third vote plus one). That procedure soon changed, and a two-thirds vote was required to overturn a rating. Over time, the membership of the Appeals Board changed. The IFIDA, which represented independent filmmakers and distributors, declined and by the late 1970s had few representatives in the appeals process. The independents' representation was restored when the American Film Marketing Association was given a place on the Appeals Board in 1995. Also the Appeals Board added a representative from the Video Software Distribution Association once video rentals became a thriving enterprise during the 1980s.[44]

Heffner initially liked the idea of an appeals panel and thought of it – perhaps naively – as a kind of reserve rating board, "another layer of honest rating judgments." And having at one time had aspirations to become a trial lawyer, he often enjoyed arguing CARA's case before a jury of sorts. He favored an appeals board "leavened with outsiders," people who might belong to such groups as the Parent Teacher Association. Their presence, he believed, would help to ensure that the public would be represented. But he came to believe that the process was flawed, because the only people who actually sat on the Appeals Board were in one way or another part of the movie industry. If one studio had a film in production that might be too violent for an R or PG rating, its representatives would be inclined to vote against a stringent rating for a sister studio, whose representatives they knew would later be voting on their film. Rarely did anyone disqualify himself or herself because of a conflict of interest, no matter how blatant. The appeals jury was "totally self-interested in the outcome," Heffner believed. He asked Valenti not to participate in appeals where he might have an economic interest and to forbid Appeals Board members from voting when they had interests at stake.[45]

Valenti contributed to the undermining of this appeals system in Heffner's opinion. The appeals process had a policy review board that at one time had met several times a year. Heffner understood that originally

44 See Heffner, *Reminiscences*, vol. 1, p. 96, Box 5, RDH-COHC-BL; and "Code and Rating Appeals Board," *Film Daily Yearbook*, 1969, 630.
45 Quotations, Heffner, *Reminiscences*, vol. 1, pp. 120 ("honest"), 139 ("leavened"), 129 ("totally"), Box 5, RDH-COHC-BL. See also Heffner, "Pre-Oral History Memorandum for 1980," 72–4, Box 1, RDH-COHC-BL.

the chairmanship of this review committee was intended to rotate among representatives of NATO, the MPAA, and IFIDA. Yet Valenti assumed the chair and never relinquished it. He refused to allow outsiders to sit on the Appeals Board, and he resisted efforts to give the public explanations for ratings. Perhaps most discouraging to Heffner, Valenti usually did not appear at appeals unless the interests of a major studio were at stake. For instance, he intervened in the appeals involving such films as Warner Bros.'s *All the President's Men* (1976), MGM/United Artists's *Rollerball* (1975) and *Poltergeist* (1982), and Universal's *Scarface* (1983). When he did appear at an appeals hearing, it was most often to weigh in on behalf of Krim, Wasserman, Jerry Weintraub, or other powerful studio chieftains.[46]

As for CARA, its early membership suggested continuity with an earlier time rather than a radical break with the past. At the outset, the rating board had five members, all of them married. That number soon expanded to seven permanent members. Several on the rating board had been with the PCA. Eugene Dougherty, fifty, who attended the Harvard Business School and had been with the PCA since 1941, became director. Geoffrey Shurlock, then seventy-seven, remained as a consultant, although in practice he had a vote equal to other board members and, due to his past experience, had considerable influence, which he sometimes used on behalf of the producers.[47] Also retained were Albert E. Van Schmus, forty-nine, who had been trained in the social sciences at the University of Chicago and had worked in the PCA since 1949, and Richard R. Mathison, also forty-nine, a former freelance writer, California bureau chief for *Newsweek,* and religion editor for the *Los Angeles Times,* who had joined the PCA in 1965. Other early members of the rating board included Richard McKay, who had worked in movie exhibition, and then had been director of advertising and publicity, first for American International Pictures, and then for Walt Disney Productions. McKay was chosen to represent theater owners. The first woman to join CARA was Dr. Jacqueline Bouhoutsos, a child psychologist. McKay and Bouhoutsos had not been members of the PCA. Janice M. Montgomery, Shurlock's secretary in the PCA during the 1960s, who had done research on movie

---

[46] Heffner, *Reminiscences*, vol. 1, pp. 124, 139, Box 5, RDH-COHC-BL; and Heffner, "Pre-Oral History Memorandum for 1980," pp. 79–80, Box 1, ibid.; and Heffner, interview (phone) with author, Aug. 27, 2002.

[47] Heffner recalled a disagreement among board members over a rating during which Shurlock reportedly said, "Give them [the producers] what they want . . . they pay our salaries." Quotation ("Give"), Heffner, *Reminiscences*, vol. 1, p. 55, Box 5, RDH-COHC-BL.

content for the MPAA and at one time had also been employed by
Columbia Pictures, became a permanent member of CARA in 1971. In
late 1969, Valenti added to the board a student intern, Stephen Farber,
ostensibly to have someone to represent people under thirty – the portion
of the population that made up the largest part of the moviegoing public.
Farber, who had just completed a master's degree in film history at UCLA,
stayed with CARA for only six months and then turned his experience
into a book entitled *The Rating Game* (1972). The number of interns on
CARA, though, increased, and by 1974 there were three board members
on fellowship.[48]

In addition to members who carried over from the PCA, CARA retained
other vestiges of the Production Code during its initial months. The ratings system's "Standards for Production" reflected the Code's values on
sex, crime, violence, language, and treatment of animals. Studios, even
though they were no longer required to do so, still submitted scripts to
CARA expecting them to be reviewed.[49] Through the early 1970s, members of the rating board reflected the tone of the Production Code, too,
in that they generally were much more concerned with sex, nudity, and
language than with violence: one sighting of a female nipple assured an
R, and one use of the word "fuck" automatically required an R rating.
CARA's official adoption of this automatic language rule came at the urging Marvin Goldman, president of NATO, whose theater owner members
dealt directly with the public and were usually the first to hear parents'
complaints about films. In all sections of the country, theater owners bore
the brunt of parental displeasure over profanity and sex in movies.[50]

Critics often question how closely the studios and theater owners honored the ratings. The system, which was largely voluntary, depended

---

[48] The former PCA members who were dropped included John A. Vizzard, fifty-four, who
had been educated in ethics and philosophy at Santa Clara and Gonzaga Universities, and
Morris V. Murphy, fifty-five, who also had studied philosophy and English at Santa Clara
and Gonzaga. Randall, "Classification by the Motion Picture Industry," 225; Farber,
Movie Rating Game, v, 18–19; and Canby, "For Better or Worse, Film Industry Begins
Ratings," *NYT*, Nov. 1, 1968, clipping in RG 46, Sen 90A-E6, Box 53, USSCCP-NARA 1.
See also *Annual Report: Code and Rating Administration, 1974* (hereafter cited as CARA,
Annual Report), RDHPP. See also See Stephen Farber, testimony, *U.S. House Hearings*,
April 14, 1977, 78, 83; and Appendix to Valenti, testimony, *U.S. House Hearings*, March
24, 1977, 39–40.
[49] Farber, *Movie Rating Game*, 15–19. On the connection between the Production Code
and the early rating system, see "Official Code Objectives," published by the MPAA in
1968; ibid., 112–15.
[50] Marvin Goldman, testimony, *U.S. Senate Hearings*, Oct. 24, 1985, 124. See also Heffner,
Reminiscences, vol. 1, pp. 43, 61, 94, 148, Box 5, RDH-COHC-BL.

on the integrity of those involved. NATO estimated in 1977 that about 15–20 percent of American exhibitors failed to adhere to the ratings. At a 1985 Senate hearing on drug abuse and the movie industry, Valenti, using NATO's figures, argued that only 20 percent "slippage" was a good record. But when senators challenged Valenti to explain how he had arrived at this estimate, he could not give a satisfactory answer. Senators Albert Gore (D-TN) and Sam Nunn (D-GA) maintained that the percentage of noncompliance was considerably higher. Nunn even speculated that 20 percent might more accurately reflect the proportion of theaters that actually enforced CARA's ratings. He called for an analysis independent of the industry.[51]

By the early 1970s, the rating system was floundering. Surveys done for theater owners indicated that an increasing number of people said the ratings did not help them select movies for their children. The percentage of college-educated people who used the ratings declined.[52] Moreover, whereas some people criticized the ratings for remaining too closely tied to the Production Code, others denounced the system for abandoning the Code's morality. The United States Catholic Conference (USCC) consulted with Valenti and the MPAA as the rating plan was being formulated, and it endorsed the new system in 1968. But by May 1971 it had withdrawn support. The bishops became disillusioned with what they thought were unreliable ratings, lack of compliance by theater owners, dishonest advertising, and the showing of X- and R-rated trailers at G and PG movies. Some bishops expressed indignation that the X rating was labeled "adult," and they were outraged by such entertainment because, as one bishop complained in 1985, there was "nothing adult" about those films. For many Catholic leaders, the classification system reflected more what the MPAA thought "the traffic would bear" with regard to sex, violence, and profanity than "any sense of what social values" or what "anti-social values were being transmitted." The fact that young people seemed the primary audience for movies made the ratings' shortcomings especially deplorable. Yet the MPAA and USCC tried to keep open lines of communication. USCC representatives accepted Valenti's invitations to attend rating appeals hearings. The USCC also put its own ratings on

[51] Quotation ("slippage"), Valenti, testimony, *U.S. Senate Hearings*, Oct. 24, 1985, 78. See also ibid., 79–80; and Richard D. Heffner, testimony, *U.S. House Hearings*, July 21, 1977, 203.

[52] See "Highlights of Opinion Research Corporation 1970 Survey on Code and Rating System," Folder 1, Box 5, Mss 1446, NATOR-BYU; and Jack Valenti to Martin Newman, Sept. 6, 1973, ibid.

motion pictures, often next to the MPAA's classification in order to high-light their differences of opinion.[53]

In July 1971, Dr. Aaron Stern replaced Dougherty as head of CARA. Stern, who was a psychiatrist on the faculty of Columbia University's College of Physicians and Surgeons, had been a consultant to the ratings board. Although he considered himself a liberal, he clashed with some CARA members who thought him too judgmental, intolerant of dissent, and eager to please the Catholic Church. Like the holdovers from the Production Code era, Stern seemed more concerned with sex than violence.[54]

The young interns in CARA – Farber and Estelle Changas – thought Stern was too repressive. It was not so much Stern's morality as his background in psychology that accounted for his conservatism, in their view. Farber and Changas winced when Stern criticized young people for "their impatience, their immaturity, their dangerous rebelliousness, even their liberal attitudes toward sex." Stern favored giving movies about "rebellion against the Establishment" a restricted rating even if they contained little violence or sex. Bouhoutsos, who also had a background in psychology, shared many of Stern's views and, according to Farber and Changas, worried about films with the "theme of insurrection." They charged that "these psychological newcomers [Stern and Bouhoutsos] are as delighted with their power over creative people as the old-time censors." Lacking even "one clear piece of evidence about the harmful effects of film viewing on children, these new psychological crusaders preach about oedipal fantasies, pre-pubital traumas and the inviolability of the family unit, with a sense of absolute certainty." Farber and Changas warned that soon the psychiatrists and psychologists would exercise as much leverage over Hollywood as had the Catholic Church. They claimed that fully a third of the movies made in 1969 and 1970 – such pictures as *Alice's Restaurant* (1969), *Soldier Blue* (1970), and *A New Leaf* (1971) – had been altered because of the rating board.[55]

Stern was not only dismissive of youthful sensibilities, he also irritated other people. He appeared to enjoy exercising authority and was not one to shun the spotlight. He threw "his power around,... and had inserted himself," if not into the production process, at least into the editing of

---

[53] Quotations, Bishop Norbert F. Gaughan, statement, *U.S. Senate Hearings,* Oct. 24, 1985, 130 ("adult"), 145 ("traffic," "anti-social"); see also ibid., 144.

[54] For a critical view of Aaron Stern and his approach to ratings, see Farber, *Movie Rating Game,* 19, 85, 95–100, 122–3.

[55] Quotations ("impatience," "certainty"), Changas and Farber, "Insiders Rate Film Code Board as 'Unreformed,'" *LAT,* Aug. 8, 1971 (Calendar), 1, 22–5.

films, and "had become something of a pain-in-the-ass" to the studios, recalled his successor, Heffner. Members of the rating board seemed reluctant to speak their minds – "a bunch of scared bunnies" Heffner called them – and rarely discussed among themselves why they had rated a movie they had just watched. That Stern's name – rather than Valenti's – often seemed to appear in the press when movie ratings were discussed also angered Valenti. By late 1973 or early 1974, Stern decided to leave CARA. Rumor had it that he wanted to become a producer and had arranged a deal with Columbia Pictures involving cable television.[56]

RICHARD HEFFNER

In the fall of 1973, Valenti placed a call to Heffner, then a Rutgers University professor and television broadcaster, who also had served the U.S. Department of State as an American specialist in communications. At the time, Heffner was in Europe, in Salzburg, delivering a paper on Soviet attitudes toward satellite-to-home broadcasting. A short time later, though, he and Valenti met. Valenti wanted Heffner, then forty-eight, to take over Stern's job, but Heffner seemed uninterested. However, Valenti convinced him to come to Los Angeles where he met Stern, who warned him about Hollywood's "seductiveness." Later, when Heffner returned to watch CARA in action, Valenti saw to it that he and his wife, Elaine, stayed in Elizabeth Taylor's suite at the Beverly Hills Hotel for several weeks. As Heffner learned more about the nature of the job, whatever reluctance he had felt faded, and he agreed to become chair of CARA starting on July 1, 1974.[57]

Heffner and Valenti struck a bargain, one not completely satisfactory to either party. Valenti agreed that Heffner would be independent in leading the rating board. No one would look over his shoulder, second-guess, or veto him. He pledged to Heffner that no one in the industry would be allowed to exert political pressure on him, promising him what Valenti called "political independence of the most precious kind." If anyone attempted coercion, Heffner was to refer that person to Valenti. Heffner agreed to these guidelines, but two other matters were not so easily settled. Valenti's secretary and general attorney, Sidney Schreiber, wanted Heffner to promise that, once he stepped down as CARA's chairman, he

[56] Quotations, Heffner, *Reminiscences,* vol. 1, p. 33 ("inserted," "ass"), 52 ("bunnies"), Box 5, RDH-COHC-BL. See also ibid., 31–2, 34, 52, 93–4.
[57] Quotation ("seductiveness"), Heffner, *Reminiscences,* vol. 1, p. 31, Box 5, RDH-COHC-BL. See also vol. 1, pp. 29–34, 37.

would not speak publicly or write a book or articles about his experiences. Heffner refused, although the issue would resurface later. Valenti also wanted Heffner to agree that his job was not a "public" one, and that even though he might be inundated with requests for interviews from the media, he had no obligation to explain why or how CARA arrived at its ratings. But more than this, Valenti did not want Heffner to talk publicly about the rating system at all. It was "important that the rating system speak with one voice," he explained. "The rating system is fragile because it is subjective.... If the press can drive a wedge between the Rating Board and Jack Valenti, they will exploit that seeming difference of opinion to the detriment of the system and its objectives.... What we cannot abide is a clangorous reaction on our part, that is, different signals being hoisted to the press. This is an ageless lesson," said LBJ's former assistant, "preeminent in the political arena which the White House and the State Department have learned to their dismay in several administrations." Heffner bridled at these demands because he thought Valenti was frequently uninformed about ratings decisions and spoke inaccurately about them. More than that, he suspected Valenti was too egotistical to tolerate counteropinions.[58]

Despite these tensions with Valenti, Heffner headed the rating board for twenty years, approximately the same length of time as Joseph Breen's tenure with the PCA. Heffner, however, differed sharply from Breen, not only in background but also in his approach to movie regulation. Breen, who had worked in journalism and public relations before coming to Hollywood, was a militant Catholic and anticommunist, who at one point apparently was also strongly anti-Semitic. Heffner had grown up in a Jewish home in Manhattan, the son of a bookie (neither parent had gone to high school). He had studied and taught American history, worked in professional broadcasting in radio and television, and was a professor of communications and public policy at Rutgers University. At one time he had been on the national board of directors of the American Civil Liberties Union (ACLU), although he left the board when he grew tired of "listening to the old Menshevikis battling with the old Bolshevikis." He continued to teach in New Brunswick and live in New York City as he shuttled back and forth to Los Angeles every other week to review movies. He avoided socializing in Hollywood. Unlike Breen, who wanted to be involved in

---

[58] Quotations ("political," "administrations"), Valenti to Heffner, July 1, 1981, document 81–14, with Heffner, "Pre-Oral History Memorandum for 1981," Box 1, RDH-COHC-BL.

deciding the content of each film, Heffner preferred to stay out of the production process. Although filmmakers continued to submit scripts – and CARA felt obligated to read them if asked to do so – Heffner was not keen to take on this job. He usually responded innocuously, hoping to discourage further readings.[59]

CARA's new leader represented a departure from the past in other ways too. He had been impressed by Valenti's explanation that the rating system was "based not upon certain moral precepts," as the Production Code had been, "but, rather, upon a . . . concern for what the majority of parents were thinking about in relation to movies." That approach, Heffner thought, offered a formula for avoiding censorship. And so he tried to avoid being a censor or moralist and disassociated himself from the Production Code. In order to end any confusion between his work and that of the Production Code, Heffner insisted on changing the name of the ratings system from the Code and Ratings Administration to the Classification and Ratings Administration, accepting the redundancy to keep the acronym CARA.[60] In rating movies, Heffner was not satisfied to follow routine and custom. Citing Henry Wriston, a former president of Brown University, who said, "Rules make decision easy, but they rob it of wisdom," Heffner soon began questioning the rules that automatically assigned R ratings to movies for the single use of a word or a brief glimpse of nudity. He believed that rating assignments required weighing films in their entirety.[61]

When he took over as head of CARA, Heffner was also unhappy with the composition of the rating board. He later told Valenti that he wanted a combination of old and new members, who would give CARA "both stability *and* flexibility," and who would "reflect *contemporary* parental attitudes toward film content." He favored retaining two former PCA members; Mathison, who stayed through 1979, and Van Schmus, who remained until 1982. Heffner considered Van Schmus to be the best person on the rating board; he was always reliable and thoughtful, even if they often disagreed. Mathison was also helpful, but perhaps not typical

---

[59] Quotation ("listening"), Heffner, *Reminiscences*, vol. 8, p. 1498, Box 5, RDH-COHC-BL. See also ibid., vol. 2, p. 274, Box 5, RDH-COHC-BL; Kaufman, "PG Man Hangs Up That Hat," *NYT*, June 8, 1994, B3; and Salamon, "The Famous and the Witty in a Half Century of Chats," ibid., Nov. 5, 2003, B8.

[60] Quotations ("based," "movies"), Heffner, *Reminiscences,* vol. 1, p. 42, Box 5, RDH-COCH-BL; see also ibid., 63. Also Heffner, interview with author, Aug. 13, 1999.

[61] Henry Wriston quoted ("Rules") in Heffner, *Reminiscences,* vol. 1, p. 95, Box 5, RDH-COCH-BL.

enough as a parent, Heffner thought, if only because he was such an accomplished writer. But McKay, who had been involved in exhibition, and Montgomery, who had been in the PCA, were too closely connected to the industry to represent the public interest, Heffner believed. McKay and Montgomery both remained until 1978. Moreover, three young people on fellowship, none of whom had children, had come onto the board. Valenti said they were there to represent moviegoers under age thirty, but Heffner also believed they were there because they could be hired for less money than the other board members. Although some members thought of their work as a lifetime appointment, Heffner believed turnover was essential if CARA was to reflect parental attitudes. Therefore, because no one on CARA, not even Heffner, had a contract, some members received notice. Eventually the rating board consisted of a combination of members who were long-termers and members, perhaps half, who served only one to three years and then were replaced. By 1979, CARA had seven members, only two of whom (Van Schmus and Mathison) had been there when Heffner arrived.[62]

A decade later, the rating board had grown to ten people – six women and four men – plus Heffner, all of whom were parents. Nine members were married, and one was divorced. They ranged in age from thirty-four to sixty-eight and their average age was forty-five (seven of the ten were in their forties). Six members had children thirteen years old or younger. Three members had children between the ages of fourteen and seventeen. All of the board members except one had some college education and six members held B.A. degrees. Two members had had some postgraduate training, and one person – a college teacher – held a Ph.D. For CARA's purposes, these members sufficiently represented the attitudes of most American parents about film content, in Heffner's view.[63] Heffner also considered it important to keep the membership of CARA anonymous. Despite criticism from moviemakers, film critics, and such groups as the American Civil Liberties Union, he resisted revealing

[62] Quotations ("stability," "content"), Heffner to Valenti, Nov. 18, 1986 (memorandum), Exhibit 86-13, with Heffner, "Pre-Oral History Memorandum for 1986," Box 4, RDH-COHC-BL. Also Heffner, *Reminiscences*, vol. 1, pp. 61, 63, 85, 101–2, 103, 105, Box 5, RDH-COCH-BL; and Heffner, interview (phone) with author, Aug. 27, 2002. See also CARA, *Annual Reports, 1974–1983* (esp. *Annual Reports* for 1977, 1978, 1979), RDHPP.

[63] See "CARA BOARD MEMBERS," Oct. 25, 1988, document 88-13, Box 4, Heffner, "Pre-Oral History Memorandum for 1988," Box 4, RDH-COHC-BL; and Heffner, interview (phone) with author, Aug. 27, 2002.

their names. He felt certain that if their identities had been known, the studios, with their considerable resources, would have lobbied them intensively.[64]

Despite clear dissimilarities, Heffner and Breen had at least two things in common. First, both shared a distaste for Hollywood culture and for many of the people who made movies. Breen entered the film industry with these prejudices firmly in place, his distrust rooted in his Catholicism and anti-Semitism. Heffner's dislike evolved over many years and out of several bruising confrontations with movie producers. He appears to have started with an open mind but grew increasingly negative. There "was so much essential dishonesty in Hollywood," he said shortly after retiring from CARA. "I...didn't really have much regard for most of the people in Hollywood or for the whole industry, with some major exceptions." It was a business without principled leadership and where greed regularly trumped concerns about public welfare.[65] Second, both men surely felt that despite their best efforts the entertainment industry had overwhelmed the values they held in highest regard. Breen's retirement in 1954 came as the Production Code began to unravel. Already by then the movies were dealing with such themes as abortion and sexuality in ways that he could not control. When Heffner retired four decades later, he believed that Hollywood had little respect for a society based on the rule of reason, and he had come to doubt the wisdom of self-regulation and whether entertainment-for-profit deserved the same First Amendment protections as did serious political speech.

Heffner's background helps to explain his approach to rating motion pictures. He had taken interest in American history during the late 1940s and 1950s. He had earned his undergraduate and master's degrees from Columbia College, where he encountered Richard Hofstadter, Henry Steele Commager, Allan Nevins, Lionel Trilling, and Jacques Barzun. At Columbia, he had read Thomas Hill Green's *Principles of Political Obligation* in a philosophy course taught by Charles Frankel and remembered Green saying that the "purpose of government is to hinder the hindrances to human development." For his graduate work, he had considered studying with the intellectual historian Merle Curti at the University of Wisconsin but instead accepted a fellowship at Columbia. After completing the master's degree, he undertook study of American history at the University of California, Berkeley, and became a teaching assistant to historian

---

[64] Heffner, *Reminiscences,* vol. 10, p. 1910, Box 5, RDH-COHC-BL.
[65] Quotations ("dishonesty," "regard"), ibid., vol. 2, p. 204, Box 5, ibid.

Kenneth Stampp. There he thought about writing a doctoral thesis on movies and American life, but he never completed the dissertation.[66]

Heffner did edit two books about American history. In *A Documentary History of the United States,* first published in 1952, he revealed his admiration for Presidents Thomas Jefferson, Abraham Lincoln, and Franklin D. Roosevelt, a belief that American expansion was related to industrial capitalism, and a conviction that the New Deal had saved American democracy from chaos and perhaps totalitarianism. In 1955, Heffner published an abridged version of Alexis de Tocqueville's *Democracy in America.*[67]

After teaching history at Sarah Lawrence College and the New School for Social Research, Heffner turned to being a writer, producer, and commentator/narrator on radio and television, primarily in New York City. Edward R. Murrow helped him get started in broadcasting. He had been introduced to Murrow in a letter from Earl Warren, written when Warren had been governor of California. Murrow inspired Heffner to believe that "television could be as important an educational force as the printed word and perhaps as the classroom itself... if used as it could and should be used."[68] He admired Murrow's strong "condemnation of the commercialization of television," and when Murrow "spoke generally about television and the *public* interest," not about the interests of network owners and other media moguls, he took notice.[69] Heffner started a weekly TV program, *The Open Mind,* in 1956, that explored the ideas of intellectuals and political leaders, and aired off and on for more than four decades. He became the founding general manager of New York's principal public broadcasting station, Channel 13, in 1962.[70]

---

[66] Heffner quoting Green ("purpose"), interview with author, Aug. 10, 2000. See also Heffner, *Reminiscences,* vol. 1, pp. 1–2, Box 5, ibid.

[67] Heffner, *Documentary History of the United States* (1952, 1965), 209, 269. This work has gone through several editions, including a fiftieth anniversary edition published in 2002.

[68] Quotation ("television"), Heffner, *A Conversational History,* xiii. Heffner had had Earl Warren's daughter as a student when he taught at Berkeley in 1948. Heffner later had lunch with Warren in 1952. Warren wrote a supporting letter for Heffner to J. Raymond Bell, then at Columbia Pictures, who later contacted Murrow about the young broadcaster/historian. Heffner, interview with author, Aug. 16, 2002.

[69] Quotations, Heffner, *Reminiscences,* vol. 1, pp. 15–16 ("condemnation"), 16 ("*public:* emphasis in original text); see also ibid., p. 6, Box 5, RDH-COHC-BL.

[70] Heffner was a newsman on ABC radio, a producer of local television public affairs programs on NBC in New York, and a director and consultant for CBS. As of 2004, "The Open Mind" still aired on WNET, Channel 13, in New York City. For Heffner's background, see Heffner, testimony, *U.S. House Hearings,* July 21, 1977, 195–6.

Over the years, Heffner became ambivalent about television. *The Open Mind* was testimony to his faith that the medium could be used for thoughtful discourse. In the early days of television, he recalled, the medium was "a conduit, a channel" where "people were more themselves. They'd actually . . . talk, think about ideas." Occasionally people would even change their opinions on camera.[71] But he recognized the medium's limitations and became apprehensive about the direction commercial television might take. During the late 1950s, when many people urged greater use of TV in the classroom, Heffner doubted that a "soul-satisfying atmosphere" could be created and warned that television's widespread use could bring a "dangerous shift in values" to American education.[72] Later, as cable channels proliferated and programs vied to appeal to the lowest common denominator, he became more pessimistic about television's ability to serve as a forum for genuine conversation. The form had become too "rigid," he said in 1978. Now "cosmeticized" people showed up in "intellectual makeup" to represent unyielding points of view.[73] Heffner never completely gave up on television and continued to believe it could be helpful in what Murrow called the "great and perhaps decisive battle to be fought against ignorance, intolerance, and indifference." The problem with television, Heffner said in 2003 (again using Murrow's words) was that it was "rusting in the scabbard during a battle for survival."[74]

The title of the television program *The Open Mind* also captured something of Heffner's approach to movie regulation. He believed that freedom demands tolerance – even of deplorable opinions. "In the area of creative expression ultimately the only truly responsible society is one built upon freedom, not control," he said. Freedom required rejecting "even

---

[71] Quotations ("conduit," "ideas"), Greenfield, "'The Open Mind': A Talk Show with Real Talk," *LAT*, April 24, 1978. See also Kaufman, "PG Men Hangs Up That Hat," *NYT*, B3.

[72] Quotation ("soul-satisfying"), from Heffner's commentary in "Design for Learning," *Saturday Review* 42 (Feb. 14, 1959), 17; see also ibid., 19. Quotation ("dangerous"), Heffner, "A Gadget Cure" [book review], ibid. 41 (May 24, 1958), 38. See also Heffner, "TV as Teacher: Of Adults, Too," *NYT Magazine*, Aug. 17, 1958, 19, 74.

[73] Quotations ("rigid," "makeup"), Greenfield, "'The Open Mind.'" See also Heffner, *Reminiscences*, vol., 7, p. 1285, Box 5, RDH-COHC-BL. Between 1972 and 1974, Heffner participated in studies funded by the Ford Foundation that examined the way television entertainment programs and advertising portrayed environmental concerns, age-related issues, and business. See Richard Heffner Associates, "Network Television's Environmental Content" (June 30, 1972); ["Report and Proposal Concerning the Identification of Entertainment Television's Aging-Related Content"] (Dec. 1973); and "Network Television's Business-Related Content" (Spring 1974), RDHPP.

[74] Quotations ("great," "rusting"), Heffner, *A Conversational History*, xiv.

the controls that persons of presumably good will choose to impose upon those who presumably are less well intentioned." The responsibility for deciding what could be seen lay with the viewer, not the creator of a message or work of art. "Basically, I believe that when restraints are placed upon communication, just so long as it is technically possible the *receiver* should take the responsibility for placing those restraints upon himself and not impose them instead upon the freedom of the *sender*. It is legitimate for listeners, viewers, *not* to listen, *not* to view. It is *not* legitimate to insist instead that speakers not speak."[75] This approach to regulation set Heffner apart not only from his predecessors who had censored movies in the United States but from his contemporary counterparts in other countries. He disagreed with the British Board of Film Censors, whose members often intervened to change film content even before giving an X, and who sometimes banned movies outright. The American system existed, he thought, to "*minimize* control, not to maximize it."[76]

Heffner found John Milton, John Stuart Mill, and Tocqueville influential. He sometimes quoted Milton, who in *Areopagitica* had asked, "Who ever knew truth put to the worse, in a free and open encounter?" Rarely, though, did the contest for truth occur in a fair arena, Heffner believed. He liked Mill when he wrote, in *On Liberty*, that "If all mankind minus one, were of one opinion, and only one person were of the contrary opinion, mankind would be no more justified in silencing that one person, than he, if he had the power, would be justified in silencing mankind."[77] During the McCarthy era, Heffner found *Democracy in America* pertinent. Tocqueville's warning about the tyranny of the majority struck him then "with particular force."[78]

The specter of a repressive majority figured prominently in Heffner's thinking about movie classification. He saw ratings as a way to defuse this potential problem. In theory, the plan allowed the marketplace to regulate what was shown. If enough people would pay to see certain kinds of films,

---

[75] Quotations, Richard D. Heffner, "Freedom and Responsibility in Mass Communications," Address delivered in London, March 22, 1982, 5–6 ("not," "intentioned"), 23–4 ("Basically," "speak"; emphasis in original text); see also ibid., 9, copy in RDHPP. This address provides one of the most concise statements of Heffner's views on freedom, censorship, and entertainment.

[76] Quotation ("*minimize*"; emphasis in original text), ibid., 9. See also Jonas, "The Man Who Gave an 'X' Rating to Violence," *NYT*, May 11, 1975, sec. 2, p. 13.

[77] Quotation ("encounter"), Richard D. Heffner, "Jefferson Revisited," address delivered in Toronto, Sept. 18, 1984, 4; see also ibid., 5, RDHPP. John Stuart Mill quoted ("mankind") by Heffner, "Freedom and Responsibility in Mass Communications," 25.

[78] Quotation ("force"), Heffner, *Alexis de Tocqueville, Democracy in America*, 21.

it seemed less likely that censorship advocates would gain enough support to pass legislation. He feared, though, that changes in communication technology threatened to make this rating system obsolete.

One key to avoiding censorship was protecting children. Classification was not intended to limit what adults watched, but it did try to restrict what children could see. Drawing a distinction between entertainment for adults and for the young was "the beginning of wisdom," Heffner told a British audience in 1982. It helped to ensure that the rating system would work over the long term, and it made sense for two reasons. For one thing, legitimate concerns existed about the impact on children of watching sex and violence in films and on television. For another, even if one disagreed that movies could damage the young, many parents assumed that some kinds of entertainment were harmful, and it made little sense from the industry's perspective to anger those parents. "A majority of Americans seem to feel that their young children should be shielded from certain experiences, such as watching explicit sexual acts or seeing brutal murders on the screen," he told a reporter in 1975. By failing to respect "the will of the majority, you may quickly turn it into a tyranny of the majority."[79]

Heffner thought of rating board members as surrogate parents. "My colleagues and I apply ratings only as we truly are led to believe they reflect parental attitudes," he told Congress in 1977. Just one criterion guided deliberations: "Will most – not will any, a few or some, but will most – American parents think this film most appropriately classified G, or PG, or R, or X?" The rating board occupied a critical position between the motion picture industry, which desired freedom from government control, and parents who wanted information about movie content. Informed parents, not government agencies, made the best decisions about what children should watch. Ratings touched adults, so the argument went, only insofar as they gave them early warnings about content.[80]

[79] Quotation ("wisdom"), Heffner, "Freedom and Responsibility in Mass Communications," 22. Quotation ("majority"), Jonas, "The Man Who Gave an 'X' Rating to Violence," 13.

[80] Quotations, Heffner, Testimony, *U.S. House Hearings,* July 21, 1977, 197 ("colleagues"), 198 ("appropriately"); see also ibid., 196; Heffner, "Freedom and Responsibility in Mass Communications," 4–5, 8; and Kaufman, "PG Man Hangs Up That Hat," *NYT,* B3.

2

Sex, Profanity, and Violence

The adoption of the rating system in 1968 was an acknowledgment that American opinion about entertainment was changing. The system also accelerated changes in cinema by removing many of the barriers to expression imposed by the Production Code and PCA. Hollywood's new leaders sought to give movie fans what they wanted, and they tolerated, even encouraged, filmmakers who challenged convention. Valenti welcomed Hollywood's new freedom and embraced what he said was "a new kind of American movie."[1]

CARA came to adopt a much more liberal approach to sex than had the PCA. Although during the 1970s and 1980s critics complained that CARA gave harsher ratings for sexual transgressions than it did for acts of violence, in fact, the rating board largely retreated from trying to regulate motion picture sex. During the Production Code years a central goal had been to control the depiction of sexuality, and even though sexually oriented films had been shown on the exploitation circuit, this kind of entertainment had largely been confined to the underground theater market. To be sure, old attitudes persisted, especially among members of the rating board who had been associated with the PCA, but from the outset, CARA's efforts were minimal in comparison to those of Joseph Breen. Heffner was more open-minded about nudity and sexually oriented themes, and before he accepted the chairmanship of CARA, he told Valenti that his mother had not raised him "to count nipples."[2]

---

[1] Quotation ("new"), Jack Valenti, "The Movie Rating System – How It Began – Its Purpose – How It Works – The Public Reaction," prepared statement to *U.S. House Hearings,* March 24, 1977, 20.

[2] Quotation ("count"), Heffner, *Reminiscences,* vol. 1, p. 30, Box 5, RDH-COHC-BL.

The movies also treated other subjects more candidly. Barriers against profanity and the use of violence fell. And many of the themes that the PCA had worked to eliminate – homosexuality, use of illegal drugs, irreverent treatments of religion – now came to be featured prominently in mainstream films.

SEX

When Breen headed the PCA, he usually reacted strongly to sexual or unconventional ideas in the movies, and had tried to forbid even the mention of such topics as abortion, incest, and homosexuality. Valenti and Aaron Stern generally indicated that they felt such themes automatically required a "restricted" rating. In contrast, Heffner was much more accepting of sexuality and controversial ideas and believed that no subject should be summarily rejected or automatically rated. "I couldn't accept the idea that any idea or theme could, by itself, be rated R, whether it was divorce or abortion. Mention abortion and the picture should be rated R! I couldn't accept that and I wouldn't let that be," he stated. As for Stern, "he never quite appreciated the difference between rating a film contextually in terms of its overall content, and rating a film because of its theme alone," Heffner said. For Heffner, whether a movie received an X, R, PG, or G all depended on how the movie treated any given theme.[3]

Few people understood or really believed that Heffner was serious about rating films according to the manner in which they treated themes and not according to the themes alone. During his early years at CARA, he became embroiled in several rating controversies during which critics accused him of imposing an R or X rating because of the picture's subject matter. George C. Scott challenged the R rating given to his film *The Savage Is Loose* (1974), a story that dealt with incest. Woody Allen was unhappy with the same rating of *Manhattan* (1979), in which a forty-something-year-old man had an affair with a high school student. Homosexuality was at issue in the bitterly contested film *Cruising* (1980), which the rating board initially rated X, and in *Nijinsky* (1980), to which CARA accorded an R.

No sooner had Heffner joined CARA than he was confronted in his office by an irate Scott objecting to the R rating of *The Savage Is Loose*.

---

[3] Quotation ("accept"), ibid., vol. 1, p. 135; see also 34, 134, Box 5, RDH-COHC-BL. Quotation ("contextually"), Heffner, "Pre-Oral History Memorandum for 1980," p. 10, Box 1, RDH-COHC-BL.

Scott, who had won an Oscar for his 1970 title role in *Patton,* had just finished filming *The Savage Is Loose* with his wife, Trish Van Devere. The film is about a family stranded on an island for many years, and Scott was certain that the mere fact that the movie dealt with incest had been the reason for the R rating. Heffner contended that it was the treatment of the theme – not the theme itself – that led to the rating. The movie had placed major emphasis upon incest, and some members of CARA had noted "the wondrous kiss of mother" given to the son at the end. They had also reacted to a wooden sculpture "with its legs spread and vagina visible for presumed masturbatory activity."[4]

At the appeal hearing, Heffner lauded Scott as "a creative artist of unparalleled brilliance," but argued that his movie should be considered as a whole, a "singular work of art," and not as "a pastiche or a jumble of unrelated scenes."[5] He then quoted from an interview that Scott had given to the *New York Times* in which he had said that the film could be seen as a story having several levels: a tale of adventure, a family's psychological survival, man versus nature, and "a sexual odyssey in the psychiatric/Freudian sense."[6] Heffner followed this quotation by citing anthropologist Margaret Mead, who had written that "Essentially, the incest taboo does only one thing: It protects the integrity of the family." Mead, Heffner said, was only expressing "the common sense of our complicated, convoluted lives. All we are saying, in applying this R classification, is that most American parents of young children will feel that if such a dramatic, demanding, forceful treatment of the major taboo of our lives is to be considered by their young children in such a vital, living setting as this motion picture provides, a parent or other mature adult should experience Mr. Scott's presentation along with them."[7] The Appeals Board upheld the R rating, but it was a "horrendous" experience for Heffner. Scott and his wife were unpersuaded and bitter. Some time later Heffner encountered the couple in a New York

---

4 Quotations ("wondrous," "vagina"), Heffner, *Reminiscences,* vol. 2, p. 222, Box 5, RDH-COHC-BL.

5 Quotations ("singular," "scenes"), ibid., p. 220.

6 George C. Scott quoted ("psychiatric/Freudian"), ibid.

7 Heffner quoting ("Essentially," "common") from his appeals statement for *The Savage Is Loose,* in ibid., vol. 2, p. 221, Box 5, RDH-COHC-BL. Margaret Mead had argued for at least minimal controls on pornography, or erotica, to protect children under age twelve. Mead, "Can We Protect Children from Pornography?" *Redbook,* 138 (March 1972), 74–80.

restaurant and overheard Van Devere say: "A bad smell just wafted into the room."[8]

Another divisive rating appeal involved *Manhattan*. One controversial aspect of this critically acclaimed movie was the affair between a middle-aged man (Allen) and a seventeen-year-old girl, played by Mariel Hemingway. Heffner had not attended the first screening of the film when the rating board voted to give the picture an R because of the automatic language rule (one character, played by Diane Keaton, used the "f" word on three occasions). At the appeal, one of the vice presidents from United Artists argued that the R rating meant that Hemingway herself would most likely be prevented from watching the picture in a theater. He compared the situation to a time when he had been in high school and had wanted to write a paper on the Nobel Prize–winning author John Steinbeck. The librarian had locked away suspect books, including *The Grapes of Wrath*, in a kind of "literary jail," and before any student could use them he or she had to get letters from their parents and teachers. This argument almost persuaded the Appeals Board to overturn *Manhattan*'s R rating, but the appeal lacked one vote to obtain the needed two-thirds majority. (Heffner believed, in fact, that had there not been confusion over the way in which the first appeals vote had been conducted, the film would have been changed to a PG.) This argument so impressed Heffner that he scheduled a second appeal. In the meantime, he watched the film for the first time and was dumbfounded by the reasoning behind the rating board's decision. In his opinion, *Manhattan* deserved the R rating, not for language, but because it depicted the affair between Allen and Hemingway. Part of the movie had been filmed at the exclusive Dalton School on the city's Upper East Side, where Hemingway was still a student and where the parents of another student there had complained about the movie. Heffner believed that their reactions reflected how most parents would feel about the film. At the second appeals hearing, held a week after the first, Heffner angered UA executives when he defended the R rating. This time, almost two-thirds of the Appeals Board voted to uphold Heffner and the rating board.[9]

---

[8] Quotations ("smell"), Heffner, *Reminiscences*, vol. 1, pp. 133 ("horrendous"), 135 ("smell"); see also 134, Box 5, RDH-COHC-BL.

[9] Quotation ("jail"), Bach, *Final Cut*, 228; also 235. See also Heffner, "Pre-Oral History Memorandum for 1979," p. 2; also ibid., pp. 3–14, Box 1, RDH-COHC-BL. Bach was a vice president at United Artists.

Rating films that dealt with homosexuality became a contentious issue during the early and mid-1980s when several mainstream movies dealt with this topic. Some of these films provoked public controversy. Religious groups condemned them for their theme and gay and lesbian groups denounced them for stereotyping. One of the ugliest ratings controversies involved *Cruising* (1980), which was originally rated X (discussed later in this chapter). *Windows* (1980), starring Elizabeth Ashley and Talia Shire, featured a homicidal lesbian and was rated R for its violence. *American Gigolo* (1980), starring Richard Gere and Lauren Hutton, was about a male prostitute. Homosexuality was a minor theme and the movie's heavy emphasis on sexuality earned it an R rating. Other films such as *Personal Best* (1982), which starred Mariel Hemingway as a college track star who had a lesbian relationship, offered more sympathetic portrayals of homosexuality. CARA rated the movie R for its nudity, drug use, and strong language rather than for the relationship. *Desert Hearts* (1986), perhaps the first feature-length movie about lesbianism directed and written by a woman, starred Helen Shaver and was a richly textured film that was rated R presumably for its nudity. *Making Love* (1982), starring former "Charlie's Angel" Kate Jackson as a woman who discovers that her husband has fallen in love with another man, received an R because of profanity and implicit sex, not because of the homosexuality theme alone.

Even though these films all received restricted classifications, Heffner denied that the ratings were based on the themes alone. It is likely that he was sincere on this point. In 1956, long before most Hollywood studios and television programs dared to deal with the topic, he had done a series of programs on homosexuality for *The Open Mind*, with Margaret Mead, columnist Max Lerner, and various psychiatrists.[10]

Homosexuality was involved in the ratings controversy over Paramount's *Nijinsky* (1980), a movie, directed by Herbert Ross, about the legendary dancer Vaslaw Fomich Nijinsky. Heffner called the picture an "extraordinarily beautiful film," but the rating board gave it an R, not because Nijinsky was homosexual, but because of a heterosexual sex scene and because of such dialogue as "you fucking little pederast whore," which provoked the application of CARA's automatic language rule.[11]

---

[10] Heffner, *Reminiscences*, vol. 1, pp. 134–5, Box 5, RDH-COHC-BL.

[11] Quotation ("beautiful"), Richard Heffner to Frank Mancuso (Paramount), March 4, 1980, document 80-29; quotation ("pederast"), Heffner to Valenti (interoffice memo), March 13, 1980, document 80-34; exhibits with Heffner, "Pre-Oral History Memorandum for 1980," Box 1, RDH-COHC-BL. For Heffner's explanation for the rating of

Nudity, masturbation, and the simulation or actual depiction of intercourse ("humping," as CARA members sometimes referred to it) invariably raised questions about where to draw rating lines. Shots of nipples, pubic hair, full frontal nudity, and simulated sex often moved films into restricted territory for many rating board members. Heffner, though, preferred to set such scenes into the broader context of the film rather than adhering to oversimplified rules. One of the first appeals cases in which he participated involved what he considered a rather innocuous documentary by David Wolper entitled *Birds Do It, Bees Do It* (1974) that dealt with copulation in the animal kingdom – birds, bees, elephants, and so forth – and that had been rated R. "I just had a very difficult time thinking how that should remain an R," Heffner recalled, but a majority of the Appeals Board voted to keep the rating. Heffner and Wolper conferred quietly and a few minor changes were made, enough so that Heffner could then argue before the rating board for a PG. Years later, Wolper approached CARA about having the original R rating restored, but Heffner dissuaded him from doing so.[12]

When human sexuality was involved, however, assigning a rating that would satisfy all parents proved impossible. In 1980, Heffner received a letter complaining about Shirley MacLaine's moaning and "self-induced orgasm" in Peter Sellers's wickedly funny satire *Being There* (1979). Despite the masturbation scene, most rating board members thought the movie was appropriately rated at PG, and Heffner dismissed the complaint. But in the context of the early 1980s, as religious groups mounted protests against permissiveness in mass entertainment, the woman who objected to the rating given to *Being There* could hardly be considered an isolated example.[13]

PROFANITY

Closely related to the representation of sexuality – and to a range of other issues including the depiction of violence – was the use of obscene or profane language. CARA's automatic language rule required giving a film

---

Nijinsky, see his six-page letter to Paramount's Barry Diller, March 17, 1980, document 80-35, ibid.

[12] Quotations ("humping," "difficult"), Heffner, *Reminiscences*, vol. 2, pp. 216–17, Box 5, RDH-COHC-BL.

[13] Quotation ("orgasm"), Frances Healy to MPAA (Mr. Heffner), May 14, 1980, document 80-D; and Heffner to Healy, May 19, 1980, document 80-D, exhibits with Heffner, "Pre-Oral History Memorandum for 1980," Box 1, RDH-COHC-BL.

an R if the four-letter word for intercourse was used even once. By 1976, the automatic language rule had come under attack and Heffner favored relaxing its enforcement. The movie that proved to be the turning point was Alan J. Pakula's Academy Award–winning film about the Watergate scandal, *All the President's Men* (1976). No movie since Warner Bros.'s *Who's Afraid of Virginia Woolf?* (1966) was more significant in the use of off-color language on screen.

All the President's Men, which reenacted the investigation by *Washington Post* reporters Bob Woodward and Carl Bernstein of the Watergate scandal that brought about the downfall of President Richard Nixon, has stood up well over time. Starring Robert Redford, Dustin Hoffman, and Jason Robards, the film depicts events that followed the break-in at the Watergate Hotel in Washington, DC in June of 1972. For a Hollywood production, it was an unusually good historical drama. Robards won an Academy Award for his portrayal of *Post* editor Ben Bradlee. From the rating board's perspective, the film posed a problem. Under the automatic language rule, which had with rare exceptions been strictly enforced until 1976, the movie plainly required an R rating. At a congressional hearing in 1977, Valenti implied that the problem with this picture centered on only one word. In fact, the rating board had found several violations of the automatic language rule. As Heffner recalled, it had "'rat fucking' and 'mother-fucker' and 'cocksucker' and everything else in it."[14]

All the President's Men was too good, both as entertainment and as recent history, to restrict its viewership with an R rating. The studio appealed. At the time, there was no rating between R and PG (the PG-13 rating did not come until 1984). The appeal was heavily attended by those associated with the film, and Redford, producer Frank Wells, and director Pakula made presentations. The Appeals Board agreed to change the rating to PG.

The new rating seemed perfectly rational at the time to Heffner, who had recommended giving the movie a PG in the first place, but as he looked back on this episode, he felt that it was a decisive moment in ratings history. Henceforth, it would be very difficult to deny a PG rating to any film just because it used the "f" word. In fact, in early 1982, Heffner told Valenti that after the decision on *All the President's Men*, out

---

[14] Quotation ("rat"), Heffner, *Reminiscences*, vol. 1, p. 176, Box 5, RDH-COHC-BL. See also appendix (p. 4) to Valenti, testimony, *U.S. House Hearings*, March 24, 1977, p. 47. Before 1976, the movie *Saturday Morning* (1971) was one of the rare films that had received an R under the automatic language rule only to have its rating changed to PG on appeal.

of thirty-five appeals of automatic language rule ratings, thirty-three had been reversed. Eventually, Heffner counted fifty-five R rating reversals.[15] For some of these films, such as Woody Allen's movie *The Front* (1976), about blacklisting, Heffner himself argued that the automatic restricted rating should be overturned. Among the other R movies whose ratings were changed to PG in the first year after *All the President's Men* were *Small Change* (1976), a François Truffaut film about the lives of children in a French town, and *The Last Tycoon* (1976), an F. Scott Fitzgerald story about a movie producer featuring several stars, including Robert De Niro and Jack Nicholson. Some of those fifty-five movies, no doubt, deserved to have their ratings changed. Heffner thought that the World War II drama *A Bridge Too Far* (1977) deserved a PG; he had only voted for an R, he said, because of the language rule (indeed, the film was later re-rated PG).[16]

Not all movies that appealed the language rule were successful. The makers of *Hopscotch* (1980), which starred Walter Matthau and Glenda Jackson, was given an R because of its language. In this comedy-drama, Matthau plays a maverick CIA spy who takes revenge on his self-important superior, played by Ned Beatty, by publishing a tell-all memoir. The filmmakers wanted the movie rated PG, but here Heffner argued successfully to keep the R rating because of the sheer volume of objectionable language: "What the fuck is he doing?" "He must be out of his fucking mind," "He's out of his fucking mind," "It's his fucking suicide note," "I don't fucking believe this," "Shut the fuck up," "fucking ball-busting imbeciles," "You bet your fucking ass." Even had there not

[15] Heffner to Valenti, Feb. 24, 1982 (interoffice memo), 82–22, Box 1, exhibit with Heffner, "Pre-Oral History Memorandum for 1982," Box 1, RDH-COHC-BL. See also Heffner, *Reminiscences*, vol. 1, pp. 183–4, 186; and vol. 7, 1522, Box 5, RDH-COHC-BL.
    Between 1968 and 1985, the Appeals Board heard 190 ratings appeals. The Appeals Board upheld CARA's rating 101 times, or in about 53 percent of the cases, and it overturned the rating board in 89 appeals, according to Valenti in 1985. Many of the successful appeals, Heffner said, involved challenges to the automatic language rule after *All the President's Men* in 1976. He speculated that only about 12 percent of CARA ratings not involving the language rule (perhaps 22 or 23 cases) had been overturned. See Valenti, statement, *U.S. Senate Hearings*, Oct. 24, 1985, 94; and Heffner, testimony, *U.S. Senate Hearings*, Oct. 24, 1985, 119. In 1980, Heffner maintained that during the first half-dozen years of his leadership (1974–80), out of about 2,500 films that CARA rated, only seven appeals resulted in changes. This number did not count cases involving the automatic language rule. See Heffner, "What G, PG, R and X Really Mean," *TV Guide*, Oct. 4–10, 1980, 40, 46.
[16] At the end of *The Front*, Woody Allen said "Go fuck yourself!" Allen quoted ("Go") in Heffner, *Reminiscences*, vol. 8, p. 1541, Box 5, RDH-COHC-BL. See also appendix (p. 4) to Valenti, Testimony, *U.S. House Hearings*, March 24, 1977, 47.

been an automatic language rule, he said, "it would be just plain wrong for the Rating Board to give this charming film a PG rating *with* this language."[17]

But most of the automatic language R's were overturned on appeal in the months after *All the President's Men,* and because of this fact, Heffner recommended to Valenti that the rule be abandoned as a way to save money. Even though nothing immediately came of the suggestion, Heffner came to regret the recommendation, as he did the outcome of the *All the President's Men* appeal. Even if the changed rating for *All the President's Men* was reasonable, Heffner had underestimated filmmakers' willingness to use this decision to exploit the rating system. One movie viewed in a vacuum would hardly change manners and morals, Heffner believed, but an accumulation of such pictures surely contributed to the growing coarseness of public language in America. The metaphor that showed up so frequently in letters to editors and other expressions of citizen outrage was that a "floodgate" had been opened to profanity. Heffner came to believe that he shared responsibility for this development.[18]

For Heffner, the language problem in *All the President's Men* (Fig. 3) pointed to the need for a new rating category between R and PG. As early as March 1976 he began to urge Valenti to create a "middle rating" that would remove restrictions for certain movies for high school students but not for preteens. He wanted this new category to be restricted, perhaps called "R-13," meaning that preteens needed to be accompanied by a parent or guardian. Over the years, Heffner periodically submitted lists of films that would have been moved from the PG or R categories to PG-13. But Valenti resisted this change, and it would not be until 1984 that the industry adopted the PG-13 – a new rating that was not restricted as Heffner had recommended.[19]

---

17 Quotations ("what," "language"), "RHD Appeal Statement...*Hopscotch*," Sept. 2, 1980, document 80-49, with Heffner, "Pre-Oral History Memorandum for 1980," and ibid., pp. 68–71, Box 1, RDH-COHC-BL.

18 Quotation ("floodgate"), Charles Champlin in Heffner, *Reminiscences,* vol. 1, p. 185; see also ibid., 123–24, 127, 183, 186, Box 5, RDH-COHC-BL. See also Heffner to Valenti, Feb. 24, 1982 (interoffice memo), document 82-22, Box 1, exhibit with Heffner, "Pre-Oral History Memorandum for 1982," Box 1, RDH-COHC-BL.

19 Quotation ("middle"), Heffner to Valenti, March 11, 1976, document 80-38, Box 1, exhibit with Heffner, "Pre-Oral History Memorandum for 1980," Box 1, RDH-COHC-BL. For additional recommendations from Heffner and lists of films that would have had their ratings changed, see Heffner to Valenti, April 11, 1977 (interoffice memo), document 80-38, ibid.; and Heffner to Valenti, March 24, 1980 (interoffice memo), document 80-38, ibid.

FIGURE 3. Dustin Hoffman, Jack Warden, and Robert Redford in *All the President's Men* (1976). Profanity in this movie about the Watergate scandal set off a rating controversy that led to a relaxation of CARA's rules about language. Photograph courtesy of Wisconsin Center for Film and Theater Research.

After the creation of the PG-13 category, the language rule evolved to have two parts. First of all, one use of a forbidden word automatically made the movie PG-13 – not R as before. More than one use of such language, or if the word was used sexually, moved the film into the R category. The second part of the rule, though, stated that if a substantial majority of the rating board members – say two-thirds – believed that the movie "cried out" for a less severe rating, then the automatic R or even automatic PG-13 could be set aside. For Heffner, both parts of this rule were equally important.[20]

Studios manipulated language to gain advantageous ratings. During the 1970s, moviemakers realized that the most profitable rating categories for films were PG and R. In many cases, producers sought to

---

[20] Quotation ("cried out"), Heffner, *Reminiscences*, vol. 8, p. 1520; see also 1519–20, Box 5, RDH-COHC-BL.

avoid the G rating. One way to accomplish this objective was to add profane language. For example, in the production of Robert Altman's *Popeye* (1980), starring Robin Williams, the studio added "Oh, shit" to the dialogue to avoid the G rating. Paul Maslansky, who produced a series of comedies entitled *Police Academy* aimed at the youth market, acknowledged that the G was undesirable because it was associated with older Disney films and "the kind of entertainment" young people had "grown out of." For *Police Academy 3* (1986), Maslansky admitted that if it looked as though the picture would receive a G, the studio "put in some modest foul language on the off-screen soundtrack" in order to obtain a PG.[21] The G rating became almost as undesirable for large-budget films as the X. Valenti acknowledged in 1985 that most producers looked upon it as the "kiss of death." There was no shortage of G films, he told Senator Nunn, but there was "a terrific shortage of G-rated audiences."[22]

During the mid-1970s, the PG rating was often thought to be the most saleable at the box office, and some producers sought to avoid the restricted rating. But the trend, so Hollywood came to believe, was moving rapidly away from even the PG, and the percentage of R movies rose steadily. During CARA's first year, only about a quarter of the movies rated received the R label. The proportion of R-rated pictures increased substantially thereafter but, through the 1970s, remained less than half of the films classified, ranging from about 36 percent in 1971 to a little more than 47 percent in 1973. During the first half of the 1980s, the percentage of R-rated films jumped significantly and rose yet again during the latter half of the decade and during the 1990s. Between 1981 and 1986, between 55 and 60 percent of CARA's rating were Rs. Beginning in 1987, the number exceeded 60 percent and remained above that level for the remainder of the century, surpassing 69 percent in 1999.[23]

VIOLENCE AND HORROR

Unlike his predecessors, Eugene Dougherty and Aaron Stern, Heffner was more interested in restraining violence than sex or profanity. When Stern

---

[21] Quotation ("Oh"), Heffner, "Pre-Oral History Memorandum for 1980," pp. 78, Box 1, RDH-COHC-BL. Paul Maslansky quoted ("kind," "grown" "soundtrack") in S. Mitchell, "The X Rating Gets Its Day in Court," *LAT*, June 21, 1990, F1.

[22] Quotations, Valenti, Testimony, *U.S. Senate Hearings*, Oct. 24, 1985, 82 ("kiss"), 81 ("terrific").

[23] Statistics from CARA, *Annual Reports*, RDHPP.

had been in charge, the joke about CARA (sometimes attributed to Jack Nicholson) had been that if the rating board saw "a nipple it's R, unless it's cut off, in which case it's only violence, and it's PG." Stern's rule of thumb, said Heffner, was "that if a knife went in, that was PG, but if it also came out and you saw blood, that was R. It didn't make any difference how many knives went in."[24]

Early on, Lew Wasserman told Heffner that he believed CARA was too lax. He thought that the Warner Bros. hit *The Exorcist* (1973) and the film *Shampoo* (1975), which starred Warren Beatty and Julie Christie, had both deserved an X – the former for horror, the latter for sex. To get a sense for what was controversial, Heffner persuaded Al Van Schmus – over Valenti's objection – to assemble a few films that had given CARA trouble before his arrival. He watched a 16-mm version of *The Exorcist* at home and agreed that it should have been given an X. Another film, Kirk Douglas's *Scalawag,* had also been improperly rated, he thought, because it had too much violence for young children, and should have been given a PG instead of the G that it had received on appeal.[25]

Heffner also had personal experiences with movies that convinced him that stronger ratings needed to be given for violence. He took his son, then perhaps twelve or thirteen, to see the Charles Bronson film *Death Wish* (1974), a story about a man who turned vigilante after muggers broke into his New York apartment to murder his wife and rape his daughter (Fig. 4). In the film, the murder and rape take place on Riverside Drive, only a few blocks from where the Heffners lived. Heffner's son was deeply frightened by the movie, so much so that he later urged his father to buy a gun. Heffner's reaction was that of a parent – he was angry because he had not been forewarned about the content of *Death Wish* and thought it should have been rated X rather than R.[26]

Wasserman, Heffner discovered, was generally more enthusiastic about strong restricted ratings for movies produced by studios other than his own company, Universal. In 1975, Wasserman agreed to finance a twenty-seven-year-old director named Steven Spielberg to make the movie *Jaws.* Based on Peter Benchley's best-selling novel, the film is about a huge, man-eating great white shark. The movie, which became a blockbuster hit, starred Roy Scheider, Richard Dreyfuss, and Robert Shaw. Heffner

---

[24] Quotations, Heffner, *Reminiscences,* vol. 1, pp. 125 ("nipple," Jack Nicholson quoted), 93 ("knife"); see also ibid., 148, Box 5, RDH-COHC-BL.

[25] Ibid., vol. 1, pp. 53, 58; and Heffner, interview (phone) with author, Aug. 27, 2002.

[26] Heffner, *Reminiscences,* vol. 7, pp. 1234–7, vol. 7, Box 5, RDH-COHC-BL.

FIGURE 4. In *Death Wish* (1974), the wife and daughter of the character played by Charles Bronson are attacked in their home. Here Jeff Goldblum struggles with Hope Lange as Christopher Logan attacks Kathleen Tolan on the floor. The scene so upset Heffner's young son that he urged his father to buy a gun for protection. Photograph courtesy of the Wisconsin Center for Film and Theater Research.

admitted that it was a scary picture and that his own wife "was practically under the seat" for part of the film. Critics such as Charles Champlin of the *Los Angeles Times* thought the picture was far too frightening for children – essentially because it showed children menaced by the shark – and believed that it should not have been rated PG. At the time, the PG was regarded as the rating best suited for drawing a large audience, and studios pushed for this classification for their big budget productions. Heffner rationalized the PG for *Jaws,* arguing that the movie's violence was unlikely to be imitated.[27]

Because of their political clout and their close connections with Valenti, studio executives like Wasserman and United Artists's Arthur Krim could exercise great leverage over ratings when their own projects were involved. Usually they got what they wanted, but not always. Krim, dubbed the industry's éminence grise by one Hollywood chieftain, headed United

[27] Quotation ("seat"), ibid., vol. 2, p. 207; see also ibid., 208.

Artists until 1978 when he became chair of Orion Productions. Those who fell out of favor with Krim could find him imperious, dictatorial, overbearing, and cold.[28]

United Artists, Krim's studio, made the movie *Rollerball* (1975). It was based on William Harrison's story *Roller Ball Murders,* starred James Caan, John Houseman, and Maud Adams, and was filmed in Munich and London (Fig. 5). Set in a future world controlled by cartels, the film was about a vicious form of Roller Derby that took the place of warfare. When Heffner first watched it, he believed the film deserved an X. He could envision "parents being horrified" by it because their children could imitate the movie's violence, he recalled. But Van Schmus and a majority of CARA members thought an R rating was appropriate. Krim, however, demanded a PG. At the appeal in July 1975, he denounced Heffner as a "fanatic about violence," just as Stern had been a "fanatic about sex." The appeal went against Krim by a vote of ten to nine. Valenti then intervened to get Krim a second hearing two weeks later, a step not usually allowed. Again, Heffner came under attack, and again Krim lost. Later, at a party, Heffner learned why Krim had been so impassioned. The difference at the box office between a PG and an R was then about $5 million. Krim, Heffner concluded, simply wanted the PG *"because it would be a key for United Artists to make more money or at least to lose less money on this film. All for the dollar!"* Years later Heffner encountered Krim on Fifth Avenue in New York and found him still focused on *Rollerball.*[29]

Although movie ratings frequently reflected political pressures and economic calculations beyond CARA's control, Heffner continued to push for classifying violent films more stringently. CARA initially gave Xs to several violent pictures. In some cases, these ratings were changed by the Appeals Board after producers argued that, even if their films were extremely violent, they did not deserve Xs because of that rating's association with pornography. In the end, usually filmmakers cut or edited scenes in order to attain a better rating.

The Appeals Board sometimes overruled CARA. One of the first challenges to an X rating that Heffner faced came in 1974, soon after he had become chairman. The challenge involved a low-budget picture which Heffner remembered being called *Wheels of Death* (1974?), about a

[28] Bach, *Final Cut,* 59–61, 419.

[29] Quotations, Heffner, *Reminiscences,* vol. 1, pp. 145 ("horrified"), 146 ("fanatic," "sex"); see also ibid., 142–7, Box 5, RDH-COHC-BL. On box-office gross for PG and R films, see ibid., 147. Quotation (*"because,"* "dollar"), Heffner, "Pre-Oral History Memorandum for 1980," p. 2 (emphasis in original text), Box 1, RDH-COHC-BL.

FIGURE 5. Richard Heffner and Arthur Krim, who headed United Artists, clashed over what rating should be given to the movie *Rollerball* (1975). Heffner believed the violence merited an X, while Krim wanted a PG. The Rating Board settled on an R. Photograph courtesy of the Wisconsin Center for Film and Theater Research.

motorcycle gang that invaded a small town. The violence was much too strong for children of any age, Heffner thought, yet the board voted to give the film an R. Stunned by this decision, Heffner began to suspect that the board could not be counted on for support on this kind of film.

The judgment also put Heffner on an uncertain footing with other rating board members who were reluctant to use the X for violence except in the most extreme cases.[30]

Heffner did make one X rating for violence stick, however, and it earned him something of a reputation. The film to gain this dubious distinction was Shigehiro Ozawa's *Street Fighter* (1974), a martial arts movie from New Line Cinema featuring a castration scene that seemed gratuitous even by the more permissive standards of the time. The *New York Times* ran an article about Heffner, calling him "The Man Who Gave an 'X' Rating to Violence." But the classification for *Street Fighter* also led to charges that CARA and the MPAA were biased against small producers, rating their movies more harshly than those made by the large studios. In early 1977, a subcommittee of the United States House of Representative's Committee on Small Business held hearings on the film ratings and independent producers. The committee subpoenaed Valenti and Heffner. Valenti, who wanted only one voice talking about the ratings – his own – did not wish to have Heffner testify before Congress and tried to prevent him from doing so, until the subpoena arrived. Valenti then traveled from Washington to New York to accompany Heffner to the hearings. On the way to the capital, he let Heffner know that he would be getting a ten-thousand-dollar-a-year salary increase. Heffner took it as Valenti's way of saying: "Pal, don't go off the handle here. Don't be a hostile witness." Valenti's offer was unnecessary, because at

---

[30] Heffner, *Reminiscences*, vol. 1, p. 149, Box 5, RDH-COHC-BL. See also e-mail, Heffner to author, Aug. 21, 2001. Another film that had its X rating overturned on appeal was *When the Screaming Stops* (1974). The story involved a woman who occasionally turned into a monster, who then ate human hearts. All but one member of CARA voted for the X. The studio, Independent Artists Corporation, argued that the movie was no more violent than such earlier horror films as *Night of the Living Dead*, *The Texas Chainsaw Massacre*, and *Andy Warhol's Frankenstein* (1974). (The appeal did not mention that *Texas Chainsaw Massacre* and *Warhol's Frankenstein* had originally been rated X but had made cuts to get the R.) The studio pleaded its case to Valenti and argued that *When the Screaming Stops* was "obviously fantasy," and "not designed to be disturbing" in the way that such movies as *Death Wish* (1974) or *Taxi Driver* (1976) had been. Those films, the studio contended, could have been "psychologically damaging to children as well as adults" because they attempted "to deliver a message and manipulate the audience in a way that could possibly result in anti-social behavior." *When the Screaming Stopped* was "just a good scare," so the appeal went. Quotations ("psychologically," "scare"), Miles Nelson (studio vice president) to Valenti, Sept. 27, 1978, with Heffner, "Pre-Oral History Memorandum for 1978, Box 1, RDH-COHC-BL; and Heffner, "Pre-Oral History Memorandum for 1978," p. 47, Box 1, ibid. See also e-mail, Heffner to author, Aug. 21, 2001.

this time Heffner believed in the rating system and had no intention of damaging it.[31]

Requests to re-rate films after they had already circulated were not unusual. Some producers discovered, though, that by the late 1970s, the criterion for rating movies had changed under Heffner. Stanley Kubrick's *A Clockwork Orange* (1971) had originally been rated X. After he deleted a short sex scene it was reclassified as an R. The word had gotten around that Heffner tended to be more liberal on sexuality than his predecessors, and in 1979 Kubrick approached him to see if the scene could be reinserted and the film retain its R. The sex scene would cause no problem, Heffner said, but went on to explain, with his colleagues' approval, that if the movie were to be reclassified, parents now would insist that the picture be rated X for its violence. Kubrick quietly withdrew the film.[32]

The system depended on the good faith and voluntary compliance of moviemakers and was therefore a system that sometimes failed. Motion pictures actually shown in theaters sometimes differed from the version that had been classified – a circumstance that "happened many more times than I'd like to think," Heffner admitted. *The Texas Chainsaw Massacre*, originally rated X, was cut by several minutes and resubmitted to CARA (then under Stern) to get an R. After Heffner became chair, he learned that a distributor had reinstated all the deleted material that had led to the X rating, but the movie still played at a Loew's Theater in the Bronx with an R.[33]

Even when CARA succeeded in bringing offending filmmakers into line the damage lingered. *I Spit on Your Grave* (1978;1981), a movie about a brutally raped woman who takes revenge on her attackers, received an X rating. By trimming the film to about forty-eight minutes, the producer managed to have the classification changed to R. But when the movie was shown, the public saw the uncut, X-rated version. The MPAA and

---

[31] Heffner quoting Valenti ("hostile"), Heffner, *Reminiscences*, vol. 1, p. 100; see also ibid., 99, Box 5, RDH-COHC-BL. Also Heffner, interview (phone) with author, Aug. 27, 2002. See also Jonas, "The Man Who Gave an 'X' Rating to Violence."

[32] Heffner, "Pre-Oral History Memorandum for 1979," pp. 27–28, Box 1, RDH-COHC-BL. Some violent movies, such as *Dawn of the Dead*, were purposely designed for an X-rated audience. The distributor booked this movie into as many midnight showings as possible, and once that X market dried up, the film was then heavily edited and resubmitted to CARA, where it received an R. Later, the distributor returned to CARA, chagrined that apparently no one wanted to see the tamer version. It recirculated as an X or possibly unrated. Ibid., 20.

[33] Quotation ("happened"), Heffner, *Reminiscences*, vol. 1, p. 110, Box 5, RDH-COHC-BL. Also e-mail, Heffner to author, Aug. 21, 2001.

CARA sued the filmmakers and forced them to apologize in ads taken out in *Variety* and the *Hollywood Reporter.* Still, movie critics inaccurately reported that CARA had allowed a film that should have been given an X to be shown with an R rating. Subsequently, makers of other violent pictures, such as *Scarface* (1983), argued that they did not deserve an X because *I Spit on Your Grave* had been given an R.[34]

Such motion pictures as *A Clockwork Orange* and *I Spit on Your Grave* combined sexual themes and violence, a combination of two elements that became more prominent during the 1970s. The rating controversy that Heffner considered the "most disillusioning" and the "ugliest episode" revolved around *Cruising* (1980), a film by director William Friedkin and producer Jerry Weintraub that dealt with gay sadomasochism in Manhattan. In it Al Pacino starred as an undercover cop who infiltrated S & M clubs in attempts to catch a killer who preyed on homosexual men. Gays protested against the way in which the film accentuated sadomasochistic practices and implied that the victims deserved their fates. What dismayed Heffner was not the subject matter of *Cruising* but the fact that, after Friedkin, Weintraub, and Valenti had exerted what he believed was inappropriate pressure on him, the filmmakers then exhibited a version of the movie that had never been rated. He called the dispute over this picture "more damaging than any other event" during his time with CARA.[35]

Weintraub's influence was considerable and he was a powerful opponent. He had been the executive producer of director Robert Altman's acclaimed movie *Nashville* (1975) and Carl Reiner's *Oh, God!* (1977), which starred singer John Denver and comedian George Burns. In 1976, *Newsweek* called Weintraub the "Wiz of Showbiz." "He treads softly in Guccis and wields one of the toughest fists in show business," the article began. "I'm into Americana and entertainment," Weintraub maintained.

---

[34] Other movie ratings were withdrawn or challenged because the films were shown in versions that had not been rated. John Schlesinger's *Honky Tonk Freeway* (1981), a comedy about life in a small town starring William Devane and Beverly D'Angelo, had its PG revoked when it restored dialogue that required an R under the automatic language rule. Heffner complained to Valenti that *Hard Country* (1981), a contemporary Western staring Jan-Michael Vincent and Kim Basinger, was being shown in something other than the PG version given by CARA. Heffner, "Pre-Oral History Memorandum for 1978," p. 53, Box 1, RDH-COHC-BL; and Heffner, "Pre-Oral History Memorandum for 1983," pp. 32, 35–7, Box 2, RDH-COHC-BL.

[35] Quotations, Heffner, "Pre-Oral History Memorandum for 1980," p. 3 ("damaging"), 31 ("disillusioning," "ugliest"); see also ibid., 2–33, Box 1, RDH-COHC-BL. See also Prince, *New Pot of Gold*, 344–8.

But he was "more a power broker than a producer," according to one competitor. A recording executive remembered him as "an aggressive, greedy, pushy, grabby person. When you shook hands with him you'd count your rings, but he exuded an aura of know-it-all that carries weight with artists." For the clients he represented in the music world – including Denver, Neil Diamond, and the Carpenters – he seemed to work wonders. Any number of people in Hollywood for whom he had done favors were thought to be in his debt.[36]

Weintraub and Friedkin asked Heffner to read the script for *Cruising* in May 1979, which he did. The automatic language rule required at least an R, and maybe an X, he said. The script also included fellatio, murder, and an undercurrent of sadomasochistic violence. Heffner could not predict how the rating board would vote. It depended on what the cameras showed and the overall treatment of the movie's themes. He did not want to get involved in the production of the film. On December 7, the rating board watched *Cruising* for the first time and voted to give it an X. Weintraub reacted angrily, "and at that moment there began," Heffner recounted the following July, "the extraordinary bluster, cajolery, assault, pressure and attempted intimidation, etc. that have characterized the *Cruising* rating situation to this moment."[37]

Weintraub and Friedkin demanded that Heffner work with film editors to make cuts, but he refused. They then retained Stern, who recommended cutting sex scenes and apparently told Weintraub and Friedkin that the movie should be given an R. The rating board viewed different versions of the film in late December 1979 and early January 1980, but thought it deserved an X. They found a brutal murder scene at the beginning of the picture particularly troubling. Stern's involvement was ill-advised, Heffner thought, because, during the years he had been away from CARA, the rating board had come to reflect a tougher stand on violence. Stern's interference made it less likely that Friedkin would make the necessary changes to obtain an R. When the rating board held firm to its decision to give the film an X rating, Heffner claims he received abusive phone calls and threats to destroy the system. Then, unexpectedly, Weintraub and Friedkin indicated that they would make whatever cuts CARA wanted.

---

[36] Quotations ("treads," "artists"), Orth, "The Wiz of Showbiz," *Newsweek*, Dec. 20, 1976, 65; also 68.

[37] Quotations ("moment," "bluster"), "RDH Summary of Major Events Relating to *Cruising*, July 7, 1980," document 80-2, p. 2; see also p. 3, with Heffner, "Pre-Oral History Memorandum for 1980," Box 1, RDH-COHC-BL.

The board watched yet another version of the film, and on January 4, 1980, voted to give *Cruising* an R.[38]

Heffner believed he had a good-faith pledge that the film would be changed and, on that basis, CARA issued the new rating. But when Heffner went to view the film in a New York theater on February 14, he saw that material that was supposed to have been cut to get the R had been left in the picture. He called Van Schmus in Los Angeles, where the movie was opening and, without telling him his own reaction, asked him to watch it. Van Schmus also thought that an unrated version of the film was being shown. "The point for us was that there was a film in distribution that literally – in terms of its content on the screen – had *not* been rated, but was carrying our rating." The filmmakers "had lied to us. Out and out lied," an outraged Heffner maintained. The rating board reconvened and unanimously agreed to revoke the R, and Heffner asked Valenti to take the necessary steps.[39]

At this point, Valenti intervened and pleaded with Heffner "over and over again with his usual business about 'being nice to these people.'" Heffner sensed that Valenti had "a very great personal stake in... Weintraub," possibly because Weintraub had political connections and could get "stars to perform for politicians Valenti wanted to influence." From Heffner's perspective, Valenti seemed to have become an advocate for Weintraub and *Cruising*. He "prevented us from getting the rating revoked," Heffner recalled, "and he and his lawyers acted all along as though the Rating Board was their enemy and Weintraub their friend!"[40]

For Heffner, the low point came on February 28–29, when he received a midnight call from Valenti, who – as Heffner recollected – played him a tape of a conversation he had had with Weintraub. As Heffner recalled the words, Weintraub had told Valenti: "I'm going to blow this fucking son-of-a-bitch right out of the water. This guy is playing around with

[38] Ibid., 3–4; and Heffner to Valenti, Dec. 31, 1979, document 80-6, Box 1, with Heffner, "Pre-Oral History Memorandum for 1980," RDH-COHC-BL.

[39] Quotations ("literally," "rating"), Heffner, "RDH Summary of Major Events Relating to *Cruising,* July 7, 1980," document 80-2, p. 6, with Heffner, "Pre-Oral History Memorandum for 1980," Box 1, RDH-COHC-BL. Quotation ("lied"), Heffner, "Pre-Oral History Memorandum for 1980," p. 19, Box 1, RDH-COHC-BL. See also Heffner to Valenti, Feb. 27, 1980, document 80-8, with ibid.

[40] Quotations, Heffner, "Pre-Oral History Memorandum for 1980," pp. 6 ("over," "Weintraub"), 7–8 ("stars," "friend"), Box 1, RDH-COHC-BL.

my livelihood. He's playing with dynamite. I'm going to put Mr. Heffner away." Afterward, Valenti reportedly said to Heffner: "He's going to sue you, Dick. I don't want anything to happen to you." The following day, February 29, Heffner, who was deeply upset, wrote to Valenti about the situation. Valenti later asked him to remove the memorandum and its attachments from his files.[41]

Heffner believed that *Cruising* inflicted a nearly mortal wound on the rating system. Aside from the protests over the movie – gays picketed theaters in New York and San Francisco – many in the press questioned why CARA had given the picture an R rating. Maybe even more troubling from the MPAA's perspective were the reactions of theater owners. Since Hollywood's economic stability depended on cooperation between the major studios and theaters, actions by the theater owners could threaten both the rating system and the industry's economic foundation. The country's largest theater chain, General Cinema Corp., which booked the film without having screened it, broke with the MPAA and refused to show the picture on the grounds that it should have been rated X. The United Artists Theater Circuit showed the movie but imposed restrictions as if it were X-rated.

The situation soured further when a San Diego exhibitor filed suit charging that CARA and United Artists (which distributed *Cruising*), had misrepresented the film by assigning it the R rating. The MPAA's attorneys – Louis Nizer (who was then outside counsel to CARA), Barbara Scott (the MPAA's general counsel), and Gerald Phillips – wanted to know how Heffner would testify. Here were ethical, if not legal, land mines, Heffner worried. Nizer and Phillips were also partners in Phillips, Nizer, Benjamin, and Krim, which represented United Artists. Nizer, in particular, believed that Heffner's insistence that "the truth is the truth" would support the plaintiff and wanted Heffner to testify that the version of *Cruising* that had been distributed had really been rated R. Considering this request an attempt "to suborn perjury," Heffner refused. Ultimately,

---

[41] Quotations ("blow," Valenti quoted, "sue"), Heffner, "Pre-Oral History Memorandum for 1980," p. 22. See also Heffner to Valenti, Feb. 29, 1980 (interoffice memo) document 80-8-A, with Heffner, "Pre-Oral History Memorandum for 1980," Box 1, RDH-COHC-BL.

Heffner gives two versions of Valenti's midnight telephone call on February 28–29, 1980. In the first, he says Valenti played a tape of the conversation. Later, Heffner said that Valenti "read to me Weintraub's statement that if I persisted in the X for *Cruising* he'd destroy me." Quotation ("read"), Heffner, "Pre-Oral History Memorandum for 1983," p. 16, Box 2, ibid. See also Box 1, ibid.

Nizer retreated and, Heffner surmised, an out-of-court deal was made with the theater owner.[42]

Only after these protests from large theater chains did the MPAA recall the movie for reevaluation. In the public bickering that followed, CARA accused filmmakers of not having made agreed-upon cuts that would have justified the R; the filmmakers denied that they had ever made this agreement and provided a refutation of these charges. Eventually, Weintraub and Friedkin announced that they had withdrawn and reedited *Cruising,* so the R rating was restored. It seemed to make little difference at the box office, where the film did poorly.[43]

---

[42] Quotations, Heffner, "Pre-Oral History Memorandum for 1980," 28 ("truth"), 30 ("perjury"); see also 23, 28, 31, Box 1, RDH-COHC-BL. See also Heffner to Louis Nizer and Barbara Scott, May 1, 1980, document 80-20; and Heffner, "Memorandum on July 22, 1980 Meeting with Lawyers Relating to 'Cruising,'" Exhibit 80-23, with Heffner, "Pre-Oral History Memorandum for 1980," Box 1, RDH-COHC-BL.

[43] See "Statement of Jerry Weintraub and William Friedkin Relative to 'Cruising' and Its R Rating," document 80-11, with Heffner, "Pre-Oral History Memorandum for 1980," Box 1, RDH-COHC-BL; and "Statement of William Friedkin and Jerry Weintraub Responding to Charges against Them Made by MPAA and the Rating Board Relative to 'Cruising' and Its 'R' Rating," document 80-12, with ibid. See also Champlin, "What Will H. Hays Begat: Fifty Years since His Code Ruled Hollywood," *American Film* 6 (Oct. 1980), 86.

3

The X Rating and the Home Entertainment Revolution

During the 1970s and 1980s, important changes occurred in the way people sent and received sexually explicit material. Before 1970, the transmission of erotica relied heavily on the printed word, black-and-white film, and still photography. This is not to say that sex films were unavailable or that color pictures and movies had not already made an impact, because so-called blue movies or stag pictures, often shot on grainy black-and-white 16 mm film, had circulated on the underground market. *Playboy* had been using color photography for its nude pictorials since the late 1950s. During the 1960s, the availability of erotic color photographs expanded rapidly, and the number of sexually explicit movies grew, too, although in 1970 it was not common to watch these films on a television set in one's home.[1]

The President's Commission on Obscenity and Pornography noted, in 1970, "a radical increase in sexually oriented motion pictures," so-called hybrid movies that combined "the sexual explicitness of exploitation films with the distribution patterns of general release films." Moreover, "an entirely new genre of highly sex-oriented films" that showed actual sexual intercourse had appeared. Whereas such explicit movies had once been confined to private or semiprivate showings, usually in sleazy locations, the new breed of hybrid film was now appearing in upscale theaters. Whereas exploitation movies had been confined to perhaps five to six

[1] For an overview of the changing character of media and pornography from the 1950s to the mid-1980s, see Robert Peters, Testimony, *Meese Commission Hearings*, Oct. 16, 1985, 37–58, Folder: "Los Angeles – 10/16/85 (Part I)," Box 3, RAGCP-NARA 2.

hundred theaters, the new-style film could anticipate exhibition in one to two thousand.[2]

During the decade of the 1970s, movies featuring explicit sexual behavior proliferated. In San Francisco, such theaters as the Screening Room, Sutter Cinema, and the O'Farrell specialized in "adults-only" entertainment, and in New York and other cities similarly well-known X-rated houses appeared. By the end of the decade, many communities had at least one theater or drive-in that showed hard-core pictures. Such films were no longer confined to seedy art houses or specialty theaters. Major studios flirted with pornography, usually labeled "soft core," with such pictures as *Emmanuelle* (1974) and *Pretty Baby* (1978).[3] Hard-core films such as *Deep Throat* (1972), *The Devil in Miss Jones* (1973), and *Behind the Green Door* (1973) played in first-run theaters and received reviews in the mainstream press.

There was a growing public for both soft-core and hard-core entertainment. *Deep Throat* created such a sensation that, according to movie critic Vincent Canby, it became fashionable "to see and to be seen at" the film. Television talk-show host Johnny Carson, director Mike Nichols, actor Jack Nicholson, and even United Nations diplomats were all seen at the picture. Ralph Blumenthal wrote in the *New York Times Magazine* about a new attitude that he called "porno chic." Some measure of just how much public attitudes toward sex in the movies had changed can be seen in the reaction to Bernardo Bertolucci's 1973 film, *Last Tango in Paris,* which dealt with an affair between a middle-aged man and a young woman and displayed full-frontal female nudity. The loudest protests came not from moralists but from disappointed women who lamented that there was no comparable exposure for Marlon Brando, the male star.[4]

During the 1970s, the money made from pornography rivaled mainstream Hollywood profits. The "X" rating – the only category that could be self-applied by a filmmaker – became synonymous with hard-core sex films. Hundreds of these movies were produced each year by companies or individuals who were not part of the MPAA. CARA reviewed only a

[2] Quotations ("radical," "films,"), "The Volume of Traffic and Patterns of Distribution of Sexually Oriented Materials," *RCOP*, 10.

[3] See Randall, "Classification by the Motion Picture Industry," 283; and Cook, *Lost Illusions*, 276–83.

[4] Quotation ("see"), Canby, "What Are We to Think of 'Deep Throat'?" *NYT*, Jan. 21, 1973, sec. 2, p. 1; and ("chic"), Blumenthal, "Porno chic," *NYT Magazine*, Jan. 21, 1973, 28; see also ibid., 30. Black, *Catholic Crusade against the Movies*, 237–8.

small percentage of these films. Indeed, the rating board had only minimal contact with this branch of moviemaking.

Part of the reason for the popularity of these films surely had to do with improvements in moviemaking technology. The soundtrack for *Deep Throat* was apparently so good that even one of the attorneys who tried to suppress the film found himself absentmindedly humming the movie's theme song. The cinematography in these hard-core movies was far superior to the amateur productions of just a decade earlier. This improved cinematography affected adult films and mainstream entertainment alike. Several light-weight 35-mm cameras appeared in the early 1970s, the most significant of which was Panavision's Panaflex 35-mm camera in 1973. Weighing twenty-five pounds, it carried 250 feet of film in its magazine and made it possible to shoot film in previously inaccessible places. As one cinematographer who had had to deal previously with a 165-pound camera put it, with a Panaflex you could move right into the bathroom and "without taking the walls out... shoot scenes in there."[5]

Improvements in technologies related to cinema are central to the history of motion pictures throughout the twentieth century, but after World War II the arrival of new media accelerated, transforming the character of entertainment and the public's relationship to it. Innovations multiplied the possibilities for expression during the 1950s and 1960s. Movies were still largely confined to theaters during the late 1960s and most people had to leave home to see them, but new technologies soon altered not only what they could see and hear, but also where and how they saw it. Improvements in television, the expansion of subscription cable TV and satellite broadcasting, and advances in video recording converged to create a revolution in home entertainment. The changes "demassified media," making it possible for people to personalize how and where they received information and entertainment. More and more often, the public began to view more diverse forms of entertainment in the privacy of their living rooms or bedrooms. The new developments made pornography and violent entertainment available to them on an unprecedented scale.

---

[5] John Alonzo quoted ("without") in Schaefer and Salvato, *Masters of Light,* 41. The Panaflex weighed thirty-four pounds when loaded with a 500-foot magazine. During the early 1970s, pornographic filmmakers also sometimes used a hand-held 35-mm Aeroflex camera. Some of the better financed pictures used a Mitchell 35-mm BNC reflex camera, reportedly costing $30,000. See Cook, *Lost Illusions,* 361, 372–3; and Turan and Zito, *Sinema,* 238, 232. For an illustrated account of sexually explicit films during the 1970s, see Muller and Faris, *Grindhouse,* 117–47. On *Deep Throat,* see also Blumenthal, "Porno chic," 30.

But the innovations also raised questions about the capability, appropriateness, and viability of the rating system. It was one thing for the public to accept sexually explicit and violent films that were limited to theaters, but would Americans remain as tolerant of the new cinematic freedom when uncensored productions came directly into their homes?[6]

X-RATED: STUDIOS AND THE COURTS

The protests over the X rating initially given to *Cruising* were perhaps more vicious than usual, but the attempt to change the rating was not exceptional. Once that rating became associated with hard-core pornography, mainstream studios soon sought to avoid the X at all costs and began to require filmmakers to produce a final product that would receive a classification no worse than R. Business calculations explain why. Many theater chains would not show X-rated films; many newspapers would not accept advertising for them. After video cassettes became popular during the 1980s, many chains would not rent X-rated films. There were exceptions of course. Occasionally, a filmmaker would ask CARA to rate a movie X because, in some parts of the country, newspapers would not advertise pictures with the self-applied X but would take the ads if CARA had made the rating.[7]

The theater owners had a hand in the adoption of the X rating, just as they had had in the automatic language rule. Valenti did not want to have the X. He preferred to have the ratings stop at the R. In effect, he would have allowed children to see any type of movie so long as their parents approved. But the National Organization of Theatre Owners objected, fearing that local obscenity laws would make them susceptible to prosecution if no X rating existed, so they pushed Valenti to include the X. The decision not to copyright the X rating was apparently made after lawyers advised that a "closed system would invite restraint of trade suits."[8]

At the outset of the rating system, the X had a broad meaning; it was intended as more than just a warning signal of explicit sex. The British Board of Film Censors had adopted the X for adult pictures during the early 1950s. Although many of the early X certificates had been issued to French and Italian movies with sexually adventuresome themes, the

[6] Quotation ("de-massified"), Toffler, *Third Wave*, 181; also 171–83.
[7] Heffner, *Reminiscences*, vol. 1, p. 74, Box 5, RDH-COHC-BL; and Prince, *New Pot of Gold*, 122.
[8] Quotation ("suits"), Mathews, "Oct. 3 Marks the Spot for Movie Showdown," *LAT*, Sept. 15, 1990, F1. See also Valenti, testimony, *U.S. Senate Hearings*, Oct. 24, 1985, 76.

FIGURE 6. Maria Schneider in Bernardo Bertolucci's *Last Tango in Paris* (1973). The United Artist film, the last movie produced by a major, mainstream studio to receive an X rating, also starred Marlon Brando. Photograph courtesy of the Wisconsin Center for Film and Theater Research.

board wanted the rating to be applied, not solely to "sordid films dealing with unpleasant subjects, but films which, while not being suitable for children, are good adult entertainment and films which appeal to an intelligent public." In the United States, CARA took a similar approach, assigning X ratings to nonpornographic movies that dealt with adult themes, such as *Midnight Cowboy* (1969), *Myra Breckenridge* (1970), *A Clockwork Orange* (1971), and *Last Tango in Paris* (1973, see Fig 6).[9] But then, as pornographers increasingly self-applied the X to their work,

[9] Arthur T. L. Watkins quoted ("sordid") in Hunnings, *Film Censors and the Law*, 145; also 129, 143–4. Watkins had been Secretary of the British Board of Film Censors. The first three movies to receive an X rating in the United States were *The Girl on a Motorcycle* (1968), a British-French picture dealing with adultery; *Birds of Peru* (1968), concerning nymphomania; and *Sin with a Stranger* (1968), a French-Italian film about a young woman who commits murder. See Canby, "For Better or Worse, Film Industry Begins Ratings," *NYT*, Nov. 1, 1968, clipping in Box 53, USSCCP-NARA 1. See also Farber, *Movie Rating Game*, 46–54.

American mainstream studios shunned the rating. Not until 1990, when Universal produced *Henry and June,* did a major studio risk turning out a movie with adult-oriented subject matter that went beyond the R. By then Hollywood had abandoned the X altogether in favor of a new category called NC-17.

This did not mean that CARA stopped using the X – far from it. Numerous films were initially rated X on first screening. Heffner wanted to use the X more frequently, not just to indicate adult themes or explicit sex but also to indicate extreme violence. Violence, in combination with sex, figured in many films during the 1970s and 1980s. However, moviemakers resisted using the X for violence because of the rating's association with pornography. Occasionally, a filmmaker would be so absolutely candid about his intentions that Heffner found it refreshing. In late 1975, Richard Dreyfuss appealed the X rating given to his film *Inserts* (1975), which dealt with a legitimate movie director who turned to making pornography. The movie had been given the X because of a violent sex scene in which a woman was strangled during intercourse. It was not the sex scene per se that had elicited the rating, Heffner said, but rather the way it had been handled. At the appeal, Dreyfuss argued that he had been brought up in Brooklyn to believe that "a man's worth is measured by his wealth, by his . . . material success." If his movie had to be shown with an X, it would fail. He needed at least an R. Although Dreyfuss lost the appeal and apparently cut the film to get the R, it still did poorly in the theaters.[10]

Heffner clung to the view that the X could and should indicate more than hard-core pornography. When the creators of *Bad Timing: A Sensual Obsession* (1980) appealed its X rating, he defended the classification. *Bad Timing* was a British film starring Art Garfunkel and Theresa Russell and dealt with a serious theme, obsessive love. In the movie, Garfunkel's character, Alex, is an American psychoanalyst who has a passionate affair with a woman named Milena (Russell). Milena is not willing to commit herself to one man, and as she becomes involved with others, Alex grows increasingly possessive. The story is told as a series of flashbacks after Milena is admitted to the hospital for a drug overdose and police are investigating whether her case is something more than an attempted suicide. As with *Last Tango in Paris,* there were explicit sex scenes. Heffner asked the Appeals Board to reaffirm the position it had taken years earlier when it ruled on *Last Tango,* namely that X was not synonymous with

---

[10] Heffner quoting Dreyfuss ("worth"), in Heffner, *Reminiscences,* vol. 1, p. 137, Box 5, RDH-COHC-BL.

pornography. "Any effort to say that we will be labeling *Bad Timing* as porno if you sustain our X is sophistry," Heffner argued. "Worse, you will be *endorsing* the idea that X means porno!"[11]

By this time, Heffner believed that there should be a better way to rate adult material. Just as there needed to be a category between PG and R, so there should be a rating between R and X. In fact, as Heffner confided to Frank Mancuso of Paramount Pictures in 1982, he and many of his rating board colleagues were "deeply sympathetic" to creating this new category. The problem, as he told the Appeals Board in the *Bad Timing* hearing, was that the R rating was already heavily burdened and might well be destroyed if it was continually forced to accept "the strongest sex or violence that *is* adult" but not pornographic.[12]

The peak year for CARA's use of the X rating came in 1976 when sixty films were so classified, about 12 percent of the total number of pictures the rating board reviewed that year. During the next five years, CARA used the rating less frequently, assigning only 22 Xs in 1978 and 34 in 1979. With the arrival of the video revolution, it all but abandoned the rating. Between 1982 and 1989, only 15 out of 3,339 films rated received an X. CARA discarded the X in 1990 in favor of the NC-17, a new rating that also would be used sparingly.[13]

While the major studios tried to distance themselves from the X rating, the judicial system tried with only limited success to impose legal restraints on X-rated films and the theaters that showed them. Here, the United States Supreme Court's focus was on sex, not violence. In 1973 and 1974, the Court grappled with regulations on obscenity, which had

---

[11] Quotations ("Any," "porno"), Heffner, "Statement on the Appeal of *Bad Timing: A Sensual Obsession*," Sept. 25, 1980, document 80-52, with Heffner, "Pre-Oral History Memorandum for 1980," (emphasis in original text) Box 1, RDH-COHC-BL. The film eventually received an R rating.

[12] Quotation ("strongest"), ibid. Quotation ("sympathetic"), Heffner to Frank Mancuso, Jan. 25, 1982, document 82-15, with Heffner, "Pre-Oral History Memorandum for 1982," (emphasis in original text) Box 1, RDH-COHC-BL.

[13] The number of films rated X together with the percentage of X-rated films in the total number of feature films rated by CARA is as follows: 1969: 89 (6.3% of 325 films rated); 1970: 42 (10% of 431 rated); 1971: 49 (9.6% of 513 rated); 1972: 11 (2% of 540 rated); 1973: 28 (4.8% of 584 rated); 1974: 24 (4.6% of 523 rated); 1975: 25 (5.4% of 459 rated); 1976: 60 (12.3% of 486 rated); 1977: 24 (6.3% of 378 rated); 1978: 22 (6.6% of 334 rated); 1979: 34 (9.4% of 361 rated); 1980: 30 (9% of 330 rated); 1981: 27 (8% of 336 rated); 1982: 4 (1.3% of 318 rated); 1983: 1 (0.3% of 342 rated); 1984: 3 (0.9% of 326 rated); 1985: 1 (0.3% of 356 rated); 1986: 0 (0% of 391 rated); 1987: 3 (0.6% of 483 rated); 1988: 2 (0.4% of 556 rated); 1989: 1 (0.2% of 567 rated). Taken from the CARA, *Annual Reports*, RDHPP. For statistics on the use of the NC-17 rating from 1990 to 1999, see Chap. 8, n. 72.

fallen into disarray since the *Roth* (1957), *Jacobellis* (1964), and *Memoirs* (1966) cases. The Court's leadership had passed from Earl Warren, who was chief justice from 1953 to 1969, to the more conservative Warren Burger, who hoped to make prosecuting pornography easier. In *Miller v. California* (1973), the Court upheld, in a 5 to 4 decision, a California law banning the knowing sale of obscene material. In that decision, Chief Justice Burger rejected the Warren Court's test for obscenity, which required the matter in question to be "utterly without redeeming social value" – a standard that had made it almost impossible to obtain convictions. Burger noted that the "redeeming social value" test, which Justice William J. Brennan Jr. had articulated in *Memoirs v. Massachusetts* (1966), had never been supported by more than a plurality of the Court (usually by no more than three justices at any one time). In the *Miller* decision, Burger's Court also rejected the idea of a national standard for defining pornography and ruled instead that local community standards could be used by trial courts in obscenity cases.[14]

In *Paris Adult Theatre I v. Slaton*, a case decided on the same day as *Miller,* the Supreme Court upheld (again 5 to 4) the right of states to prevent the showing of hard-core pornographic films in adult theaters even if the owner had limited the audience to adults. The case, which originated in Georgia, involved two movies. A lower court had thrown out the complaints on the grounds that the theater had not admitted minors and that exhibiting the films to consenting adults was permissible under the Constitution. The Georgia Supreme Court reversed this decision. Using *Miller,* the United States Supreme Court upheld the Georgia high court, holding that even though "conclusive proof is lacking," states could conclude that "a nexus does or might exist between antisocial behavior and obscene material." Moreover, it said that showing obscene matter in a public place was "not protected by any constitutional doctrine of privacy." Whatever right to privacy that an adult might have at home did not extend to a commercial theater. Nor was everything shown to consenting adults constitutionally protected; Georgia's obscenity laws and their relation to the First Amendment could therefore be reinterpreted in light of the standards set out in the *Miller* case.[15]

One might assume that these cases should have made it easier for prosecutors to suppress hard-core pornography. Indeed, many theater owners

---

[14] Chief Justice Burger's opinion in *Miller v. California*, 413 U.S. 15 (1973) (online version).
[15] Quotations ("conclusive," "privacy"), *Paris Adult Theatre I v. Slaton*, 413 U.S. 49 (1973) (online version).

feared that a "new atmosphere" had been created by the decision, one favorable to the aggressive prosecution of obscenity, and that the X rating would be "an invitation for attack." In fact, a number of cases did come to trial. In 1974, Herbert Streicher (a.k.a. Harry Reems), the male star of *Deep Throat,* became the first movie actor to be prosecuted at the federal level for his performance in a film. A Memphis jury convicted him in 1976 for being part of a national conspiracy to carry "an obscene, lewd, lascivious, and filthy motion picture" across state lines. His attorneys appealed on ground that, although Streicher's work was done before the *Miller* decision by the Supreme Court, the Memphis judge had given instructions to the jury that applied the *Miller* guidelines. The federal government did not bring Streicher to trial again.[16]

Obtaining convictions even in small communities where, it was presumed, local standards for obscenity were narrower, remained problematic, as evident in another 1974 case. A theater owner in Albany, Georgia, Billy Jenkins, had been convicted for showing Mike Nichols's film *Carnal Knowledge* (1971), starring Jack Nicholson, Art Garfunkel, Ann-Margret, and Candice Bergen. The film, which contained nudity and frank dialogue, offered a thoughtful treatment of the sexual relationships of two men who had been college roommates (Nicholson and Garfunkel) over an extended period. The Georgia Supreme Court was divided, but held that the conviction was within the guidelines set down in the *Miller* case. The test for obscenity in *Miller* required that the work in question "portrays, in a patently offensive way, sexual conduct specifically defined by the applicable state law; and, taken as a whole, does not have serious literary, artistic, political, or scientific value." It was difficult for prosecutors to argue that *Carnal Knowledge,* which was not a hard-core film, fell into that category. The MPAA backed Jenkins's appeal to the United States Supreme Court, where Louis Nizer argued that the film merited protection under the First Amendment. The Court agreed and, in setting out the decision, Justice William H. Rehnquist said that "juries do not have unbridled discretion in determining what is 'patently offensive.'" In short, the First Amendment, which the Court uniformly applied across the nation without consideration for any cultural

---

[16] Quotations, Peter D. McKenna to Salah M. Hassanein, memorandum: "Ramifications of Recent Supreme Court Decision on Obscenity," July 27, 1973, pp. 19 ("atmosphere"), 20 ("attack"), Folder 2, Box 5, Mss 1446, NATOR-BYU. Indictment quoted ("obscene") in De Grazia and Newman, *Banned Films,* 142; also 143. See also Goldstein, "Obscenity Law: Standards Vary," *NYT,* Feb. 10, 1977, clipping in Folder 4, Box 6, Mss 1446, NATOR-BYU.

differences that might exist from one locale to another, took precedence over community standards.[17]

Recognizing that the *Miller, Paris Adult Theatre,* and *Jenkins* cases by themselves would not enable them to eliminate adult movie houses, some communities tried a different approach that involved controlling land use and limiting adult theaters to "combat zones." The goal was to prevent locating the theaters in areas where residential neighborhoods and businesses might be adversely affected. The United States Supreme Court upheld this method of control in two cases, *Young v. American Mini Theatres* (1976) and *City of Renton v. Playtime Theatres, Inc.* (1986). Neither case involved criminal penalties or completely suppressing films.[18]

Nothing could slow down the proliferation of pornographic films and other X-rated materials in the nation's urban areas. It was not that the federal government's efforts to suppress pornography ceased with the *Carnal Knowledge* and *Deep Throat* cases. On the contrary, in 1977, the United States government initiated 40 prosecutions for obscenity and won 57 cases, most of which had been started earlier. The U.S. Postal Service also managed to obtain 11 convictions, and the U.S. Customs Service seized and destroyed 15,000 items. But ultimately, these actions amounted to little more than harassment against the pornography industry. "For the most part," acknowledged one prominent attorney, "if material is distributed to willing adults under discreet circumstances, there is very little prosecution."[19]

The difficulties involved in suppressing adult films can be illustrated by the case of the film *Caligula,* released in early 1980 by Robert Guccione, the publisher of *Penthouse* magazine. A movie about the debauched Roman emperor whose reign began in A.D. 37, *Caligula* starred Malcolm McDowell, Peter O'Toole, and Sir John Gielgud, and featured sadism, bestiality, necrophilia, and explicit sexual activity. Initially, Guccione did not submit *Caligula* to CARA and attached his own "Mature Audiences" rating, with instructions to theater owners not to admit anyone under eighteen. Distributors tried to keep *Caligula* out of theaters that

---

[17] Quotation ("portrays"), *Miller v. California,* 413 U.S. 15 (1973) (online version). Quotation ("juries), *Jenkins v. Georgia,* 418 U.S. 153 (1974) (online version). See also De Grazia and Newman, *Banned Films,* 139–40, 145.

[18] See *Young v. American Mini Theatres* 427 U.S. 50 (1976), and *City of Renton v. Playtime Theatres, Inc.* 475 U.S. 41 (1986).

[19] Stanley Fleishman quoted ("For," "prosecution"), in Cook, "The X-rated Economy," *Forbes* 122 (Sept. 18, 1978), 82.

specialized in pornography and targeted, instead, houses that catered to foreign and art cinema. When the movie opened in New York, the group Morality in Media – an organization that fought pornography in mass media – attempted to file suit against federal officials because they had not declared the film obscene after U.S. Custom's officials seized it in 1979, when Guccione first brought it into the United States. The complaint, which was unsuccessful, claimed to represent more than 3,300 Roman Catholic clergymen and 2,200 prosecutors in the United States. In Boston, authorities seized the film, which was then being shown outside the city's X-rated "combat zone." In Atlanta, prosecutors threatened action if the film were shown there. Experts testified in court, in both cities, on behalf of the film, however. In Boston, professor Andrew Hacker said the movie had serious political content because it showed that "absolute power corrupts absolutely." In Atlanta, film historian Robert Sklar defended the public's right to see the film. After hearing the testimony, judges in Boston and Atlanta declared that the movie was not obscene under the standards set out in the *Miller* case.[20]

Clearly, the *Miller* case did not afford prosecutors an effective means to fight films of this nature – that is, movies with serious content in addition to sexual themes and violence. And the viewing public was far from unanimous in their opinions about the film – many people who saw *Caligula* thought the most offensive parts of the movie involved violence rather than sex. But the *Miller* ruling defined obscenity as an issue of sex and said nothing about violence. Showing violent conduct, one prosecutor observed, was "not in any way prohibited by the criminal law."[21]

A major industry had come into being. *Forbes* reported in 1978 that pornography grossed $4 billion a year, "about as much as the conventional motion picture and record industries combined." This figure included not only movies but also magazines, adult bookstores, peep shows, and other commercial ventures. The pornographic movie industry developed outside the auspices of mainstream Hollywood and the Motion Picture

---

[20] Some groups explored strategies that did not rely on obscenity law. In Ohio, a private organization known as Citizens for Decency through Law (CDL) forced Guccione to withdraw *Caligula* in Fairlawn rather than face a civil proceeding that the film's showing constituted a "public nuisance." Andrew Hacker quoted ("absolute"), De Grazia and Newman, *Banned Films,* 150; see also ibid., 148–51, 378–9; and Prince, *New Pot of Gold,* 348–50.

[21] Madison, WI, district attorney quoted ("prohibited") in Prince, *New Pot of Gold,* 350. In marketing *Caligula* for other countries in the Western Hemisphere, *Penthouse* used Vestron Video to distribute the movie with an R rating, an edited version of the X-rated film shown in American theaters. Ibid.

Association of America. By the end of the 1970s, there were about 780 adult movie theaters in the United States (out of 16,827 theaters) that took in more than $365 million annually. As will be seen in later chapters, pornography became an even larger business during the 1980s and 1990s, thanks in part to new media.[22]

HOME ENTERTAINMENT

Adult theaters were to remain entrenched in communities throughout the 1970s, despite the efforts of courts and prosecutors, only soon to be virtually eliminated by new technologies. Major changes were under way in home entertainment. More lenient regulatory standards, improvements in color TV, the expansion of cable and satellite broadcasting, and videotaping all opened new worlds of television viewing possibilities, with the result that, by the early 1980s, it was not unusual for people to watch uncensored films on television in the privacy of their homes. Valenti and Heffner considered these technological innovations as, at best, mixed blessings and, at worst, harbingers of catastrophe. Valenti saw in them an economic threat to Hollywood; Heffner feared they could endanger freedom of expression and threaten the rating system.

It became difficult to separate movies from TV. Like motion pictures, television relaxed its standards during the 1970s, although the medium remained more closely regulated than the cinema. The National Association of Broadcasters (NAB) had established a code for TV programming and advertising in 1952, part of post–World War II efforts to reform broadcasting. Like the Production Code and 1968 rating system of the movie industry, the NAB's programming guidelines were a form of self-regulation calculated to prevent government interference. The three major networks and most television stations subscribed to them. The guidelines, which were not strongly enforced, were eventually abandoned after an attempt was made in 1975 to amend the code to create a "family viewing" time between 7 p.m. and 9 p.m. The change, which the Federal Communications Commission (FCC) supported, would have curtailed program content containing sex and violence during this time slot. Hollywood producers and writers successfully challenged this family viewing requirement on the ground that it violated the First Amendment. The NAB's response

---

[22] Quotation ("conventional"), Cook, "The X-Rated Economy," 81. See also De Grazia and Newman, *Banned Films*, 145. On the growth of pornography, see also Chapters 5, and 6.

was to suspend all of its code's standards for programming. In 1982, the NAB also eliminated its advertising guidelines after a federal court judge ruled that sections of the code restrained trade. With the elimination of the NAB code and deregulation during the 1980s by the FCC and the Federal Trade Commission (FTC), networks found themselves free to broadcast just about anything they chose, provided, of course, that they did not provoke legislators or offend advertisers. As code guidelines eroded, the networks cut back on the size of their "standards and practices" departments, where employees reviewed advertising and edited (i.e., censored) programming.[23]

One strategy was adopted that brought edited versions of R-rated, and even X-rated, movies to television: the so-called PG letter. The major networks were reluctant to show restricted films, and ABC had even promised not to show R-rated pictures. Similarly, many cable stations hesitated to show movies that had been X rated. To help overcome this reluctance, CARA adopted a policy whereby a studio could surrender the original restricted rating for a film, withdraw that version from theatrical release for ninety days, and then receive a PG rating for a revised version of the picture – assuming, of course, that the studio had made enough changes to merit the new classification. A letter would then go to the network indicating the changed rating. If critics questioned why an R-rated movie had been shown on network TV, executives could pull from their files the PG letter to prove that changes had been made. A similar procedure was followed when a Los Angeles cable station wanted to show the X-rated *Last Tango in Paris*. At Valenti's request, a new version of the United Artists film was rated R and shown on cable TV.[24]

All the while, TV was becoming technologically more sophisticated. During the 1970s, color television improved and the number of sets burgeoned. In 1969, only about 32 percent of U.S. households had a color TV; four years later more than 55 percent had one; and by 1975 more than two-thirds of American households had color television. By the mid-1980s, the percentage had risen to more than 90 percent, and by the end of the 1990s, it stood at about 98 percent. The realism and visual qualities that color provided, something largely limited to movie theaters during the 1960s, became part of home entertainment. Quality continued to improve with the arrival of digital television and with the introduction in 1984 of High Definition TV (HDTV), although at the end

[23] See Liebert and Sprafkin, *Early Window*, 55–8, 125–7.
[24] See Heffner, *Reminiscences*, vol. 7, pp. 1379–80, Box 5, RDH-COHC-BL.

of the century, HDTV had yet to make major headway in the television market.[25]

As networks loosened their standards and the quality of television pictures improved, cable and satellites greatly expanded what could be seen on television. Cable made possible "narrowcasting," or providing specialized programming to a particular audience (e.g., children, adults only). Unlike broadcast television, which sent its transmissions through the airwaves to anyone in the area who owned a TV, cable providers used a closed-circuit wiring system, buried underground or strung along utility poles, that entered consumers' homes in much the same manner as telephone lines. Broadcast television stations needed to have a license from the Federal Communications Commission, whereas cable systems, which contracted with state or local governments, did not. In general, the FCC held considerably less regulatory power over cable than over broadcast TV, and even that authority seemed to recede during the 1970s. In a case involving Home Box Office (HBO), a United States Court of Appeals held that the FCC had exceeded its authority when it attempted to limit the right of cable systems to show certain kinds of movies and sporting events. The decision eliminated the commission's restrictions on pay TV's use of feature-length movies.[26] Pornographers also found new opportunities on cable. Al Goldstein, who in 1968 had started a magazine called *Screw*, exploited "leased public access" television in Manhattan to begin *Midnight Blue* in 1975, a cable program that featured interviews with porn stars, topless women, and ads for escort and telephone sex services.[27]

Cable and satellite systems greatly expanded the availability of uncensored programming. Cable television subscriptions grew rapidly during the 1970s when providers increased the number of channels and the diversity of programming, and when cable companies started using satellites

[25] On color television sales in the United States, see Berinstein, *Statistical Handbook on Technology*, 140 (Table 7.15). See also Marlow and Secunda, *Shifting Time and Space*, 20. On HDTV, see Winston, *Technologies of Seeing*, 88–108.

[26] See *Home Box Office, Inc., et al. v. Federal Communications Commission*, No. 77-1878. 190 U.S. App. D. C. 351 (1978); and *Federal Communications Commission v. Home Box Office*, Inc., 434 U.S. 988 (1977). The United States Supreme Court further eroded the FCC's power in 1979 when it said that the commission had exceeded its authority by requiring cable televisions systems with more than 3,500 subscribers to offer at least twenty channels by 1986 and to make available some of those channels for educational, governmental, and public uses. See *Federal Communications Commission v. Midwest Video Corp.*, No. 77-1575. 440 U.S. 689 (1979).

[27] Quotation ("leased"), Friedman, "The Fat Cat of Porn; Al Goldstein Claims He's Misunderstood," *Newsday*, Sept. 4, 1990, pt. 2, p. 8.

to transmit programs to local cable providers.[28] Satellite transmissions proved helpful to such pay cable services as HBO, Showtime, and Cinemax that allowed subscribers to watch uncut R-rated films – movies that ordinarily would be censored on network television. ("Pay" cable usually involved subscriber fees beyond those required to receive the channels available through "basic" cable service.) In 1975, HBO, then a company about three years old with approximately three hundred thousand subscribers, began distribution of uncut movies to cable television using RCA's satellite, Satcom I. Within five years, aided by satellites and by the favorable court ruling that voided the FCC's restrictions on showing feature films, HBO had six million subscribers. The availability of pay channels such as HBO, which used satellite distribution, proved to be an enormous stimulus to cable use. In 1972, fewer than 10 percent of American homes had cable television – about six million subscribers. The number of subscribers to basic cable had grown to almost eighteen million by 1980. By 1985, more than sixty-five-hundred cable systems provided at least a basic hookup to about forty million American homes. By then, 22.8 million households (more than one-fourth of the homes with television sets) subscribed to pay cable, and some estimates indicated that more than 14.5 million households subscribed to channels that carried R-rated programs. It was also possible for those with cable or satellite TV to subscribe to pay channels that provided X-rated entertainment.[29]

Cable and satellite installations continued to increase after 1985. By 1992, there were more than eleven thousand cable systems operating in more than thirty thousand communities. For people with a receiving dish, it was possible to get home programming directly from satellites. Although direct-to-home satellite systems were not nearly as commonplace as cable during the 1980s, Americans installed more than a quarter of a million linkups each year during the second half of the decade. (Not until near the end of the century did satellite television penetration approach

---

[28] On the FCC and the expansion of cable during the 1970s, see *Final Report,* 361. The Cable Communications Policy Act of 1984 established a national policy on how the cable television industry would be regulated at the federal, state, and local levels. For background on the FCC and television, see Baughman, *Television's Guardians.*

[29] For households in the United States with basic cable, see *MPAA Worldwide Market Research, 2002 US Economic Review* (http://www.mpaa.org/useconomicreview/). For pay cable households, see ibid. For households receiving R-rated and X-rated programs, see *Final Report,* 362, also 361–4. For cable subscriptions in 1972, see Sterling and Haight, *Mass Media,* 56 (Table 190-A). For HBO, see Cook, *Lost Illusions,* 414–15. For the expansion of pay cable between 1980 and 1983, see also Prince, *New Pot of Gold,* 96.

10 percent of households in the United States.) In 1990, almost 55 million households had basic cable and at least 27 million subscribed to pay channels. By 2000, those numbers had increased to almost 70 million and 34 million, respectively.[30]

While cable television expanded what people could watch, videotape and affordable video recorders promised even greater changes. During the latter half of the 1980s, the increase in cable TV was nowhere as spectacular as the spread of video recorders. The VCR penetrated American homes more rapidly than radio had; of communication technologies only television entered households faster. By 1989, half again as many people owned a VCR as subscribed to pay cable television. In 1982, Valenti had predicted that by the end of the decade there would be 35 to 38 million VCRs, most of Japanese manufacture, in the United States. His estimates were far too low.[31] During the 1980s, the price of VCRs dropped from more than $800 per machine to about $200. In 1985, Americans were reportedly buying 25–30,000 video recorders every day, and more than 75 million were sold in the United States during the decade. Where in 1979, fewer than 1 percent of Americans owned a VCR, by 1986, 30 percent of households had one, and by 1990, almost 70 percent (more than 62 million households). By the late 1990s, this figure approached 90 percent.[32]

Not surprisingly, the sale and rental of videocassettes grew rapidly during the 1980s. Early in the decade, home recording seemed most prominent, and retail sales of blank cassettes rose from about 24 million in 1982 to almost 300 million by 1986. By mid-decade, though, most people were using VCRs to watch prerecorded movies. Patterns of movie watching changed. Instead of going to a theater or waiting for a film to come to network television, many viewers now rented the movie on cassette. By

---

[30] For basic and pay cable households in the United States after 1985, see *MPAA Worldwide Market Research, 2002 US Economic Review.* (http://www.mpaa.org/useconomic-review/); *Final Report,* 362; and Wasko, *Hollywood in the Information Age,* 82. For satellite usage, see Berinstein, *Statistical Handbook on Technology,* 139 (Table 7.13); *Final Report,* 361; and MPAA Worldwide Market Research, "Satellite Households," *2002 US Economic Review* (http://www.mpaa.org/useconomicreview/). Slightly different figures appear in Prince, *New Pot of Gold,* 96. See also Wasko, *Hollywood in the Information Age,* 82, 95; also ibid., 71–112.

[31] Putnam, *Bowling Alone,* 217, 223; Prince, *New Pot of Gold,* 96; Valenti, testimony, *U.S. House Hearings,* April 12, 1982, 22; and ibid., 459–60.

[32] On American VCR ownership, see Berinstein, *Statistical Handbook on Technology,* 141 (Table 7.17); Prince, *New Pot of Gold,* 94–6; and Lane, *Obscene Profits,* 33. See also Wasko, *Hollywood in the Information Age,* 124–5.

the early 1990s, there were more than 30,000 video stores in the United States, and in addition to these outlets, many businesses – groceries, service stations, bookstores – rented out cassettes. By some estimates, more than 300 million videos were being rented each month. More than three times as many people rented cassettes as went to the theaters, and income from video rentals more than doubled box office revenues.[33]

Videocassettes were just part of a larger story involving magnetic recording. The impact of videotape (and audiotape) on world and American culture merits more study. Although the Quadruplex video recorder – the prototype for VCRs – first appeared in 1956, and television stations quickly adopted videotape, the technology at first was simply too expensive and cumbersome for most moviemakers. By the late 1960s, however, consumer electronics experts agreed that there was an enormous potential home video market, and it seemed as though almost every company that manufactured videotape was trying to make new video products for use in the home. In 1971, Sony, a Japanese company, introduced the three-quarter-inch U-matic videocassette, a development that eventually would make the technology much more accessible to the public because it eliminated the need for a technician. Recording and playback involved simply inserting a cassette into a machine. In 1975, Sony launched its Betamax one-half-inch video recorder. Two years later, RCA followed with a VCR in VHS format.[34]

Not only a boon to television news, videotape soon offered several advantages to moviemakers. Because video cameras recorded images directly onto magnetic tape, in much the same way tape recorders stored sound, the videotape could be viewed and edited immediately after shooting. For motion pictures, photographic film was normally used to record images on a negative, which then required processing before the images could be edited. With the aid of a computer, a movie recorded on videotape could be edited in just a few days, as compared to the weeks required for editing film. With the immediate playback that videotape made possible, it was often not necessary to reconvene actors and crews to reshoot scenes. Videotape was cheaper than film, and the improved equipment was usually less expensive. It was also relatively inexpensive to transfer

[33] See Numungwun, *Video Recording Technology,* 161; Wasko, *Hollywood in the Information Age,* 113–14, 130; and Prince, *New Pot of Gold,* 96–7 (Prince cites a study done by Columbia Pictures).

[34] See Numungwun, *Video Recording Technology,* 150; also 143–64. See also Marlow and Secunda, *Shifting Time and Space,* 19, 22–3, 113.

images from film to videotape, a fact that had important implications for the distribution of all movies, including those made by pornographers.

Videotape also empowered the viewers of moving pictures. Before the VCR, they were generally limited to watching movies in theaters or on network TV. They had little or no choice of pictures. With the arrival of video rental stores during the 1980s, viewers could suddenly choose from a staggering array of movies that reflected different styles, time periods, and cultures. The power held by studios and network stations to determine what movies were seen was sharply diminished. With the advent of the VCR, viewers also gained control over where and when they watched movies or other programs. The VCR gave them the ability to "shift" time and space.[35]

Certainly one important dimension of videotape was its impact on the production of pornographic movies. Videotape, along with other innovations in communication, made it both easier to produce pornography and more difficult for authorities to police it. During the 1980s, videotape accelerated the growth of pornography, already a multibillion dollar business, and played a part in the shift of the industry's center from such cities as San Francisco and New York to Los Angeles. VCR owners shunned the porn theaters and watched at home.[36]

Thus pornographers found videotape advantageous. It made their movies easier and cheaper to make. In 1972, the hard-core movie *Behind the Green Door* cost Jim and Artie Mitchell about $60,000 to shoot using 16-mm film.[37] Less sophisticated 60- to 90-minute movies shot on film during the early 1980s still usually cost somewhere between $50,000 and $75,000 to produce. The same movies could be shot on videotape for perhaps $4,000 to $20,000 and edited quickly. Thousands of copies of pornographic films could be reproduced from a master videotape. The cost to the distributor during the early 1980s usually ran from $8 to $15 per copy for buying, copying, packaging, and advertising the movie. The distributor would then sell the product to the wholesaler for about $31, making a 100 percent to almost 400 percent profit.[38] The potential

---

[35] Marlow and Secunda, *Shifting Time and Space,* 141; and Prince, *New Pot of Gold,* 124.

[36] Prince, *New Pot of Gold,* 122; Hubner, *Bottom Feeders,* 110, 202, and 252; and Heidenry, *What Wild Ecstasy,* 213.

[37] Hubner, *Bottom Feeders,* 198–9. In addition to Hubner's book, Muller and Faris, *Grindhouse,* is also informative on hard-core filmmaking.

[38] See early drafts of Meese Commission Report in Folder 7, pp. 26–8, Box 56; and Folder 14, pp. 114–15, Box 56, RG 60, RAGCP-NARA 2. See also *Final Report,* 347, 353–4; and Lane, *Obscene Profits,* 33.

market for adult videocassettes was also much larger than it was for adult films. One survey in 1987 estimated that 75 percent of establishments renting cassettes carried X-rated videos.[39]

An additional advantage of videotape for pornographers was the privacy it afforded viewers. No longer did they have to go to a public place, a theater or drive-in, to watch pornography. Video's greater accessibility and portability brought hard-core entertainment into areas beyond the reach of traditional cinema. Pornography became available not only to many more men but also to many more women, who had avoided the adult theaters and sex shops because they were usually located in unsavory urban areas. Indeed, women made up a large percentage of viewers who rented hard-core tapes. The video store, often centrally located and with an "adults only" section, became a fixture in most American communities during the 1980s.[40]

The new technology contributed to more than just movie watching. The availability of cheap video cameras and VCRs also brought changes to home movie making. As people moved away from using 8-mm cameras in favor of video, it became easier for ordinary people to create their own movies. Sony's camcorder came onto the market in 1983 at a price easily within the reach of middle-class Americans. By 1985, more than a half-million camcorders had been sold; by 1990 that figure had climbed to almost three million. While these innovations were most commonly used to capture family histories and other everyday activities, those with a bent for pornography seized the opportunity. For "little more than the cost of a blank videotape, a bottle of wine, and some baby oil" amateurs could now make their own movies without the need for them "to be developed and vetted by the local chemists."[41]

---

39 For percentage of stores renting X-rated videos, see O'Shaughnessey, "Boycott Aimed at Stores with X-Rated Films," *LAT,* July 12, 1987, pt. 1, p. 1.

40 "View in Privacy of Home; Women Form Big Market for Hard-Core Porn Tapes," *LAT,* Dec. 22, 1985, 13 (Metro); Lane, *Obscene Profits,* 33, 50-1; Prince, *New Pot of Gold,* 122; and O'Toole, *Pornocopia,* 103–4, 172.

41 Quotations ("wine"), Lane, *Obscene Profits,* 51. Quotation ("vetted") O'Toole, *Pornocopia,* 283. Sony demonstrated the first consumer camcorder in 1980. After the camcorder came on the market, many families abandoned 8-mm and Super-8 formats for home movies, preferring to use videotape instead. Because videotapes were more convenient to use, they also replaced 16-mm film in many nontheatrical outlets such as schools, TV stations, and airlines. There were significant differences between videotape and film, though. Videotape was a poorer archival medium for home movies, deteriorating more rapidly than film. Aesthetically, celluloid retained an actual image on its surface, whereas videotape held only magnetic signals that needed decoding. Many found the image quality of film superior to videotape. See Marlow and Secunda, *Shifting Time and Space,* 19;

New technology also led to an explosion in the number of pornographic pictures. Whereas only a hundred new porn movies appeared in 1976, and four hundred new adult titles appeared in 1983, the number quadrupled two years later to sixteen hundred. In subsequent years, these numbers continued to multiply.[42]

By the mid-1980s other technologies were making it more difficult for authorities to locate and control the production of pornography. In addition to videotape and camcorders, pornography's technological underpinnings also included other forms of magnetic recording and the telephone system. Audiocassettes, which since the 1970s had become influential in many areas, including music, politics, and education, became a source of inexpensive, homemade pornography. After the deregulation of telephone service in 1982, prerecorded messages sometimes known as "Dial-a-Porn" began to appear. Within a year, hundreds of thousands of calls were being made each day to these sexually explicit message services in cities such as New York, generating millions of dollars in revenue. Dial-a-Porn services also included sexually explicit live conversations with paid performers. These services could be used by adults and children alike.[43]

By the early 1980s, the personal home computer had shown extraordinary possibilities for revolutionizing access to sexually oriented material, although electronic mail, the Internet, and the ability to transfer erotic images were still in their infancies. Already by 1981, a government report indicated that "evolving computer-based systems are crossing over and blurring traditional regulatory boundaries." If one could afford a personal computer in 1985 – and about 15 percent of American households had them – one could subscribe to SEXTEX, a service that allowed subscribers to buy pornographic videos and magazines, provided a bulletin board for posting messages, and offered electronic mail with other subscribers. The boom in personal computer use came during the late 1980s and 1990s, and Internet use began to soar in the mid-1990s. Then it became possible to watch X-rated films on one's computer screen.[44]

---

and Prince, *New Pot of Gold*, 94, 123–4. On camcorder sales, see Berinstein, *Statistical Handbook on Technology*, 138 (Table 7.12).

[42] See Chapter 6.

[43] See chapter draft, p. 16, Folder 7, Box 56, RAGCP-NARA II; and *Final Report*, 364–7, 375–6.

[44] Quotation ("blurring"), OTA, *Computer-Based National Information Systems*, x. See also Putnam, *Bowling Alone*, 223; and *Final Report*, 367–9. On households with person computers, see Berinstein, *Statistical Handbook on Technology*, 109 (Table 5.7). In 1991, about one-quarter of American homes had a personal computer; by 1994, one-third had them. Two years later, 40 percent of homes had a personal computer.

Other developments well under way by 1985 also brought controversial entertainment into homes. Video games that combined violence and sex increased in sophistication and popularity. Graphic lyrics and provocative advertising that coupled sex and violence in rock music led to congressional hearings at which parents asked for warning labels, not unlike movie ratings, to be put on records and cassettes. Opponents of sexual permissiveness argued that rock music was one of the main ways in which explicit, hard-core pornography was delivered to children. Its arrival was "unrestrained," said one critic. Parents had "absolutely no control over what their very, very young children would...listen to for many hours a day."[45]

NEW MEDIA, VALENTI, AND HEFFNER

At first, Valenti found the innovations of the 1970s and 1980s threatening. By the mid-1970s, he was alarmed by the use of video to pirate films overseas. Before 1975, movie piracy had been confined largely to the theft or unlawful reproduction of film prints. The problem was especially pronounced in France and Great Britain. There was also a lesser problem with so-called 16-mm collectors in the United States and Canada. By 1975, one-fourth of the pirated films were being videotaped; by 1979, 97 percent of the contraband appeared on this medium.[46]

Video piracy initially seemed especially egregious abroad, particularly in areas where there was a certain level of wealth, poor local TV service, and few other recreational opportunities. It was common in the Middle East, South Africa, areas in the South China Sea region, and in the Caribbean, Colombia, and Venezuela. European hotels, Italian television stations, and Malaysian coffeehouses openly showed pirated videotaped films. To make matters worse, local authorities abroad were often reluctant to act against the culprits and generally regarded video piracy as a "necessary evil." By the end of the 1970s, though, it became clear that

---

By 2002, personal computers had penetrated about two-thirds of American households, and more than 60 percent of American households had access to the Internet. Ibid. See also *MPAA Worldwide Market Research, 2002 US Economic Review* (http://www.mpaa.org/useconomicreview/).

[45] Quotations ("unrestrained," "day"), Bruce Ritter in Meeting of the Attorney General's Commission on Pornography, Oct. 18, 1985, 61; also ibid., 58–9, Folder: "Los Angeles – 10/18/85," Box 4, RAGCP-NARA 2.

[46] See Jack Valenti to The Chief Executives of the Member Companies, Aug. 30, 1979: "Report on the Worldwide Operation of Our Film Piracy, Program," 1–5, in Folder: "Motion Picture Association of America: Rating Sheets," MPTRR-LC.

America was the largest potential outlet for pirated movies. Valenti estimated in 1979 that there were about three million home video recorders worldwide, almost two-thirds of them in the United States.[47]

Video piracy quickly assumed large dimensions. One estimate in 1982 placed the revenue lost by the video industry in the United States at about $700 million worldwide. By 1987, Valenti maintained that the American film industry lost $1 billion a year from pirated videocassettes. Twenty percent of that loss ($200 million) came from Japan, where an estimated nine to ten thousand video stores did business in pirated tapes.[48]

As the sale of VCRs escalated in America, Valenti predicted that the technology would irreparably damage the American entertainment industry. It would undermine the intellectual property rights of writers and performers. It also threatened Hollywood's normal distribution patterns: the industry did not serve all markets at the same time, but distributed motion pictures sequentially – that is, films went first to theaters, then to pay TV, network TV, home video, hotels, airlines, schools, and so on. The time shifting that videotape made possible gave consumers the freedom to choose when to view a film, and that feature, together with the fast-forward function by remote control that allowed viewers to edit out commercials, would destroy the advertising revenue that undergirded commercial television and filmmaking.[49]

Valenti attempted – unsuccessfully – to prevent the spread of Sony VCRs in America. He warned Congress in 1982 of a new Japanese invasion. "The video recording machine and its blank tape are on the threshold of an invasion into the American marketplace so massive we cannot adequately forecast its impact," he said. Always fond of similes, he reportedly

---

[47] Quotation ("evil"), ibid., 7; see also ibid., 1–2.

[48] During March 1982, the movie industry undertook several efforts to curb piracy. In the United States, Warner Home Video (part of Warner Communications Company and a MPAA member) initiated civil lawsuits against video retailers in Chicago and California on behalf of itself and other large studios (Columbia, Embassy, MGM, Paramount, 20th Century Fox, United Artists, Universal, Disney, and Lucasfilm). Chicago was then thought to be a major center for piracy, with more than 40 percent of the rental stores suspected of trading in illegally copied tapes. Later in the year, Universal Pictures initiated civil action on behalf of MPAA companies in the United Kingdom, which resulted in September raids conducted simultaneously in fourteen locations. The raids netted about 4,000 pirated tapes. See *PR Newswire*, March 16, 1982, and ibid., Oct. 7, 1982. See also "Japanese Urged to Control Video Cassette Tape Piracy," *Journal of Commerce*, Feb. 18, 1987, Foreign Trade Section, A4.

[49] Valenti, testimony and statement, *U.S. Senate Hearings*, April 21, 1982, 459–63. On videotaping's disruption of distribution patterns, see Valenti memo, Aug. 30, 1979, p. 7, MPTRR-LC.

FIGURE 7. Jack Valenti.

told legislators that the VCR "is to the American film producer and the American public as the Boston Strangler is to the woman alone."[50] "Now like a great tidal wave just beyond the shore line, this video recording machine and its tape threaten, profoundly, the life-sustaining protection on which the U.S. film and television industry depends: *its copyright.*" Video recorders were like "tapeworms" that would invade millions of homes, "eating away at the very heart and essence of the most precious asset the copyright owner has, his copyright."[51] He proposed imposing a royalty fee on VCR purchases. In 1984, the United States Supreme Court ruled that home taping was protected by fair use and did not violate copyright protection.[52] When it became apparent that efforts to limit the

[50] Valenti quoted ("video," "alone") in *NYT*, Sept. 2, 2000, A19.

[51] Quotation ("*copyright*"; emphasis in original text), Valenti, statement, *U.S. Senate Hearings*, April 21, 1982, 467; also 468. Quotations ("tapeworms," "eating"), Valenti, testimony, ibid., 459. See also Valenti, testimony, *U.S. House Hearings*, April 12, 1982, 8.

[52] Valenti, testimony and statement, *U.S. Senate Hearings*, April 21, 1982, 459–63. See also Wasko, *Hollywood in the Information Age*, 126–30. In 1975, Universal and Disney studios filed suit against Sony, maintaining that Sony's VCRs encouraged copyright infringement. The case went to the United States Supreme Court, which ruled against the studios in early 1984. The Court said that home taping was protected by fair use and did not violate copyright. At the same time that this case wound its way through the judicial system, Universal, Disney, and the other major studios moved aggressively into the home video market, placing many of their titles on cassettes for sale or rent. See Prince, *New Pot of Gold*, 99–103.

spread of video technology were futile, Valenti eventually concluded that it might not be all bad for Hollywood. By 1986, evidence suggested that the main reason people used the VCR was not to time shift TV programs but to watch rental movies. By the end of the decade, Valenti and others had come to believe that videocassettes had actually stimulated the public's appetite for feature-length motion pictures. "The trend is that the more a person watches a movie on a VCR, the more that person seems to be drawn to wanting to see a movie in a theater," Valenti told an audience at the Consumer Electronics Show in Las Vegas in early 1989. Instead of seeing the VCR industry as a parasite draining the life from the film industry, Valenti now urged cooperation in the fight against piracy.[53]

While Valenti brooded over economic issues, Heffner saw cable channels, satellites, and VCRs as threats both to the rating system and possibly even to freedom of expression. The classification system had been designed for films that were shown in theaters, not for the new media used in homes. Much of the post-1968 entertainment clashed with the values that Americans traditionally had considered acceptable for the home. By 1980, it had become easy to watch R-rated movies in one's living room or bedroom, Heffner said, and X-rated films had become accessible "to any person – young or old – who can turn the switch to 'On.'" He wondered if most people would tolerate this material.[54]

The new media bypassed many of the means used to regulate motion pictures and TV. When movies were shown in theaters, the box office acted as "an intermediary." Market forces regulated commercially sponsored television. Stations broadcasting over the air were naturally limited by the space and time spectrum. When a station or network had only one signal, questionable content was either permitted or rejected, and selecting content acceptable to most viewers was relatively simple.[55] By 1980, cable's "blue programs" and X- and R-rated videocassettes and videodisks circumvented Hollywood's rating system. Narrowcasting through cable permitted the tailoring of entertainment to individual tastes. Like the movie industry, "with its thousands of theaters," Heffner explained, "the new home media can employ a multiplicity of 'screens' and an almost

---

[53] Valenti quoted ("trend") in "In Brief: Valenti Seeks VCR Collaboration," *LAT,* Jan. 9, 1989, Business Section, pt. A, p. 3. See also Wasko, *Hollywood in the Information Age,* 130.

[54] Quotation ("switch"), Heffner, "'Narrowcasting' and the Threat to Morals," *NYT,* Aug. 17, 1980. See also Heffner, "Freedom and Responsibility in Mass Communications," address delivered March 22, 1982, 16, 18, RDHPP.

[55] Quotation ("intermediary"), Heffner, "Freedom and Responsibility in Mass Communications," 23; also 16, 21.

infinite number of inputs. Unlike the single-channel, single-screen traditional broadcaster, these new media can at any one moment offer in our
homes clearly labeled, alternative fare that may be either family-oriented
or mature, that may be suitable either for children or for adults, that
may reflect either traditional values or those at the cutting edge of social
acceptability." [56]

Not only did the new media change home entertainment, they complicated Heffner's work at CARA. It was clear to him by 1987 that videocassettes were beginning to strain, if not weaken, the rating system. While
CARA was primarily concerned with rating movies created for theatrical
distribution, Heffner thought it was important to rate cassettes if the makers of videos requested it. But this decision presented several problems.
First, there was the question of whether cassettes designed for home use
should be judged by the same standards as movies shown in theaters. The
British also had to confront this problem during the late 1980s and early
1990s, when they were inundated with violent and pornographic videos
which they called the "nasties." There the government required the British
Board of Film Censorship (later British Board of Film Classification) to
rate perhaps five to six thousand videos, and a royal commission was
designated to study the question of standards. Some people argued that
because "a man's home is his castle," the ratings should be more lenient
for cassettes. But psychologists argued that, in fact, the videos should
be rated more severely, because they were brought into the home where
children could watch violent and sexually provocative material again and
again. Heffner was sympathetic to arguments about the possible damage
these cassettes could cause, but he favored retaining a single standard. By
the mid-1980s, most Americans had become accustomed to what G, PG,
R, and X meant, and it would be too confusing, he felt, to adopt yet a
new set of standards. [57]

A second difficulty arose from the fact that rating videos increased
CARA's workload. In early 1986, the rating board generally watched no
more than two films per day. This schedule gave members the opportunity to discuss the movies and extra time to consider the most appropriate
classification. Votes were sometimes tabled for a day or two to give members time for reflection. It "was a professor's delight," Heffner said of the

[56] Quotations ("thousands," "acceptability"), ibid., 21–2. See also Heffner, "'Narrowcasting' and the Threat to Morals."
[57] Quotations ("nasties," "castle"), Heffner, *Reminiscences*, vol. 7, p. 1206; see also 1204–
7, Box 5, RDH-COHC-BL.

timetable in the pre-cassette era. By early 1988, as the number of requests for video ratings increased, CARA was often scheduled to review at least three movies each day. Moreover, rating the videos, which tended to be more violent and sexually explicit (many of them were made for men who wanted a "stag show at home," Heffner said), was usually more time-consuming than rating the 35-mm prints designed for theatrical release. The videos were often resubmitted several times before CARA settled on a final rating. The increased workload gave rating board members less time to consider each movie and increased the possibility that they would choose an inappropriate classification.[58]

Another problem associated with CARA's increased workload was that fewer people evaluated each movie. As the number of requests to rate videos continued to mount, it became impossible for the full rating board to watch each picture. This development required adopting a two-platoon system in which half the members might watch one movie while the other half saw another film. This change weakened the effectiveness of the rating system, in Heffner's estimation. There had always been safety in numbers, he felt. The more qualified raters involved in the process, the less likely the ratings were to be biased by the prejudices of one person or a small group of people. It became apparent to Heffner that CARA needed more members and to expand its facilities. At first, Valenti objected and questioned the need to rate cassettes at all – CARA's business was simply to classify movies scheduled for theatrical release. CARA did equip itself with both a video room and a film projector theater in order to facilitate a two-platoon system, but the change came "almost over Jack's dead body," Heffner recalled. Valenti opposed spending the money. Slowly, though, he came to see the wisdom of rating videos.[59]

CARA did not become involved in rating hard-core pornography. X ratings on videos were usually self-applied by the makers of the cassettes. But videocassettes most certainly blurred the line between pornography and what was commonly considered permissible entertainment during the 1980s. Heffner worried that developments in pornography and violence had serious implications for freedom of expression. Americans had accepted the content of post–Production Code movies during the late 1960s and 1970s, he believed, "only because they could be kept

[58] Quotations, Heffner, ibid., vol. 8, pp. 1403 ("delight"), 1401 ("stag"); see also ibid., 1401–5, 1407–8, Box 5, RDH-COHC-BL.
[59] Quotation ("dead"), Heffner, ibid., vol. 8, p. 1404; see also 1403–5, Box 5; and vol. 7, p. 1207, Box 5, RDH-COHC-BL.

much more at a distance." That the theater provided a wall of separa-
tion between movies and where one lived had been "freedom's saving
grace, for words and deeds commonly perceived as beyond the pale have
often been tolerated in our democratic society just because they have been
kept largely out of sight, far from our homes and families. Make them
now more visible, thrust them before our children, and we run the risk
that angry Americans will devise formulas of protest and techniques of
self-protection that could prove over-reactive and dangerously hostile to
free expression and free choice for all." The protection of freedom of
expression required self-restraint on the part of moviemakers and the
"voluntary mechanism of marketplace intervention," he thought.[60] Furthermore, the problems posed by these new media were global issues, in
Heffner's opinion. As satellites beamed the century's "continuing behavioral revolution" into homes around the world, clashes over the nature of
American entertainment would inevitably occur in other countries. The
free flow of information would likely suffer.[61]

Heffner's reflections brought criticism from civil libertarians, who questioned the possibility of, or indeed the need for, distinguishing between
more and less important forms of expression. Who was capable of drawing that line? If one rejected the concept of the government as surrogate
parent to protect children from harmful entertainment, was it any wiser
to allow an American business, acting through self-regulation, to assume
that role? If some entertainment so deeply offended Americans that it
led them to support censorship, that risk had to be taken. Even restrictions designed only to shield children were ill-advised, according to some
critics.[62]

Some of these arguments, especially those relating to children, gave
Heffner pause. By 1980, as pornography and violent entertainment were
entering homes on an unprecedented scale, he had begun reconsider his
absolutist views about freedom. "No restrictions . . . no prohibitions for
even *our* younger children's movie-going?" he inquired of his critics.

---

[60] "The will of an angry majority whose standards and tastes are too long or too flagrantly
violated may turn into the tyranny of the majority," Heffner warned. Quotations, Heffner,
"Freedom and Responsibility in Mass Communications," address delivered March 22,
1982, 17 ("distance," "all," "angry"), 19 ("marketplace"); see also ibid., 20, RDHPP.
See also Heffner, "'Narrowcasting' and the Threat to Morals."

[61] Quotation ("continuing"), Heffner, "Freedom and Responsibility in Mass Communications," 21; see also ibid., 24–5, RDHPP.

[62] See Ian D. Volner to Heffner, Sept. 11, 1980, document 80-I; and Volner to Heffner,
Oct. 30, 1980, document 80-I, with Heffner, "Pre-Oral History Memorandum for 1980,"
Box 1, RDH-COHC-BL.

"Instead *all* films – the most violent, the most abusive, the most explicit – *all* of them literally wide open at the box office for *all* children of *all* ages? Why is it that you find it so difficult for civilized adults at least to try to draw a protective, nurturing line between ourselves and our younger children?" The problem, as he saw it, amounted to a balancing act. Society had a responsibility to protect children, and that had to be weighed against the encouragement of creativity. "Our need is to reconcile what may seem to be conflicting thrusts, but what are, in reality, different sides of the same coin of civilization."[63]

Although the criticism from civil libertarians annoyed Heffner, at the beginning of the 1980s he was more concerned that a counterattack by those who wanted to limit the freedom of filmmakers seemed to be materializing. He had reason to be concerned. More technological innovations were on the way to change moviemaking further, rendering it possible to portray sex and violence more graphically and realistically than ever before. And now a rapidly growing body of research argued that depictions of sex and violence in mass media indeed do have harmful effects on society. Heffner was ambivalent about the research, but he understood that there might be a core of truth in it and did not hesitate to use it in defending some of CARA's rating decisions. But although he recognized the potential impact of the home entertainment revolution, he did not fully grasp the extent to which technology was changing moviemaking.

[63] Quotation ("restrictions," "children"), Heffner to Volner, Nov. 3, 1980, document 80-I, with ibid. (emphasis in original text). Quotation ("reconcile"), Heffner to Volner, Sept. 22, 1980, document 80-I, with ibid.

4

The Technology of Special Effects and the Effects of Screen Violence

Since the end of World War II, and especially since 1968, the trend in motion pictures, and indeed in most popular entertainment, has been toward ever greater violence. As a result, researchers, always concerned about the possible effects of entertainment on society, turned toward examining the effects of this increase in depictions of violence. By the early 1980s, numerous empirical studies had argued that watching violence on television, in motion pictures, and in other forms of mass entertainment could have damaging social effects on children and even adults. Most researchers did not claim that watching a single violent TV program or film, or even a number of them, was the primary problem; rather, it was the cumulative effect of witnessing hundreds of acts of violence in movies and television shows that was damaging.[1] Their studies indicated that by the time the average child became a teenager, he or she had seen thousands of murders and other acts of violence in entertainment media. Furthermore, many researchers asserted, the more realistic the depiction of violence witnessed by either a child or an adult, the stronger the viewer's response would be, and the more likely the depiction of violence would elicit aggressive behavior.[2]

This body of research literature was, and continues to be, hotly contested. Claims about the number of studies (as of 2005) purporting to

---

[1] Most researchers "would not *deny*" that watching a single violent movie, or small number of them, could also "trigger violence," according to Jack McLeod, a well-known scholar on media effects. "Experimental research," he notes, has "controlled exposure and studied *immediate* effects though often delayed effects as well." Quotations, e-mail, Jack McLeod to author, Aug. 30, 2004 (emphasis in original text).

[2] See *National Television Violence Study: Volume I*, 28.

show a link between media violence and aggression range from 1,000 to 3,500. Critics have rightly attacked these figures as exaggerated. A more realistic figure – confirmed by recent meta-analyses – would be that, as of 2003, between 200 and 300 studies have confirmed that media violence can have potentially harmful effects on some people. As one authority in this field observes, however, even the lower number of studies remains a formidable body of research. By comparison, she writes, "the finding that calcium intake increases bone mass is based on thirty-three studies," and "the conclusion that exposure to lead results in low I.Q. is based on twenty-four studies."[3] Whereas some people have exaggerated the number of studies linking violence in mass media to violence in the real world, some scholars of media effects have "shied away from overly strident claims." They have done so, explains one of the leading authorities in this area, "not so much from doubting the research but more from worrying about bringing about censorship and repressive measures."[4]

One of the most wide-ranging attacks on research connecting media violence and aggressive behavior came from Jonathan Freedman, a professor of psychology at the University of Toronto. Freedman, whose work was supported by the MPAA and who had not done firsthand research on media violence, claimed to have "looked at all this research." He concluded that these studies do not support the conclusion "that exposure to media violence causes children or anyone else to become aggressive or to commit crimes"; nor do they support the view that media violence causes insensitivity to real-world violence. Moreover, he argued, despite the fact

---

[3] Quotation ("calcium"), from Joanne Cantor's review of Freedman's *Media Violence and Its Effect on Aggression*, in *JMCQ* 80 (Summer 2003): 468. Also Joanne Cantor, interview with author, Jan. 20, 2003. See also Bushman and Anderson, "Media Violence and the American Public: Scientific Facts versus Media Misinformation," 477–89. In 1982, one work maintained that, up to that time, about 2,886 studies had been done on TV and social behavior (although not all of the studies dealt with violence). See the 1982 edition of Liebert and Sprafkin, *Early Window*, 106.

[4] Quotations ("shied," "measures"), e-mail, McLeod to author, Aug. 30, 2004. The case for connecting violence in mass media with real-world violence, according to McLeod, "is based on the *convergence* of evidence of three very different types: experimental . . . ; cross-section/single time point surveys . . . ; and panel-studies over time. . . . Each type of research design has strengths and weaknesses. Experimental studies are strong in controlling exposure thus controlling extraneous influences but can be criticized for being 'artificial' in various ways. Cross-section surveys are strong in being able to generalize and reach all types of families, etc., but must rely on self-report measures and statistical controls over extraneous influences. Panels have the advantages of surveys but have better control over time-order by having both violence exposure and aggressiveness measures at different points in time. They too have weaknesses," because they sometimes wait "too long (10 years or so) to take 'after' measures." Quotations, ibid. (emphasis in original text).

that many scientific and health organizations – the American Medical Association, American Psychiatric Association, the National Institute of Mental Health, the American Academy of Pediatrics – endorsed the view that media violence could be harmful, it was "almost certain that not one of these organizations conducted a thorough review of the research."[5] Some supporters of Freedman's conclusions went further. Marjorie Heins, who has been a leader in the ACLU and a staunch advocate for media literacy, doubted "whether quantitative sociological or psychological experiments" could "tell us much about the effects of something as broad and vague in concept as 'media violence.'"[6]

Although Freedman and Heins dismiss this research too readily, Freedman makes a valid and important point. Too few people actually read the research available, preferring instead to rely on what others say about it. This tendency to depend on others is perhaps unavoidable in an age of specialization. Still, it can lead to mischief and confusion. Separating first-rate, dispassionate scholarship, in which the goal is the pursuit of truth for its own sake, from lesser research – or worse, from endeavors influenced by funding agencies or other pressure groups – is difficult for the nonspecialist. Here, good journalism is particularly needed. It is in providing an interpretive bridge between the work of scholars and the public that journalism can make an important contribution to our understanding of media violence and its effects on society. In the absence of this bridge, it is relatively easy for special-interest groups to confuse public considerations of this important issue by simply presenting conflicting testimony from so-called experts.

Richard Heffner, who taught in the communications program at Rutgers University, was well aware of the studies that social scientists had been doing on violence in mass media. His wife was a psychotherapist who worked with the parents of troubled children. Over the years on his TV show, *The Open Mind,* he interviewed several people – Fredric Wertham and Neil Postman, to name two – who had written about

---

[5] Quotations, Freedman, *Media Violence and Its Effect on Aggression*, x ("looked," "exposure"), 9 ("certain").

[6] Text quotation ("quantitative"), see Marjorie Heins's review of Freedman's book *Media Violence and Its Effect on Aggression* in *The Nation*, 275 (July 22–9, 2002), 29. Another recent critic of media effects research, and a defender of Freedman's conclusions, writes: "Media violence literature has become a jumble of unrelated excursions into empirical science, narrative analysis, and communication studies. . . . Nothing could be further from scientific research than the disciplines of film and communication studies." Note quotations, Trend, "Merchants of Death: Media Violence and American Empire," 292 ("jumble"), 294 ("Nothing").

media effects (although neither had conducted original research in this area). He acknowledged that entertainment industry leaders and other critics could always show that the research was inconclusive. He thought that some researchers overstated the connection between violence shown in mass media and violence in real life and, in so doing, made themselves vulnerable to attack by those people such as Valenti who wanted to absolve Hollywood of responsibility for antisocial behavior. Yet the high level of violence in movies troubled him, and he came to believe that the cumulative impact of witnessing intense violence, even if fictionalized in film or on TV, was not only harmful to children but also to adults.[7] He also suspected that it made little difference what the experts thought if most people believed that viewing media violence damaged the young. He worried that violent, pornographic movies would anger a large part of the viewing public to such a degree that, incensed, they would demand censorship.[8]

Heffner wanted the MPAA to survey parents about their attitudes toward the rating system and violence in the movies. He pushed for more restrictive ratings on violent films. He recommended adding new rating categories between PG and R and between R and X, and giving parents more information about the rating decisions.

In these endeavors, he received little support from Valenti. Despite the growing body of research that pointed to the harmful effects of media violence on society, Valenti, throughout his tenure at the MPAA, adhered to the view that such studies were inconclusive. He opposed polling parents on the subject. As Heffner recalled: "Valenti absolutely prevented it, saying to me, 'Dick,...If you find out that people are concerned about violence in films, then you're going to have to rate violence more harshly.'" "Precisely," Heffner replied. "I thought that's what our job was to do." Valenti resisted calls for new rating categories and for giving explanations for ratings. When the MPAA's member studios invested heavily in films that contained high levels of violence, he supported their appeals for lenient ratings.[9]

---

[7] See Elaine Heffner, *Mothering*. Also Heffner, interview (phone) with author, Aug. 27, 2002. Many of Heffner's television interviews on *The Open Mind* can be seen at the Museum of Television and Radio, New York.

[8] Heffner, *Reminiscences*, vol. 2, p. 250, Box 5, RDH-COHC-BL; and Jonas, "The Man Who Gave an 'X' Rating to Violence," sec. 2, p. 13.

[9] Quotations ("Valenti," "do"), Heffner, *Reminiscences*, vol. 1, p. 90, Box 5, RDH-COHC-BL. For Jack Valenti and research on media violence, see Arar, "Movie-Ratings Boss Says System Works," L3.

The level of violence in movies continued to rise during Heffner's tenure, and so did the number of disagreements over how to rate violent films. Valenti's lack of leadership on the issue appalled Heffner, who came to question whether voluntarism and self-regulation could work for commercial entertainment. He summed up the problem bluntly: "if we're going to save our collective asses from the censor, we'd better recognize film violence as one of the things that parents hold most against us."[10]

THE TECHNOLOGY OF SPECIAL EFFECTS

As movies became noticeably more violent during the late 1960s and early 1970s, advances in special effects technology helped to make the violence more realistic and sensational. Arthur Penn's *Bonnie and Clyde* (1967), set in the 1930s, was about a gang of desperados led by Clyde Barrow and his girlfriend, Bonnie Parker, and starred Warren Beatty, Faye Dunaway, and Gene Hackman. In filming the movie's finale – in which Bonnie and Clyde die in a brutal machine-gun ambush by Texas rangers – Penn created the illusion of a graphic, bloody massacre by using multiple cameras to show the scene from many angles and dozens of "squibs" (condoms containing fake blood hidden in the actors' clothing and rigged to explode to simulate the effect of bullets striking their bodies). In addition, to emphasize the realism of the visual effects, he showed the massacre scene in slow-motion. In *The Wild Bunch* (1969), a hard-edged Western about outlaws set in the early 1910s and starring William Holden and Robert Ryan, director Sam Peckinpah carried Penn's techniques further. Attempting to stylize the violence, Peckinpah used slow-motion and multicamera montage, as well as telephoto lenses. Many people, including Heffner, believe that *The Wild Bunch* marked a turning point with regard to violence in films.[11]

Horror movies especially became much more gruesome than they had been in previous decades, in both story lines and special effects. Many were relatively low-budget films. A few achieved cult status. George Romero's *Night of the Living Dead* (1968), an independently distributed film in

---

[10] Quotation ("collective"), Heffner, "Pre-Oral History Memorandum for 1982," p. 60, Box 1, RDH-COHC-BL.

[11] See Heffner, *Reminiscences*, vol. 1, pp. 44–7, Box 5, RDH-COHC-BL. Peckinpah modeled *The Wild Bunch* in some ways on Akira Kurosawa's *The Seven Samurai* (1954). On *Bonnie and Clyde* and *The Wild Bunch*, see Prince, "Graphic Violence in the Cinema," in Prince, ed., *Screening Violence*, 10–12. On Peckinpah, see also Prince, "The Aesthetic of Slow-Motion Violence in the Films of Sam Peckinpah," in ibid., 175–201; and Prince, *Savage Cinema*.

black and white, presented a tale of dead people rising from their graves, hunting the living, and devouring the flesh of their victims. Romero's sequel, *Dawn of the Dead* (1979), was filmed in color and showed people in a shopping mall fighting zombies who could only be killed by having their brains destroyed. Early in the movie, one particularly graphic scene showed a zombie's head being shot off. Effects specialist Tom Savini created the scene by molding a plaster skull and covering it with latex skin fitted with more than a dozen squibs filled with blood, corn chips, and apple core bits to simulate bone and brain. He then used a blast from a real shotgun to make the "head" explode into gory bits. Tobe Hooper's *Texas Chainsaw Massacre* (1974), a low-budget film about cannibalism, based loosely on the story of Wisconsin serial killer Ed Gein, used similar techniques to great effect. To create scenes showing a chainsaw slicing into the flesh of the killer's victims, actors wore sheet metal for protection and covered it with packets of blood and raw steak under their clothing. A big-budget, mainstream horror picture by William Friedkin about demonic possession, *The Exorcist* (1973), starring Max von Sydow, Linda Blair, and Ellen Burstyn, took special effects to a new level. Effects specialists Marcel Vercoutere and Dick Smith created a series of lifelike masks for Blair to wear in her role as a child possessed by the devil. In one scene, the words "Help Me" appeared to rise on Blair's abdomen. To achieve the effect, the words were written in cleaning fluid (Trichloroethylene) on a layer of latex placed on Blair's stomach. As the fluid evaporated, the words disappeared. In perhaps the most sensational scene in the film, the possessed Blair appeared to rotate her head 360 degrees. To create the effect, a replica of the star's head was mounted on an axle and the eyes were operated by remote control. A riveting story with startling special effects, *The Exorcist* (Fig. 8) became a box-office blockbuster, earning ten Academy Award nominations and winning two, one for best sound, the other for best adapted screenplay. Virtually every major Hollywood studio rushed to copy Warner Bros.'s film, hoping to have the same success.[12]

Many kinds of movies other than horror, of course, made use of the improvements in special effects, and it is worth digressing briefly to consider some of the innovations that raised the technical quality of most motion pictures. Many of these technological advances – for example, computer-assisted motion control – helped to make the fantasy worlds

---

[12] See Schecter and Everitt, *Film Tricks*, 98–100, 202, 205; and Cook, *Lost Illusions*, 222–3, 226.

FIGURE 8. Special effects transformed Linda Blair's character who is possessed in Warner Bros.'s blockbuster hit *The Exorcist* (1973). Many moviemakers attempted to imitate Warner Bros.'s success. Both Richard Heffner and Lew Wasserman thought *The Exorcist* should have been rated X for horror. Photograph courtesy of Photofest.

created by movies seem more realistic. From the 1920s onward, a key process in special effects was traveling matte, or "blue-screen" photography. In this process, miniatures were manipulated frame-by-frame in front of a blue screen so that the camera shots would leave the background unexposed. Then, through double exposure during the printing process, the background was superimposed, or "matted in." In the film *Star Wars* (1977), George Lucas improved on this technique by combining it with a computerized motion-control system. As a result, *Star Wars* transformed special effects, making them at once more sophisticated and less expensive to produce. This movie thus set the standard for other films for about two decades. Another innovation occurred in a 1982 Disney project, *Tron,* which used digital effects and blended several minutes of computer animation with live-action shots. Within a few years, computer-generated images came to dominate special effects.[13]

There were also technical advances in cinematography during this period. In the 1970s, cinematographers benefited from changes that some in the field thought amounted to "a quantum leap over the past." Lighter, smaller, and more powerful lighting equipment, and improvements in color film stock accelerated the trend away from shooting movies on studio sets to shooting them on location. The introduction of faster lenses permitted filming at much lower levels of light than had been possible with the older Technicolor stock, and the overdevelopment ("pushing") of film in the lab increased its speed. As a result, American moviemaking attained a new aestheticism, which the cinematographer Nestor Almendros, who used the techniques in making *Days of Heaven* (1978), likened to the change brought to late-nineteenth-century painting by the introduction of premixed oil paint that came in tubes. That innovation increased the artist's ability to capture changing light conditions outdoors and contributed to the rise of Impressionism. Just as the improved paint had given artists greater freedom to paint on location, so developments in film and camera equipment during the late 1960s and 1970s made it easier to shoot evocative scenes in much lower levels of light.[14]

By the early 1980s, processing techniques had improved so much that low-budget movies made with 16-mm film had become much more appealing to the eye. Before this time, 16-mm films had often had a grainy

---

[13] During the late 1970s, computer graphics and computer animation were still in the early stages of development. See Cook, *Lost Illusions,* 383–4, 386. See also Finch, *Special Effects,* 142–51.

[14] Quotation ("quantum"), Cook, *Lost Illusions,* 361; also 355–6. For Nestor Almendros, see Oumano, *Film Forum,* 85–6.

quality that made them look cheap by comparison to the more expensive 35-mm pictures.[15] Improvements in emulsion technology during the 1980s by the Eastman Kodak Company helped to make the quality of 16-mm prints almost the equal to that of 35-mm film. Louis Malle's *My Dinner with André* (1981), Stephen Frears's *My Beautiful Laundrette* (1985), Spike Lee's *She's Gotta Have It* (1986), and Ann and Jeanette Petrie's *Mother Teresa* (1987), all of high quality, were first shot on 16-mm film and then enlarged to 35-mm for theater viewing. Not only could this new and improved film be used for art films, but it was also "all the better to show slimy alien creatures gnawing on hapless humans in the dark," one independent film maker is reported to have said.[16]

There were other developments in camera technology during the 1970s. Improved zoom lenses were used: by Robert Altman in the antiwar picture, *M*A*S*H* (1970) and in the film *Nashville* (1975), his treatment of country music, mass media, and politics; by Stanley Kubrick in the epic *2001: A Space Odyssey* (1968) and in the visually stunning *Barry Lyndon* (1975). Steven Spielberg used the light-weight Panaflex 35-mm camera to make *Sugarland Express* (1974), and Roman Polanski used it in filming *Chinatown* (1974). The Louma crane (first developed in France) featured a remote-controlled camera that could be guided into previously inaccessible areas and was used in filming *Superman* (1978) and the James Bond film, *Moonraker* (1979). Another significant improvement in cinematography was "floating" camera mounts that were used to stabilize portable 35-mm cameras while they were in motion. The technology derived, in part, from an antivibration helicopter mount used during the late 1960s. The camera known as the Steadicam, which connected to the user's waist and chest by a harness, was first used by Haskell Wexler in *Bound for Glory* (1976). It gave cameramen greater freedom of movement and made possible motion shots in new locations. For example, it was used to film the running scenes in *The Marathon Man* (1976) and *Rocky* (1976), and in such horror films as *Halloween* (1978), *Friday the 13th* (1980), *The Shining* (1980), and *Wolfen* (1981).[17]

---

[15] Most moviemakers still preferred 35-mm film, though. The "magic" in 35-mm made it more desirable for feature-length movies and commercials, said the head of one New York film laboratory. "There's a lot more you can do with the film." Irwin Young, chairman of DuArt Film Laboratories, quoted ("magic") in Lewis, "Business Technology: Advances in Film; Low-Budget Movies Get a High Gloss," *NYT,* Feb. 11, 1987, D6.

[16] Quotation ("slimy"), Dan Diefenderfer (president of Shriek Company, independent film studio in Kansas City, MO), paraphrased in ibid.

[17] Cook, *Lost Illusions,* 362–5, 372–80.

As cinematography became more sophisticated so did sound reproduction. Here, too, *Star Wars* marked a turning point by using to great effect the Dolby stereo optical sound system. This system had been tried two years earlier in 1975, but it was the popularity of *Star Wars* that convinced studios that theaters equipped with Dolby sound would attract large audiences. Other blockbuster films to use the new sound system included *Close Encounters of the Third Kind* (1977), *Saturday Night Fever* (1977), and *Superman*. Studios rushed to install Dolby sound, and by the end of 1977 about two hundred theaters were equipped with it. That number quadrupled in 1978. Less than a decade after *Star Wars* only a few of the nation's fifteen thousand theaters lacked Dolby sound systems. Before 1977, most theater sound systems were monaural. Films that played in stereo generally used magnetic prints that were expensive and tended to degrade with use. The Dolby stereo optical system produced high-quality sound, and it usually required only a modest outlay ($5,000) from studios to convert to this technology.[18] It is interesting to note here that it was the realistic Dolby sound in Spielberg's *Poltergeist* (1982) that would be at the center of one of the most important rating controversies of the early 1980s.

Along with the improvements in visual and sound effects, the number of so-called slasher films increased sharply during the late 1970s and early 1980s, alarming critics who feared the potential effects they might have on some viewers. Many of these films "showcased the splatter effects that prosthetics and latex had brought to cinema," often combined violence and sex, and depicted women as helpless prey. Many adopted a technique that John Carpenter exploited in his film *Halloween* (1978), using the portable Steadicam to give viewers the illusion that they were seeing the scene through the eyes of a stalker as he chased his victim. The camera seemed to invite viewers to accompany the murderers and to participate in their elaborate rituals. Critics argued that this technique aroused those viewers already prone to sadism and was morally inexcusable. The film *Friday the 13th* (1980), another featuring the work of makeup artist Tom Savini, followed the same pattern and inspired numerous sequels.[19] That the victims in many movies of this kind were women stirred charges of misogyny (see Fig. 9). Women's groups protested and film critics condemned CARA for not giving X ratings to more of these pictures. Heffner believed that *Friday the 13th* "diminished the Board's

[18] See ibid., 386–8.
[19] Quotation ("showcased"), Prince, *New Pot of Gold,* 351; see also 352. For the increase in horror films, see ibid., 298 (chart 7.1).

FIGURE 9. That the victims in many horror movies were women led to charges of misogyny. Here actress Betsy Palmer is "enmeshed in total terror" by a deranged killer in *Friday the 13th* (1980). Photograph courtesy of the Wisconsin Center for Film and Theater Research.

sensitivity to violence and allowed everything else to build further and further and further on it." When Paramount made the first sequel, *Friday the 13th: Part II* (1981), CARA initially gave it an X because of half a dozen gruesome scenes (totaling about 4,700 feet of film). Although the producers resisted cutting the violence, they did finally edit the film enough to get an R. More violent movies would be receiving X ratings, Heffner told Paramount's Frank Mancuso, "if the world were a better place. But of course, if it were, then audiences wouldn't be rushing to see these films; nor, hopefully, would producers rush to produce them."[20]

THE EFFECTS OF SCREEN VIOLENCE

The increasing violence in motion pictures and its accompanying realism concerned researchers, health professionals, and any number of other

---

[20] Quotation ("diminished"), Heffner, "Pre-Oral History Memorandum for 1980," p. 36, Box 1, RDH-COHC-BL. Quotation ("world"), Heffner to Frank Mancuso, Feb. 13, 1981, doc. 81-24, with Heffner "Pre-Oral History Memorandum for 1981," Box 1, RDH-COHC-BL.

critics. Paralleling the growing explicitness of movies, and the improvements in filmmaking technology that helped to make it possible, was a large growth in research studying the effects of mass media. Concerns about the harmful effects of violence in mass media are long-standing, but the devastation caused by World War II and the technological innovations that followed served as catalysts for the investigation of this issue. The ubiquitous presence of television by the 1960s literally brought the problem home to Americans. As motion pictures became more violent, and as more and more of them appeared on TV, it became impossible to separate movie mayhem from television. Moreover, TV programming itself was a problem. The percentage of television shows and cartoons that contained violence was very high by the late 1960s and remained consistently so through the 1990s. Furthermore, because TV is also a window on the real world, news coverage of the bloody war in Vietnam and domestic crime at home brought brutality directly into American living rooms.[21]

The effects that TV violence and, more generally, violence in popular culture might have on the young had been debated for some time. A UNESCO study in 1952 speculated that the average twenty-year-old had seen at least eighteen thousand murders and beatings in comic books alone without even considering what was shown at the movies.[22] Senate hearings in 1954 and 1955 by Senator Estes Kefauver's Subcommittee to Investigate Juvenile Delinquency, and in the early 1960s by Senator Thomas J. Dodd's Subcommittee on Juvenile Delinquency, had criticized the level of violence in motion pictures and on TV and suggested that it was unhealthy for society.[23] In 1968, in the aftermath of the Robert Kennedy and Martin Luther King, Jr. assassinations, the National Commission on the Causes and Prevention of Violence held hearings, and one of the topics covered was the effects of mass media. The commission judged the United States to be the most violent of all the Western democracies. It also concluded that motion pictures and television were "profoundly educative for their viewers, teaching them that the world is a violent and untrustworthy place," and showed them how to use violence to cope with this unfriendly environment. It did not matter whether the programs

---

[21] For the percentage of violent television programs and cartoons through the mid-1980s, see Liebert and Sprafkin, *Early Window,* 116–18.

[22] See Siepmann, *Television and Education in the United States,* 105.

[23] See *U.S. Senate Hearings [TV],* 1954–5: June 5, Oct. 19–20, 1954; April 6–7, 1955; and *U.S. Senate Hearings [Motion Pictures],* 1955: June 15–18, 1955. For a critical assessment of the hearings chaired by Senator Thomas J. Dodd, see Boddy, "Senator Dodd Goes to Hollywood," Spigel and Curtin, eds., *Revolution Wasn't Televised,* 161–83. See also Liebert and Sprafkin, *Early Window,* 59–64.

were fact or fiction; children assimilate into their own behavior the adult conduct they see.²⁴

However, empirical studies linking the violence in motion pictures and TV programs to actual violent behavior were relatively rare at this time, and movie and television executives exploited this weakness at the hearings. Some executives promised to reduce entertainment violence and to fund research that would uncover the true relation between watching and behavior. Valenti, though, cast doubt on the value of scholarship. He claimed that the previous forty years of social science research on whether screen violence is harmful to children was "ambivalent . . . contradictory" and simply "not conclusive." Most experts, he said, were "reluctant to conclude that the portrayal of violence in motion pictures results in harmful social behavior." Valenti was not the first movie industry leader to question the work of social scientists who argued that movies could have harmful effects. During the 1930s, Will Hays had turned to the philosopher Mortimer Adler for ammunition to help him discredit the Payne Fund Studies. Adler attacked the methodology used by the Payne Fund Studies and argued that social science was inadequate to evaluate the influence of movies.²⁵

In 1968, Maine Senator Margaret Chase Smith called for hearings on film classification. She turned to a new generation of authorities who had witnessed the brutality of World War II and the Holocaust. The psychiatrist Fredric Wertham condemned the comic-book industry and criticized television in his book *Seduction of the Innocent* (1953). "What all media need at present is a rollback of sadism," he argued. In his work *A Sign for Cain* (1966), he considered violence in a broad social context and indicated that mass communication was only one factor in the problem, but a critical factor because, for the young, mass media (films, TV, radio, comic books, magazines) had become schools for violence.²⁶ Children were being "conditioned to an acceptance of violence as no civilized nation has ever been before." The most dangerous effect of movie

---

²⁴ Quotation ("profoundly"), Baker and Ball, *Mass Media and Violence. Volume IX: A Report to the National Commission on the Causes and Prevention of Violence,* 282; also 280–1, and in general chap. 12, "The Effects of Media Violence on Social Learning," 261–83. See also article on the National Commission on the Causes and Prevention of Violence in the *St. Louis Post-Dispatch,* June 5, 1969, A1, A13.

²⁵ Quotations ("ambivalent," "behavior"), Valenti, statement, Dec. 19, 1968, before the National Commission on the Causes and Prevention of Violence, reprinted in Prince, ed., *Screening Violence,* 67; see also ibid., 68.

²⁶ Quotation ("sadism"), Wertham, *Seduction of the Innocent,* 361. See also Wertham, *A Sign for Cain,* 193–228.

mayhem, Wertham believed, was that it made viewers indifferent to the "devaluation of human life."[27] Senator Smith also heard from Leonard Berkowitz, a professor at the University of Wisconsin, who maintained that children who were frustrated socially and prone to fantasy were more likely to be incited to aggressive acts by viewing media violence than to be purged of their hostility (i.e., through catharsis). Psychiatrist Robert Glyn suggested that at least one-third and maybe more than half of the young people who watched movies would be affected by film violence. Children from broken homes were particularly vulnerable, he felt.[28]

And then there was the problem of what Senator Smith called the unrelenting portrayal of "sex without love, love without marriage, the harmlessness of infidelity, the glorification of the prostitute and the normalcy of rape." Films often presented women as weak, "evil" creatures and as the victims of male brutality. The social consequences of these portrayals, Smith believed, could be staggering. Illegitimate births and venereal disease among teenagers were rising dramatically. Syphilis among teens had more than doubled during the past decade. Violence against women would likely increase. "It is no wonder that children exposed to such violence might well tend toward a more aggressive attitude when confronted with life's frustrations," she pointed out.[29]

If in 1968 there had been a lack of research showing that entertainment violence could have harmful effects, all that soon changed. The following year, Congress funded the surgeon general's Scientific Advisory Committee on Television and Social Behavior, and, in 1972, the investment yielded a five-volume examination of TV's effects on social learning, adolescent aggressiveness, and daily life. Several of the studies in this report indicated that what children learned from television could be good or bad, and that the effects of this learning could be strongly influenced by parents. The studies showed that even though parents were uneasy about what their children learned from TV, they often failed to provide supervision for even the youngest children. The thrust of this research, which was conducted

[27] Wertham quoted ("conditioned"), unlabeled newspaper clipping dated June 14, 1968, p. 4, in MCSP-NISM. Wertham quoted ("devaluation") in Coe, "Senator Smith vs. Violence in Films," Feb. 4, 1968, *WP*, copy in MCSP-NISM.

[28] See Berkowitz, *Aggression*, 234, 236, and generally, 229–55. See also M. C. Smith, "'Sick Movies' – A Menace to Children," 140; and Robert Glyn cited in Smith, "My One Year War for Better Movies," 5, MCSP-NISM.

[29] About 600 new cases of venereal disease were reported each day, Smith said. Quotations ("sex," "evil"), Smith, "My One Year War for Better Movies," 10, MCSP-NISM. Smith quoted ("wonder") in Larrabee, "Violence in Movies: Sen. Smith's Crusade," clipping labeled "*MST*," June 23, 1968, p. D-7, MCSP-NISM.

in experimental settings, confirmed that "more overt aggressive behavior follows exposure to violent content than to nonviolent content or no content."[30]

From the outset, the surgeon general's report became embroiled in controversy. The TV industry had tried to prevent researchers they suspected would be critical from participating in it.[31] Some scholars who did participate thought that the report's summaries of the research were "wishywashy being clouded over by the politics of the Advisory committee."[32] Others called the report "a masterpiece of evasiveness." Its "conflicting conclusions" were worded in such a manner that "if taken out of context," said one historian, they "could be adduced to either side of the effects debate." Small wonder that the press coverage of the final report was confusing. The initial summary of the report in the *New York Times*, which led with the headline "TV Violence Held Unharmful to Youth," misrepresented the studies. Other stories unambiguously linked television entertainment "to the aggressive behavior of many normal children."[33]

The report became a catalyst for new investigations. In the decade following its publication, hundreds of studies appeared – about 90 percent of all the research done up to that time on the topic – making it a "golden age" for social science research on television's influence on behavior. Government and corporate money poured into research. The National Science Foundation as well as the Ford and Markle Foundations provided funding. The medical establishment and civic organizations became involved when the American Medical Association (AMA), the American Psychological Association (APA), and the National Parent Teacher Association (PTA) enlisted in the effort to curb media violence. In early 1977, *Newsweek* extrapolated from part of this research to estimate that the average teenager by high school graduation had watched

---

[30] Quotation ("overt"), Greenberg, "Televised Violence: Further Explorations (Overview)," in Comstock, Rubinstein, and Murray, eds., *TSBRP*, vol. 5: *Television's Effects: Further Explorations, in TRSGSACTSB*, 20. See also Lyle, "Television in Daily Life: Patterns of Use Overview," in Comstock, Rubinstein, and Murray, eds., *TSBRP*, vol. 4: *Television in Day-to-Day Life: Patterns of Use, TRSGSACTSB*, 24.

[31] The television industry attempted to exclude some researchers who were known to have linked viewing screen violence and violent behavior. On blackballing, see Rowland, Jr., *Politics of Violence*, 156; and Liebert and Sprafkin, *Early Window*, 82–3; also ibid., 85.

[32] Quotation ("wishy-washy"), e-mail, McLeod to author, Aug. 30, 2004.

[33] Quotations ("evasiveness," "conflicting," "debate"), Rowland, Jr., *Politics of Violence*, 163. Quotation ("Unharmful"), from Gould, "TV Violence Held Unharmful to Youth," *NYT*, Jan. 11, 1972, 1, 75. Quotation ("aggressive"), see UPI's coverage as reported in the *Indianapolis Star*, Sept. 4, 1971, 1.

15,000 hours of television, had been subjected to 350,000 commercials, and had "vicariously participated in 18,000 murders."[34]

By the mid-1970s, violence in the American mass media had become a problem for other countries as well. In Canada, American movies and television programs dominated the market – more than 90 percent of the films for which Canadians paid rental fees came from the United States. In 1977, Ontario's Commission on Violence in the Communications Industry concluded that the "great weight of research into the effects of violent media contents indicates potential harm to society." It found that Canadians – including children – were watching increasing amounts of American-made TV programming, which had "much higher levels of violence" than programs produced in Canada or elsewhere, and television's "escalation of violence" was "drawing other sections of the media along like the tail of a comet."[35]

By the early 1980s, in the United States, a consensus had started to emerge among researchers who studied media effects and from psychiatric and medical professionals who had to treat the results of sexual abuse and other types of violence. In 1982, on the tenth anniversary of the surgeon general's report, communication scholars published a two-volume work that synthesized the research done during the preceding decade on TV's influence on society: *Television and Behavior: Ten Years of Scientific Progress and Implications for the Eighties* (1982). These volumes, published by the National Institute of Mental Health (NIMH), discussed the research and concluded that a large literature now existed that confirmed the findings of the surgeon general on TV and violence. Substantial evidence demonstrated "a causal relationship between televised violence and later aggressive behavior." No longer could television be considered merely harmless entertainment or a negligible factor in daily living; it had become an important "part of the total acculturation process."[36] Moreover, with the advent of cable TV, pay channels, and VCRs, the numbers

---

34 Quotation ("vicariously"), "What TV Does to Kids," *Newsweek*, 89 (Feb. 21, 1977), 63. Quotation ("golden"), Liebert and Sprafkin, *Early Window*, 115. See also ibid., 109, 115–16, 119–24. See also Herbert Pardes, "Foreword," in Pearl, Bouthilet, and Lazar, eds., *Television and Behavior: Ten Years of Scientific Progress and Implications for the Eighties* (hereafter cited as *Television and Behavior*, 1982). *Volume I: Summary Report*, iii.

35 Quotations ("great," "comet"), *Report of The Royal Commission on Violence in the Communications Industry. Volume I: Approaches, Conclusions and Recommendations*, 53; see also ibid., 19.

36 Quotations, Pearl, Lazar, and Bouthilet, eds., *Television and Behavior. Volume I: Summary Report*, 37 ("relationship"), 87 ("process").

of television movies shown had greatly proliferated and were thereby rapidly assuming greater importance. And television programs increasingly treated politically controversial subjects and such previously taboo themes as divorce, unmarried cohabitation, and single parenting. However, *Television and Behavior* stated that the research done during the previous decade had focused not just on the potentially negative effects of television but also on how the medium could be used to promote positive behavior. It concluded that "children learn from watching television and what they learn depends on what they watch," but that the beneficial effects of television were undermined by an unrelenting diet of violence. The studies were clear about the consequences of violence. "After 10 more years of research, the consensus among most of the research community is that violence on television does lead to aggressive behavior by children and teenagers who watch the programs.... In magnitude, television violence is as strongly correlated with aggressive behavior as any other behavioral variable that has been measured. The research question has moved from asking whether or not there is an effect to seeking explanations for the effect."[37]

The NIMH's report treated the question of whether television violence increased aggression as though it was a closed question. Some scholars contended, though, that the NIMH was "too complacent" in making this case. In 1983, Thomas D. Cook, a professor of psychology and urban affairs at Northwestern University, maintained that, while there was some linkage between TV violence and aggression, it was "highly unlikely that television plays more than a minor role in directly producing violence and violent crime in the U.S." Cook also noted that most previous studies had made a stronger connection between TV violence and "incivility" than between TV violence and actual physical aggression with intent to harm.[38]

Later criticism of the NIMH's report was more strident and misleading. In 1994, Freedman argued that the NIMH had failed to make a comprehensive, unbiased review of the literature and that the literature review had been done by L. Rowell Huesmann, who was "one of the most avid true believers" of the claim that TV produced harmful social effects.

---

[37] Quotations, ibid., 6 ("After," "effect"), 51 ("children," "watch"). See also ibid., iii, 2, 74. For research after 1984, see Chapter 9.

[38] Quotations, Cook, Kendzierski, and Thomas, "The Implicit Assumptions of Television Research: An Analysis of the 1982 NIMH Report on Television and Behavior," *POQ* 47 (1983): 193 ("unlikely"), 194 ("complacent," "incivility"); see also ibid., 179–94, 198–9.

However, this opinion contrasted sharply with Cook's earlier conclusion in 1983 that Huesmann's literature review had "accurately" reflected "the opinion of many other scholars" and that, overall, the NIMH's report had presented "a reasonable summary of current knowledge about television, its effects and its potential." Freedman contended, however, that Huesmann "referred to a few articles" and spent most of his literature review discussing his own work. This critique was an oversimplification. It is true that Huesmann did discuss his own research – about a dozen studies in which he had been involved – but he also covered more than eighty other references. Moreover, Freedman in his arguments chose to ignore the summarizing chapter of volume 1 of the NIMH's report on "Violence and Aggression." In that summation, Huesmann's work comprised but a fraction of the research on which the chapter was based.[39]

RATING CONTROVERSIES AND PG-13

As one would expect, the debate over research on the effects of violence in mass media spilled over into movie rating controversies. Several movies made by well-known filmmakers during the early 1980s – *Dressed to Kill, Blade Runner, Scarface, Body Double, Poltergeist,* and *Indiana Jones and the Temple of Doom* – provoked protests and embroiled the ratings board in controversy over the levels of violence and terror in these films. Brian De Palma made three of the films, Spielberg two, and Ridley Scott one. The controversies revealed a clearly flawed appeals process in which conflicts of interests were common. The use of so-called expert witnesses by the studios to support their arguments for more lenient ratings raised questions about the reliability of testimony-for-hire. Eventually, public criticism of the ratings reached such a crescendo that even Valenti was forced, for the first time, to agree to changes in the system.

In De Palma's *Dressed to Kill* (1980), a murderous cross-dressing psychiatrist, played by Michael Caine, kills his victims by slashing them with a razor. One especially brutal murder scene, in which the victim was played by Angie Dickinson, takes place in an elevator. Some critics and viewers found the scene reminiscent of the shocking stabbing scene in Alfred

---

39 Quotations ("avid," "referred"), Freedman, "Viewing Television Violence Does Not Make People More Aggressive," *Hofstra Law Review* 22 (Summer 1994): 836. Quotations, Cook, Kendzierski, and Thomas, "The Implicit Assumptions of Television Research," 180 ("accurately," "opinion"), 198 ("reasonable"). Marjorie Heins also follows Freedman's lead in her attack on the NIMH's report. See Heins, *Not in Front of the Children*, 236, 359n48.

Hitchcock's *Psycho* (1960), which had starred Anthony Perkins and Janet Leigh. But where much of the actual violence in Hitchcock's black-and-white film had been left to the imagination, in *Dressed to Kill* the attack was more graphic and more prolonged. The movie was also filmed in color, which, according to some research, makes many viewers find the blood and violence more disturbing than in black-and-white. Some critics objected to the movie because of the violence against women.[40] Members of the rating board considered the original version of *Dressed to Kill* so "intensely adult" that all of them voted to give the film an X. The "over-the-brink quality of the elevator murder and the throat-slashing at the end" made it inappropriate for children, Heffner concluded. But Heffner had no objections to the overall theme, or to the possibility of gratuitous violence toward women that it showed. In fact, he called the picture a "masterpiece." He was not, however, certain what to make of De Palma, who seemed intent on "cynically playing the game of using the press" to attack CARA. In the end, *Dressed to Kill* was edited to make it R-rated.[41]

A new controversy arose from Ridley Scott's movie *Blade Runner* (1982), which was based on Philip K. Dick's novel *Do Androids Dream of Electric Sheep?* (1968). In it, the main character, played by Harrison Ford, is a former policeman hired to hunt down renegade androids, known as replicants, in a future Los Angeles of the year 2019. A dark and violent film, *Blade Runner* nevertheless had serious things to say about artificial intelligence and the future.[42] When it received an R rating instead of a PG, the studio challenged the rating and called on the head of UCLA's

[40] For research indicating that color depictions of blood and violence in news photographs are more disturbing than the same pictures in black-and-white, see Detenber and Winch, "The Impact of Color on Emotional Responses to Newspaper Photography," *VCQ* 8, no. 3, (2001): 7; also 4–8, 14. The effects of color images on viewers merit additional research. There are few, if any, empirical studies on what impact color moving images in films and on TV have upon attention. See Detenber, Simons, and Reiss, "The Emotional Significance of Color in Television Presentations," *Media Psychology* 2 (2000): 333; also 331–55. On violence against women and *Dressed to Kill*, see Prince, *New Pot of Gold*, 353.

[41] Quotations, Heffner, "Pre-Oral History Memorandum for 1980," pp. 53 ("intensely," "masterpiece"), 54 ("cynically"), Box 1, RDH-COHC-BL. De Palma understood publicity's capacity to mask the true nature of events. He later said that "what you see represented in the media and books written about show business is false – and you get so sick of this public relations machine surrounding it – you want someone to say the truth about something." De Palma quoted ("false") in Salmon, "Looking Back at the Bonfires, Personal and Professional," *NYT,* June 16, 2002, sec. 2, p. 28.

[42] At least two alternate versions of this film were created in addition to a "director's cut" released in 1993 that contained added footage and a changed ending.

psychology department, Seymour Feshbach, to testify for them. Feshbach testified in favor of the PG rating by claiming that the violence was a form of catharsis and fantasy. The catharsis theory held that experiencing violence vicariously through the media of television or movies often has the effect of helping to purge viewers of aggression. While this theory continues to have spirited defenders, by 1982 most communication researchers had concluded that little evidence supported it. The NIMH's *Television and Behavior* summarized the research on catharsis theory by stating: "Since practically all the evidence points to an increase in aggressive behavior, rather than a decrease, the theory is contradicted by the data."[43]

Heffner used the NIMH's report to defend the R rating for *Blade Runner*, and also referred to Leonard Berkowitz. In a *New York Times* article about the movie, Berkowitz had said that violent actions on screen increased some people's indifference to real-life violence, taught them that such actions were acceptable behavior, and stimulated violent activity in some people. Warner Bros. lost its appeal of *Blade Runner*'s rating by a decisive 15 to 4 vote. It is difficult to know how much weight Heffner's use of media effects research carried, since the movie's violence would have made obtaining a PG a hard sell in any event.[44]

Indeed, it seems that research on violence and media, no matter how voluminous or carefully done, was rarely sufficient to carry the day in rating appeals. Such was the case with De Palma's critically acclaimed but extremely violent *Scarface* (1983). A remake of Howard Hawks's 1932 classic that had starred Paul Muni, De Palma's *Scarface* starred Al Pacino as a Cuban refugee drug dealer in Miami. The first rating the remake received was an X. Heffner was less bothered by the violence and profanity (by one count, the "f" word was used 175 times) in the movie than were the women on the rating board, but he felt that, given the film's overall content, most parents would consider the X rating appropriate. "It wasn't the most violent movie I had ever seen by any means," he said, but "it was violent, very violent," and "it should have been edited further or rated X." Universal, which was not inclined to risk exhibiting a

---

[43] Quotation ("evidence"), [Pearl, Bouthilet, and Lazar, eds.], *Television and Behavior. Volume I: Summary Report*, 40. In addition to Feshbach, Dr. Gordon Berry of UCLA's Graduate School of Education also testified on behalf of Warner Bros. at the appeals hearing. For a recent defense of the catharsis theory, see Heins, *Not in Front of the Children*, 228–53.

[44] See Heffner, "Pre-Oral History Memorandum for 1982," pp. 56, 58–9, Box 1, RDH-COHC-BL. For Berkowitz's interview, see *NYT*, June 30, 1982, copy in doc. 82-7, Heffner, "Pre-Oral History Memorandum for 1982," Box 1, ibid.

big-budget film with an X rating, appealed. Because of Lew Wasserman's involvement, Heffner expected Valenti to intervene on behalf of the studio, and indeed, three weeks before the appeal, Valenti told Heffner that "it was terribly important that Universal get an R."[45]

Valenti presided over the appeal in early November 1983. Universal's president, Robert Rehme, appeared at the hearing, as did De Palma. The studio used several expert witnesses, including two psychiatrists who specialized in children and adolescents, to argue that the film merited re-rating. The head of the Organized Crime Division from Broward County, Florida, testified. *Time* magazine's former film critic, Jay Cocks (who had collaborated on films with moviemakers De Palma and Martin Scorsese), read a letter to De Palma from fellow movie critic, Roger Ebert, who had condemned CARA for giving *Scarface* an X after it had given an R to the more repulsive *I Spit on Your Grave*. (Ebert did not mention, or may not have known, that in the latter case the distributor had substituted the X-rated version for the edited movie that had been rated R.) Alan Friedberg, who headed both Sack Theaters and NATO, maintained that, although *Scarface* might be too violent for children, it did not deserve an X because that rating was used for pornography.[46]

Heffner realized that the deck was stacked. "If you lie down with the psychiatrists," he said in a jab at the experts, "you wake up with the Fliess of their discontent." (Wilhelm Fliess was a psychiatrist who had turned against Sigmund Freud.) He knew, though, that only the psychiatrists would get that point. He considered calling Matilda Cuomo, wife of the New York governor Mario Cuomo, as a witness. She would be effective in speaking about how most parents regarded the violence in *Scarface*. But he resisted calling her, fearing that even had he been able to save the X rating, it would have alienated Wasserman and other executives to the point of mortally wounding the rating system. The outcome was never in doubt. The Appeals Board voted 17 to 3 to give *Scarface* the R.[47]

[45] Quotation ("Universal"), Heffner, "Pre-Oral History Memorandum for 1983," p. 5; see also ibid., 3-4, 20, Box 2, RDH-COHC-BL. Quotation ("violent"), Heffner, *Reminiscences*, vol. 1, p. 132, Box 5, ibid. See also ibid., vol. 7, pp. 1241-3, Box 5, ibid.

[46] Heffner, "Pre-Oral History Memorandum for 1983," pp. 19-20, 33, Box 2, RDH-COHC-BL; Heffner, interview (phone) with author, Aug. 27, 2002; and Corliss, "He Lost It at the Movies," *Time,* 139 (March 23, 1992), 64. Major Nick Navarro headed the Organized Crime Division in Broward County, FL.

[47] Quotation ("Fleiss"), Heffner, *Reminiscences*, vol. 1, p. 132, Box 5, RDH-COHC-BL. See also Heffner, "Pre-Oral History Memorandum for 1983," pp. 3-42, Box 2, RDH-COHC-BL. For Heffner's appeals statement, see doc. 83-5, Box 2, ibid.

The fallout from this appeal had several effects. Relations between Heffner and Valenti deteriorated further. Heffner believed that Valenti had undermined him in the press when Valenti was quoted as saying that he wanted his own teenage daughter to see *Scarface* because of its anti-drug message. More than this, Valenti had revealed that his loyalty would always be to the large studios even if it meant "diminishing and demeaning his own system." In the absence of "honest and responsible and public interest-charged leadership," Heffner doubted that self-regulation would work.[48]

In the long run, the appeals decision on *Scarface* set a precedent that influenced the ratings of other violent movies. For example, when in 1990 director Abel Ferrara made *King of New York,* CARA initially gave it an X. The film starred Christopher Walken as the drug lord over a gang of black drug dealers who regularly killed off their Colombian, Chinese, and Italian rivals. The intensity of Walken's performance impressed critics, but violence in the film was frequent and graphic. At the appeal hearing, experts hired by the studio criticized the rating board's decision to give the movie an X. One expert, then the director of the psychology department at New York's inner-city Metropolitan Hospital, was especially persuasive when she testified that most of her patients were gunshot or drug abuse victims and that the film offered a "perfect picture of urban life." Only "nice, white, middle-class Midwest families," would find *King of New York* shocking or offensive. Heffner countered that this criterion for judging the movie was beside the point. CARA did not rate pictures on how accurately they showed inner-city life but rather on how most parents might react to the films. The X rating was barely overturned by a 6 to 3 vote. As one Appeals Board member asked Heffner, how could they give *King of New York* an X when *Scarface* had received an R?[49]

Soon after the ratings dispute over *Scarface,* De Palma voiced his displeasure with the rating system and was quoted as saying that he planned to make a real X-rated film. "You wanna see violence? You wanna see sex? I think it's about time to blow the top off the ratings," he told *Moviegoer*. In his movie *Body Double* (1984), he demonstrated what he meant. In *Body Double,* Craig Wasson plays an unemployed actor who while house-sitting uses a telescope to spy on an attractive woman in a nearby home

---

[48] Quotations, Heffner, "Pre-Oral History Memorandum for 1983," pp. 6 ("demeaning"), 28 ("honest"); see also ibid., 29, Box 2, RDH-COHC-BL.

[49] Quotations ("perfect," "families"), Heffner, "Pre-Oral History Memorandum for 1990," pp. 38–9; see also ibid., 3, Box 2, RDH-COHC-BL.

and witnesses her murder by an assailant who uses a large power drill. De Palma believed that the electric drill would be more frightening and exciting to viewers than more traditional murder weapons. Critics charged that the prolonged murder scene was little more than sexual sadism; antipornography feminists called De Palma a misogynist. De Palma, who invoked the First Amendment, denied that his films promoted violence against women. Heffner hoped to avoid another confrontation, but the rating board voted initially to give *Body Double* an X, not for violence but "basically for sexuality of a 'porno level'" and profanity. Despite De Palma's bluster, he agreed to edit the film in order to get an R.[50]

Although the rating board's decisions prevailed regularly with smaller studios and low-budget films, the rating system tilted sharply in favor of studios with big-budget productions. Steven Spielberg's enormously popular movies are cases in point, and they did perhaps more than anything else to change the rating system.

Spielberg's *Poltergeist* (1982), directed by Tobe Hooper and distributed by MGM/United Artists (UA), is a ghost story about a suburban family whose home is invaded by malevolent spirits that kidnap their five-year-old daughter. It features flashy special effects and takes full advantage of the Dolby Sound system. The rating board gave the picture an R, not for violence *but for terror*. The raters believed that some scenes, especially those in which the Dolby sound magnified frightening situations, were too intense for small children to see without a parent or guardian. MGM challenged the rating, and the subsequent hearing may well have been the first appeals case in which sound was a major factor.

CARA's counsel, William Nix, warned Valenti that potential conflicts of interest existed. In 1981, MGM purchased United Artists from Transamerica, and Nix suggested that if the UA representative were allowed to vote in the *Poltergeist* appeal it would open CARA and the industry to damaging criticism. "There were a *lot* of peculiar goings-on here," Heffner remembered. "The pressure that was put upon me was unbelievable." Compared to the other major studios at the time, MGM/UA was a marginal player, and the rating on *Poltergeist* could potentially have had a huge impact on box-office revenue. Heffner recalled that, at the appeal, studio president Frank Rosenfelt indicated that "the economic consequences" of an R "would be devastating." While MGM

50 Liz Smith in the *New York Daily News* (Nov. 11, 1983), quoting De Palma ("You," "ratings"), quoted in Heffner, "Pre-Oral History Memorandum for 1983," p. 30, Box 2, RDH-COHC-BL. Quotation ("porno"), Heffner, "Pre-Oral History Memoradum for 1984," p. 63, also ibid., 62, Box 1, RDH-COHC-BL. See also Prince, *New Pot of Gold*, 353–6.

tried to argue that the film was not excessively violent, Heffner insisted that violence was not so much the issue for the rating board as was the level of terror that was increased by the Dolby Sound system. At the time, there was little research available on the effects of horror films on children that Heffner could use to strengthen his case. Subsequently, though, research showed that such movies as *Poltergeist,* and the earlier *Jaws,* did leave lasting and sometimes troubling impressions on many children under ten who saw the films.[51]

Valenti, who had tolerated conflicts of interests on such other appeals cases as *Blade Runner,* insisted that United Artists's vote be counted in the *Poltergeist* appeal.[52] The studio brought in a child psychologist, Dr. Alfred Jones, to bolster its case. As it turned out, MGM/UA probably did not need the help, because the Appeals Board voted 20 to 4 to give *Poltergeist* a PG. CARA bore the brunt of the criticism when parents complained about this rating. "People 'in the know' came to believe that we could be 'had,'" Heffner said. Rosenfelt was clearly irritated that Heffner had so vigorously defended the R rating, and Valenti let him know that the resentment might surface again at an upcoming meeting of the studio executives. Concerned that he would be fired, Heffner asked Valenti to extend his severance pay from six months to a year.[53]

One result of the *Poltergeist* controversy was to push Hollywood toward adopting a new rating classification between R and PG. Heffner had been advocating this step since *All the President's Men* in 1976 when he urged creating a restricted category called R-13. By 1980, he felt even more strongly that the rating system had not kept pace with changes in film content since the late 1960s. After the ratings fiasco over *Cruising,*

---

[51] Quotations, Heffner, "Pre-Oral History Memorandum for 1982," pp. 22 ("*lot,*" "unbelievable"; emphasis in original text), 24 ("economic," "devastating"); see also ibid., 43–4, Box 1, RDH-COHC-BL. See also William Nix to Jack Valenti, May 6, 1982, p. 3, doc. 82-1, with Heffner, "Pre-Oral History Memorandum for 1982," ibid.; and Prince, *New Pot of Gold,* 15, 71. For research discussing the possible effects on children that such movies as *Poltergeist* and *Jaws* might have, see Cantor, "*Mommy, I'm Scared,*" 9–10, 14–15, 34; and Cantor, "'I'll Never Have a Clown in My House!'" – Why Movie Horror Lives On," *PT* 25, no. 2, (2004): 283–304. Among the deleterious effects were "long-term problems," including "sleep disturbances" and "lifelong phobic behaviors." Cantor, interview with author, Jan. 20, 2003.

[52] For example, the Ladd Company, which made *Blade Runner,* had worked out an arrangement for Warner Bros. to distribute this picture. Nevertheless, Valenti insisted that Warner Bros. be allowed to vote on the appeal of *Blade Runner*'s R rating. Heffner, "Pre-Oral History Memorandum for 1982," pp. 23–4, Box 1, RDH-COHC-BL.

[53] Quotation ("People"), Heffner, "Pre-Oral History Memorandum for 1982," p. 53; see also ibid., 22, 47, 51, Box 1, RDH-COHC-BL. See also Heffner to Valenti, June 29, 1982, doc. 82-28, with Heffner, "Pre-Oral History Memorandum for 1982," ibid.

he told Wasserman that if the system's credibility were to be maintained, new rating categories were needed and the public should also be given more information that explained the ratings.[54]

In late 1980 and 1981, CARA conducted an experiment in Kansas and western Missouri in which explanatory language was added to the ratings for PG and R films. PG movies had descriptions such as "violence," "sensuality," or "language," with further qualifiers such as "minor" or "some." R films carried the same descriptions but without the qualifiers. In movie advertising, CARA publicized these changes and exhibitors used them in theaters. CARA then conducted interviews with parents who had children between the ages of five and seventeen.[55] Valenti resisted giving the fuller explanations and decided to stop the Kansas-Missouri experiment in early 1982. Perhaps worried that parents would use the additional information to prevent children from attending films, he argued that no language could adequately explain what kind of violence was in a movie and that the added descriptions would actually confuse the public.[56] Heffner believed this argument was evasive and that Valenti wanted to turn him into an "intellectual eunuch." He also doubted that fuller explanations would harm attendance. Surveys had shown that parents either were unable or did not try to control which movies their teenagers saw and did not believe theater owners enforced restricted admission policies anyway. But they did like to have the additional information about ratings, if for no other reason than it made them feel as though they could give better advice to their children. Heffner believed that the rating system required revision in order to meet the needs of the 1980s. "The real question," he told Valenti, was "whether intelligent, rational, reasonable, and appropriate responses to the changes that have taken place in our industry might not protect both the industry and the public interest *better* than will a rigid adherence to the patterns of the past."[57]

---

54 Heffner to Lew R. Wasserman, Oct. 10, 1980, doc. 80-J, with Heffner, "Pre-Oral History Memorandum for 1980," Box 1, RDH-COHC-BL. See also Heffner, ibid., pp. 79–80.

55 William Nix to Chuck Barnes, Oct. 27, 1980, doc. 80-56; and Mike Linden to Jack Valenti, Will Nix, Dick Heffner, Griff Johnson, Barbara Scott, Nov. 25, 1980, doc. 80-58, with Heffner, "Pre-Oral History Memorandum for 1980," Box 1, RDH-COHC-BL.

56 Valenti to Richard Orear, Jan. 5, 1982, doc. 82-17, with Heffner, "Pre-Oral History Memorandum for 1982," Box 1, RDH-COHC-BL.

57 Quotation ("eunuch"), Heffner to Jack [Valenti], June 24, 1981 (inter-office memo), document 81-11, with Heffner, "Pre-Oral History Memorandum for 1981," Box 1, RDH-COHC-BL. Quotations ("real," "*better*"; emphasis in original text), Heffner to Valenti, Feb. 12, 1982, doc. 82-21, with Heffner, "Pre-Oral History Memorandum for 1982," Box 1, ibid. See also Heffner to Frank Mancuso, Jan. 25, 1982, doc. 82-15; and Heffner

There were powerful people in Hollywood who were also ready for a change, including Wasserman's protégé, Spielberg. Shortly before the *Poltergeist* appeal, in late April 1982, the influential director drove Heffner to the Los Angeles airport and along the way indicated that he wanted a rating that distinguished between teenagers and preteens. Heffner, who now favored calling the new category "PG-M," offered to lobby other industry leaders discreetly. He knew that some of them, including Paramount chair Barry Diller, supported a new rating. But Heffner had to tread carefully, because every time his name appeared in the press favoring a change in the system, Valenti "went ballistic." With the new category, Heffner told Valenti in 1982, a number of PG films would receive new, more restrictive ratings: Chevy Chase's *Modern Problems* (1981), Spielberg's *Raiders of the Lost Ark* (1981), Warner Bros.'s *Salem's Lot* (1981), and Universal's *Four Seasons* (1981). Similarly, there were R films that would be rerated to the less restrictive rating, and some of these movies would include Universal's *Blues Brothers* (1980), Warren Beatty's *Reds* (1981), and Paramount's *Mommie Dearest* (1981).[58]

It was not until 1984, after another Spielberg film, *Indiana Jones and the Temple of Doom* (Fig. 10), created a furor when it received a PG rating, that change came. In the movie there is a scene where the villain reaches into the chest of a living man and pulls out his beating heart for all to see. Many parents and critics believed that the film was too violent for preteens. It was in the aftermath of this picture, when the industry faced intense criticism from the public and Valenti met with pressure from exhibitors, that he reluctantly agreed to adopt the PG-13.[59]

By this time, Valenti also appears to have been leaning toward giving the public more information. In October 1984 he sent a memo to the MPAA's advertising and publicity committee saying, "I am now convinced the time has come for us to provide explanations for ratings." He hoped

to Valenti, July 29, 1982, doc. 82-33, with Heffner, "Pre-Oral History Memorandum for 1982," Box 1, ibid.

[58] Quotation ("ballistic"), Heffner, *Reminiscences*, vol. 2, p. 211; see also ibid., 210, Box 5, RDH-COHC-BL. See also Heffner to Steven Spielberg, July 23, 1982, doc. 82-2, with Heffner, "Pre-Oral History Memorandum for 1982," Box 1, ibid.; and Heffner, interview (phone) with author, Aug. 27, 2002. See also Heffner to Valenti, Feb. 12, 1982, doc. 82-21; and Heffner to Valenti, May 12, 1982, doc. 82-24, with Heffner, "Pre-Oral History Memorandum for 1982," Box 1, ibid.

[59] Heffner, "Pre-Oral History Memorandum for 1982," p. 30, Box 1, RDH-COHC-BL. On *Poltergeist*, see ibid., 21–38. See also S. Mitchell, "The X Rating Gets Its Day in Court," F1; and Fox, "Jack Valenti Says Change Possible for Film Ratings," *LAT*, Aug. 10, 1990, F1.

FIGURE 10. A scene from *Indiana Jones and the Temple of Doom* (1984) where the villain extracts the heart from a living man. Protests from parents and other critics convinced the movie industry to adopt a new rating category, PG-13. Photograph courtesy of Photofest.

that after Bethlyn Hand, who was in charge of publicity, and her group commented on the memo, he would be able to show the plan to the studio executives and then make the announcement later in the fall at the National Association of Theatre Owners convention. The advertising people reacted negatively, however, and argued that explanations would hurt the marketing of films. Although Heffner countered that the added information would defuse calls for censorship, Valenti turned his back on the plan.[60]

New technologies helped to alter the public's relationship to cinema during the 1970s and early 1980s. Innovations expanded production techniques, improved special effects, and helped to move horror, science fiction, and fantasy films into the mainstream of production. They made motion picture violence more realistic, gruesome, and visceral.[61] These advances, in combination with cable, satellite television, and videotape, brought explicit entertainment directly into people's homes on an unprecedented scale. Such films as *Dressed to Kill, Scarface,* and *Body*

[60] Jack Valenti memo, Oct. 8, 1984, quoted ("convinced"), in Heffner, *Reminiscences,* vol. 7, p. 1211; see also ibid., 1210–12, 1214–15, Box 5, RDH-COHC-BL.
[61] See Cook, *Lost Illusions,* 370–2, 374–80.

Double, as well as many other violent movies, played uncensored via cable and satellite television. Their appearance coincided with a period when videocassette rentals began to grow exponentially in the United States. Often movies originally rated X but edited to get an R would have the original X-rated material restored to the cassette version. When *I Spit on Your Grave* was released on videocassette, for example, most versions contained the X-rated material.[62] Video merchandisers liked to let it be known that the movies they sold or rented might have been R-rated when they played in the theaters but that they now had X-rated content. Eventually, many low-budget horror movies bypassed theaters in favor of straight-to-video distribution. During the 1980s, as one historian observed, the "blood epics, like sex films, shifted to video and the private home as the preferred site for consumption."[63]

As the cable and video market became virtually unrestricted, network television, one may speculate, began to show movies that would have been banned or heavily censored prior to the home entertainment revolution. In 1985, as Valenti testified before Congress, Senator Al Gore (D-TN) questioned the wisdom of an ABC affiliate (WJLA) in Washington, DC, showing *The Exorcist* and other R-rated films during prime time.[64]

The problem became widespread even outside the United States. Video piracy and the expansion of American movies abroad through legitimate means meant that this kind of entertainment was projected worldwide. Just as sexually explicit videos infiltrated even the most traditional and closed of societies, so too did the violent pictures of the 1970s and 1980s.

Despite the growing evidence that violence in entertainment could be harmful to children and to other members of society, during the 1970s and 1980s, Hollywood moguls professed to be unconvinced. In 1985, when Valenti testified before the Meese Commission, which was then investigating pornography, he talked about violence in motion pictures and on television and about the industry's position on the problem. His testimony was hardly reassuring to people who were worried about the effects of mass media. He admitted that there had been a sharp increase in movie violence, including "bestiality and sadomasochism," during the past decade, but he clung to the position he had taken in 1968 before

---

[62] See Heffner to Valenti, Jan. 6, 1982; and Heffner to Valenti, June 22, 1981, doc. 82-8A, with Heffner, "Pre-Oral History Memorandum for 1982," Box 1, RDH-COHC-BL.

[63] Quotation ("epics"), Prince, *New Pot of Gold*, 353. See also Heffner, "Pre-Oral History Memorandum for 1983," pp. 80–1, Box 2, RDH-COHC-BL; and O'Toole, *Pornocopia*, 118–19.

[64] See Valenti, Testimony, *U.S. Senate Hearings*, Oct. 24, 1985, 77–8.

the National Commission on the Causes and Prevention of Violence. Despite the large number of studies on media violence that had appeared since that time, he continued to argue that evidence from social science research was inconclusive.[65] "What is too much violence?" he asked the commission. "I have examined that question with some of the – I think the most ingenious scholastic academic minds in this country. . . . Is it John Wayne storming the beaches at Iwo Jima and machine-gunning 200 Japanese, one man garroting another in an alley, a man killing a wife with a revolver. Or is it the sheriff shooting it out at the OK Corral. How do you deal with that?"[66]

Unlike scientific research that proved that cigarettes cause cancer, social science research on movie effects was unreliable, he asserted.

Now, I believe the Surgeon General on cigarettes. I have not found any responsible – well, any great body of scientific and medical scientists who will dispute the single statement that if you smoke enough cigarettes you have a high percentage risk of getting cancer.

On the other hand, I have not seen any certifiably redeemable data, confirming data, that proves [sic] that watching films is a causal relationship for doing something you wouldn't already be tempted to do because of some other, somebody jostling you on the subway or someone saying an offensive remark to you, because of the dislocation of your own brain and mind. I haven't seen that. I have found in this field, it's much like a murder trial, where the defense says that my client is incompetent to stand trial. So he has six psychiatrists who swear on their mother's grave that this man is certifiably insane.

Then the prosecution brings six psychiatrists who say precisely the opposite. That's what we have found. Exactly that. But I haven't been able to assemble data which confirm this causal relationship.[67]

There was simply too much money to be made from entertainment that traded in violence and sex for a free market society to be able to restrain it. Because violent movies were often highly profitable, and because the major filmmakers dominated the appeals process, there were powerful forces that worked against efforts to curb violence in mainstream motion pictures. Hollywood resisted taking even such minimal steps as reforming the rating system. Finally, in 1984, studios agreed to add a new category between PG and R, but there was still nothing to categorize the area between R and X. Moreover, Valenti remained reluctant to offer the public

[65] Quotation ("bestiality"), Jack Valenti, testimony, *Meese Commission Hearings,* Oct. 17, 1985, 36; see also ibid., 24, Folder: "Los Angeles – 10/17/85 (Part I)," Box 4, RAGCP-NARA 2.
[66] Quotation ("What," "Corral"), ibid., 27.
[67] Quotation ("Surgeon," "relationship"), ibid., 42–3.

more information explaining why the ratings were given to individual films. "Courts and judges don't have to explain and while ours is not a judicial system, it has some similarities," Valenti told Heffner in the aftermath of the criticism that followed *Cruising* and *Dressed to Kill*.[68]

The addition of the PG-13 rating neither mollified critics, who were mobilizing to take action on several fronts, nor satisfied Heffner, who thought the system needed additional reforms. The events of the early 1980s troubled Heffner. Appalled by what he and other rating board members were seeing each week, dismayed that the self-restraint needed from moviemakers to make voluntarism work seemed in short supply, he acknowledged his "own sense of shame for humanity that other human beings actually create and distribute and exhibit media content that so taints everything and perhaps everyone it touches." To a London audience in 1982, and again in Toronto two years later, he said, "I do dearly wish the earth would just open up to swallow whole some of the dreadful things we see . . . perhaps even some of the dreadful persons who make them."[69]

---

[68] Quotation ("Courts"), Valenti to Heffner, July 1, 1981, doc. 81-14, with Heffner, "Pre-Oral History Memorandum for 1981," Box 1, RDH-COHC-BL.

[69] Quotations ("shame," "them"), Heffner, "Jefferson Revisited," Address delivered Sept. 18, 1984, 5, RDHPP. See also Heffner, "Freedom and Responsibility in Mass Communications," Address delivered March 22, 1982, 6, 16, RDHPP.

5

Pornography

The effects of sexuality in mass media pose issues no less interesting than the ones raised by violence. As the nation moved away from a culture that was largely oriented to print toward one that is more image- and audio-oriented, the use of photography and then moving pictures during the late nineteenth and early twentieth centuries brought important changes in the ways people experience sexuality. As the technologies of communication became more sophisticated and proliferated, interest in what influence these developments might have in this area of human conduct grew. During the early 1950s, Alfred Kinsey and his associates studied the effect of media on sex and noted that people often reacted differently depending on the medium (e.g., text, still pictures, moving pictures) through which they received erotic stimuli. Some years later, the 1970 *Report of the Commission on Obscenity and Pornography* (hereafter referred to as 1970 *Report*) pointed to research that showed that erotic films tended to produce more sexual arousal among viewers than photographs or written text. A more recent study of pornography reached a similar conclusion when it stated that "pictorial stimuli tend to be more arousing than textual, and cinematic stimuli more arousing than still graphics."[1]

As explained in the preceding chapters, after the 1970 *Report* appeared, significant changes occurred in the way erotic stimuli were transmitted and received, and they deserve more scholarly attention than they have been given. A flawed effort to examine these changes was undertaken in 1985 and 1986 by the Attorney General's Commission on Pornography – better

---

[1] Quotation ("stimuli"), Randall, *Freedom and Taboo*, 95. See also Johnson, et al., "The Impact of Erotica," 169; also 167–74; and Kinsey et al., *Sexual Behavior in the Human Female*, 652–63, 669–75, 687–9.

known as the Meese Commission, after President Ronald Reagan's attorney general, Edwin Meese III. The Meese Commission began its investigation with the assumption that much had changed in the media environment since the work of the 1970 President's Commission on Obscenity and Pornography. Unfortunately, some Meese Commission members had already made up their minds about the influence of pornography well before the 1985–6 hearings started. The witnesses called by the commission were heavily skewed in favor of those who talked about harmful effects. Moreover, the press, on the whole, covered the issues surrounding pornography poorly. Still, it is worth examining these hearings because a good deal of testimony focused on the potential effects of sexually arousing materials in mass media.

Some of the research and testimony about harmful effects implicated mainstream entertainment. It was not just hard-core pornography that was potentially damaging to children, the experts explained; some Hollywood movies and television programs might also have serious consequences for the young. Furthermore, researchers argued, certain kinds of material that appeared in such publications as *Playboy* and *Penthouse* were problematic.

In his testimony at the Meese Commission hearings, Jack Valenti expertly deflected criticism of mainstream movies and TV shows. However, Valenti, Heffner, and others in the movie industry knew that if the Meese Commission succeeded in its efforts to suppress pornography, pressure would likely increase on mainstream Hollywood. Indeed, the Reagan administration and its supporters did attempt to change the way motion pictures portrayed a number of subjects, including sex, drug abuse, and religion.

The Meese Commission is interesting for another reason. Although it made more than ninety recommendations for fighting pornography, and although there were successes in this battle to be sure, overall its impact on eradicating pornography was at best marginal. The question is why were these results so minimal? Had communication technologies become so sophisticated and widespread by the late twentieth century that it was no longer possible for any agency to control depictions of sexuality, violence, and other controversial themes?

THE MEESE COMMISSION

Just as important changes altered the media environment after the 1970 *Report,* so significant developments also occurred in the political and cultural arenas. American politics and culture shifted in a more conservative direction, first with the Richard Nixon and Gerald Ford administrations during the 1970s, and then with the Reagan and George H. W. Bush presidencies during the 1980s and early 1990s. Conservative religious groups gained strength during this period and their leaders exercised considerable political clout, especially during the Reagan administration. To many people on the political and religious right, pornography was both a symbol and a cause of America's moral decline. Hollywood was also part of the problem, many conservatives believed, but some of them thought that if the mainstream movie industry could be changed, it could be a force for reversing the nation's moral downward slide.

The 1970 *Report*, which had been started in 1967 during the Lyndon B. Johnson administration, issued several significant, if controversial, findings. A majority of the commission's members concluded that there were few or no harmful effects from pornography and recommended removing restrictions for adult consumers. It said that long-term exposure (fifteen days or more) to erotic materials usually resulted in satiation, characterized by a marked decline in sexual arousal and interest in such stimuli. One long-term result of loosening legal controls, therefore, would be to reduce interest in pornography. The 1970 *Report* maintained that exposure to pornography seemed to have little or no effect on established attitudes toward sexual morality or sexuality, and in young people it "had no impact upon moral character over and above that of a generally deviant background." It concluded that being exposed to explicit sexual material played no "significant role" in causing "delinquent or criminal behavior among youth or adults."[2]

Considerable support existed for these conclusions when they appeared. Some writers concurred that pornography was essentially harmless and could even be considered an art form.[3] Researchers found little or no connection between erotic material and antisocial behavior. The historian E. J. Hobsbawm, for example, argued that there were "no good grounds" for the belief that "permissiveness in public sexual or other personal behavior" led to "social-revolutionary movements," or that "a narrow sexual morality" was "an essential bulwark of the capitalist system."[4]

---

[2] Quotations ("impact," "adults"), "The Effects of Explicit Sexual Material," *RCOP*, 27; see also ibid., 25–6; and Randall, *Freedom and Taboo*, 97.

[3] See Michelson, *Aesthetics of Pornography*; and Simons, *Pornography without Prejudice*.

[4] Quotations, Hobsbawm, "Revolution Is Puritan," in Nobile, ed., *New Eroticism*, 36 ("no," "movements"), 38 ("narrow," "capitalist"). See also Moos, "The Effects of Pornography: A Review of the Findings of the Obscenity and Pornography Commission."

One review of more than three dozen studies concluded that pornography could be beneficial to the development of normal sexuality.[5] Supporters of the 1970 *Report* pointed to Denmark, where pornography had been legalized and where the more liberal laws appeared to have contributed to a decrease in child molestations.[6] The legalization of pornography in Denmark, one researcher even predicted, spelled "the doom of a multi-million dollar industry." Others thought it unlikely that in the United States a "vast ... untapped audience" was ready to buy pornography once legal restrictions were repealed. The 1970 *Report* also gained enthusiastic endorsements from Hugh Hefner and *Playboy,* as well as from other like-minded publishers.[7]

But from its publication, the multivolume 1970 *Report* was also denounced by many. President Nixon called the conclusions of the commission's majority "morally bankrupt," and the U.S. Senate voted sixty-five to five to reject the 1970 *Report.* About the time the 1970 *Report* appeared, social, legal, and political conservatives issued dire warnings that pornography dehumanized society, eroded self-restraint, undermined democratic government, and, when disseminated through mass media, could even destroy civilization. They urged stronger state and local regulation.[8] Their condemnations of pornography and of the 1970 *Report* reached a broad popular audience through the pages of such publications as the *Reader's Digest,* where articles questioned the commission's objectivity and its assertion that no connection existed between erotica and sex crimes.[9]

---

[5] See Money and Athanasiou, "Pornography – Review and Bibliographic Annotations."

[6] Buckley, "Oh! Copenhagen," *NYT Magazine,* Feb. 8, 1970, 32–46; and Kutschinsky, "The Effect of Easy Availability of Pornography on the Incidence of Sex Crimes: The Danish Experience."

[7] Quotations ("doom"), Gilmore, "Preface," in Kemp, ed., *Illustrated Presidential Report of the Commission on Obscenity and Pornography,* 9. Quotation ("vast"), Monroe, "Introduction," ibid., 7. This work was an unauthorized version of the 1970 Commission's Report.

[8] See, for example, Berns, "On Pornography: I – Pornography vs. Democracy: The Case for Censorship"; Bickel, Kauffmann, McWilliams, and Cohen, "On Pornography: II – Dissenting and Concurring Opinion"; Kristol, "Pornography, Obscenity and the Case for Censorship," *NYT Magazine,* March 28, 1971, 24; and Bonniwell, "The Social Control of Pornography and Sexual Behavior." See also the essays by George Elliott, George Steiner, and Ernest van de Haag in Hughes, ed., *Perspectives on Pornography.* Quotation ("bankrupt"), Boyer, *Purity in Print,* 309. For conservative reaction to the 1970 Report, see also ibid., 306–10, 321–3.

[9] See Keating, Jr., "The Report That Shocked the Nation"; and Schultz, "What Sex Offenders Say about Pornography."

These currents of criticism found a champion in Ronald Reagan. During the 1980 presidential campaign, he called for restoring "traditional moral values" and appealed to a loose coalition of groups that denounced "secular humanism" and promoted a "pro-family" agenda. The many evangelical Christians and other conservatives who made up these groups were deeply upset by the political and social turmoil of the 1960s and 1970s. They were opposed not only to pornography but also to permissiveness in mass entertainment, abortion, homosexuality, drug abuse, and the federal equal rights amendment for women.[10] They wanted to reassert the Judeo-Christian values that they believed modern culture had abandoned.

When President Reagan signed legislation to strengthen the enforcement of laws against child pornography in May 1984, he also announced that a national commission would reassess the conclusions of the 1970 *Report.* "I think the evidence that has come out since that time," Reagan said, "plus the tendency of pornography to become more extreme, shows that it is time to take a new look at this conclusion." Early in 1985, Reagan directed Attorney General William French Smith to establish a new commission. In May, Edwin Meese III, who had replaced Smith, announced the names of the eleven people who would serve on what became known simply as the Meese Commission. Its findings were entitled the *Final Report of the Attorney General's Commission on Pornography* (1986; hereafter referred to as *Final Report).*[11]

Opponents of pornography nationwide found a sympathetic audience in the attorney general's commission, where conservatives, many of whom were in law enforcement, strongly influenced the hearings. The chair, Henry E. Hudson, a Republican in his late thirties, was an attorney who had successfully prosecuted pornography in Arlington County, Virginia. Reagan lauded his work at a meeting with leaders of Morality in Media in March 1983 and later nominated him to be U.S. Attorney for the Eastern District of Virginia. Hudson's main interest on the commission lay in developing legal strategies to proscribe pornography. The commission's executive director, Alan Sears, was a prosecutor in the U.S. Attorney's office for western Kentucky. Although not a voting member, he was influential on the commission and consistently supported

[10] See Bennetts, "Conservatives Join on Social Concerns," *NYT,* July 30, 1980, A1; and Briggs, "Evangelicals Debate Their Role in Battling Secularism," *NYT,* Jan. 27, 1981, A12. See also Boyer, *Purity in Print,* 315.

[11] Ronald Reagan quoted ("evidence") in "Child Pornography Law Enacted," *NYT,* May 22, 1984, A20.

strengthening laws for prosecuting pornographers. Harold (Tex) Lezar, who played an important part in the creation of the Meese Commission, had worked for William F. Buckley, Jr., written speeches for Nixon, and been Assistant Attorney General for Legal Policy under U.S. Attorney General Smith. Another commission member, Edward J. Garcia, was a U.S. district judge in California who had been appointed by President Reagan.[12]

Other members are more difficult to categorize. They agreed that shared moral values were important, but they differed over the extent to which sexual morality should be considered an "essential part of the social glue" that made civilization possible. Most of them believed pornography was subversive. Diane D. Cusack, who served on the City Council of Scottsdale, Arizona, thought that pornography, if left unchecked, would "undermine our social fabric" and favored vigorous prosecution. The Reverend Bruce Ritter, president and founder of Covenant House, an international child-care agency that helped runaways and operated centers in the United States, Canada, and Guatemala, believed that all forms of sexually explicit materials degraded the "very nature of human sexuality." For Ritter, sexual privacy, no less than personal liberty, was a God-given right, fundamental to human dignity and citizenship; in his opinion, the invasion of this privacy by pornography was profoundly subversive. (Ritter's emphasis on privacy sadly assumed a new dimension a few years later when he was forced to leave Covenant House following a scandal that involved charges that he had had homosexual relationships with some of the young men in his care.)[13] James C. Dobson, who held a Ph.D. in child development, was a licensed psychologist and family counselor, and president of Focus on the Family, a California-based organization that produced a syndicated radio program. Dobson had written several books, including *Dare to Discipline* (1970) and *Hide or Seek* (1979), the latter about self-respect in children. A devout Christian, he considered pornography harmful in many ways and felt that it

---

[12] On Henry E. Hudson, see Transcript of Proceedings, Meeting of the Attorney General's Commission on Pornography, June 18, 1985, p. 26, Folder: "Washington – 6/18/85," Box 1, RAGCP-NARA 2; Hoffman, "Reagan Hears Pleas to Battle Pornography," *WP*, March 29, 1983, A5; and Scannell, "Arlington's Prosecutor Tapped for U.S. Attorney," *WP*, March 29, 1986, B1. For Alan Sears, Harold Lezar, and Edward J. Garcia, see McManus, "Introduction," *Final Report*, xxxvii–xxxviii.

[13] Quotations, ("glue"), *Final Report*, 46. Quotation ("fabric"), "Statement of Diane D. Cusack," ibid., 486. Quotation ("nature"), "Statement of Father Bruce Ritter," ibid., 512; see also ibid., 512–13.

threatened the "future of the family itself."[14] Park Elliott Dietz, an M.D.
and Ph.D., taught courses at the University of Virginia on law and psychiatry, and crimes of violence, and had published research in the *Journal of Forensic Sciences* about sexual sadism in detective magazines, a
theme he traced back to the seventeenth century. Dietz thought most
forms of pornography were "immoral" and corrupted the family and
society's moral fabric. But he stopped short of supporting a commission
resolution that named the family society's most important unit, because he
believed that the government should not try to dictate ideal living arrangements. Frederick Schauer also opposed this resolution. A law professor
at the University of Michigan, Schauer had written a book for legislators, judges, and prosecuting attorneys entitled *The Law of Obscenity*
(1976). Although earlier in his career he had defended the producers of
the movie *Deep Throat,* he was considered a middle-of-the-roader on the
commission. He wrote the "Overview and Analysis" section of the *Final
Report.*[15]

The members of the commission who were perhaps the most skeptical about the claims concerning the alleged harms caused by pornography were three women. Deanne Tilton-Durfee, who began her career
as a social worker in Los Angeles and was president of the California
Consortium of Child Abuse Councils, was most worried about the potentially damaging effects of pornography on children. Ellen Levine edited
Woman's Day and was vice president of CBS Magazines. Trained in journalism, she believed that she had "become attuned" to what concerned
"most American women." Judith Veronica Becker, who received a Ph.D.
from the University of Southern Mississippi, taught clinical psychology at
Columbia University's College of Physicians and Surgeons and had spent
the past decade working with victims of sexual abuse and sex offenders.[16]

---

[14] Quotation ("future"), "Personal Comments by Commissioner James Dobson," ibid.,
508. For other harms, see ibid., 506–8.
[15] Quotation ("immoral"), "Statement of Park Elliott Dietz," ibid., 492. See also ibid., 488–
91; Dietz, Harry, and Hazelwood, "Detective Magazines: Pornography for the Sexual
Sadists?"; and McManus, "Introduction," *Final Report,* xl. On Frederick F. Schauer, see
McManus, "Introduction," *Final Report,* xxxviii; and Schauer, *Law of Obscenity.*
[16] Quotations ("attuned," "women"), Ellen Levine, in Transcript of Proceedings, Meeting
of the Attorney General's Commission on Pornography, June 18, 1985, p. 25, Folder:
"Washington – 6/18/85," Box 1, RAGCP-NARA 2. For Tilton-Durfee and Becker, see
ibid., 22–4. Also on background for commission members, see *Final Report,* 477–546;
Nobile and Nadler, *United States of America vs. Sex,* 16–22; and Kurtz, "Pornography
Panel's Objectivity Disputed; Critics Call Meese Commission Overzealous," *WP,* Oct. 15,
1985, A4.

The Meese Commission operated on assumptions, largely underappreciated by its detractors, that important changes in technology had occurred since 1970, and that along with those changes the nature of pornography itself had changed. Few aspects of modern society, the commission argued, were untouched by cable TV, satellite transmissions, magnetic recording, computers, and competition in telecommunications. Even the commission members most critical of the *Final Report* acknowledged "the stunning change in the way in which people now receive erotic stimuli." As Levine told Valenti, "we are now breeding a new society, a society that is very accustomed to visuals." She and Becker urged more research on the "shift from print to video," and especially on how video's influence on children and adolescents might differ from print's influence on the young. For other commission members, pornography seemed to be growing more violent and more focused on previously taboo subject matter. These two developments alone made the 1970 *Report* "starkly obsolete," the commission maintained.[17]

Defining just what constituted pornography, of course, was no easy matter. The ancient Greek word *pornographos* meant "writing about harlots," but its modern usage, which includes not only written communications but visual images, began to emerge sometime between the mid-eighteenth and mid-nineteenth centuries. By the late-nineteenth century, pornography had become associated with prostitution, obscenity, and licentious wall paintings such as those recovered in the excavations of the ancient city of Pompeii. During the second half of the twentieth century, pornography became identified with explicit depictions of sexuality. By the late 1960s, references to a "pornography of violence" appeared in the criticisms of films and television.[18] Some press accounts inaccurately reported that the Meese commission failed to define what it meant by pornography, but the commission's records indicate that the members did deliberate about the term and gave a clear definition of it in their *Final Report*. They defined it to mean "only that . . . material [which] is predominantly sexually explicit and intended primarily for the purpose of sexual arousal." The commission often used the term interchangeably with

[17] Quotation ("stunning"), "Statement of Dr. Judith Becker and Ellen Levine," *Final Report,* 542. Quotation ("breeding"), Ellen Levine from Jack Valenti's testimony in Public Hearing before the Attorney General's Commission on Pornography, Oct. 17, 1985 (in Los Angeles), p. 54, Folder: "Los Angeles – 10/17/85 (Part I)", Box 4, RAGCP-NARA 2. Quotation ("starkly"), *Final Report,* 6.
[18] Quotation ("harlots"), Kendrick, *Secret Museum,* 1; see also ibid., 2. Quotation ("violence"), *Oxford English Dictionary* (http://dictionary.oed.com/cgi/entry/00184357).

"sexual materials." Recognizing that "pornography" was a pejorative term for most people, the commission attempted to eschew its negative connotations by stating: "Where we do use the term, we do not mean for it to be, for us, a statement of a conclusion.... Whether some or all of what qualifies as pornographic under this definition should be prohibited, or even condemned, is not a question that should be answered under the guise of definition."[19]

For Meese Commission members as well as for many others, pornography, whatever its definition, entailed the commercialization of sex, and with it an invasion of sexual privacy. Members disagreed over the extent to which sexual privacy was "more than a matter of individual choice." Many thought that in the past sex had been "somewhat too private" and a topic too readily avoided, but most now thought that the pendulum had swung too far in the other direction. To those who believed that sexual intimacy should remain private, any public exhibition was harmful in and of itself.[20]

TESTIMONY ON THE EFFECTS OF PORNOGRAPHY

By the late 1970s, not only did attacks on pornography come from evangelicals, social conservatives, and feminists, but an increasing number of scholars were challenging key conclusions of the 1970 *Report.* Studies criticized the methodology used in the 1970 *Report,* its inadequate examination of sexual violence in motion pictures and television, and its inability to measure the effects of erotica on children.[21]

The claim made in the 1970 *Report* that repeated exposure to pornography led to satiation or to declining interest in erotic materials appeared dubious; the conclusion rested on a slim evidentiary base.[22] Subsequent research was much less clear-cut, especially when subjects were allowed to masturbate following exposure to pornography. Under those conditions, studies indicated, interest in pornography did not decline and in fact arousal actually increased with repeated exposure.[23]

---

[19] Quotations ("predominantly," "definition"), *Final Report,* 7.
[20] Quotations, *Final Report,* 44 ("choice"), 45 ("private").
[21] See Wills, "Measuring the Impact of Erotica." For cinema, TV, and the harmful effects of pornography, see Eysenck and Nias, *Sex, Violence and the Media.*
[22] One experimental study used fewer than three dozen college-age males. See "The Effects of Explicit Sexual Material," *RCOP,* 25. See also Howard, Reifler, and Liptzin, "Effects of Exposure to Pornography," *TRCOP, Vol. VIII,* 97–132.
[23] See Randall, *Freedom and Taboo,* 97–99.

The explosive growth in pornography from a $10 million-a-year business in 1970 to a multibillion dollar industry by 1985 also seemed to belie the 1970 *Report*'s conclusion about satiation. Since 1970, there had been a massive increase in the volume of pornographic materials produced. In addition to being distributed through the new media already mentioned, porn was featured prominently on newsstands, in bookstores, and in video shops. Whereas only eighteen bookstores sold adult material in Los Angeles in 1969, by 1984 there were about four hundred bookstores and video outlets where it was not unusual for hard-core films to be displayed alongside Walt Disney movies. The *Final Report* suggested the dimensions of the problem by listing the titles of some 2,325 magazines, 725 paperback books, and 2,370 movies found in just sixteen stores in a half-dozen major U.S. cities in 1985. Nationwide, the Meese Commission estimated, 50–60,000 different sexually explicit publications were on the market, and these figures did not include what could be seen on cable television and in video arcades, or heard on audiocassettes or Dial-a-Porn services.[24]

Critics challenged the 1970 presidential commission's assertion that pornography was generally benign. The nature of pornography, they argued, had changed radically since 1970, when the market had consisted largely of nudity and simulated sex acts. During the 1970s, explicit depictions of varied heterosexual and homosexual sex acts increased. More troubling to critics was a sharp increase in materials showing sadomasochism, bestiality, child pornography, and aggressive, violent sex involving women. This type of material was relatively rare when the 1970 commission had conducted its investigation, and as a result its findings had been based, for the most part, on nonviolent pornography. Evidence now indicated, critics maintained, that some of this more explicit and violent material did have negative effects.[25]

What influence did this deluge of sexually explicit and often violent imagery have? What harm, if any, did it cause? The Meese Commission devoted attention to these questions, although it had only one year

[24] See Robert Peters, testimony, *Meese Commission Hearings*, Oct. 16, 1985, 22, 36, 60B, Folder: "Los Angeles – 10/16/85 (Part I)," Box 3, RAGCP-NARA 2; and *Final Report*, 360, 387–424 (for titles), and 425–39.
[25] Both law enforcement officials and communication researchers testified that the nature of pornography had changed significantly since 1970. See, for example, Peters, testimony, *Meese Commission Hearings*, Oct. 16, 1985, 36–50, 60B–60C, Folder: "Los Angeles – 10/16/85 (Part I)," Box 3, RAGCP-NARA 2: and Malamuth and Donnerstein, "The Effects of Aggressive-Pornographic Mass Media Stimuli," in Berkowitz, ed., *Advances in Experimental Social Psychology*, 15: 105–6. See also Court, "Pornography and Sex Crimes," 129–57.

in which to prepare its report, about half the time that had been spent preparing the earlier 1970 *Report,* and its budget (about $500,000) was also considerably smaller than the budget for the earlier commission. The Meese Commission had little money even to pay honoraria to the expert witnesses it called. From June 1985 through January 1986, the commission held hearings in several cities. In Houston, social scientists testified on the connection between pornography and behavior. In Los Angeles, the hearings covered production, distribution patterns, and technology. In Miami, the hearing was devoted to child pornography; in New York, to organized crime. (Most commission members believed that organized crime controlled much of the pornography business.) Testimony in Chicago dealt with law enforcement and the First Amendment. One important fact the commission discovered was that few people were prosecuted for pornography during 1984–5, even in such centers of production as New York and Los Angeles.[26]

As it tried to assess effects, the Meese Commission divided pornography into five categories along a scale of potential harmfulness. At one end of the spectrum was child pornography, which all members agreed was harmful and should be outlawed. At the other end of the spectrum was simple nudity, which had become virtually omnipresent even in mainstream media. Between these two poles were three categories that commission members found more ambiguous and difficult to evaluate. The category closest in ranking to child pornography in its potentially harmful effects was "sexually violent material," which included sadomasochism or scenes in which violent, forced sexual relations resulted in the sexual arousal of the unwilling victim (usually a woman). This category also included materials commonly available in the mainstream that showed "sexual activity or sexually suggestive nudity coupled with extreme violence, such as disfigurement or murder." In 1986, the commission argued that this kind of material was becoming the most widespread type of pornography. The next class of pornography included nonviolent depictions of sex involving "degradation, domination, subordination, and humiliation." Many feminists argued that, because most pornography showed women being subordinate to men and implied that women existed only to satisfy men sexually, this type of material could only weaken respect for women's rights. But Becker and Levine cautioned that the commission's assumption about the volume of nonviolent,

---

[26] See Transcript of Proceedings, Meeting of the Attorney General's Commission on Pornography, June 16, 1985, 106–7, Folder: "Washington – 6/18/85," Box 1, RAGCP-NARA 2; and Kelley, "Meese Outlines New War on Pornography," *LAT,* Feb. 11, 1987, pt. 1, p. 1.

degrading pornography might be exaggerated. Moreover, they thought the commission's efforts to quantify each of the different categories of pornography were, at best, only "guesstimates." Among these guesstimates they included the final category – "non-violent and non-degrading materials" – which, the commission maintained, existed only in relatively small quantities.[27]

Differences over how to determine the degree of potential harm divided the commissioners. The more liberal members, including Becker and Levine, tended to dismiss conclusions not grounded in serious social science research. The commission did hear testimony from several social scientists who asserted that certain types of pornography could be damaging, and it incorporated the findings of these researchers into its conclusions. Still, some members questioned whether social science could answer the important questions about pornography. Dietz, Ritter, and Hudson thought that social science research was inadequate to the task, even though they accepted its findings about the adverse effects of pornography. Dietz was a psychiatrist and sociologist who praised behavioral science research techniques to the commission, but he concluded that social science research was "too new on the historical scene to have developed adequate data on every important social problem, too little funded to have amassed all the data desired, and too positivistic to tell us what we should do, particularly when competing interests are at stake."[28] For Ritter, the commission's heavy reliance "on evidence of harms drawn from the empirical and social sciences to the virtual exclusion of other kinds of 'evidence'" was a "fatal flaw." Hudson believed that only some harmful effects could be documented clinically and that much of pornography's influence defied scientific analysis. Some commission members even felt confident that they could "intuitively" assess the likely impact of pornography.[29]

[27] Dietz apparently suggested these categories, although Becker and Levine thought they did not correspond to the classifications used by social scientists. As a result, Becker and Levine argued, it was difficult to apply social science research to the question of harm. Quotations, *Final Report,* 39 ("sexually," "murder"), 43 ("non-violent"); see also ibid., 43–7. Quotation ("guesstimates"), "Statement of Dr. Judith Becker and Ellen Levine," ibid., 545. See also ibid., 543; and McManus, "Introduction," ibid., xxxix.

[28] Quotation ("positivistic"), "Statement of Park Elliott Dietz," *Final Report,* 487. See also "Statement of Dr. Judith Becker and Ellen Levine," ibid., 543–4; and Transcript of Proceedings, Meeting of the Attorney General's Commission on Pornography, June 18, 1985, 21–2, Folder: "Washington – 6/18/85," Box 1, RAGCP-NARA 2.

[29] Quotations ("evidence," "flaw"), "Statement of Father Bruce Ritter," *Final Report,* 511. Quotation ("intuitively"), ibid., 44. See also "Statement of Henry E. Hudson, Chairman," ibid., 485.

Questions about the long-term historical significance of sexual imagery were especially difficult to measure empirically. Consider the possible influence of the least controversial of the commission's pornography classifications: nonviolent, nondegrading depictions of explicit sex, and nudity. Most commission members believed intuitively that a connection existed between behavior in society and the activities shown on film and television, although they differed in their assessments of the degree of this influence. Most agreed that little or no link existed between sexual violence and nonviolent, nondegrading sexually explicit materials. Nevertheless, most of them thought that these materials contributed to promiscuity. In the opinion of those who believed that marriage, the nuclear family, fidelity, and equality in sexual relationships were crucial to society – Cusack, Ritter, Dobson, Dietz, and the members with prosecutorial backgrounds – even nonviolent, nondegrading pornography was harmful. It was not unreasonable to conclude, the *Final Report* hypothesized, "that materials depicting sexual activity without marriage, love, commitment, or affection bear some causal relationship to sexual activity without marriage, love, commitment, or affection. There are undoubtedly many causes for what used to be called the 'sexual revolution,' but it is absurd to suppose that depictions or descriptions of uncommitted sexuality were not among them."[30]

Most commissioners found confirmation of their opinions in the work of researchers Dolf Zillmann and Jennings Bryant, among others, whose studies concluded that prolonged exposure to nonviolent pornography made both men and women more accepting of pre- and extramarital sex, generated discontent with one's sexual partner, created doubts about marriage being one of society's essential institutions, and undermined trust between spouses or friends. Moreover, heavy use of pornography promoted a lack of sensitivity toward the victims of sexual violence, because it tended to trivialize rape and the sexual abuse of children, led people to believe that unusual sexual activities were normal, and decreased the belief that women should be equal to men in intimate relations. Dietz carried these conclusions further, arguing that pornography was a menace to public health and linking it to the spread of AIDS and other medical and social ills.[31]

[30] Quotation ("materials," "them"), ibid., 44.
[31] See ibid., 41n46, 42–4; Dolf Zillmann, testimony, *Meese Commission Hearings*, Sept. 11, 1985, Folder: "Houston – 9/11/85 (Part I)," Box 2, RAGCP-NARA 2; and Zillmann, "Effects of Prolonged Consumption of Pornography," in Zillmann and Bryant, eds., *Pornography*, 154. The latter piece was originally part of the material the commission

Some commission members rejected these conclusions, however. Becker and Levine believed that most research showed that nonviolent, nondegrading pornography did "not have a negative effect on adults." The commission's *Final Report* acknowledged these differences of opinion by concluding that more research needed to be done on the impact of pornography on marriage as well as on sexual appetites and practices.[32]

On one point the commissioners were unanimous. Children were vulnerable to harmful effects from all categories of pornography, including those that might have no negative effects on adults. This was another area where judgments rested on common sense or intuition, and perhaps, too, on what the commissioners assumed were long-standing societal norms. For obvious reasons, little research was done on what effects pornography might have on the very young. Information about sexuality should be introduced by the family, not through pornography, the *Final Report* stated. "For children to be taught by these materials that sex is public, that sex is commercial, and that sex can be divorced from any degree of affection, love, commitment, or marriage is for us the wrong message at the wrong time."[33]

As for simple nudity, the commission commented on it only briefly, and while few, if any, believed that viewing the naked body per se was harmful, some members nevertheless worried that it could influence children's attitudes about women, gender relationships, and sex in general. They did agree, however, that nudity in art and for educational purposes probably did not cause harm.[34]

It is interesting to note that the commission distinguished between pornography that appeared solely in print and that which appeared in nonprint media. With the exception of material involving children, the commission excluded printed pornography (without images) from the materials it recommended for prosecution. The issue of this exclusion divided members. Ritter favored the exclusion because he believed that First Amendment values were "crucial to American life and the virtual

---

used to prepare its *Final Report*. See also Zillmann and Bryant, eds., *Pornography*, xvi; Zillmann, *Connections between Sex and Aggression;* and "Statement of Park Elliott Dietz," *Final Report*, 492; and ibid., 488–91.

[32] Quotation ("negative"), "Statement of Dr. Judith Becker and Ellen Levine," *Final Report*, 544; also 47. Commission members united in saying that nonviolent, nondegrading pornography "in some settings and when used for some purposes can be harmful. None of us think that the material in this category, individually or as a class, is in every instance harmless." Quotation ("settings"), *Final Report*, 46; also 45.

[33] Quotation ("wrong"), *Final Report*, 45; also 47.

[34] Ibid., 46–7.

sanctity and integrity of the printed word" was "central to the absolute freedom of political debate and dissent." Dietz, who agreed, thought
research had established that the printed word caused little harm. Hudson
doubted that this type of material warranted action but saw little reason
to limit the options of prosecutors.[35]

The commission focused most of its attention on violent and degrading depictions of sex and on portrayals that were nonviolent but nevertheless degrading – categories, the *Final Report* asserted, that made up
the greatest part of pornography. Most research appeared to show that
viewing pornography, either on an occasional or long-term basis, heightened sexual arousal. Whether this effect had long-term consequences
and whether those consequences harmed society were subjects of disagreement. Pornography did not change arousal patterns in viewers, one
researcher noted, but a "surprising percentage of the population" was
already prone to arousal by the combination of violence and sexuality
and found violent pornography exciting.[36]

Did watching such pornography lead to violent and antisocial behavior
in the real world? As explained in Chapter 4, by the early 1980s many
people believed that significant research showed that watching television
violence could increase the likelihood of aggressive behavior, especially
among teenagers and children.[37] The Meese Commission heard testimony
from several researchers who now linked violent pornography to harmful
social effects. Victims of sexual abuse also testified, as did such feminists
as Andrea Dworkin and Catharine MacKinnon, who denounced pornography for its deleterious effects on women.

Most testimony from researchers emphasized the potentially harmful effects of violent pornography. Among those to testify were Edward
Donnerstein of the University of Wisconsin, Madison, and Neil A.
Malamuth of UCLA. In 1982, they had published an article about the
research on the effects of the aggressive forms of pornography that
had appeared since the 1970 *Report*. Because violent pornography was

[35] Quotations ("crucial," "dissent"), "Statement of Father Bruce Ritter," *Final Report*, 514.
See also "Statement of Henry E. Hudson, Chairman," ibid., 485. For Dietz on the printed
word, see Meeting of the Attorney General's Commission on Pornography, Oct. 18, 1985,
110–11, Folder: "Los Angeles – 10/18/85," Box 4, RAGCP-NARA 2.

[36] Quotation ("surprising"), Neil Malamuth, testimony, *Meese Commission Hearings*, Sept.
11, 1985, Houston, TX, p. 72, Folder: "Houston – 9/11/85 (Part I)," Box 2, RAGCP-
NARA 2. See also ibid., 94.

[37] See Pearl, Bouthilet, and Lazar, eds., *Television and Behavior, Vol. I: Summary Report*,
6, 36–44.

relatively rare before the late 1960s the 1970 *Report* had made little assessment of its effects, but during the 1970s aggression in sexually explicit movies and publications increased dramatically (in both hard-core and soft-core magazines, e.g., *Playboy* and *Penthouse*).[38] Most research now indicated, Malamuth and Donnerstein concluded, that society had "ample reasons for concern about the effects of aggressively toned pornographic stimuli." Particularly troubling were images of women "responding favorably to male aggression." They could "easily . . . affect . . . beliefs, attitudes, and behavior," influence the way some viewers perceived rape and the victims of rape, and help to "foster a cultural climate that is relatively tolerant of acts of aggression against women."[39]

Donnerstein and Malamuth's views were well known. Donnerstein had testified at the public hearing in Minneapolis in December 1983, where an antipornography ordinance proposed by Dworkin and MacKinnon was being considered, and he and Malamuth appeared before the Meese Commission in September 1985, in Houston. In Minneapolis, Donnerstein stated that many men were aroused by depictions of women enjoying rape and other forms of aggression. Even short exposures of five to ten minutes could affect the attitudes of "very normal types of males" and make them more inclined to accept myths about rape. If one assumed that children learned "from Sesame Street how to count one, two, three, four, five, believe me," he said, "they can learn how to pick up a gun and also learn . . . about male/female relations." If you could "measure sexual arousal to sexual images" and measure the attitudes males held about rape, you could "predict aggressive behavior with women, weeks and even months later," Donnerstein suggested. Indeed, some researchers would argue, he said, that the connection between watching some kinds of violent images and callous and aggressive behavior toward women was "much stronger statistically than the relationship between smoking and cancer."[40]

Yet Donnerstein felt that the opponents of pornography misused his research. A point often missed was his finding that images showing women who did not enjoy rape failed to arouse most men. Moreover, simply

[38] Malamuth and Donnerstein argued that in hard-core paperbacks, the depiction of rape doubled between 1968 and 1974. See Malamuth and Donnerstein, "The Effects of Aggressive-Pornographic Mass Media Stimuli," 104–6, 108–9.

[39] Quotations, ibid., 106 ("ample," "behavior"), 113 ("foster").

[40] Quotations, Edward Donnerstein, testimony, *Minneapolis Hearings,* Dec. 12, 1983, 15 ("normal"), 29 ("measure," "predict"), 30 ("statistically"), 40–1 ("Sesame," "relations"), Folder 14, Box 69 ("Exhibits – Chicago"), RAGCP-NARA 2.

erotic images – explicit nonviolent, nondegrading depictions – did not produce aggressive behavior. He told the Meese Commission when it met in Houston that "it was really the violent component in violent pornography which was the issue, not the sexual nature of the material." But even in considering violent materials, one had to be careful about what conclusions could be drawn, he warned.[41]

The testimony of Donnerstein and Malamuth should have made the commission consider seriously the nature of Hollywood films and other mainstream entertainment. It was not just the violent sexually explicit materials that could desensitize men to the plight of real sexual assault victims and increase aggressive behavior. It was also violent commercially shown R-rated movies such as *I Spit on Your Grave, Texas Chainsaw Massacre,* and *The Toolbox Murders* that could produce equally powerful effects. "The strongest reactions we get are from the popular slasher films, not the X-rated materials," Donnerstein said.[42]

Perhaps even more insidious in their effects were the less obvious depictions of sexual violence in media other than film. Scenarios showing women enjoying sexual assault could be found in television soap operas and prime-time programs, in images on Rolling Stones album covers, and in the pages of *Playboy, Penthouse,* and *Hustler* magazines, Donnerstein observed.[43] In addition, Malamuth argued, popular fiction portrayed aggression against men and women differently. Aggression against women generally included a sexual component that was not present in assaults against men. Men were portrayed as wanting to avoid being victimized,

[41] Quotation ("violent"), Edward Donnerstein, testimony, *Meese Commission Hearings,* Sept. 11, 1985, Houston, TX, p. 10, Folder: "Houston – 9/11/85 (Part I)," Box 2, RAGCP-NARA 2. See also Donnerstein, testimony, *Minneapolis Hearings,* Dec. 12, 1983, 21, 27, 31, Folder 14, Box 69 ("Exhibits – Chicago"), ibid.; and Kurtz, "Pornography Panel's Objectivity Disputed," *WP,* Oct. 15, 1985, A4.

[42] Edward Donnerstein quoted ("strongest") in Kurtz, "Pornography Panel's Objectivity Disputed," A4. See also Donnerstein, testimony, *Meese Commission Hearings,* Sept. 11, 1985, Houston, TX, 11–13, 16, 24, Folder: "Houston – 9/11/85 (Part I)," Box 2, RAGCP-NARA 2; and Donnerstein, testimony, *Minneapolis Hearings,* Dec. 12, 1983, 33–6, Folder 14, Box 69 ("Exhibits – Chicago"), ibid.

[43] Malamuth and Donnerstein argued in 1982 that the materials "most likely to cause anti-social effects . . . were clearly not X-rated pornographic films," but movies that might be shown nationally on television or depictions of "sexual aggression within such 'legitimate' magazines as *Playboy* or *Penthouse.*" Quotations ("antisocial," "*Playboy*"), Malamuth and Donnerstein, "The Effects of Aggressive-Pornographic Mass Media Stimuli," 130; also 131. See also Donnerstein, testimony, *Meese Commission Hearings,* Sept. 11, 1985, 17–18, 25, Folder: "Houston – 9/11/85 (Part I)," Box 2, RAGCP-NARA 2; and Donnerstein, testimony, *Minneapolis Hearings,* Dec. 12, 1983, 16–17, Folder 14, Box 69 ("Exhibits – Chicago"), ibid.

whereas women often seemed to invite victimization and hence, by impli-
cation, bore some responsibility for their treatment. These themes, so bla-
tantly depicted in hard-core pornography, were subtly portrayed in mainstream fiction and advertising, and differed only in degree. They appeared
in such PG-rated movies as Sam Peckinpah's *The Getaway* (1972) and
Lina Wertmuller's R-rated *Swept Away* (1975) – movies shown widely
on television. The same type of violent images and themes appeared in
such publications as *Penthouse*, which, Malamuth charged, had accented
violence and sex in recent years, and in the advertising of other *Penthouse*-
owned magazines such as *Newlook*. This type of material, including that
found in mainstream outlets, could bring "relatively long lasting attitude
changes" even when people are "not aware that they are being affected
or they are being changed," Malamuth's research indicated.[44]

It was one thing to show a connection between pornography and
changed attitudes, but it was more difficult to establish a link between
changed attitudes and behavior. Here, nonspecialists might be forgiven for
being confused. Despite his earlier testimony in Minneapolis suggesting
a strong connection between watching violent pornography and aggression toward women, in October 1985 Donnerstein said that, although he
believed that exposure to sexually violent materials might change people's attitudes, there was no evidence to indicate that it changed their
behavior. It was "impossible," he said, to prove that pornography caused
sexual crimes. "The evidence just isn't that clear-cut."[45] Malamuth, however, argued before the Meese Commission that changes in attitudes in
some cases could affect behavior. His data showed "that attitudes, in
combination with other factors, do certainly predict and seem to cause
actual behavior...such as aggression against women." Pornography,
when isolated as a factor by itself, might have "weak effects...in an
absolute sense," but in combination and interaction with other factors
"will have powerful effects." Some people are more susceptible to its
effects than others. "Those individuals, to begin with, [who] are more
aggressively inclined, are more attracted to media stimuli that involve
sexual violence...[and are] also more likely to be influenced by it."
Malamuth emphasized context and the complex nature of behavior. He
concluded that mass media and pornography in themselves were hardly

[44] Quotations ("relatively," "changed"), Malamuth, testimony, *Meese Commission Hearings*, Sept. 11, 1985, 82; see also ibid., 75–80, Folder: "Houston – 9/11/85 (Part I),"
Box 2, RAGCP-NARA 2.
[45] Donnerstein quoted ("impossible," "clear-cut") in Kurtz, "Pornography Panel's Objectivity Disputed," A4.

inconsequential, but they were also not the only factors, nor were they, perhaps, even major causes of aggression against women. Rather, they comprised part of a complicated interaction. Thus Malamuth backed away from giving Hudson the answer he wanted when Hudson asked if "in very basic terms, you would agree that someone who might be predisposed to commit a violent sexual act may very well, as a result of reading pornography, be incited into the actual commission of that act?" No, Malamuth replied, "I would have to say that at this point I don't think there is sufficient data to answer that question one way or the other, because the laboratory is a situation where we create sanction for aggression, where aggression to some degree is justified or at least given a context where it is acceptable." More research was necessary before Hudson's question could be answered definitively.[46] However, Malamuth agreed that violent pornography, and even in some circumstances nonviolent, nondegrading pornography, could be harmful.[47]

Where Malamuth had been disinclined to draw conclusions unsupported by research data, other researchers were less reluctant. Surgeon General C. Everett Koop stated unambiguously that pornography was "an accessory to the crime of child abuse" and to other antisocial behavior. "We suspect that for men who are even slightly predisposed to such behavior, this material may provide the impetus that propels them from the unreal world of fantasy to the real world of overt action."[48]

John Court, clinical psychologist and director of the Spectrum Psychological Counseling Center at Flinders University of South Australia,

---

[46] Quotations, Malamuth, testimony, *Meese Commission Hearings*, Sept. 11, 1985, 82 ("predict"), 86 ("aggression"), 91 ("weak," "powerful"), 92 ("individuals," "influenced"), 108 ("predisposed," "acceptable"); see also ibid., 69–71, 74, 109, Folder: "Houston – 9/11/85 (Part I)," Box 2, RAGCP-NARA 2. See also ibid., 109.

[47] As for nonviolent, nondegrading depictions of sex, Malamuth concluded "that sexually explicit stimuli that emphasize love, mutual respect and so forth, do not increase any aggressive tendencies and under certain circumstances may even reduce them." But earlier, he said: "When you talk about sexual material devoid of violence, I think that involves a great deal of different kind of stimuli. Again the context is very important. If a person is raised to believe that sex is taboo, that somehow he can't engage in sex; outside of the context of an accepted manner it is something that is bad; then showing sex between, supposedly between two consenting adults, can be a whole power trip and have elements in it that may evolve aspects of violence." Note quotations, Malamuth, testimony, *Meese Commission Hearings*, Sept. 11, 1985, Houston, TX, 89–90 ("when," "violence"), 102 ("reduce"), Folder: "Houston – 9/11/85 (Part I)," Box 2, RAGCP-NARA 2. For Malamuth on the harmful effects of violent pornography and some television programs, see ibid., 106–7.

[48] C. Everett Koop quoted ("accessory," "action") in Kurtz, "Pornography Panel's Objectivity Disputed," A4.

reiterated an earlier critique he had made of the 1970 *Report*. Contrary to the conclusions presented in 1970, he found that crime did not decline where erotica was readily available; pornography could not be kept away from children; little research existed to prove that pornography had therapeutic effects; and people did not lose interest in explicit materials when they were easily obtainable. Moreover, the 1970 *Report* had made little study of violent pornography, and its conclusions had relied heavily on the discredited catharsis theory. In Australia, as in America and many other countries, video had "effectively sexualized the home environment," and research had not begun to explore the full dimensions of the problem, Court said. Laboratories that studied effects had not kept up with technology and still used slides and 16-mm film. Few studies had been done on pornography's effects on teenagers and children. Court had no doubt, he told Hudson, that pornography was "one of the causal factors" in rape, in spousal and child abuse, and in the spread of AIDS. "If action is delayed until the research evidence is in, we shall wait forever," he said.[49]

A majority of the commission found such testimony persuasive. The *Final Report* had little trouble concluding that "substantial exposure to sexually violent materials" bore "a causal relationship to antisocial acts of sexual violence and, for some subgroups, possibly to unlawful acts of sexual violence." Sexually violent pornography contributed not only to an increase in "aggressive behavior towards women" but also to the acceptance of rape myths and other negative attitudes. Violent pornography as well as the nonviolent but degrading variety were underlying causes for discrimination against women. Even though social science research backed these conclusions, the commissioners confidently said, it did not take volumes of empirical investigations to make these judgments, and in fact the *Final Report* acknowledged that some of the commission's conclusions required "assumptions not found exclusively in the experimental evidence." Simple "common sense" suggested that "the images that people are exposed to bear a causal relationship to their behavior."[50]

---

[49] Quotations, John Court, testimony, *Meese Commission Hearings*, Sept. 12, 1985, 17 ("sexualized"), 18 ("delayed"), 20 ("causal"); see also ibid., 3, 5–6, 19, Folder: "Houston – 9/11/85," Box 2, RAGCP-NARA 2. See also Court, "Pornography and Sex Crimes – Re-Evaluation in Light of Recent Trends around the World," 129–57.

[50] Text quotations ("substantial," "behavior"), *Final Report*, 39–40; also 41–2. This was not to say that "all people with heightened levels of aggression" would commit sexually violent acts, but "over a sufficiently large number of cases" there would be increasing aggression aimed at women. Repeated exposure to pornography which showed women saying "no" but really meaning "yes," and which portrayed women secretly enjoying

CRITICS

Although the Meese Commission skewed its witness list to those who emphasized the negative effects of pornography, it did receive some testimony from individuals who offered alternative views, even though their voices were in the minority. Richard Green, founding editor of *Archives of Sexual Behavior* and a past president of the Society for the Scientific Study of Sex, argued that some types of sex-related crimes had decreased in Denmark and Germany as people bought more erotica. Pornography combined with masturbation, he said, provided "an outlet for anti-social sexual impulses," and he contended that erotica could be educational and therapeutic. He also criticized laboratory research that used student subjects – the kind of studies done by Donnerstein and Malamuth, for example – saying that it was an unreliable way to predict behavior.[51] *Playboy*'s counsel, Burton Joseph, presented a survey of studies prepared in 1984 for Canada's Department of Justice that stated flatly that "no systematic research evidence available" suggested a causal relationship between morality and pornography in Canada. Nor did research show that there was a link between explicit materials and such crimes as rape, or that viewing such materials harmed the average adult. This survey found "considerable evidence of conceptually cloudy thinking related to virtually every aspect of the work on the impact of pornography."[52] Another report summarizing more than forty articles that appeared between 1970 and 1985, including work by Donnerstein, Malamuth, and Zillman, and apparently submitted with the Canadian survey, also offered a message suggesting that answers to questions about the harmful effects of pornography were not clear-cut. But for most members of the Meese Commission, such opinions were insufficient to

rape, led to attitude changes, with consequences of the "most serious proportions." Those who watched a great deal of violent pornography were less inclined to view the victims of real-life rape or other forms of sexual aggression as victims who had suffered serious injury or degradation. They were also less inclined to hold the rapist responsible for his or her actions, or to believe that he or she deserved harsh punishment. Note quotations, ibid., 39 ("heightened," "cases"), 41 ("proportions").

[51] Quotation ("outlet"), Nobile and Nadler, *United States of America vs. Sex*, 89–90. Richard Green, a professor in the Department of Psychiatry and Behavioral Science at the State University of New York at Stony Brook, testified before the Meese Commission in Houston on September 11, 1985.

[52] Quotations, McKay and Dolff, "The Impact of Pornography: A Decade of Literature" (prepared under contract with the Department of Justice, Canada, 1984), 93 ("systematic"), 96 ("cloudy"); see also ibid., 94, Folder 22, Box 70 ("Exhibits – Chicago"), RAGCP-NARA 2.

refute the work of researchers who testified that pornography could be harmful.[53]

Of course, in this relatively new area of research there was much that remained unknown, and there were legitimate criticisms to be made of the Meese commission. The commission did not offer convincing evidence that the great majority of pornography was violent and/or degrading, nor did it provide a satisfactory definition of what constituted "degrading" pornography. It largely ignored violence against women in mainstream media. It drew conclusions that went beyond social science research.[54] The *Final Report*'s confident assertions that "common sense" suggested a linkage between pornography and certain attitudes and behavior, that it was possible to determine "intuitively" that there was a linkage, opened the commission to attack. Moreover, it was true that a majority of the members of the commission were most interested in prosecution, and that their efforts surely encouraged censorship and vigilantism.

Critics of the Meese Commission argued that the data on the effects of pornography were inadequate and that the lack of scientific consensus made it difficult to formulate a sound national policy. Donald L. Mosher, a professor of psychology at the University of Connecticut who had contributed three studies to the original 1970 *Report*, told the commission as much when he testified in 1985. One did not have to share Mosher's civil libertarian views to concede that he had a point.[55] The research on several important questions was inconclusive. It had not yet proven that exposure to explicit materials led to increased sexual activity or to significant changes in established sexual conduct. Indeed,

---

[53] See Morris (prepared by), "Contemporary Research between 1970 through 1985 Relating to Exposure to Explicit Sexual Material and Aggression or Anti-Social Consequences," (July 1985), Folder 22, Box 70 ("Exhibits – Chicago"), RAGCP-NARA 2. This work, and the survey by McKay and Dolff, are attached to Joseph, "Presentation to Attorney General's Commission on Pornography," July 24–25, 1985, ibid.

[54] Becker and Levine made these points, and they disagreed with several of the commission's recommendations for prosecution. See "Statement by Dr. Judith Becker and Ellen Levine," *Final Report*, 542, 544; also 540–6; and Tavris, "The Illogic of Linking Porn and Rape: Meese Commission Overlooks Proper Reasoning in Findings," *LAT*, July 7, 1986, pt. 2, p. 5.

[55] See Nobile and Nadler, *United States of America vs. Sex*, 92–4. Donald L. Mosher testified before the Meese Commission in Houston on September 11, 1985. For his work on the 1970 Commission on Obscenity and Pornography, see Mosher, "Psychological Reactions to Pornographic Films," *TRCOP, Volume VIII: Erotica and Social Behavior*, 255–312; Mosher, "Sex Callousness toward Women," ibid., 313–25; and Mosher and Katz, "Pornographic Films, Male Verbal Aggression against Women, and Guilt," ibid., 357–79.

it suggested that pornography was not a primary agent in the formation of patterns of sexual behavior, although here the results were not
definitive. Whereas research tended to be strong in showing a connection between pornography and arousal, it was less certain on attitude
formation. It suggested a relation between pornography and more tolerant views about sexual behavior, and a greater readiness to believe rape
myths and accept aggression toward women. But how strong and persistent such attitudes were, and what their relationship to actual behavior might be, required additional study. The link between exposure to
pornography and antisocial or criminal behavior still appeared tenuous
to many who examined this literature. On the Meese Commission, Becker
and Levine argued that the research had "not been designed to evaluate
the relationship between exposure to pornography and the commission of
sexual crimes." Similarly, social science research did "not speak to harm,"
but to "a relationship among variables or effects that can be positive or
negative."[56]

If the research did not prove a connection between pornography and
the above effects, neither did it disprove the connection; it was just
inconclusive. However, by 1985 it was not unreasonable to conclude
that numerous studies had shown that a steady diet of violence in mass
media could have damaging effects – at least for a segment of society.
Furthermore, major research on television violence conducted between
the late 1950s and 1990 did show that a significant correlation existed
between erotica – both violent and nonviolent – and aggressive behavior.
This research tended to back the contention of Zillmann and others who
argued that even nonviolent erotica portraying women as promiscuous
could "encourage callous attitudes or behavior toward women among
males."[57]

In the *Final Report*, the lengthy lists of video and publication titles – so
explicit in themselves that even antipornography crusaders shunned the
report – provided clear evidence that since the 1960s mainstream culture
had been and was being inundated with new forms of sexually provocative materials. By focusing on this kind of material, the Meese hearings
on pornography in 1985 and 1986, despite their several flaws, provided
an opportunity to educate the public about what was then known – and

---

[56] Quotations ("designed," "negative"), "Statement by Dr. Judith Becker and Ellen Levine,"
Final Report, 543. See also ibid., 544. For a discussion of the research literature, see
Randall, *Freedom and Taboo*, 102, 104, 106–7, 111–15.

[57] Quotation ("callous"), Paik and Comstock, "The Effects of Television Violence on Antisocial Behavior: A Meta-Analysis," 537; see also 522, 538.

unknown – about the influence of sexually explicit materials in the mass media. Regrettably, the American press for the most part failed to offer to the public a full and dispassionate account of this complex issue. In the heated atmosphere of the time, oversimplifications were rife. Members of the Meese Commission who wanted to attack not only hard-core pornographers but also certain mainstream publications were not interested in the nuances of research or in findings that were inconclusive. Opponents of the commission denounced the hearings as merely a front for censorship.

For Valenti, the areas of uncertainty about what research could show provided ample maneuvering space for Hollywood. By the time he testified in Los Angeles on October 17, 1985, the commission had heard plenty of testimony that condemned not only hard-core pornography but also violent mainstream motion pictures. Eager to disassociate Hollywood from the hearings, Valenti branded pornography an "outlaw industry" and contended that the rating system effectively shielded children from explicit materials. He pronounced pornographic movies tedious and predicted that interest in them would decline once the novelty had worn off. But when Ritter asserted that the gap between PG-13- and R-rated films had narrowed and that many R films amounted to soft-core pornography, Valenti admitted that the values behind the ratings had changed with time. *Midnight Cowboy* was given an X rating when it appeared in 1969, for example, but now, he said, it probably would receive no more than a PG-13. Asked if an X-rated movie in 1985 might not in the future become an R-rated picture, Valenti thought it doubtful, but acknowledged that because the system depended on consensus from many groups, "you have to lower sometimes the standards you might employ."[58]

The Meese Commission could have been much tougher on Hollywood. The very definition of pornography that it used – sexually explicit materials "intended primarily for the purpose of sexual arousal" – could easily have been applied to many Hollywood films. Even though Hollywood had contributed enormously to the commercialization of sex, the *Final Report* had little to say about mainstream cinema's use of nudity and its depictions of nonviolent, nondegrading sex. Buried in the commission's discussion of sexually violent materials was a brief mention of the possible harmful effects of watching slasher movies, but virtually nothing appeared on the

---

[58] Quotations, Jack Valenti, testimony, *Meese Commission Hearings*, Oct. 17, 1985, 4 ("outlaw"), 55 ("lower"); see also ibid., 34–35, 47, 48, Folder: "Los Angeles – 10/17/85 (Part I)," Box 4, RAGCP-NARA 2.

consequences of depicting violence against women in other mainstream films, television programs, and popular fiction.[59] Nor did the commission explore the possibility raised by people like Richard Heffner (who did not testify) that the new home entertainment media might be making the classification system obsolete. Heffner, who earlier had made a point of not wanting "to count nipples," was coming to believe that the heavy emphasis on sex in films and on television, brought directly into homes by new media, had repercussions. "I can't ignore the fact," he later said, "that the AIDS epidemic, the plague of AIDS, has to a large extent been a function of the sexual permissiveness that was fostered by the nature of the motion pictures, to which we gave R rather than X, or to which we gave PG rather than R."[60]

Although Hollywood escaped the Meese Commission hearings largely unscathed, it was not unintimidated. Although the mainstream movie industry was not the immediate target of the Reagan Justice Department, clearly there were signals to make Valenti and other Hollywood leaders nervous. As it developed, the campaign against pornography involved not just an attack on hard-core moviemakers but also attempts to remove such magazines as *Playboy* and *Penthouse* from the newsstands. If the efforts to restrict these publications – by then widely accepted by many Americans as legitimate – proved successful, it was certainly possible that more vigorous efforts in the future would be made to get the studios to clean up mainstream motion pictures. Throughout the remainder of the decade, supporters of the antipornography crusade attacked the rating system for its lax standards, not only on sex, but also on the issues of substance abuse and the treatment of religion, among others.

[59] *Final Report*, 39–41.
[60] Quotation ("epidemic"), Heffner, *Reminiscences*, vol. 1, p. 173, Box 5, RDH-COHC-BL.

6

The Antipornography Crusade

The Meese Commission's conclusions about the influence of sexually explicit materials had never been in doubt. Most commission members focused on what practical steps could be taken to eliminate pornography, and to that end they made more than ninety recommendations. There followed an aggressive campaign by the Reagan administration not only to prosecute hard-core pornographers but also to intimidate the producers of such soft-core publications as *Playboy* and *Penthouse.* The Meese Commission's formulation of legal strategies to fight pornographers followed efforts by feminists who pushed for legislation to ban pornography in two American cities, Minneapolis and Indianapolis.

To First Amendment proponents, the growing strength and numbers of antipornography partisans and the creation of the Meese Commission appeared ominous. Richard Heffner had long suspected that the public's tolerance for certain types of movies was conditional. He knew the conservatives' position well; he had used Victor Cline's book *Where Do You Draw the Line?* (1974) in his classes at Rutgers. Cline, a Mormon and a psychotherapist, had assembled essays by Irving Kristol, Norman Podhoretz, James Q. Wilson, and others, and himself and had concluded that pornography and media violence assaulted taboos on sex and violence that were "intrinsic to social order." Because they undermined the institution of the family, they were "enemies of our kind of society," said Cline, who advocated a stronger test for what constituted obscenity and restrictions on some kinds of expression. Cline criticized the movie ratings. Although Heffner tried to persuade him of the system's value, he suspected that Cline's views on censorship might actually be relatively moderate when compared to those held by other conservatives.[1] In 1980, Heffner wrote an article for the *New York Times* in which he stated that violent, sexually explicit material shown via cable, satellite, and VCRs could provoke a strong public reaction. Two years later, he told an audience of film censors in London that "a violent counterrevolution in morals and manners could endanger all free expression." Although he confessed that his own belief in freedom for commercial entertainment was being severely tested, he was not yet ready to abandon the American rating system, which he believed was still preferable to the more restrictive systems elsewhere in the world. It was "better by far to tolerate media atrocities," he told an audience in Toronto in 1984, "than to commit the ultimate atrocity of censorship upon tolerance itself."[2]

The antipornography crusade of the 1980s had the backing of a popular president (Ronald Reagan) and included a small army of zealous federal, state, and local prosecutors, a judicial system staffed with a growing number of Reagan-appointed justices, and grassroots support from many religious and civic organizations. Despite all their combined efforts, the availability of hard-core pornography was not greatly reduced; in fact, it achieved new levels of growth and prosperity during the 1990s. The same can be said about the frequency of sex and violence shown in mainstream media – movies, TV programs, video games, and the Internet.

For the Reagan administration, the problem of pornography did not exist in isolation. The White House linked sexual permissiveness with substance abuse and declining respect for religion. In the battle for public morality Hollywood was considered pivotal. Indeed, as the Meese Commission hearings proceeded, Nancy Reagan and others in government were already trying to force Valenti to do something about depictions of drug use in the movies. Many Christians also became highly critical of the ways in which motion pictures portrayed religion. Alarmed by this pressure, Valenti and other leaders in the entertainment and publishing industries mounted a formidable defense of the First Amendment by enlisting the help of public relations and advertising experts.

---

[1] Quotations ("intrinsic," "society"), Cline, *Where Do You Draw the Line?* 357. See also ibid., 355–8; and Heffner, *Reminiscences*, vol. 7, pp. 1216–17, Box 5, RDH-COHC-BL.

[2] Quotation ("violent"), Heffner, "Freedom and Responsibility in Mass Communications," address delivered March 22, 1982, 19; also 16, RDHPP. Quotations ("atrocities," "itself"), "Jefferson Revisited," address delivered Sept. 18, 1982, 6, RDHPP; also 5. See also Heffner, "'Narrowcasting' and the Threat to Morals." Heffner wanted the *New York Times* to use a different title, one indicating that he worried most about the "threat to freedom" posed by new home entertainment media.

ANTIPORNOGRAPHY OFFENSIVES

At the forefront of efforts to eradicate pornography during the early 1980s were conservatives, many of whom were evangelical Christians, and feminists, who were angry about the depictions of women. Most of these people had been opposed to the growing permissiveness and violence of American culture since the 1960s. The dramatic way in which the new technologies of the 1970s and 1980s had altered the transmission of words, sounds, and images now imbued their concerns with a new urgency.

Several organizations mobilized Christians. These groups included Morality in Media, established in 1962 by Father Morton A. Hill, S.J., to fight obscenity in the media, and the Arizona-based Citizens for Decency through Law (CDL), a militant antipornography organization started in 1957 by financier Charles H. Keating, Jr. (Both Hill and Keating had been members and critics of the 1970 Commission on Obscenity and Pornography.) Also joining in the battle were the Moral Majority, founded by the evangelist and reverend Jerry Falwell, which lobbied for conservative political candidates until it disbanded in 1989, and the Campus Crusade for Christ, in existence since the 1950s. Active, too, was the National Federation of Decency (later known as the American Family Association), founded by the Reverend Don Wildmon in 1977, which promoted family values, the "Biblical ethic of decency," and warned about the influence of television, movies, and other mass media. (Pornography in mass media, Wildmon argued in 2000, had been an accomplice in the rise in abortions, whose total over three decades had exceeded the population of Canada.)[3] Evangelical Christians found natural allies in such organizations as the National Coalition on Television Violence, founded in 1980, which not only focused on prime-time television programs, but in 1981 charged that the film industry had flooded the country with violent movies.[4]

Ronald Reagan articulated the views of these groups. As president, he spoke about bringing a "spiritual reawakening" to America. Part of this goal involved turning Americans away from the popular culture of the

---

[3] Quotation ("Biblical") AFA: American Family Association of New York. http:// www.Afany.org/. See Don Wildmon, "That's What Christians Do Now" http://www. alliance4lifemin.org/ThatswhatChristiansdonow.html. (Accessed March 17, 2005). President Nixon had appointed Charles H. Keating, Jr., to the 1970 commission. See Kemp, ed., *Illustrated Presidential Report of the Commission on Obscenity and Pornography*, 15, 17. Other information taken from Web sites for different groups. See also Boyer, *Purity in Print*, 323.

[4] On the National Coalition on Television Violence, see Prince, *New Pot of Gold*, 366.

1960s and 1970s, which, in Reagan's opinion, had caused the country to lose its "religious and moral bearings." Pornography and drug abuse were high on the list of social ills to be remedied. Early in his presidency, Reagan told the Association of Independent Television Stations that there was too much nudity and profanity in contemporary movies. "I liked it better when the actors kept their clothes on," he said, as he reminisced about *The Winning Team*, a movie he had made in 1952. So when leaders from Morality in Media met with the president and called for the government to be more aggressive in fighting pornography, they found Reagan receptive. In early 1984, Reagan told the National Religious Broadcasters' convention that he favored a constitutional ban on abortion; he also linked abortion with child pornography, drugs, and the American Civil Liberties Union. A few weeks later, at a meeting of the National Association of Evangelicals, he lamented that pornography, drug abuse, and sexual promiscuity had "spread through the nation like a fever" since the 1960s.[5]

Just how much President Reagan wanted to reform the mainstream movie industry that traded in its own brand of commercialized sex and violence needs qualification. Reagan was a product of Hollywood. In addition to being an actor, he had been president of the Screen Actors Guild and a leader of the Motion Picture Industry Council, which was formed in early 1948 in order to create a better image for the movie industry after the House Committee on Un-American Activities hearings of 1947. He had considerable experience not only in front of cameras and microphones but also behind the scenes, where he worked in public relations, often in cooperation with Valenti's predecessor at the MPAA, Eric Johnston. Reagan wanted to convince Americans that Hollywood people deserved respect, and, as the public became more tolerant of movies after World War II, he voiced few objections when the rules about nudity and other once forbidden themes in the Production Code were gradually

---

[5] Quotations ("spiritual," "bearings," "fever"), "Excerpts from President's Address," *NYT*, March 7, 1984, A20. Reagan quoted ("clothes") in Raines, "Reagan Calls New Movies Too Risqué," *NYT*, Jan. 28, 1982, B8. (Reagan starred in *The Winning Team* with Doris Day.) See also Hyer, "Evangelical Broadcasters Define Role in Politics," *WP*, Feb. 4, 1984, B6; and Clines, "Reagan Sees U.S. Regaining 'Moral Bearings,'" *NYT*, March 7, 1984, A1. Following the meeting between Reagan and leaders of Morality in Media, more than a hundred Roman Catholic and Eastern Orthodox bishops wrote letters asking for a federal monitor to oversee the enforcement of obscenity laws and to curb what was then a $6 billion (U.S. billion) industry. See Hoffman, "Reagan Hears Pleas to Battle Pornography," *WP*, March 29, 1983, A5; and Austin, "Bishops in Plea against Smut," *NYT*, May 25, 1983, A19.

relaxed. Many of the stories on which his own motion pictures were based had been at odds with the code's morality. Moreover, violence had been an important ingredient in his movies from the start of his career in 1937. He played characters who were ready with "smashing fists . . . when guns are not handy!" Warner Bros. advertised his films as having "the red meat that the thrill fans go for," and as averaging "one fight for every thousand feet" of film. His movies were typical of Hollywood in that era and would have been even more violent if Joe Breen and the PCA had not intervened. Reagan preferred action films, and during the 1950s, gravitated toward Westerns. On television, he hosted *Death Valley Days.* During the 1980s, he showed little interest in curbing the growing violence in American movies, despite mounting evidence that it might have harmful effects.[6]

There was little doubt, though, that Reagan opposed the commerce in pornography that flourished outside mainstream Hollywood. As California governor in 1969, he tried to rally the public against pornography, and he signed legislation to help prosecutors. As president, he wanted not only tougher laws but a more activist judiciary. He tried to fill vacancies on the Supreme Court and in the federal courts with justices sympathetic to his views on pornography and abortion. In 1986 he told the Knights of Columbus that by the end of his second term he would have appointed almost half of the federal judges, and he predicted that they would have a long-term impact.[7]

Evangelical Christians and other conservatives were natural constituents for Reagan, but by the mid-1980s the war on pornography had also enlisted groups not normally allied with the president. Feminists and lesbians who were disillusioned with the sexual revolution of the 1960s and 1970s, alarmed by growing brutality toward women, and appalled at the increasing commercialization of sex in the United States, denounced violence and pornography in the media. They saw inherent dangers in explicit imagery and believed that the very existence of pornography degraded and damaged women and children. In 1977, *Ms.* editor Gloria Steinem attacked child pornography, but added that all pornography involved "the obscene use of power" in which the powerful took pleasure

---

[6] Quotations, Vaughn, *Ronald Reagan in Hollywood,* 71 ("smashing"), 72 ("meat," "feet"). On Reagan and the Production Code, see ibid., 219–26, 230. See also Hoffman, "Reagan Hears Pleas to Battle Pornography," A5; and Cockburn, "Violence Has Become the Pornography of the '80s," *WSJ,* June 19, 1986, sec. 1, p. 31.

[7] See Weinraub, "Reagan Predicts Impact of Judicial Appointees," *NYT,* Aug. 6, 1986, A13. See also Davies, "Reagan Promises to Rid Campuses of 'Anarchists,'" *NYT,* Jan. 8, 1969, 36; and "Reagan Signs Two Laws to Combat Pornography," *NYT,* June 27, 1969, 42.

in "the humiliation and dehumanizing of the powerless." Although many feminists favored a total ban on all pornography (adult as well as child porn), the National Organization for Women (NOW) stopped short of this position. However, NOW did pass a resolution at its 1984 convention in Miami Beach stating that pornography was "a factor in creating and maintaining sex as a basis for discrimination" and that it violated the "civil rights of women and children."[8]

Women made several organized efforts to oppose pornography. Feminists in Los Angeles established Women Against Violence Against Women (WAVAW) in 1976 in response to a sadistic film entitled *Snuff* (1973), a low-budget, independent production that billed itself as "the *bloodiest* thing that *ever* happened in front of a camera!" The producer of *Snuff*, Allan Shackleton, exploited rumors circulating in 1971 that a South American film had been made showing the actual murder of a girl on camera by taking an Argentine slasher movie called *Slaughter* (1971) and adding a scene that showed the rape and dismemberment of a woman. The picture was released in 1975 under the title *Snuff* and did reasonably well at the box office in 1976.[9] Although a police investigation indicated that the murder in the film had been simulated and that the actress in the film was alive and well, WAVAW succeeded in shutting down the movie in many theaters in Southern California and elsewhere, and WAVAW chapters sprang up across the United States. WAVAW considered brutality toward women, whether depicted in films or occurring in real life, to be the most urgent problem in society. It opposed violence in all forms of media and denounced corporate sponsorship that made such entertainment possible.

Other organizations also mobilized women. A few months after the creation of WAVAW in 1976, feminists in San Francisco started Women Against Violence in Pornography and Media (WAVPM). In 1979, with the founding of Women Against Pornography (WAP), the feminist antipornography movement gained national momentum. The membership

---

[8] Quotations ("obscene," "powerless"), Steinem, "Pornography – Not Sex But the Obscene Use of Power," *Ms.* 6 (August 1977), 44; see also ibid., 43. NOW resolution quoted ("factor," "children"), in Goodman, "Battle on Pornography Spurred by New Tactics," *NYT*, July 3, 1984, A8. See also Hunt, *Governing Morals,* 206–7; and Bronstein, "Porn Tours," 122.

[9] Quotation ("*bloodiest*"; emphasis in original text), Lyons, *New Censors*, 67; see also ibid., 63–68. On *Snuff*, feminists' reactions, and box-office performance, see Bronstein, "Porn Tours," 120–9; and Williams, *Hard Core,* 189–95. Americans Roberta and Michael Findlay made *Slaughter*.

of WAP included the well-known feminist Susan Brownmiller, and the organization tended to overshadow WAVAW. Not all feminists supported this group, however; WAP's pro-censorship stance alarmed feminists who were civil libertarians and women who favored a more "pro-sex" approach.[10]

Feminists inveighed against both the hard-core porn industry and mainstream Hollywood. Feminist literature argued that pornography dehumanized women, reflected hatred against them, and condoned violence.[11] WAVPM pressured corporations over newspaper advertising for films, demanding that they tone down lurid ads for violent movies and eliminate advertising for pornographic pictures. Its members protested against porn theaters in San Francisco and New York, demonstrated against such magazines as *Hustler* that specialized in crude sex, and held a national conference to organize strategy. During the early 1980s, they, together with other feminists, also condemned violence against women in mainstream Hollywood films. Brian De Palma's films *Dressed to Kill* (1980) and *Body Double* (1984) led critics to charge that pornography had become part of mainstream cinema. When *Dressed to Kill* appeared, WAP and WAVPM picketed theaters in New York, Hollywood, and other cities.[12]

Feminists sought tougher laws against pornography. In Minneapolis, Andrea Dworkin, author of *Pornography: Men Possessing Women* (1981), and Catharine MacKinnon, a law professor, proposed a law that would make it easier to prosecute pornographers. The two women had been at the University of Minnesota in 1983, where they co-taught a law school course on pornography. Their plan differed from previous obscenity law in that it defined pornography as "the sexually explicit subordination of women, graphically or in words" and treated pornography as "discrimination against women." This legal strategy placed the administration of the law under the city's Civil Rights Commission, not the Criminal Justice Division. Whereas obscenity in the *Miller* decision held that material was not obscene unless a work, "taken as a whole," lacked "serious literary, artistic, political, or scientific values," the measure devised by Dworkin and MacKinnon allowed no such qualification. In Minneapolis, the city council passed the Dworkin-MacKinnon measure, but Mayor

---

[10] Quotation ("pro-sex"), Bronstein, "Porn Tours," 242; also 2–3, 5, 16, 247, 328–71. For other grassroots feminist antipornography groups during this period, see ibid., 5n4.

[11] Such feminist works included Barry, *Female Sexual Slavery*; Lederer, ed., *Take Back the Night*; Griffin, *Pornography and Silence*; and Dworkin, *Pornography*. See also Prince, *New Pot of Gold*, 356–7; and Bronstein, "Porn Tours," 250.

[12] See Lyons, *New Censors*, 74–7: and Bronstein, "Porn Tours," 178–89, 193–207.

Donald Fraser vetoed it on grounds that it violated the First Amendment. The Indianapolis city council approved a similar measure, and it was signed by Mayor William Hudnut before an appeals court overturned the legislation.[13]

PORNOGRAPHY – ATTACK AND COUNTERATTACK

If the measures attempted in Minneapolis and Indianapolis had only limited success, a combination of aggressive government prosecutions and citizen action during the late 1980s did make inroads into the business of pornography. Despite efforts to convince President Reagan otherwise, there seems little doubt that he accepted the Meese Commission recommendations and intended to act on them. In October 1986, he told an antipornography action group, Chicago Statement, that pornography was "vicious and dangerous" and that it harmed women and children. A few weeks later, he signed a bill that strengthened federal prosecution of child pornography, and a few days after that he told the interdenominational Religious Alliance against Pornography that a national crusade against pornography would be a top priority. Christian conservatives, including Falwell's Moral Majority and Wildmon's National Federal of Decency (NFD), embraced the crusade.[14]

Attorney General Meese established a ten-person National Obscenity Enforcement Unit in March 1987. The unit's Federal Obscenity Task Force worked with the FBI, Internal Revenue Service, Customs, and Postal Service, and assisted local and state prosecutors. The unit moved aggressively. More than eighty federal indictments for obscenity came in the seven months following the creation of the Enforcement Unit, an 800 percent increase over indictments for the previous year. Between 1987 and 1991, the Enforcement Unit investigated 222 adult porn cases and 1,422 child pornography cases (more than double the number that had been conducted between 1980 and 1985) and won 135 convictions.[15]

13 Quotations ("sexually," "women"), Downs, *New Politics of Pornography*, xi. See also *Miller v. California*, 413 U.S. 15 (1973); and Prince, *New Pot of Gold*, 357.

14 Reagan quoted ("vicious") in "The Nation," *LAT*, Oct. 26, 1986, pt. 1, p. 2. See also "Toughened Child Pornography Bill Signed by Reagan," ibid., Nov. 8, 1986, pt. 2, p. 3; and "Clerics Say President Vows a Major Drive to Curb Smut," *NYT*, Nov. 15, 1986, sec. 1, p. 9.

15 "There's an alarming step-up in activity around the country through the encouragement of the Justice Department," Leanne Katz, the executive director of the National Coalition against Censorship, observed in August 1987. "The call for censorship of sexually explicit materials we're seeing all over the country results from that." Note

The Reagan administration's strategy involved both intimidation and legal initiatives. In February 1986, well before the Meese Commission released its findings, Executive Director Sears wrote a letter – without informing commission members – to twenty-six companies that sold such magazines as *Playboy* and *Penthouse* stating that the commission had heard testimony that their enterprise was "involved in the sale or distribution of pornography." The twenty-six firms included 7-Eleven, Rite-Aid, Thrifty, and Dart.[16] The charges had been made by Wildmon, who had been pressuring advertisers to withdraw support from movies, TV programs, and publishers that traded in what he considered to be pornography. Sears's letter came at a time when sales and advertising for *Playboy* and *Penthouse* were already declining, in part because of pressure from such groups as the Moral Majority and NFD, and in part because of changing entertainment patterns brought about by the development of videocassettes and other new technology. Word circulated that the Meese Commission's report would list some ten thousand stores in the United States that had been identified as selling pornographic magazines. By July 1986, more than sixteen thousand outlets had decided to take *Playboy, Penthouse,* and other materials off their shelves. The Curtis Circulation Company, then the largest distributor of magazines in the United States, announced that Wal-Mart would even pull rock-and-roll magazines from its eight hundred stores.[17]

The Meese Commission encouraged citizens to take "private action" that might involve "on-site or near-site protesting" and boycotts. The

quotation ("alarming"), Leanne Katz quoted in Bishop, "Justice Dept. Team Leading Broad Effort on Obscenity," *NYT,* Aug. 22, 1987, 6. See also Brigman, "Politics and the Pornography Wars," *Wide Angle* 19, no. 3 (1997), 162; and United States Department of Justice, *Beyond the Pornography Commission,* 43–50. The size of the National Obscenity Enforcement Unit was increased from ten to thirteen prosecutors, and it also had an Obscenity Law Center that coordinated antipornography efforts across the United States.

[16] Letter quoted ("sale") in Scot, "Wildmon, NFD Finally Get Some Respect," *Adweek,* June 30, 1986 (Southeast Edition). See also Thomas, "Spectrum: The White House versus Penthouse," *The Times* (London), July 14, 1986, Issue 62508; McManus, "Introduction," *Final Report,* xxxii; "Defeated by Pornography" (editorial)," *NYT,* June 2, 1986, A16; Cohen, "Pornography: The 'Causal Link,'" *WP,* June 3, 1986, A19; Kurtz, "Pornography Panel's Objectivity Disputed," *WP,* A4; Yardley, "The Porn Commission's Hidden Agenda," *WP,* July 14, 1986, C2; and "Penthouse Fights Moral Majority," *Financial Times* (London), April 21, 1986, 24I.

[17] See Sitomer, "Battle Lines Are Drawn over US Pornography Study," *Christian Science Monitor,* July 8, 1986, 3; and McDaniel, "A Salvo in the Porn War," *Newsweek,* July 21, 1986, 18.

Catholic Church endorsed this strategy.[18] In Los Angeles, where 2.5 million Catholics made up the country's largest archdiocese, Archbishop Roger M. Mahony advocated action on many fronts and sought to cooperate with national organizations including Morality in Media, Citizens through Decency in Law, and the National Religious Alliance against Pornography. "We all stand in shame as our city is acknowledged as one of the pornography centers of the world," he said. He urged followers to picket 7-Eleven stores and other convenience outlets, to start a letter-writing drive to cable television companies that carried channels with adult films, and called on legislators to enact laws against pornography. Recognizing that the X-rated movie theater had become a "dinosaur," Mahony called for a boycott of stores that traded in X-rated videotapes. Pornographic videos, he said, provided "a training manual for how to get and give AIDS." The boycotts would not erode civil liberties, because "Pornography does not fulfill any of the purposes for which we protect free speech." It was not "a constitutional right, but a civil wrong." It was clear that Church leaders were not content merely to target the adults-only industry but planned to clean up Hollywood and other mainstream media as well. Archbishop John P. Foley of Philadelphia, who headed the Vatican's Pontifical Commission for Social Communications, urged citizens to organize against sexually explicit television soap operas and sadistic martial arts films.[19]

Such calls for citizen action had an effect. They surely helped to convince theater-chain owners of the wisdom of not showing X-rated films and to persuade studio executives to enforce contracts that required them to produce feature films that would receive nothing worse than an R rating. Many video outlets stopped carrying X-rated and unrated movies.

The Reagan administration's legal initiatives were also effective. The Meese Commission recommended ninety-two ways to fight pornography at the federal, state, and local levels, and called for changes in federal law. One recommendation proposed asking Congress to pass a forfeiture

---

[18] The Meese Commission also warned that if legitimate works of art or literature such as James Joyce's *Ulysses* or Sinclair Lewis's *Elmer Gantry* were suppressed because of their sexual explicitness, "society would, quite simply, be the worse for it." Quotations, *Final Report,* 72, ("on-site"), 73 ("worse," "encourage"); see also ibid., 71–4.

[19] Archbishop Roger M. Mahony, quoted ("shame," "manual," "protect") in O'Shaughnessy, "Boycott Aimed at Stores with X-Rated Films," *LAT,* July 12, 1987, pt. 1, p.1. Bruce Taylor, quoted ("dinosaur") in ibid. See also Haberman, "Vatican Condemns Kung Fu Films and Sex on TV," *NYT,* May 17, 1989, A3; and "Archdiocese Demands Stronger Anti-Porn Laws and Prosecution," *LAT,* March 15, 1987, sec. 1, p. 32.

statute modeled on laws used to combat drug trafficking. The commission urged stronger measures to control obscene cable and satellite television programs and "dial-a-porn" telephone services, and it asked judges to impose harsher sentences for recurrent violators of obscenity statutes. Of the recommendations, forty-nine, or more than half, concerned child pornography and advocated tougher laws and more vigorous prosecution by the Department of Justice.[20]

The Meese Commission also recommended that state legislatures amend obscenity laws to set a less stringent standard than the then current requirement that material be "utterly without redeeming social value." The United States Supreme Court, of course, had rejected this criterion in 1973 in the *Miller* case, but some states, including California, where about 80 percent of X-rated films and videos were made, had retained it. In 1987, California legislators did change the state's obscenity law to make it easier to prove obscenity. Instead of having to show that material was "utterly without redeeming social importance," prosecutors now had only to demonstrate that it was "without significant literary, artistic, political, educational or scientific value."[21]

One tactic used by the Justice Department during both the Reagan presidency and the George H. W. Bush administration involved threatening businesses with indictments in multiple jurisdictions. This tactic had been advocated by Keating, Jr.'s Arizona-based Citizens for Decency through Law. In 1983, its general counsel, Bruce A. Taylor, had suggested to President Reagan that prosecutors in the nation's ninety-four federal judicial districts be assigned to indict pornographers. Under the 1973 *Miller* three-part test for obscenity, one part asked if "'the average person, applying contemporary community standards' would find that the work depicts or describes, in a patently offensive way, sexual conduct specifically defined by the applicable state law." This provision meant that federal prosecutors could, in theory, bring indictments against

---

[20] Other recommendations included passage of legislation to make it an unfair labor and business practice to hire anyone to take part in commercial sexual activities; imprisonment for a minimum of eight months for a first-time conviction of violating federal obscenity laws involving the depiction of adults, and a minimum one-year sentence for subsequent convictions; aid to the victims of pornography, including civil remedies for damages; and stricter regulations on "adults only" establishments. See *Final Report,* 77–193; and United States Department of Justice, *Beyond the Pornography Commission,* 19, 20, 27.

[21] Quotation ("utterly"), Recommendation 7, *Final Report,* 77; also 94–5. California law quoted ("significant") in Bishop, "Justice Dept. Team Leading Broad Effort on Obscenity," *NYT,* Aug. 22, 1987, A6.

the same company for selling exactly the same material in each of the ninety-four districts. "Multiple, simultaneous prosecutions at both federal and local levels," said former Utah prosecutor Brent Ward, would "test the limits of pornographers' endurance" and potentially "undermine profitability to the point that survival of obscenity enterprises" would be threatened. Although the CDL had no formal connection with the Reagan administration, the National Obscenity Enforcement Unit adopted a strategy that resembled Taylor's recommendation. In 1987, Meese revised the guidelines for federal prosecutors. Prior to that time, the guidelines had discouraged prosecutors from using multiple-district prosecutions except in unusually egregious cases. Meese's revisions, circulated in September, encouraged multiple prosecutions in obscenity situations.[22] In selecting mail-order distributors of X-rated movies and sexually explicit magazines to pursue, prosecutors usually chose conservative districts where they anticipated that community standards would support their efforts. Between 1987 and 1991, the National Obscenity Enforcement Unit obtained fifty convictions involving mail-order businesses. First Amendment advocates called this approach "forum shopping."[23]

The antipornography forces seemed to be gaining momentum. In October 1986, the *New York Times* reported that the X-rated industry was in a "slump." "Erotica is under siege. In the last few years, at least half of the nation's adult movie theaters have closed down. *Playboy Magazine*'s circulation has tumbled, and its cable television channel is losing subscribers. Its female counterpart, *Playgirl Magazine*, is reorganizing its finances in Chapter 11 bankruptcy proceedings. Even sales of X-rated videos, once the industry's best hope, have leveled off." In March, 1987 *Playboy* reported that newsstand sales had dropped by more than 700 thousand copies, a 42 percent decline, and *Penthouse* announced similar losses. It all appeared to be part of a larger trend. By some accounts, sales of adult magazines had dropped about 25 percent since 1981, and during the same period the number of advertising pages in *Playboy* and

---

[22] Quotation ("average"), from *Miller v. California*, 413 U.S. 15 (1973). Brent Ward quoted ("multiple," "test") in McGee, "U.S. Crusade against Pornography Tests the Limits of Fairness," *WP*, Jan. 11, 1993, A1. See also Howe, "U.S. Accused of 'Censorship by Intimidation' in Pornography Cases," *WP*, March 26, 1990, A4; and Hentoff, "The Justice Department's Tainted Fruit: Harassing Those Engaged in Lawful Activity Is Not a Proper Function of Government," *WP*, July 25, 1992, A21.

[23] Herald Price Fahringer quoted ("forum") in Howe, "U.S. Accused of 'Censorship by Intimidation' in Pornography Cases." See also Brigman, "Politics and the Pornography Wars," 162.

Penthouse had declined by more than a third. Even the mainstream movie industry seemed changed. *Premiere* magazine reported in 1988 that "Explicit sex may be a thing of the past as a new puritanism sweeps Hollywood."[24]

Critics of the Meese Commission and the antipornography crusade attempted to refute claims about the harmful effects of pornography but soon realized that these arguments alone would be ineffectual in the climate of the late 1980s. They turned instead to the First Amendment and soon found that it provided, not only a line of defense, but also, when combined with an effective public relations campaign, a powerful weapon to discredit the commission and its supporters.

Representatives of the American Civil Liberties Union and other opponents of censorship had testified or submitted statements to the Meese Commission, but they quickly learned that their advice carried little weight. Harvard law professor Alan Dershowitz blasted the commission's "self-selected, self-serving" witnesses when he testified in January 1986. Earlier, *Penthouse* had hired Dershowitz to defend the rights of pornographers in a debate with conservative columnist William F. Buckley, who hosted the television program *Firing Line*. Dershowitz continued his defense before the Meese Commission and argued that its members had "no right to shut down the marketplace . . . from which dissenting ideas come."[25] Burton Joseph testified that *Playboy* had "always eschewed violence" and compared efforts to ban obscenity in the United States to the censorship in such repressive regimes as the Soviet Union and Iran.

---

[24] Quotations ("slump," "siege"), Kristof, "X-Rated Industry in a Slump," *NYT*, Oct. 5, 1986, sec. 3 (Financial), p. 1. *Premiere* magazine quoted ("puritanism") in Connors, "Real Erotica More Than Skin Deep," *Cleveland Plain Dealer*, Jan. 24, 1993, H1.

    Penthouse, which claimed the 7-Eleven stores were its most significant outlet, reported sales losses of more than 777,000 copies, about a 27 percent decline. See *Adweek*, The Magazine Life sec., March 23, 1987. In April 1986, after the Meese Commission released its *Final Report*, Southland Corporation announced that its 7-Eleven stores would no longer carry *Playboy* and *Penthouse*, which, estimates said, would cause the publications to lose about 100,000 sales per month (*Adweek*, April 21, 1986 [Western Advertising News Edition]). Estimate on sales of adult magazines since 1981 was made by the Council of Periodical Distributors Association. See Scot, "Wildmon, NFD Finally Get Some Respect," *Adweek*, June 30, 1986 (Southeast Edition). For advertising, see Richter, "Thrifty Drug to Quit Selling Adult Magazines," *LAT*, May 2, 1986, sec. 4, p. 1.

[25] Alan Dershowitz quoted in Nobile and Nadler, *United States of America vs. Sex*, 110 ("self-selected"), 111 ("marketplace"). In addition to Dershowitz, among the opponents of censorship who testified or submitted written statements were writer Kurt Vonnegut and American Library Association president Beverly Lynch. For witnesses appearing before the commission and those who submitted statements, see *Final Report*, 465–70, 472–4.

"Censorship of 'pornography' – whatever that is to you – is unwise and unenforceable. It is bad law and bad public policy," he said. His opposition to censorship was grounded in the ideas of John Stuart Mill, who had written:

The only freedom which deserves the name is that of pursuing our own good in our own way, so long as we do not attempt to deprive others of theirs or impede their efforts to obtain it. Each is the guardian of his own health, whether bodily, or mental or spiritual. Mankind are greater gainers by suffering each other to like as seems good to themselves, than by compelling each to like as good as seems good to the rest.[26]

Certainly the antipornography crusade led the adult film industry into a renewed appreciation of the U.S. Constitution. In many adult films, producers began to include a statement about the importance of the First Amendment.

Appeals to the First Amendment went hand-in-hand with a public relations strategy that attempted to discredit the Meese Commission by portraying it as a group of "self-appointed censors and moral vigilantes." *Playboy* and *Penthouse* joined with the ACLU, the American Booksellers Association, the Association of American Publishers, and the Association of American University Presses, and announced in July 1986 that they had hired one of Washington's most influential lobbying firms, Gray & Company, to assist them. The group formed an association known as Americans for Constitutional Freedom (ACF). One Gray & Company executive recounted how they had arrived at the name: "You sit down with a sheet of paper and some very smart, crazy, creative people, and you play with words. You try to come up with an organization whose name will be as attractive to as many people as possible and sounds like something you'd like to be involved in and support.... You register the name. Register with Congress, if you're going to lobby."[27]

Gray & Company, which was in the process of being acquired by Hill & Knowlton (then the second-largest public relations corporation in the world), had acted as lobbyists for several foreign countries, including the communist-led government in Angola, Turkey, and Canada. Despite this

[26] Quotation ("unwise") and John Stuart Mill quoted ("freedom") in Joseph, "Presentation to Attorney General's Commission on Pornography," July 24–5, 1985, p. 18, Folder 22, Box 70 ("Exhibits – Chicago"), RAGCP-NARA 2. Quotation ("eschewed"), ibid., 16; see also ibid., 6, 9.
[27] Quotation ("vigilantes"), in Thiel, "Gray & Co. Hired to Rebut Meese Panel," *WP*, July 28, 1986, (Washington Business sec.), 5. Unnamed executive quoted ("sit") in Trento, *Power House*, 197; also 196, 407n7.

odd mix of clients, it also had clout in the White House. Its founder, Robert Keith Gray, had been vice-chairman of Hill & Knowlton, director of communications for the 1980 Reagan campaign, and co-chair for the president's inauguration. Gray was among the attorney general's friends, but he was not averse to working against causes supported by Meese and the president. Part of Gray & Company's plan was to convince Reagan, Meese, and leaders in both political parties that the commission work was "so flawed, so controversial, so contested and so biased that they should shy away from publicly endorsing the document." (Indeed, Meese did try to distance himself from the commission's *Final Report*.) The other goal, as explained by John M. Harrington, the executive vice president for the Council for Periodical Distributors Association and one of the ACF's founders, was to convince the American public that these "self-appointed censors have a wider agenda on their minds," and that their efforts were not simply confined to magazines. The publicity campaign attempted to preempt the commission's findings by making several other arguments: there was no scientific foundation for the assertion that sexual materials caused crime or violent activity; trying to control pornography wasted national resources that could be allocated to more pressing social and economic problems; the commission was driven by religious zealots who would repress all rights; and, if the antipornography crusade succeeded, its supporters would then move to impose their illiberal agenda on the majority of Americans. Finally, Gray & Company recommended driving home the idea that one did not have to agree with every type of publication in order to support the right of all citizens to peruse them.[28]

The strategy to sell these ideas to the public was multifaceted. Part of it involved an intensive media campaign to place advocates on talk shows, news reports, and other television and radio programs. News conferences in several cities would be used to point out mistakes made by the commission. Press releases and "advertorials" (presumably paid ads that were essentially editorials) were used.[29]

Books were another means of refuting the Meese Commission. Philip Nobile and Eric Nadler, editors at *Forum* (a magazine published by

---

[28] John M. Harrington quoted ("agenda") in Thiel, "Gray & Co.," 5. Quotation ("flawed"), Stephen Johnson (Senior Vice President, Gray & Company) quoted in letter to John M. Harrington, June 5, 1986, in McManus, "Introduction," *Final Report,* xlvi; see also ibid., xlviii; Dougherty, "Hill & Knowlton to Buy Gray, the Lobbyists," *NYT,* June 4, 1986, D1; and Trento, *Power House,* 198.

[29] Quotation ("advertorials"), Trento, *Power House,* 197; see also 196–9.

Penthouse), provided a book-length account of the Meese Commission's work, aided by *Penthouse*'s marketing and public relations staff. The title alone of their 1986 work, *United States of America vs. Sex: How the Meese Commission Lied about Pornography*, left little doubt about its thesis. Nobile and Nadler considered themselves "journalists of sexual politics." In 1970, Nobile had assembled an interesting collection of writings entitled *The New Eroticism* that included work by Herbert Marcuse, Norman O. Brown, and Eric Hobsbawm. In 1986, Nobile and Nadler accused the Meese panel of being biased and superficial, and of reaching conclusions regardless of the evidence. According to their account, the evidence showing that exposure to pornography caused violent sexual crimes was unconvincing. The authors denounced the commission for ignoring the positive qualities of erotica and for threatening First Amendment rights. It was a "scary enterprise in censorship," said the authors, who argued that "erotica is an idea. And when the government joins forces with special-interest groups to repress freedom of thought, it is time to protest their not-so-silent scream." Minotaur Press, a part of Penthouse International, published more than a hundred thousand copies of *United States of America vs. Sex* and sold the paperback edition for only $3.95.[30] The ACLU also issued a 188-page critique of the Meese Commission entitled *Polluting the Censorship Debate*. It argued that the commission was promoting government censorship and "moral mob rule" by setting forth a "panorama of unconstitutional proposals" that violated not only the First Amendment but privacy, choice, and due process.[31]

Another part of the public relations campaign were ad hominem, or personal, attacks. "We attempted to call into question the motives, the values of the people on the Commission, raise questions about their own backgrounds," a Gray & Company executive revealed.[32] One particularly inviting target was the founder of Covenant House, Bruce Ritter. In a 1990 article for the *Village Voice*, Nobile wrote about allegations that Ritter had engaged in sexual misconduct and misused funds at Covenant House. Nobile himself was a Catholic who had studied theology, contributed articles to the *National Catholic Reporter* and *Commonweal*, and thought of himself as part of the "rise of the Catholic left." He disagreed strongly with Ritter's views about sex. Nobile had first caught scent

---

[30] Quotations ("journalists," "scary," "scream"), Nobile and Nadler, *United States of America vs. Sex*, 7; also 369–70. See also McDowell, "Some Say Meese Report Rates an 'X,'" *NYT*, Oct. 21, 1986, C13.

[31] Quotations, Lynn, *Polluting the Censorship Debate*, 2 ("mob"), 3 ("panorama"); see also 4.

[32] Unnamed executive quoted ("attempted") in Trento, *Power House*, 198.

of a possible scandal as he was finishing his 1986 book. A man who had formerly received help from Covenant House contacted him and claimed that he and Ritter had had a sporadic fourteen-year sexual relationship. The encounters had continued, the man asserted, even while Ritter sat on the Meese Commission. Nobile's editors were unconvinced in 1986 that the man was credible, but by early 1990 at least three other men who been under Ritter's supervision had come forward to say publicly that they had also had sex with the Franciscan priest. *Village Voice* made Nobile's exposé its cover story with the title "The Secret Life of Father Ritter." Although Ritter denied wrongdoing, private investigators hired by Covenant House confirmed his misconduct. In the wake of the scandal, Ritter resigned as head of Covenant House. To rebuild its image, Covenant House turned to Hill & Knowlton.[33]

To what extent did journalists and publishers allow the work of public relations and marketing people, whose endeavors were largely hidden from public view, to frame the coverage of the pornography hearings? What was the impact of this publicity on opinion? And what, if anything, did the MPAA and Hollywood contribute to this strategy?

If such questions are difficult to answer, it is clear that few reporters covered the issues in depth, and that the major publishing houses and a number of religious publishers refused to handle the *Final Report*. Even the *New York Times* and the *Los Angeles Times* incorrectly implied that the *Final Report* failed to provide a definition of pornography.[34] The *New York Times* accused the commission of "appealing more to sensibility than evidence" and faulted it for "recklessly encouraging censorship." A *Washington Post* columnist dismissed the *Final Report*'s conclusions as "more a wish than a scientific finding," hardly more than a "foregone conclusion."[35] Unable to find a large press to publish its work, the

---

[33] Philip Nobile quoted ("rise") in Sennott, *Broken Covenant*, 202; see also 203, 283–4, 296. See also Gambardello, "Ministry Barred for Ritter," *Newsday*, March 30, 1990 (City Home Edition), 8; Nobile, "Body and Soul," *Village Voice* 35 (Jan. 30, 1990), 25; Plummer, "Sex Charges Pit Four Young Men against the Revered Founder of Covenant House," *People's Weekly* 33 (Feb. 26, 1990), 38–40; "Ritter Resigns," *Christian Century* 107 (March 14, 1990), 273; "Ritter Probe Ends," ibid., 107 (May 9, 1990), 487; "Sex Reports on Priest Called Confirmed," *LAT*, Aug. 4, 1990, A21; "Charity's Report Back Allegations That Priest Engaged in Misconduct," ibid., Aug. 5, 1990, B3; and Goodell, "What Hill & Knowlton Can Do for You, (And What It Couldn't Do for Itself)," *NYT*, Sept. 9, 1990, sec. 6, p. 44.

[34] See "Defeated by Pornography" (editorial), *NYT*, June 2, 1986, A16; and Tavris, "The Illogic of Linking Porn and Rape," *LAT*, July 7, 1986, (Metro sec.), 5.

[35] Quotations ("appealing," "censorship"), "Defeated by Pornography," Quotations ("wish," "conclusion"), Cohen, "Pornography: The 'Causal Link,'" *WP*, June 3, 1986, A19.

Meese Commission eventually turned to Rutledge Hill, a small concern in Nashville, which published about forty thousand copies of the *Final Report* in an abridged version. Some Christian bookstores would not stock the work because of its graphic descriptions of movies and lengthy quotations from pornographic literature. Rutledge Hill distributed the work in a wrapper with a warning label stating it contained "extremely explicit content" that most people would find "offensive."[36]

THE FAILURE TO REGULATE SEX AND VIOLENCE

In assessing the reasons why the antipornography campaign failed to accomplish more, one should not underestimate the formidable part played by sophisticated public relations and advertising strategies. There are also several other reasons. First, there were judicial setbacks. Some of the Reagan court appointees appeared not to share the views of Meese and the prosecutors who pushed aggressively to outlaw explicit sexual materials. In Indianapolis, the antipornography measure passed by the city council and signed by the mayor was overturned by an appeals panel headed by Reagan appointee Frank Easterbrook on grounds that the law violated the First Amendment and amounted to "thought control."[37]

Other setbacks followed.[38] Playboy Enterprises and Penthouse International, together with the Council for Periodical Distributors Associations and the American Booksellers Association, sued Meese and Alan Sears, charging that the commission had circulated a blacklist of establishments and distributors of *Playboy* and other publications that were protected by the Constitution. Backed by the ACLU, these groups asked that the federal court issue an injunction to end circulation of the blacklist and to inform distributors that the sale of the publications in question was protected by the First Amendment. A federal judge blocked the Meese Commission

---

[36] Quotations ("extremely," "offensive"), McDowell, "Some Say Meese Report Rates an 'X,'" C13.
[37] Measures introduced in California, Massachusetts, New York, and Wisconsin also failed. Frank Easterbrook quoted ("thought") in Downs, *New Politics of Pornography*, 139; see also ibid., xiii, 137–9, 153; Bronstein, "Porn Tours," 389–90; and Whitman, "Are Reagan's New Judges Really Closet Moderates?" *WP*, Aug. 9, 1987, C1.
[38] For judicial setbacks involving the Child Protection and Obscenity Enforcement Act of 1988, see Thompson, "Part of Child Pornography Law Struck Down," *WP*, May 17, 1989, A19; "Librarians in Court, Again" (editorial), *WP*, Feb. 26, 1991, A20; "Court Upholds Porn Film Law," *Pittsburgh Post-Gazette*, Sept. 21, 1994, A6; Deibel, "Court Supports Laws to Prevent Porn Using Kids," *Denver Rocky Mountain News*, June 27, 1995, A21.

from naming stores that sold adult magazines. By April 1987, dozens of 7-Elevens in Las Vegas and Detroit were trying to put *Playboy* back on their shelves in response to requests for the issue that had nude photographs of game-show hostess Vanna White.[39] This is not to say that boycotts and other economic pressures were completely ineffective. These types of tactics did manage to limit mainstream outlets for X-rated movies, and later, as will be seen, NC-17–rated pictures.

Although the strategy of multiple prosecutions put several national distributors of sexually explicit materials out of business, critics denounced the practice as "censorship by intimidation" and accused the government of harassing businesses involved in legal activities. Three federal courts ruled the tactic unconstitutional as a violation either of due process or of the First Amendment. In 1993, the Justice Department under President Bill Clinton announced that it was abandoning this strategy.[40]

A second weakness in the campaign against sexually explicit materials was that the antipornography coalition – if it could be called that – between feminists and Christian conservatives had little chance of long-term durability. Many feminists and nonfeminist Christian women who opposed pornography found it awkward to cooperate with one another. After an effort to combine forces with Methodists in South Carolina, feminists and their supporters realized that Christian women were also likely to oppose feminism. Beyond the basic differences between these two camps on issues, the feminist movement, and Women Against Pornography in particular, were torn by internal tensions. Susan Brownmiller alienated lesbian feminists and gained a reputation for being homophobic. A pro-sex countermovement among feminists emerged. (Some lesbians, for example, endorsed sadomasochism.) Feminists and other foes of pornography who leaned toward civil libertarianism pulled back from WAP. By

---

[39] See "Playboy Sues Meese, Porn Panel, Cite 'Blacklist,'" *Adweek*, May 26, 1986 (Southeast Edition). See also Blodgett, "Porno Blacklist? Magazines Fight Meese Panel," *ABA Journal* 72 (July 1, 1986): 28; Kurtz, "Pornography Panel's Objectivity Disputed," *WP*, Oct. 15, 1985, A4; "Tests that Pornography Fails" (editorial), *Christian Science Monitor*, July 10, 1986, 15; "7-Elevens Drawn Back to 'Playboy' by Vanna Issue," *Adweek*, April 13, 1987, National Newswire sec.; and "The Playboy Philosopher," *Newsweek*, Aug. 4, 1986, 3, 50.

[40] Quotation ("intimidation"), Howe, "U.S. Accused of 'Censorship by Intimidation' in Pornography Cases," *WP*, March 26, 1990, A4. See also Hentoff, "The Justice Department's Tainted Fruit," *WP*, July 25, 1992, A21; McGee, "U.S. Crusade against Pornography Tests the Limits of Fairness," *WP*, Jan. 11, 1993, A1; and McGee, "U.S. Reviews Reagan-Bush Obscenity Tactic; Justice Department May End Multiple Prosecutions of Pornographers," *WP*, Nov. 24, 1993, A1.

the mid-1980s, the feminist antipornography movement had fractured and lost much of its power.[41]

Even if these judicial setbacks and the breaking of the antiporn alliance had not occurred, the media environment of the 1980s and 1990s made it extraordinarily difficult to regulate depictions of sex. New technology – first video, cable, and satellites, then personal computers and the World Wide Web – frustrated antipornography endeavors. These new means of communication helped to make pornography simply too lucrative to be repressed. Despite the policies of Blockbuster, K-Mart, and Wal-Mart not to rent X-rated entertainment, adult material remained widely available on video. When the Meese Commission had begun its work in 1985, about 1,600 new adult movies were being produced each year (a figure, as noted, that represented a 400 percent increase over just two years earlier). Production leveled off during the next few years and remained at a rate of under 2,000 movies annually until 1992. During the 1990s, the adult entertainment business entered a boom period. In 1995, about 5,000 sex videos were produced. Two years later that number exceeded 8,000 titles, and by 2000 it stood at about 11,000 (a figure for one year that was well in excess of the total number of stag films made during the 1950s and 1960s combined, and far more than the 400 mainstream Hollywood films made in 2000). At the turn of the century, Americans rented more than 700 million X-rated videotapes annually.[42]

Corporate America took advantage of this gold mine by providing pay-per-view adult entertainment over satellite and cable television providers. General Motors, EchoStar, AT&T, Marriott International, Hilton, and Time Warner were among the corporations offering such services. General Motors' subsidiary DirecTV had 8.7 million subscribers in 2000 who paid almost $200 million a year for adult movies provided by satellite.

---

[41] By 1981, leaders in WAVAW and WAVPM had concluded that legal strategies for controlling pornography could endanger feminist speech. Bronstein, "Porn Tours," 287–8, 342, 385–6, 393, 394. See also *WP*, 292–398; and Goodman, "Battle on Pornography Spurred by New Tactics," *NYT*, July 3, 1984, A8.

[42] Estimates put the number of explicit films made between 1955 and 1967 between 2,000 and 5,000. See Sampson, "Commercial Traffic in Sexually Oriented Materials in the United States (1969–1970)," *TRCOP: Volume III*, 186 and 189. Between 1985 and 1990, about 1,250 to 1,500 new pornographic movies appeared each year; Prince, *New Pot of Gold*, 121–3. During 1999, 711 million hard-core sex movies were rented, according to *Adult Video News*, as reported in Egan, "Technology Sent Wall Street Into Market for Pornography," *NYT*, Oct. 23, 2000, A20. See also Rich, "Naked Capitalists," *NYT Magazine*, May 20, 2001, sec. 6, p. 52; O'Toole, *Pornocopia*, 214; Lane III, *Obscene Profits*, 51; and Petersen, *Century of Sex*, 380. Petersen provides a lower estimate of about 100 million X-rated rentals per year (ibid.).

EchoStar Communications Corporation, one of the country's major satellite providers, made more money from sex films than did all of *Playboy's* cable, Internet, and magazine interests combined. The country's largest communication corporation, AT&T, provided adult films over a broadband cable service known as the Hot Network. AT&T also owned a company that marketed such entertainment to almost a million hotel rooms. Marriott hotels provided adult films even in such conservative states as Utah. The widespread availability of pornographic movies in hotel chains in conservative communities made it more difficult for prosecutors to argue that the rental of explicit videos violated community standards.[43]

Explicit sexual entertainment comprised much more, of course, than just videos, cable programs, and satellite TV. By the 1990s, Internet web sites, video games, and DVDs could be added to the technologies discussed by the Meese Commission. The availability of explicit sex on the World Wide Web fueled the Internet's growth. Videocassettes, cable, and satellite transmissions had eliminated the need to go to an adult theater. The Internet made it unnecessary to go even to the local video store, providing an almost unlimited variety of pornography, much of it free.[44]

Despite the work of prosecutors, in September 1989 *The Economist* could report that "Today, Los Angeles remains safe for pornographers." Nationwide, pornography continued to thrive. Where in 1970 the American market in hard-core pornography yielded perhaps $5 to $10 million annually, and by 1985 $6 to $10 billion (U.S. billion), by the end of the century it had become a $10 to $14 billion-a-year business, bringing in more money than all of professional baseball, football, and basketball combined, and more than the American public spent on mainstream movie tickets.[45]

Sexuality in entertainment, as noted earlier, did not comprise just pornography. It also pervaded mainstream materials and remained a staple of most movies and television programs. Though the antipornography campaign pressured mainstream moviemakers into toning down motion picture sex during the late 1980s, by the early 1990s Hollywood had reverted to form. Such movies as *Whore* (1991), *Basic Instinct* (1992), *The*

---

[43] See Egan, "Technology Sent Wall Street into Market for Pornography," *NYT,* Oct. 23, 2000 A20.

[44] See Lane III, *Obscene Profits,* 34–5.

[45] Quotation ("safe"), "Pornography: Smut City," *The Economist,* Sept. 23, 1989, 28 (World Politics and Current Affairs: American Survey); U.K. ed., 58. See also Egan, "Technology Sent Wall Street Into Market for Pornography," A20; and Rich, "Naked Capitalists," 51.

Lover (1992), *Damage* (1993), and *Body of Evidence* (1993) promised audiences experiences that were "fiercely erotic," "erotic and intense," and "shocking." In early 1993, a film critic for the *Cleveland Plain Dealer* observed that "after a brief – but heralded – pause during the ascendancy of both the Reagan era and AIDS, the industry went right back to the business of merchandising sex."[46] As for television, by the 1990s it was not unusual to watch evening television programs that only a few years earlier would have been rated at least an R had they been shown in a movie theater. The American Academy of Pediatrics (AAP) reported in 1995 that the average teenager saw and heard fourteen thousand sexual references and innuendos each year on television, and only about 1 percent of them made any mention of contraception, responsibility, or abstinence.[47]

If the campaign to control sexually arousing materials achieved only limited success, efforts to contain violence in the media met with abject failure. Here there was no counterpart to the antipornography crusade, although health professionals, researchers, and parents were outspoken in their dismay. Legally, there was little legislation to regulate motion picture or television violence. Obscenity laws usually did not forbid excessive violence in mass media. And there was scarcely more than lip service paid to the possibility of reform from entertainment leaders.

The aggressive campaign launched by government prosecutors and antipornography crusaders, the calculated public relations offensive on the part of their opponents to discredit the Meese Commission and its findings, and the failure of the press to cover the issues fully, virtually ended any chance of an extended, thoughtful public exploration of what influence sexually explicit materials in mass media might have. Dashed in the furor was Frederick Schauer's hope that the *Final Report* would "be read rather than summarized, ... be thought about rather than used as rallying cry or flag of battle, and ... be as much the beginning of serious discussion and debate rather than the end of it."[48]

---

46 Quotations ("fiercely," "heralded"), Connors, "Real Erotica More Than Skin Deep," H1.
47 Heffner, *Reminiscences*, vol. 1, p. 173, Box 5, RDH-COHC-BL; and Shelov et al., "Children, Adolescents, and Television," *Pediatrics* 96, no. 4 (Oct. 1995), 786–7.
48 Quotation ("read"), "Personal Statement of Commissioner Frederick Schauer," *Final Report*, 535.

7

Hollywood, Drugs, and Religion

Pornography was only one problem confronting Jack Valenti and the MPAA during the mid- and late-1980s. Of immediate concern was the entertainment industry's association with illicit narcotics. The White House under presidents Ronald Reagan and George H. W. Bush wanted to enlist movies and television programs into the war on drugs, and antidrug advocates called for a new rating category that would indicate substance abuse in films. Then there were conflicts with religious groups that harbored resentments, not only about the way movies showed sex, violence, and drugs, but also about the ways in which motion pictures portrayed religion. These groups organized protests against movies and videos, and they were often suspicious of the motives behind the movie ratings. In addition to these difficulties, festering among moviemakers was a growing discontent with the rating system. By 1990, their disenchantment had become so great that some of them mounted legal challenges to the system, while others urged the creation of a new category to replace the X.

Richard Heffner had long believed that the system needed reform. He wanted to give parents more information about why the various ratings were issued, and he favored creating a new category between the R and X. He also worried that some proposals for adding a new rating, together with complaints and pressures to do something about pornography, drug abuse, and other ills, threatened to change the nature of CARA and transform it from a ratings agency into a censorship board. By 1985, he was frustrated. He had been chair of CARA for a decade but felt that he had had only minimal impact on the system.[1]

---

[1] Heffner, *Reminiscences*, vol. 7, p. 1233, Box 5, RDH-COHC-BL.

The events of this period led Heffner to reconsider the meaning of the First Amendment and impelled Valenti to make an eloquent defense of the rights it guaranteed. These events also surely contributed to public cynicism about the entertainment industry's use of the First Amendment. As noted, pornographers adopted it as a line of defense, and it became the basis of a public relations campaign to discredit the Meese Commission. Studios used it to market films. In Hollywood it was not easy to distinguish between opportunism and authentic commitment to civil liberties.

RATINGS AND THE WAR ON DRUGS

The Reagan administration linked pornography to other social ills that included substance abuse, rock-music lyrics, and more broadly, the president said, mass media that corrupted children with a "glorification of drugs, violence and perversity." It was all part of "a failed and exhausted liberal ideology," that erected barriers to keep God away from children but had "trouble locking up drug pushers, thieves and murderers."[2]

The administration took direct aim at Hollywood. At or near the top of the list of things to change was the depiction of drug use in movies and television programs. The White House pressured Valenti and the MPAA to join the fight against illegal narcotics. First Lady Nancy Reagan assumed a prominent role in the war on drugs. The arm twisting unsettled Valenti. He was "practically hysterical with fear for what Mrs. Reagan was going to do because of the drug content of American movies," Heffner recalled after a ride down Madison Avenue with him in a limousine. Heffner was alarmed, too, because he saw White House interference as an unwarranted intrusion by the government into the ratings process.[3]

The entertainment industry was important to any campaign against substance abuse if for no other reason than that so many young people went to the movies and watched television. If one accepts estimates about movie attendance by the United States Catholic Conference (USCC) – and many in government found little reason to doubt them – about half of the film industry's projected $4 billion (U.S. billion) ticket sales in 1985 went to moviegoers whose ages ranged between ten and twenty-four. At that time, about 60 percent of the motion pictures were rated R. These same

---

[2] Reagan quoted ("glorification," "murderers") in Weinraub, "Rock Lyrics Irk Reagan," *NYT*, Oct. 10, 1985, C17.
[3] Quotation ("hysterical"), Heffner, "Pre-Oral History Memorandum for 1985," p. 23, Box 2, RDH-COHC-BL.

movies often appeared on television, sometimes uncut, where they were seen by millions.[4]

Hollywood faced considerable negative publicity over its connection to illicit drug use. *Parade,* a publication with a mass circulation, reported on its July 21, 1985, cover that in "recent months, Goldie Hawn, Jane Fonda, Dolly Parton, Lily Tomlin and JoBeth Williams have been shown smoking marijuana in millions of American homes." They had done so in movies that played on television. Prior to the late 1960s, drug use was rarely shown and then almost always in a disapproving way, *Parade* maintained. All this began to change with such movies as *Easy Rider* (1969) and *M*A*S*H* (1970), and with drug humor that came to television in such programs as *The Tonight Show,* starring Johnny Carson, and *Saturday Night Live.* Since the late 1960s, only a handful of films had treated substance abuse in a negative way. In contrast, during the early 1980s, *Parade* pointed out, at least sixty motion pictures had depicted drug use in a favorable, even upbeat, manner. Movies most commonly showed actors using marijuana, but cocaine and other illegal drug usage (although usually not heroin) was also shown. Several of the films were box-office hits, and one, *Terms of Endearment* (1983), won five Academy Awards. Many of these films were aimed at the youth market: *Animal House* (1978), *Caddyshack* (1980), *Airplane!* (1980), *National Lampoon's Class Reunion* (1982), *Risky Business* (1983), and *Revenge of the Nerds* (1984). *Parade* quoted Valenti in a way that made him seem to trivialize marijuana use. "I don't know of a single film where drugs are glamorized," he said. "To me, drugs are things like heroin and cocaine," he said. "I'll wager marijuana is used by half the people on Capitol Hill and Wall Street.... Yuppies are the biggest users of pot."[5]

CARA came under attack. The USCC criticized the PG ratings given to Spielberg's *Poltergeist* in 1982, Universal's *Sixteen Candles* in 1984, and Atlantic's *Teen Wolf* in 1985, all films heavily marketed to teenagers. In *Poltergeist,* the parents, who otherwise were portrayed as good role models, giggled as they shared a marijuana cigarette – a gratuitous and ill-advised scene, according to the bishops. (That the father was seen reading

---

[4] See Norbert F. Gaughan, testimony, *U.S. Senate Hearings,* Oct. 24, 1985, 130.

[5] Quotation ("smoking"), Satchell, "Does Hollywood Sell Drugs to Kids?" *Parade,* July 21, 1985, cover and p. 5. Valenti quoted ("glamorized," "pot"), ibid., 7. Among those movies that this article said showed drug abuse in a negative way were Al Pacino's *Panic in Needle Park* (1971), Gene Hackman's *French Connection* (1971), Bette Midler's *The Rose* (1979), Paul Newman's *Fort Apache – The Bronx* (1981), Burt Lancaster's *Atlantic City* (1981), and Brian De Palma's *Scarface* (1983).

FIGURE 11. During the 1980s, critics attacked moviemakers for encouraging illegal drug use, and the Ronald Reagan administration attempted to recruit Hollywood into its war on drugs. Here Tommy Chong (*left*) and Cheech Marin "get totally loaded on the world's biggest known joint" in their movie *Up in Smoke* (1978). Photograph courtesy of Photofest.

a book about Ronald Reagan also may not have played well in the White House.) The USCC rated *Sixteen Candles* morally objectionable because of its nonjudgmental depiction of teen sex and humorous treatment of alcohol abuse and drunk driving. In *Teen Wolf,* when actor Michael J. Fox turned into a werewolf, his enhanced ability to smell enabled him to sniff out a friend's marijuana stash.[6]

Other movies featuring drug use came in for condemnation. The National Council of Churches criticized *Private Benjamin* (1980) for making this topic an object of humor. *Nine to Five* (1980), which starred Fonda, Tomlin, and Parton, and *Scarface* (also denounced for violence) were often mentioned, along with *The Big Chill* (1983), which starred William Hurt and JoBeth Williams. Critics found the R-rated films of comedians Cheech and Chong, *Up in Smoke* (1978; see Fig. 11) and *Still*

---

[6] See Norbert F. Gaughan, statement, *U.S. Senate Hearings,* Oct. 24, 1985, 146–7. *Teen Wolf* also showed drinking and reckless driving. See also Brode, *Films of Steven Spielberg,* 107.

Smokin' (1983), even more offensive. For the latter movie, the advertising alluded to marijuana use, promising that you could "always smell the excitement in the air," and "they'll keep you rollin' in your seats!"[7]

In 1985, the U.S. Senate held hearings on drug abuse and the entertainment industry. It became apparent at these hearings that parents wanted more information about why and how ratings were applied to films. James Wall of the National Council of Churches and editor of *Christian Century* urged adding to the ratings a short phrase to indicate sex, violence, language, or substance abuse. The USCC called for similar information, and Marvin Goldman, who had been president of the National Organization of Theatre Owners during the late 1970s, strongly recommended giving parents more data. Heffner also cautiously indicated that he would not object if more information appeared about how CARA arrived at its decisions.[8]

Calls came for a new rating category, "SA," to indicate substance abuse. Actor William Shatner, who played Captain Kirk in the popular *Star Trek* series, threw his support behind this plan at the Senate hearings. Several organizations also lobbied for an SA category as they pressured studios to change the way they portrayed drug use. These organizations included the Scott Newman Center, founded and funded by actor Paul Newman, whose son Scott had died from an overdose of alcohol and Valium; the Caucus for Producers, Writers, and Directors; and the Entertainment Industries Council. The director of the latter group, producer Renee Valente of 20th Century Fox, formally petitioned the MPAA and CARA for the new rating.[9]

As was the case with the PG-13 rating and before that, with the Missouri-Kansas experiment, Valenti resisted giving more information about the ratings and objected to an SA category. Heffner believed that the MPAA's public relations and advertising people had counseled Valenti that a policy of not giving explanations would bring the least criticism and less bad publicity. "You couldn't give *sufficient* information," Valenti reportedly told Heffner, "so don't give any information at all." Disseminating the explanations would be a logistical nightmare, he told the press.

---

[7] Quotations ("smell," "seats") from *U.S. Senate Hearings,* Oct. 24, 1985, 65. On *The Big Chill,* see Gaughan, testimony, ibid., 133. For *Private Benjamin,* see James M. Wall, statement, ibid., 150.

[8] Wall, statement, *U.S. Senate Hearings,* Oct. 24, 1985, 149–50; Gaughan, statement, ibid., 147; Gaughan, testimony, ibid., 132; Marvin Goldman, testimony, ibid., 123, 124; Goldman, statement, ibid., 127–8; Richard D. Heffner, testimony, ibid., 121.

[9] Satchell, "Does Hollywood Sell Drugs to Kids?" 4, 6.

How would the information be distributed – by 800 telephone numbers, mailing to the twenty thousand theaters screens? There would also be confusion. In a society of almost 240 million where each person looked at matters through "his own prism," how did you define the meaning of "mild language?" As for the SA rating, "I thought it stood for sex appeal," he quipped.[10]

The overwhelming majority of movies did not make substance abuse appealing, Valenti told the Senate hearings in 1985. He had seen the Cheech and Chong ads, but testified that if one looked at the seven hundred hours of movies produced each year by Hollywood, probably less than an hour glamorized drug use. The industry had taken steps to improve its advertising copy, he claimed. "I think you'll find most of the ads are not that bad any more, because – and I use this word again with great sensitivity – we are trying to sanitize them so that nothing appears in that ad that would offend parents beyond what we think is reasonably offensive – whatever that means." Moreover, the movie and television industries had produced more mainstream entertainment to combat the "national fungus" of drug abuse than the public realized. The movie *Midnight Express* (1978) and the television series *Cagney and Lacey* (1984–5) were but two examples.[11] Even if the institutions that protected social mores – the family, school, and church – had "eroded and collapsed over the last couple of decades," Valenti remained optimistic, he told Senator Sam Nunn. He saw an "ascension, happily, of a reinforcement of some stronger values" in movies that might counter social malaise and drug culture. None of the big moneymakers in Hollywood – *Star Wars* (1977), *The Empire Strikes Back* (1980), *E.T.* (1982), *Return*

---

[10] Quotations ("*sufficient,*" "all"; emphasis in original text), Heffner, "Pre-Oral History Memorandum for 1981," p. 2, Box 1, RDH-COHC-BL. Quotation ("prism"), Valenti, testimony, *U.S. Senate Hearings,* Oct. 24, 1985, 84. Valenti quoted ("appeal") in Satchell, "Does Hollywood Sell Drugs to Kids?" 7. Heffner believed that Bethlyn Hand, who handled the MPAA's advertising and public relations, had advised Valenti against giving more information about why ratings were given. See Heffner, "Pre-Oral History Memorandum for 1980," pp. 79–80, Box 1, RDH-COHC-BL; and Hedlund, "Valenti Opposes Plan for Drug Use Rating for Films," *LAT,* Oct. 25, 1985, 8. Polls taken for the MPAA by the Opinion Research Corp. at Princeton indicated, Valenti said, that most parents liked the rating system just as it was. Seventy-two percent of parents approved of the system, while only 20 percent had a negative view of it. Valenti, testimony, *U.S. Senate Hearings,* Oct. 24, 1985, 67; and Valenti, statement, ibid., 91.

[11] In addition, other antidrug abuse productions included *Desperate Lives* (1982); *Fame* (1984); *Mr. T.* (1984); *Gremlins* (1984); *T. J. Hooker* (1985); and *Facts of Life* (1985). See Valenti, statement, *U.S. Senate Hearings,* Oct. 24, 1985, 112. Quotations, Valenti, testimony, ibid., Oct. 24, 1985, 67 ("fungus"), 70 ("sanitize"); see also ibid., 71–2, 73.

of the Jedi (1983), *Indiana Jones and the Temple of Doom* (1984), *Back to the Future* (1985), and even Sylvester Stallone's *First Blood* (1982) and *Rambo: First Blood II* (1985) – reflected the pessimism and defeatism of the Vietnam War era, explained Valenti. "*Rambo* suddenly says, 'By Jingo, we can win.'"[12]

Although Valenti resisted and ridiculed the idea of a new rating category, once the White House exerted pressure, he was more than willing to use the existing system to make the studios change their ways. He wanted the rating board to give an R to any movie dealing with drugs with no appeal possible, unless the film involved some form of "redemption." The rating should reflect a judgment about drug use in such movies as *Nine to Five, Poltergeist,* and *Scarface.* Valenti softened this position somewhat when he testified before the Senate in 1985, pledging that he would soon institute a rule that any film depicting substance abuse would be rated at least PG-13.[13]

With the help of Lew Wasserman and other powerful industry leaders, Valenti conspicuously publicized Hollywood's antidrug activities. Wasserman chaired an Entertainment Industries Council committee, which announced it would give Nancy Reagan its first annual award for outstanding work against substance abuse and that henceforth the award would be named after the First Lady. Valenti co-chaired the dinner in Los Angeles in September 1985 at which Mrs. Reagan was honored. Valenti also enlisted Jerry Weintraub and the Weintraub Entertainment Group to produce a series of antidrug commercials for the White House. The ads featured actors Dudley Moore, Clint Eastwood, Bette Midler, and Olivia Newton-John. Moore, of course, had perfected the role of the amiable drunk in the film *Arthur* (1981). Eastwood would soon direct the highly acclaimed movie *Bird* (1988), about the talented but drug-addicted jazz saxophonist Charles "Bird" Parker. The makers of this film challenged its R rating but lost their appeal, in part because of film's strong drug content.[14]

---

[12] Quotations ("eroded," "values," "Jingo"), Valenti, testimony, ibid., Oct. 24, 1985, 81.
[13] Quotation ("redemption"), Heffner, "Pre-Oral History Memorandum for 1985," p. 49, Box 2, RDH-COHC-BL. See also Heffner, "Pre-Oral History Memorandum for 1982," p. 52, Box 1, ibid.; and Valenti, testimony, *U.S. Senate Hearings,* Oct. 24, 1985, 68, 100.
[14] See Jacobs, "A Special Award for Nancy Reagan," *LAT,* Aug. 15, 1985, pt. 5 (View), p. 4; "Morning Report: Movies," *LAT,* July 13, 1987, sec. 6 (Calendar), col. 2. See also Heffner, Appeals Statement for *Bird,* July 26, 1988, document 88-19, Heffner, "Pre-Oral History Memorandum for 1988," Box 4, RDH-COHC-BL; and Heffner, *Reminiscences,* vol. 7, p. 1248, Box 5, ibid.

After the contentious rating appeal over *Scarface,* Heffner doubted that Valenti could be trusted to do the right thing on the drug issue. He felt that when the interests of the large studios were at stake, Valenti was too inclined to compromise the rating system's integrity and was willing, if need be, to use CARA as a scapegoat. That Valenti would have actually encouraged his own teenage daughter to see the violent *Scarface,* purportedly because of its antidrug message, Heffner thought was reprehensible.[15]

Heffner and Valenti also clashed over what role the ratings should play in the war on drugs. Heffner knew that parents were unhappy. He had heard protests in 1980, for example, about the PG rating given to the comedy *Airplane!* but had dismissed the complaints. When he first watched *Poltergeist,* he had been so intently focused on the movie's horror scenes that he did not pay attention to the couple smoking marijuana. He doubted, though, that most parents would have favored restricting the movie for the potsmoking scene alone. He opposed illicit drug use, to be sure, but he also was against giving automatic ratings because of theme or subject matter, and he suspected that the White House had created a climate in which even physicians were now reluctant to prescribe legitimate drugs to relieve terminally ill patients. He did not want CARA to have to distinguish between drug use and drug abuse. "Don't get us into decision-making about whether drug use is good or bad, 'gratuitous' or not," he told Valenti in 1985.[16]

Although Heffner opposed having an automatic rating for drug use, he did believe that every parent at CARA equated drug use with drug abuse, and he promised senators in October 1985 that no picture dealing with substance abuse would ever be categorized as a family film, or G-rated. But whereas Valenti wanted a rule that any narcotics use would automatically trigger no less than a PG-13 rating, Heffner favored a more flexible policy. In November he proposed a revision to the policy that lumped together Valenti's automatic drug-use rule and CARA's automatic language rule. Henceforth, the rating board would give no less than a PG-13 to movies that contained "*any* drug use-related content," unless CARA members

---

[15] See Heffner, "Pre-Oral History Memorandum for 1983," p. 29, Box 2, RDH-COHC-BL. Heffner bluntly assessed Valenti's position. You had "to be a real scudball" to do something like that, he said. Quotation ("scudball"), ibid. For *Scarface* and the rating appeal, see Chapter 4.

[16] Quotation ("gratuitous"), Heffner, "Pre-Oral History Memorandum for 1985," p. 49, Box 2, RDH-COHC-BL. See also Heffner, "Pre-Oral History Memorandum for 1982," p. 52, Box 1, ibid.; and Heffner, *Reminiscences,* vol. 7, pp. 1249–51, Box 5, ibid.

unanimously agreed that most parents would consider such classification unreasonable, in which case a less severe rating could be given. As for language, a "single use of *one* of the harsher sexually derived words, though only as an expletive," would warrant a PG-13, and more than one use of such expletives, or even a single use of such words in a sexual context, would move the pictures into the R category – unless rating board members unanimously voted otherwise. He believed that NATO leaders also favored this plan, and so was appalled the following year when Valenti's public relations department told the press that the MPAA and NATO had agreed that any movie having references to illicit drug use would automatically receive no less than a PG-13 rating. This policy violated what Valenti supposedly had been working hard to avoid, he complained.[17]

While CARA eventually did move toward a drug and language policy similar to what Heffner had proposed, the climate was not yet right for its implementation. Sentiment existed within the movie industry for even stronger guidelines than Valenti wanted. In 1988, Richard H. Frank of Walt Disney Studios and a former president of the Academy of Television Arts and Sciences, said that the "media ... have an undeniable responsibility to become a full partner with the government and citizens" in the war on drugs, and he offered a lengthy twelve-point plan that would force stricter policies on the MPAA and CARA. Heffner objected. The most effective contribution that the rating system could make to the campaign against illegal narcotics, he told Valenti, "should be rating explanations generally ... with drug content prominently included."[18]

Heffner worried that momentum for repression was increasing in 1985 and 1986. In addition to the Meese Commission and the attention given by the White House and Congress to drug abuse in movies and on TV, in the fall of 1985, a U.S. Senate committee began investigating pornography

---

[17] Quotations ("*any*," "*one*"; emphasis in original text), Heffner to Valenti, Nov. 20, 1985, doc. 85-5-2, Box 4, with Heffner, "Pre-Oral History Memorandum for 1985," Box 4, RDH-COHC-BL. See also Heffner to Valenti, April 9, 1986, doc. 86-3A, Heffner, "Pre-Oral History Memorandum for 1986," Box 4, ibid.; Heffner, testimony, *U.S. Senate Hearings*, Oct. 24, 1985, 118, 121; and Kleiman, "Films to Get Stricter Ratings," *NYT*, April 9, 1986, C18.

[18] Quotation ("media"), Frank, "Media/Entertainment White House Conference for a Drug Free America, Post Conferees Meeting Version, May 1988," attached to Jack Valenti to Richard Heffner/Simon Barsky (interoffice memo), June 16, 1988, doc. 88-11, with Heffner, "Pre-Oral History Memorandum for 1988," Box 4, RDH-COHC-BL. Quotation ("prominently"), Heffner to Valenti, June 21, 1988, doc. 88-11, Box 4, ibid. See also Heffner, *Reminiscences*, vol. 8, pp. 1491–3, Box 5, ibid.

on record albums and in music lyrics. At these hearings, the Parents Music Resource Center, whose members included Tipper Gore, wife of then Tennessee senator Al Gore, and Susan Baker, wife of then secretary of the treasury James A. Baker III, pushed to have rating labels, not unlike those used by the movies, applied to popular music. President Reagan was reported to be especially irked by the lyrics in rock music.[19]

Heffner liked Tipper Gore when he met with her at a small, out-of-the-way restaurant in 1985. She had approached him for advice on how the movie ratings worked. He believed that her worries about rock music arose from concern about her own children but sensed she was naive about how much protection ratings could provide. He thought that a plan to put lyrics on record boxes and album covers would be little more than a come-on for the recording business.[20]

Meanwhile, Heffner felt pressure from Washington and the news media to identify and rate "gratuitous drug abuse" in motion pictures. To use the ratings in this way amounted to unwarranted government intrusion, he thought. As he told Rudolph Giuliani, who was then U.S. Attorney for the Southern District of New York, this use of the ratings system would demand that CARA deal with the intentions of moviemakers, and it would move his work from film classification to film censorship. "We don't try to get inside their [filmmakers'] heads. And we are not about to do so," he said.[21]

These pressures came at a time when Heffner was already having second thoughts about the wisdom of giving legal protection to Hollywood's exploitation of violence. It seemed a good time to reassess the meaning of the First Amendment. He participated in an American Library Association round table on intellectual freedom in 1985, and there talked about how the "rights of the creative individual" needed to be respected but also balanced against the "rights of the majority . . . of parents whose primary concern is for the well-being of their own children." He still believed

---

[19] See Molotsky, "Hearing on Rock Lyrics," *NYT*, Sept. 20, 1985, C8; Harrington, "The Capitol Hill Rock War," *WP*, Sept. 20, 1985, B1; Weinraub, "Rock Lyrics Irk Reagan," *NYT*, Oct. 10, 1985, C17; and Harrington, "Is It Cleaner in the Country?" *WP*, Oct. 16, 1985, B7. See also Heffner, "Pre-Oral History Memorandum for 1985," p. 9, Box 2, RDH-COHC-BL. A subcommittee of the United States Senate Commerce, Science and Transportation Committee investigated music lyrics.

[20] Heffner, *Reminiscences*, vol. 7, pp. 1246–7, Box 5, RDH-COHC-BL.

[21] Quotations ("gratuitous," "heads"), Heffner to Rudolph Giuliani, July 23, 1985, doc. 85-7, Heffner, "Pre-Oral History Memorandum for 1985," Box 4, RDH-COHC-BL.

that, if limits needed to be placed on communication, the responsibility for imposing restraints should rest with the receiver who could choose not to listen, read, or view: Restrictions should not be imposed "upon the freedom of the *sender*."[22]

In July 1986, Heffner chaired a conference on "Liberty – the Next 100 Years" sponsored by Rutgers University and New York University that brought together prominent leaders and intellectuals to discuss First Amendment issues. One debate centered around the question "Can free speech become too costly?" Another asked, "When considering personal liberty, where does one draw the line between private interests and public well being?" Yet another discussion dealt with whether the doctrine of original intent sufficiently safeguarded liberties. Floyd Abrams, an attorney specializing in First Amendment issues, pointed out that the Constitution had been created before the invention of modern communications, and historian James MacGregor Burns observed that the Constitution was "not a sacred document" but "a charter of government that was made by man" and therefore could be "changed by man." The discussion turned to pornography. An ACLU representative argued against prior restraint on speech or restrictions on sexually explicit materials, while a writer for *The National Review* urged community action rather than legal remedies to fight the thriving sex shops then in mid-town Manhattan. Some civil libertarians applauded Tipper Gore's plan for labeling rock-music albums because it relied on community pressure rather than legal penalties. Catharine MacKinnon's call for more punitive measures to control pornography received a generally negative response. Panelists argued that a proper understanding of "liberty" would lead to a "sense of community" that would respect minority opposition.[23]

Heffner wrestled with such issues on an almost daily basis in his work. After these conferences his conviction about the need for balance between the power of the majority and the rights of the minority remained

---

[22] Quotations, Remarks by Richard D. Heffner, "ALA Conference: Caution: This Program Is Rated X," *Newsletter on Intellectual Freedom* 34 (Sept. 1985): 176 ("rights"), 178 ("*sender*"; emphasis in original text). Copy in Document 85-12, with Heffner, "Pre-Oral History Memorandum for 1985," Box 4, RDH-COHC-BL.

[23] Quotation ("costly"), Goodman, "Liberty Weekend/The People; Liberty Conferees Debate Judges' Role," *NYT*, July 6, 1986, A18. Quotation ("considering"), Blau, "A Good Time to Ask: What Do We Mean by 'Liberty'?" *NYT*, June 22, 1986, 26. Quotations ("liberty," "community"), Goodman, "Liberty Panel Ponders Wherefores of Freedom," *NYT*, July 7, 1986, B4. James MacGregor Burns quoted ("sacred," "man"), in ibid.

firm. It also seems clear that he now doubted that purely commercial entertainment unconnected to the public's welfare qualified to be ranked with the many forms of political and religious expression that had been suppressed in the past. "I continue to deplore the attitude of those who define censorship as a limitation upon their desire for riches," he told the editor of *Film Comment*. "I am too much aware of the tragic history of censorship in this country and in others not to know that it consists of a *prohibition* upon writing or speaking or otherwise expressing one's thoughts . . . not upon one's untrammeled ability to engage in commerce that is totally removed from concern for the public interest." Yet, in believing this, he faced a dilemma, for he still thought censorship posed great dangers, and he remained suspicious of those who claimed to speak for public opinion. "I will not permit others – not in the White House or elsewhere – to co-opt my deep and abiding concern for majority rule. I am not willing to reject concerns for majority rule because others inaccurately *claim* to speak for majorities. In short, I am not willing to dance to the tune of those who do not and probably could not ever understand the proper tension between majority rule and minority rights that has always characterized the best tradition of our nation."[24]

HOLLYWOOD AND RELIGION

Many religious leaders were, at best, ambivalent about modern media. In the words of Pope John Paul II, the various media held "untold possibilities for good" and "ominous possibilities for destruction." In September 1987, Lew Wasserman introduced the pope to an audience of fifteen hundred entertainment leaders that included Valenti, producer Merv Griffin, directors Peter Bogdanovich and Oliver Stone, comedian Bob Hope, actors Charlton Heston, Ed Asner, and many others. John Paul II told this group that they could produce "great beauty, revealing what is noble and uplifting in humanity and promoting what is just and fair and true." But they could just as easily "appeal to and promote what is debased in people: dehumanized sex through pornography or through a casual attitude toward sex and human life, greed through materialism and self-righteousness." If they exercised bad judgment, they would "wound consciences and human dignity" and damage "sacred fundamental rights,"

---

[24] Quotations ("dep*l*ore," "*prohibition*," "*claim*"; emphasis in original text), Heffner to Harlan Jacobson, July 23, 1986, doc. 86-15, with Heffner, "Pre-Oral History Memorandum for 1986," Box 4, RDH-COHC-BL.

the pope said. "Do not let money be your sole concern, for it, too, is capable of enslaving art as well as souls."[25]

The pope stood before a jaded group in Los Angeles, to be sure. Asking Hollywood to deemphasize money was about as likely as the possibility of John Paul II – himself a former playwright and actor – appearing in one of the industry's R-rated films. "If we had to get rid of greed," Griffin quipped, "I'd have to cancel *Wheel of Fortune* and *Jeopardy*." Valenti essentially agreed. "If we got rid of greed," he said, "there wouldn't be any projects in this town." There were many projects that never reached the screen, Valenti maintained, because "it's not responsible to do it." But, he noted, four hundred movies had been released in the United States during the previous year. "I can't be a good shepherd for all these films."[26]

Perhaps such remarks helped to account for the continuing worry conservative religious leaders felt about Valenti and Hollywood during the 1980s. Valenti, they felt, ignored their advice about drug culture, sex, and violence. But their resentment ran deeper. They were also angry over how motion pictures portrayed religion. If the movies did not actually slander religion, they believed that many films at least tried to undermine religious belief. Furthermore, it was not just the films that were problematic; their effects, often both sensational and confusing, were magnified by Hollywood publicity.

The belief that cinema can powerfully influence the way people think about religion has been present almost since the birth of cinema. In an earlier era, Daniel Lord worried about the power of cinema after he had seen D. W. Griffith's *Birth of a Nation* (1915). He feared that Griffith's favorable depiction of the Ku Klux Klan would encourage bigotry against blacks and Roman Catholics. So concerned did Lord become about Hollywood's portrayals of religion that he became an adviser on the set of *The King of Kings* (1927), where he tried to persuade Cecil B. DeMille to eliminate a segment that emphasized a love story between

[25] Pope John Paul II quoted ("possibilities," "destruction") in Champlin, "Small Screen Takes on the Big Issues – Again," *LAT*, Sept. 17, 1987, sec. 6 (Calendar), p. 1. Quotations ("humanity," "souls"), from transcript of Pope John Paul II, Address to Communication Industry Executives, Los Angeles, Sept. 15, 1987, in *NYT*, Sept. 16, 1987, A24.

[26] Merv Griffin quoted ("greed," "cancel"), and Valenti quoted ("greed," "town") in Maraniss and Jenkins, "Pope Asks Entertainers, Media to Be Forces for 'Great Good,'" *WP*, Sept. 16, 1987, A8. Valenti quoted ("responsible," "shepherd") in Stafford, "Pope Reminds the Media to Bear Good, Evil in Mind," *St. Petersburg Times*, Sept. 16, 1987, A1.

Judas and Mary Magdalene.[27] The Production Code, which Lord helped to draft, was protective of religion, and during Joseph Breen's leadership of the PCA between 1934 and 1954, one would be hard pressed to find negative images of religious leaders. During that period, many leading men played admirable men of the cloth. Spencer Tracy, one of the most popular actors of his time, played a priest in *Boys Town* (1938) and *Men of Boys Town* (1941) as did Pat O'Brien in *Angels with Dirty Faces* (1938) and *The Fighting 69th* (1940), and Bing Crosby in *Going My Way* (1944) and *The Bells of St. Mary's* (1945). Clark Gable, Frank Sinatra, and Mickey Rooney also played clergymen. Ronald Reagan portrayed a priest in the Army Air Corps movie *For God and Country* (1944). During the 1950s and into the 1960s, Hollywood's reverential treatment of religion continued in religious spectaculars with casts of thousands including *The Robe* (1953), which starred Richard Burton as a Roman involved in Christ's crucifixion who later coverts to Christianity, and the two famous Charlton Heston vehicles, *The Ten Commandments* (1956), in which he played Moses, and *Ben-Hur* (1959), which garnered eleven Academy Awards in 1959. In 1965, Max von Sydow played Jesus in *The Greatest Story Ever Told,* a film that emphasized the divine nature of Christ.[28]

Despite the respect accorded religion in the big-budget films, religion's protected place in American movies began to erode during the 1950s. Many religious leaders and film censors thought that Roberto Rossellini's film *The Miracle* (1948), which led to the 1952 Supreme Court decision giving cinema protection under the First Amendment, ridiculed the virgin birth. Then, with the demise of the Production Code, not only did more liberal interpretations of religion appear, but frankly negative images of Christianity, its leaders, and their followers became a staple in Hollywood movies. The films *Jesus Christ Superstar* (1973), *Godspell* (1973), *Brother Sun, Sister Moon* (1973), and *Nasty Habits* (1977) offended many critics. Some religious leaders condemned the last film for using a convent to satirize the Watergate scandal. Religious leaders called *The Passover Plot* (1976) a "direct attack on Jesus Christ . . . in such a way as to destroy the whole basis of Christian faith."[29] Franco Zeffirelli's 1977 television miniseries *Jesus of Nazareth* attempted to set Christ's message in the

---

[27] Lord, *Played by Ear,* 273, 280–3. Representatives from B'Nai B'rith, the Anti-Defamation League, and the Rabbinical Assembly of America also pressured DeMille to delete scenes that suggested the Jews crucified Christ. See Lyons, *New Censors,* 148–9.

[28] Dart, "Age-Old Problem: Portrayals of Christ Tempt Controversy," *LAT,* July 30, 1988, sec. 1, p. 1.

[29] Quotation ("attack"), ibid. See also Lyons, *New Censors,* 155.

context of history, but fundamentalists denounced it for portraying their Savior as "an ordinary man – gentle, fragile, simple," while ignoring his divine nature. As one critic put it, he was "a weakling – terrified, uncertain, searching, meditative, mystical, a guru-type Jesus – definitely not the strong Christ of the Scriptures." General Motors pulled its advertising from the program (although Zeffirelli estimated that because of TV and videotape his interpretation of Jesus was seen by perhaps one billion people worldwide). The British satire *Monty Python's Life of Brian* (1979), came under attack when distributed in America, because although it was supposedly about a fictional person born in a stable, the protagonist's life paralleled that of Jesus. The Archdiocese of New York called the picture "a mockery of Christ's life," and Lutherans, Episcopalians, and the National Council of Churches said it was blasphemous.[30]

During the 1980s, Hollywood displayed what one critic called an "anti-clerical impulse." In *Monsignor* (1982), Christopher Reeve (who had earlier played Superman) portrayed an unprincipled prelate who seduces a beautiful nun (Genevieve Bujold) and rises to power by conspiring with the Mafia to control the Vatican's wealth. In *Agnes of God* (1985), Meg Tilly played a young nun who gives birth in a convent and then murders her child. Anne Bancroft played the Mother Superior who attempts to cover up the crime, and Jane Fonda the psychiatrist who tries to unravel it. Pope John Paul II condemned Jean-Luc Godard's *Je Vous Salue Marie* (*Hail Mary*), a French film that opened in American art theaters in the fall of 1985. Set in modern times, it is about a teenager, the daughter of a gas station owner, who becomes pregnant without intercourse. Catholics claimed that the film demeaned Christ's birth, and they picketed theaters where it was shown. In other films, such as *True Confessions* (1981) starring Robert De Niro, and *The Mission* (1986) with Jeremy Irons, even though individual priests were shown performing good works and maintaining their faith and idealism, the Catholic Church itself appeared hypocritical. In *The Godfather, Part III* (1990) the Church appeared to be corrupt at every level, and the movie's central figure, Mafia boss Michael Corleone (played by Al Pacino) was shown receiving the highest honor a Catholic layman could obtain from Rome. The negative images spilled into other film genres. Teenage comedies such as *Heaven Help Us*

---

[30] Quotation ("ordinary"), Bob Jones III quoting Franco Zeffirelli in Forshey, *American Religious and Biblical Spectaculars*, 170. Quotation ("weakling"), Dart, "Age-Old Problem," *LAT*, July 30, 1988, sec. 1, p. 1. Quotation ("mockery"), Lyons, *New Censors*, 157. Procter and Gamble did become a sponsor for Zeffirelli's mini series. See ibid. See also Zeffirelli, *Franco Zeffirelli's Jesus*, viii–ix.

(1985) spoofed the stupidity of parochial education. Horror films such as *Silver Bullet* (1985) showed a werewolf masquerading as a man of the cloth.[31]

Protestants and Jews fared no better than Catholics. In *Crimes of Passion* (1984), which CARA first rated X for its sexual content, Anthony Perkins (who had achieved fame as Norman Bates in Alfred Hitchcock's 1960 thriller, *Psycho*), played a sleazy evangelist obsessed with a prostitute (actress Kathleen Turner). His scheme to save her soul required her to be murdered.[32] *The Handmaid's Tale* (1990), featuring Natasha Richardson, Faye Dunaway, and Robert Duvall, was alternative history about an America in which Christian fundamentalists seized power, burned books, degraded and enslaved women, and tried to eradicate ethnic minorities. In *The Rapture* (1991), Mimi Rogers played a convert to Christianity who was addicted to group sex. Her faith led her to murder her daughter while she waited for the Rapture – the end of the world at which time believers would be taken to heaven. When the Rapture did come, though, Rogers's character, who blamed God for her child's death, had become embittered and refused entry into heaven. In *The Chosen* (1978), starring Rod Steiger and Maximilian Schell, *Radio Days* (1987) and *Crimes and Misdemeanors* (1989), both directed by Woody Allen, and *Enemies, a Love Story* (1989), directed by Paul Mazursky, the caricatures or unsympathetic portrayals of rabbis and believers led critics to denounce the films.

Moviemakers sometimes even associated Christianity with sadism and other forms of violence. In *Misery* (1990), actress Kathy Bates, wearing a cross prominently displayed around her neck, made a number of references to religion as she tortured a writer, played by James Caan. In *Cape Fear* (1991), directed by Martin Scorsese, Robert De Niro played a sadistic ex-convict and rapist who threatened a family. Characterized as a Pentecostal Christian, he carried a Bible and had a large cross tattooed on his back. Although this film was a remake of a 1962 movie of the same title that had starred Gregory Peck and Robert Mitchum, the earlier version had included no religious imagery, and some speculated that the remake was Scorsese's way of getting back at the religious critics who,

[31] Quotation ("anticlerical"), Medved, *Hollywood vs. America*, 52. See also ibid., 37–49, 52–4; and Lyons, *New Censors*, 158–9.
[32] See Heffner, "Pre-Oral History Memorandum for 1984," pp. 67, 69–70, Box 2, RDH-COHC-BL. For scenes cut from the original version of *Crimes of Passion* to get an R rating, see Barry Sandler to Distribution (interoffice memo), Sept. 1984, pp. 6–8, Document 84-14, with ibid.

three years earlier, had attacked his film *The Last Temptation of Christ* (1988).[33]

Scorsese had based *The Last Temptation of Christ* on Nikos Kazantzakis's 1955 novel. Kazantzakis had written a serious and controversial book – so controversial, in fact, that the Greek Orthodox Church excommunicated him, and he was not allowed to be buried in Greece after his death in 1957. His intellectual odyssey had taken him from the ideas of Henri Bergson to Greek Orthodoxy to Friedrich Nietzsche, then to Buddha and Lenin, and finally back to Christianity. Along the way, he had written another well-known novel, *Zorba the Greek* (1946), also made into a movie in 1963.[34] The actress Barbara Hershey had given the novel to Scorsese. It took Scorsese, who was a Roman Catholic and one-time seminarian, several years to read Kazantzakis's work, but his movie followed the book rather closely. Hershey played Mary Magdalene in the movie. Willem Dafoe, who had previously appeared in Oliver Stone's *Platoon* (1986), portrayed Jesus, Harvey Keitel portrayed Judas, and rock-star David Bowie was Pontius Pilate. Paul Schrader helped to prepare the script and Jay Cocks was an uncredited collaborator. Scorsese also contributed to the final shooting script.[35]

In *The Last Temptation of Christ*, Kazantzakis portrayed a human Jesus who was constantly tempted by evil and who occasionally succumbed to the sins of the flesh. Only by showing this constant struggle, Kazantzakis believed, could Christ's rejection of evil be meaningful. In the book, as Jesus was nailed to the cross, he was tempted by Satan in the guise of a female angel. She showed him a vision of how his human life could have unfolded. He would have fathered children with Mary Magdalene. Later, he would have been confronted by Judas Iscariot, who would berate him as a coward and traitor to God. Although Jesus admitted

---

[33] For antireligious themes in these and other movies, see Chapter 4, "Comic Book Clergy," in Medved, *Hollywood vs. America*, 50–69.

[34] See Landsbaum, "Bishop, Schuller Join Voices Urging 'Temptation' Boycott," *LAT,* Aug. 10, 1988, sec. 2, p. 1; Dart, "Some Clerics See No Evil in 'Temptation,'" *LAT,* July 14, 1988, sec. 6, p. 1; and Bien, trans., "A Note on the Author and His Use of Language," in Kazantzakis, *Last Temptation of Christ*, 497–506.

[35] Scorsese made the film in Morocco on a budget of less than $7 million and with five stuntmen. See Dart, "'Last Temptation' Views Still Coming In; Boycott of 'E. T.' among Religious Reactions to Controversial Movie," *LAT,* Aug. 27, 1988, sec. 2, p. 6; Dart, "Some Clerics See No Evil in 'Temptation,'" sec. 6, p. 1; and Champlin, "Critics at Large: Scorsese in the Wake of 'Temptation,'" *LAT,* Jan. 19, 1989, sec. 6, p. 1. Barbara Hershey had worked with Scorsese earlier, in *Boxcar Bertha* (1972), and had appeared in other films such as *The Stunt Man* (1980), with Peter O'Toole, and Woody Allen's *Hannah and Her Sisters* (1986).

that he at first "lost courage and fled" crucifixion, at the end of Kazantzakis's story, he realized his mistake and chose to accept his fate on the
cross, thus overcoming temptation. All "turned out as it should, glory be
to God!"[36]

A number of things about the movie upset purists. Before filming began,
Scorsese and Universal floated an early version of Schrader's script in
which Christ has a dream that he is making love to Mary Magdalene
and tells her, "God sleeps between your legs." This scene apparently was
eliminated before filming started, but the motion picture contained other
controversial scenes. It began by showing Jesus helping to nail another
Jew to a cross; later Jesus reached into his chest and pulled out his beating
heart. There was full-frontal nudity of women who attended the baptism
of Jesus, and a nude scene showing Jesus and Mary Magdalene making
love when Satan tempted Christ by showing him what his life could have
been. Some evangelicals called Scorsese's Christ a "wimp" – weak, vac-
illating, unwilling to accept God. Morality in Media branded the movie
"sacrilegious" and objected to dialogue in which Jesus says: "Forgive me;
I've done too many bad things. . . . I am afraid of everything. . . . Lucifer is
inside of me." At the same time, critics complained, the film's strongest
characters were Judas and Satan in angel disguise. James Wall was disappointed that both Scorsese's movie and Kazantzakis's novel ended with
Jesus's death and not with his resurrection.[37] Religious broadcasters James
Dobson (the former Meese Commission member) and Pat Robertson saw
the movie as an assault on conservative Christianity and urged their followers to let Universal and MCA, the studio's parent company, know of
their disapproval. "It seems to me to be the latest example of that kind
of disrespect and insult that could not be expressed to any other minority group in the world," Dobson said. African Americans, Muslims, and
any number of other groups would not tolerate similar treatment of their
venerated leaders, he told listeners to his radio program, *Focus on the
Family.*[38]

---

[36] Quotations, Kazantzakis, *Last Temptation of Christ,* 494 ("fled"), 496 ("glory"). See
   also ibid., 492, 504.
[37] Quotations ("sleeps," "wimp"), Dart, "Some Clerics See No Evil in 'Temptation,'" *LAT,*
   July 14, 1988, sec. 6, p. 1. Quotations ("sacrilegious," "Forgive," "Lucifer"), Dart,
   "Evangelist Offers to Buy All Copies of Christ Movie," *LAT,* July 16, 1988, sec. 2, p. 3.
   See also Dart, "'Last Temptation' Views Still Coming In," *LAT,* Aug. 27, 1988, sec. 2,
   p. 6. Hershey had appeared nude or seminude in earlier movies, including *Boxcar Bertha,
   The Stunt Man, Last Summer* (1969), *The Baby Maker* (1970), and *The Entity* (1983).
[38] James Dobson quoted ("disrespect") in Dart, "Age-Old Problem," *LAT,* July 30, 1988,
   sec. 1, p. 1.

FIGURE 12. Willem Dafoe as Jesus in *The Last Temptation of Christ* (1987). Many religious groups protested against this film and Universal Studios, which produced it. Photograph courtesy of the Wisconsin Center for Film and Theater Research.

Although there were elements in this treatment of Christ's life that were open to legitimate criticism, it is doubtful that many moviegoers would have paid attention to this low-budget film, because it hardly had the makings of a blockbuster. "Had there been no protests, it would have disappeared quickly," said the editor of *Show Biz News*. "It's not a commercial picture."[39] Of importance in rescuing the film from near obscurity and putting it into the realm of public spectacle was the studio's publicity campaign. Universal's strategy sought to create a "buzz among moviegoers."[40] The news about Schrader's script that included

[39] Alex Ben Block quoted ("protests") in Easton, "Slow Release Strategy Pays Big Dividends," *LAT,* Aug. 16, 1988, sec. 6, col. 1.

[40] Quotation ("buzz"), ibid. Universal fired its advertising agency in the Dallas/Fort Worth area, Levenson & Hill, because it refused to handle promotional material for *The Last Temptation of Christ*. The studio replaced L&H with Moroch & Associates, a move worth between $500,000 and $1 million to the latter agency. Universal also reviewed its contracts with several other local advertising agencies. The studio's national agency, DDB Needham/Los Angeles, which handled $50–70 million in ad copy, was not part of the review. See Talmadge and Sharkey, "Universal Drops L&H Amid Movie Flap," *Adweek,* Sept. 12, 1988 (Southwest Edition).

Christ's controversial dream undoubtedly helped in this regard. The studio held a secret screening of the film for about thirty to forty Protestant and Catholic leaders, including representatives of People for the American Way and Fundamentalists Anonymous, both organizations known to be critical of the religious right. Most who attended the screening offered positive assessments of the movie.[41] Before releasing the film nationwide, Universal showed it in a handful of carefully selected theaters in nine American and Canadian cities. This strategy had been successful for two earlier pictures, 20th Century Fox's *Die Hard* (1988) and MGM's *A Fish Called Wanda* (1988).[42]

Universal attempted to capture the intellectual high ground. It appealed to teachers, librarians, and religious leaders with a glossy, eight-page "discussion guide" distributed by the nonprofit Cultural Information Service (CIS). CIS circulated about 200,000 copies of this mailer, but made no mention of the fact that Universal had funded it or that CIS had worked to prepare it with the studio's head of public relations, Sally Van Slyke. The guide asked readers to "think of the film as a chance to listen to the many different, even conflicting, voices inside yourself and to delve into your beliefs, values, priorities, ideals," and to consider it "as a religious journey today." In conjunction with the movie's opening, Touchstone Books – a division of Simon & Schuster – issued 200,000 paperback copies of Kazantzakis's novel with a "crown of thorns" advertising design on the book's cover.[43]

The studio sought to cast the film as a First Amendment issue – religious zealotry threatening to repress the creations of a visionary writer and a

---

[41] The Rev. Charles Bergstom of the People for the American Way said that Scorsese's use of Scripture did not offend him. Former antiwar activist Daniel Berrigan called it "a long, demanding film," and a communication official for the World Council of Churches, Andrea Cuno, said she thought it was more an art picture than a religious movie. An Episcopal bishop from New York, Paul Moore, said that he had had "a very, very positive reaction" and "saw nothing blasphemous" in the picture. All note quotations are from Dart, "Some Clerics See No Evil in 'Temptation,'" sec. 6, p. 1.

[42] *The Last Temptation of Christ* opened in Los Angeles, New York, Chicago, Washington, Toronto, Montreal, Minneapolis, San Francisco, Seattle. *Die Hard* starred Bruce Willis. Studio executives believed that he had an image problem at the time because of his television show, *Moonlighting*. But Fox played down Willis's role and the film opened to large crowds. MGM had opened *A Fish Called Wanda* in just three theaters, but word of mouth and good reviews made it a success. Both films became among the summer's top grossing pictures. See Easton, "Slow Release Strategy Pays Big Dividends," sec. 6, col. 1.

[43] Quotation ("think," "journey"), Broeske, "Outtakes: Missing Link," *LAT*, Sept. 18, 1988, Calendar sec., p. 19. An English translation of the novel had been available since 1960, and Touchstone, which acquired the rights to it in 1966, had sold 150,000 copies. See Dart, "'Temptation,' with a New Cover, Due at Bookstores, Publisher Says,"*LAT*, Aug. 19, 1988, sec. 6, p. 6.

talented director. Predictably, Christian conservatives rose to the bait. On the day the movie was released, twenty-five thousand protesters, who had been coordinated by a Christian TV station and two Southern California radio stations, showed up at the gate of Universal studios, backing up traffic for several miles on the northbound Hollywood Freeway. Bill Bright, a cofounder of Campus Crusade for Christ, offered to buy all prints of *The Last Temptation of Christ* for $10 million. Universal responded to this offer by taking out full-page ads in the *New York Times, Washington Post, Los Angeles Times, Atlanta Constitution, Daily Variety,* and the *Hollywood Reporter* that reproduced the studio's letter to Bright: "Though those in power may justify the burning of books at the time, the witness of history teaches the importance of standing up for freedom of conscience, even when the view being expressed may be unpopular," stated the letter.[44] Hollywood directors assembled to support Scorsese's right to make the film. Sydney Pollack warned that "the very essence of what we mean when we talk about a free society" was at stake. Fundamentalists had little to fear, he said, because "Christianity has survived 2,000 years; certainly Martin Scorsese's $6-million movie is not a threat to it." Twenty directors, including Oliver Stone, Clint Eastwood, John Carpenter, Peter Bogdanovich, and Billy Wilder, signed a statement backing Scorsese.[45]

Valenti supported Wasserman and Universal by issuing a forceful condemnation of censorship: "No one, no matter how passionate their opposition, no matter how strenuously they disagree, can or should prevent the entry of a point of view, whether it is political or creative or philosophical. Speak up, say what's on your mind? Of course. Protest whenever and whatever you choose? Of course. But prevent a creative work from being judged by the public? No. Not now or any time. And that's where the MPAA and its member companies take their stand: No prior censorship, ever!"[46]

In this instance there was no disagreement between Valenti and Heffner. Heffner was not particularly interested in the controversy over the life of Jesus, and there were few in his inner circle who were fundamentalists

---

[44] Letter to Bill Bright quoted ("burning") in Easton, "Studio Fires Back in Defense of 'Temptation,'" *LAT,* July 22, 1988, sec. 2, p. 1. See also Chandler, "25,000 Gather at Universal to Protest Film," *LAT,* Aug. 12, 1988, sec. 1, p. 1; and Dart, "Evangelist Offers to Buy All Copies of Christ Movie," *LAT,* July 16, 1988, sec. 2, p. 3.

[45] Sydney Pollack quoted ("essence," "threat") in Dart and Chandler, "Full Theaters, Protests Greet 'Temptation'," *LAT,* Aug. 13, 1988, sec. 1, p. 1.

[46] Valenti quoted ("passionate") in Heffner, "Pre-Oral History Memorandum for 1988," p. 66, Box 2, RDH-COHC-BL.

or conservative Christians to whom he might turn for advice. He ignored calls to give an X rating to *The Last Temptation of Christ* on the ground that it was sacrilegious. Even though he considered the picture in some ways "ludicrous," it was, in his opinion, a serious attempt to interpret Jesus. The issues it raised were exactly "the kind of free speech that Jefferson and our forefathers were concerned with."[47]

It should be noted parenthetically that Heffner approved of Valenti's statement about freedom so much that he used it against him in contract negotiations. Heffner kept a daily log of his activities – as a means of refuting inaccurate claims that moviemakers sometimes made about ratings matters – and Valenti apparently feared that these notes might some day be turned into a book. Heffner had not participated in the industry's pension plan and had begun to worry about his financial security. Knowing this, Valenti approached him with a contract offer in 1988 that offered him a large raise in exchange for a signed agreement that Heffner would not write anything about the MPAA. It was "a horrendous invitation to intellectual servitude," Heffner concluded. He refused to sign, and in so doing referred Valenti to his own defense of the First Amendment in the controversy over *The Last Temptation of Christ*. The salary increase that Heffner had expected was not forthcoming, and the episode further soured relations between the two men.[48]

With regard to *The Last Temptation of Christ*, Universal's campaign worked well at first. The film played before sell-out crowds in the nine theaters in which it opened. Many in the press concluded, and some evangelists even conceded, that the protests gave the movie free publicity and contributed to the large turnout. But success proved to be short-lived, and *The Last Temptation* soon languished in the theaters.[49] That religious leaders called on followers to boycott the film, that some theater chains refused to show it while others exhibited it only reluctantly also hurt the

---

[47] Quotations, ibid., 63 ("ludicrous"), 67 ("speech"). See also Heffner, *Reminiscences*, vol. 7, p. 1303; and vol. 8, pp. 1510–11, Box 5, RDH-COHC-BL.

[48] Quotation ("servitude"), Heffner, *Reminiscences*, vol. 8, p. 1457; see also ibid., pp. 1452–64, Box 5, RDH-COHC-BL.

[49] See Chandler, "Protests Aided 'Temptation,' Foes Concede," *LAT*, Aug. 14, 1988, sec. 2, p. 1; and Hunt, "'Temptation' Video to Rekindle Fundamentalist Ire?" *LAT*, June 2, 1989, sec. 6, p. 13. According to the *Los Angeles Times*, the movie did "record-breaking" business during its opening weekend, taking in more than $400,000. See Easton, "Slow Release Strategy Pays Big Dividends," p. 1. See also Dart and Chandler, "Full Theaters, Protests Greet 'Temptation,'" p. 1; Dart, "Church Declares 'Last Temptation' Morally Offensive," *LAT*, Aug. 10, 1988, sec. 2, p. 3; and Easton, "'Last Temptation' Draws Mostly Sold-Out Houses," *LAT*, Aug. 15, 1988, sec. 6, p. 1.

film.[50] The call to boycott extended to video sales the following year. Even though Universal released the video version of *The Last Temptation* quietly and without promotion or advertising, the American Family Association, a Mississippi-based organization, mounted a national campaign against the video. Blockbuster Video, which had about seven hundred stores nationwide, refused to stock the film, although other chains – Palmer Video, Tower Video, and Music Plus – carried it. In an effort to punish MCA/Universal, the Southern Baptist Christian Life Commission tried to persuade its fourteen million followers to boycott not only *The Last Temptation* but also the video of the studio's smash hit *E.T.* (1982) when it appeared later in the year.[51]

Issues related to both substance abuse and religion continued to beset Hollywood in the post-Reagan years. In 1989, President George H. W. Bush also reproached entertainment leaders for making light of and even glorifying narcotics use in Hollywood films and on television. His antidrug czar William Bennett considered both movies and television essential to the war on substance abuse but remained suspicious of most actors. Early in the Bush presidency, producers and filmmakers announced that Hollywood would take an active role in antidrug campaigns, a role that included sending drug experts to the studios to review scripts and

---

[50] Southern Baptist and Eastern Orthodox leaders condemned *The Last Temptation of Christ*. Protestant televangelist Robert Schuller urged his followers to boycott the film. The Reverend Billy Graham said that he would not take part in a boycott, but he denounced the movie for being "sacrilegious." The Catholic Church declared the movie "morally offensive." In Calcutta, India, Mother Teresa spoke against the film, and in Orange County, California, Roman Catholic bishop Norman F. McFarland called on the half-million Catholics in the area to avoid the picture. Note quotation ("sacrilegious"), "Religion Briefs: Billy Graham Says He Will Not See 'Last Temptation,' Calls It Sacrilegious," *LAT,* Sept. 17, 1988, sec. 2, p. 7; Landsbaum, "Bishop, Schuller Join Voices Urging 'Temptation' Boycott," *LAT,* Aug. 10, 1988, sec. 2, p. 1. Note quotation ("offensive"), Dart, "Church Declares 'Last Temptation' Morally Offensive," sec. 2, p. 3.

The unwillingness of some theater owners to show the film created uncertainty at Universal about how widely to release the picture. The Edwards Cinema Chain, which operated many theaters in Southern California, refused to show the movie, and General Cinema, the nation's fourth largest chain, was also reluctant. See "Edwards Cinemas Chain Won't Run 'Last Temptation',," *LAT,* Aug. 7, 1988, sec. 2, p. 8. See also Easton, "Slow Release Strategy Pays Big Dividends," *LAT,* sec. 6, col. 1.

[51] See Atkinson, "Home Tech: Quiet Release of Controversial 'Last Temptation of Christ,'" *LAT,* June 30, 1989, sec. 6, p. 25. See also Hunt, "'Temptation' Video to Rekindle Fundamentalist Ire?" *LAT,* June 2, 1989, sec. 6, p. 13. Despite the boycott effort, *E.T.* videos appeared to do well in the Bible Belt. See Dart, "'Last Temptation' Views Still Coming In," *LAT,* Aug. 27, 1988, sec. 2, p. 6; and Hunt, "Fundamentalists Urge 'E. T.' Video Boycott; Pre-Orders Set Record," *LAT,* Sept. 16, 1988, sec. 6, p. 4.

offer recommendations.[52] During the Clinton administration, depiction of illicit drug use appeared in more than one-fifth of popular films. About half of these movies dealt with the short-term consequences of abuse, and only one in eight pictures showed long-term effects. But although all of the films that showed illegal drugs were rated PG-13 or R, almost half of these ratings failed to mention that substance abuse appeared in the movie.[53]

It is worth noting that this war on substance abuse said relatively little about alcohol and tobacco use in motion pictures. Earlier in the century, the PCA had intervened regularly to tone down on-screen alcohol consumption. It had done little, though, to discourage smoking. Into the 1980s, movie actors were shown using alcohol and tobacco as a matter of course. Comparatively few films showed the consequences of abuse, despite substantial scientific research that had proven that both substances could pose health hazards. Indeed, some films deliberately encouraged use. In the 1992 movie *Basic Instinct*, screenwriter Joe Eszterhas, who described himself at the time as a "militant smoker," admitted that he included smoking as "part of a sexual subtext." Eszterhas created one scene in which Sharon Stone's character, a smoker, tried to seduce Michael Douglas's character, who was trying to quit, by blowing smoke in his face.[54] Smoking and alcohol use were widespread in many other movies. One study of the two hundred most popular video rentals for 1996–7 found that consumption of alcohol appeared in 93 percent of the pictures, and tobacco use in 89 percent. In more than one-third of the movies, alcohol use was associated with luxury or wealth, and also with violence or crime. In about one-fifth of the rentals, it was also associated with sexual activity. Fewer than half the movies depicted the negative consequences of alcohol use, and only 14 percent of the films showed someone refusing

---

[52] See "Bush Lashes Hollywood's Lax Attitude toward Drugs," *Toronto Star*, March 23, 1989, A28; Kelley, "Hollywood Plans Starring Role in Drug War," *USA Today*, June 23, 1989, A1; and "Bennett Urges Entertainment Industry to Join War on Drugs," *St. Petersburg Times*, Oct. 24, 1989, A3.

[53] These figures are taken from a study of video rentals during 1996 and 1997, sponsored by the Office of National Drug Control Policy. See Roberts, Henriksen, and Christenson, "Substance Use in Popular Movies and Music," *MediaCampaign* (April 1999), see "Executive Summary," and "Movie Findings" (http://www.mediacampaign.org/publications/movies/movie_partV.html).

[54] Quotations ("militant," "subtext"), Eszterhas, "Hollywood's Responsibility for Smoking Deaths," *NYT*, Aug. 9, 2002, A17. Eszterhas made this admission after he had been diagnosed with throat cancer. See also Eszterhas, *Hollywood Animal*, 726–8; also 701–36.

a drink that had been offered. Alcohol and tobacco use cut across all film genres.[55]

While critics remained unhappy with the way the entertainment industry depicted substance abuse, religious leaders also continued to express their dissatisfaction with Hollywood. Not only were they suspicious of how movies portrayed religion, they were also appalled by the rating system. Many of them had not approved of the adoption of the PG-13 rating by the industry. By 1990, though, an even more dubious change, from their perspective, was being considered: the creation of a new adult category that would reside between R and X. This plan was so outrageous in the eyes of some religious advocates that they mounted a drive to turn back entertainment to an earlier time. They hoped to revive Hollywood's Production Code, or at least a new version of it.

[55] See "Executive Summary," in Roberts, Henriksen, and Christenson, "Substance Use in Popular Movies and Music," at http://www.mediacampaign.org/publications/movies/movie_partI.html).

8

NC-17

For Jack Valenti and the MPAA, the attack by religious conservatives on the ways in which Hollywood portrayed religion was soon overshadowed by trouble closer to home. Rebellious moviemakers and exhibitors were becoming more critical of the rating system and impatient with Heffner. Their dissatisfaction peaked in 1990 when two lawsuits challenged the ratings system and some theater owners appeared ready to adopt their own movie classifications. These developments impelled the MPAA to replace the X rating with a new rating category called NC-17 and to provide – over Valenti's long-standing objections – explanations for why some ratings were given. However, these steps did not stop studios from exploiting the ratings for publicity, nor did they mollify the critics, especially those outside the industry, who had long been cynical about the rating system. In fact, the adoption of NC-17 only inflamed their already deteriorating relationship with the MPAA.

Filmmakers were unhappy that no rating existed for serious adult films that were not pornographic. The uncopyrighted X, originally designed for such adult pictures (e.g., *Midnight Cowboy* and *Last Tango in Paris*), had become synonymous with the hard-core industry. Now studios refused to accept anything worse than an R rating for their major productions. As writer-director Paul Schrader explained: "Every contract I sign says, 'I agree to submit an R film of no more than 120 minutes' – so it's a contractual obligation. The producers of a $30 million film don't want you to go out with an X. And no major release will go out unrated." As noted, to be X-rated or unclassified had several drawbacks. Many newspapers would not take advertising for such movies. It meant being excluded from desirable theater locations because some theater chains would not play X-rated films, and many malls had real-estate contracts that prohibited their showing. Television stations often would not carry such entertainment. All this amounted to economic coercion and was nothing less than censorship, moviemakers complained.[1]

The American Civil Liberties Union (ACLU), on whose national board Heffner once sat, agreed. It had also condemned the rating system, calling it an effort to "homogenize the content" of media and "a private combination of power" that limited "the marketplace of ideas in film."[2] The ACLU's executive director, Ira Glasser, said that every time a director agreed to a contract that required no less than an R-rated or PG-13-rated movie, an "episode of censorship" occurred. It was "impossible to calculate the amount of self-censorship" that took place as moviemakers struggled to stay within the rating system's boundaries. He pointed to the cuts made by Brian De Palma in *Scarface* and by Alan Parker in *Angel Heart*. If this type of cutting took place in the publishing world, few would fail to call it censorship; if the government imposed such a system, it would be "constitutionally impermissible," Glasser said.[3]

The historian in Heffner made him skeptical of this kind of criticism, and he clashed not only with filmmakers but parted company with the ACLU over this issue. Yes, he told Glasser, the contract did amount to censorship, but who was "doing the censoring? It's the damned film maker, who subjects himself – . . . for dollars, not for first amendment reasons, to this kind of garbage." If people were ready to compromise their ideas for profit, "and others are ready to buy or rent" these people, one could not seriously condemn the rating system for censorship. To those who accused CARA of censorship, he replied, "That just isn't so." CARA did not forbid subject matter or imagery. "For good or for bad, anything goes in this industry and in the system." The rating board never told anyone that a work would not be distributed unless the studio made cuts. "We don't give two hoots in hell what segments they include or don't include

[1] Paul Schrader quoted ("contract") in Collins, "Guidance or Censorship? New Debate on Rating Films," *NYT,* April 9, 1990, C11.

[2] Quotations ("homogenize," "film"), American Civil Liberties Union, "Rating Systems Sponsored by the Communications Industries, Policy #18," copy in doc. 88-14A, with Heffner, "Pre-Oral History Memorandum for 1988," Box 4, RDH-COHC-BL. See also Heffner, *Reminiscences,* vol. 8, p. 1498, Box 5, ibid.

[3] Quotations ("episode," "calculate," "impermissible"), Ira Glasser to Heffner, Nov. 3, 1988, doc. 88-14F, with Heffner, "Pre-Oral History Memorandum for 1988," Box 4, RDH-COHC-BL. Heffner, *Reminiscences,* vol. 8, p. 1501, Box 5, ibid.

in their films. We simply try, if they want a rating, to give them the one we believe most closely reflects parental attitudes." Putting matters more bluntly to Glasser, Heffner said that when it came to moviemakers he was "talking about people who rush to sell their souls. And while even whores have rights, if you must condemn anyone, condemn them." CARA did not ask filmmakers to censor their movies, he later told a reporter: "No film has to participate in the process, or even stay with the rating we give them."[4]

Moreover, Heffner understood that an X rating was not always a bad thing. Although it could be financially devastating to a large studio that invested heavily in a film, for smaller companies that could afford little advertising, the X could bring otherwise unobtainable publicity. At any rate, the issue was fundamentally not about ideas but about money. It was not a First Amendment concern, he told Glasser.[5]

CHALLENGING THE X

Several filmmakers challenged the rating system during 1990, a year Heffner considered a turning point. The films involved in the challenges included two pictures from Miramax Films, *The Cook, the Thief, His Wife and Her Lover* (1990), a dark comedy from Great Britain directed by Peter Greenaway, and *Tie Me Up! Tie Me Down!* (1990), from Spanish director Pedro Almodóvar. Also included was Maljack Productions's *Henry: Portrait of a Serial Killer* (1990). The makers of both *The Cook* and *Henry* refused to accept an X from CARA and released their pictures unrated. In addition, Maljack and Miramax went to court to contest the X ratings for *Henry* and for *Tie Me Up! Tie Me Down!*[6]

Movie critic Roger Ebert, who gave *The Cook* a favorable review, nevertheless warned that it was "not an easy film to sit through." The film is about an avaricious, sadistic husband (the thief, played by Michael Gambon) who, on most nights, can be found in a swank restaurant where, early in the film, in a fit of rage he forces the cook to eat excrement and then urinates on him. When his beautiful but frustrated and

---

[4] Quotations ("That," "hoots," "them"), Heffner to Ira Glasser, Nov. 9, 1988, doc. 88-14G, with Heffner, "Pre-Oral History Memorandum for 1988," Box 4, RDH-COHC-BL. Quotation ("participate"), Heffner quoted in Collins, "Guidance or Censorship?" C11. See also Heffner, *Reminiscences*, vol. 8, pp. 1501–2, Box 5, RDH-COHC-BL.
[5] Heffner, *Reminiscences*, vol. 8, p. 1502, Box 5, RDH-COHC-BL.
[6] See Heffner, "Pre-Oral History Memorandum for 1990," pp. 1–2, Box 2, RDH-COHC-BL; and Collins, "Guidance or Censorship?" C11.

long-suffering wife (played by Helen Mirren), begins an affair with a man (the lover, played by Alan Howard) whom she sees in the restaurant, the husband takes revenge by having his henchmen cram an entire book down the lover's throat, one page at a time. In addition, the movie featured cannibalism and male and female nudity. Some critics considered it a satire of the Margaret Thatcher regime. A *Washington Post* reviewer saw in the film "a metaphor so grand, so lavishly comprehensive, that it can stand as a final, definitive assessment of the state of Western civilization." At least four CARA members favored giving the picture an R, although Heffner thought the picture was "clearly X" and that most parents would consider it inappropriate for children. Although Ebert criticized the "timid souls" at CARA who had failed to give *The Cook* an R rating, Heffner agreed with other critics who thought the movie "would probably never have received such raves were it not for its X rating." Author Stephen Farber was not far off the mark, Heffner thought, when he had written that "the unqualified enthusiasm for...grisly films raises nagging questions about the skewed values of today's critics."[7]

Henry: Portrait of a Serial Killer, distributed by Maljack Productions, was a brutally explicit docudrama based loosely on the story of mass murderer Henry Lee Lucas. Maljack was an Illinois-based independent company involved primarily with distributing videocassettes. Filmed in 1985–6 with then little-known actors, the movie is about a psychopathic drifter, Henry (played by Michael Rooker), and his former prison buddy, Ottis (played by Tom Towles), who murder complete strangers with remorseless savagery. In one scene, the pair invade a home and videotape their murder of an entire family. The movie seemed too realistic for a typical slasher picture, and CARA gave it an X rating in March 1988 because of its violence. Early the next year, Maljack, which was not a MPAA member, surrendered its ratings certificate and released the picture unrated. When it was shown in Chicago and New York, it sparked

---

[7] Quotations ("easy," "timid"), see Ebert's review of *The Cook, the Thief, His Wife and Her Lover* (wysiwyg://142//http://www.suntimes.com/ebert/ebert_reviews/1990/01/thecook.html). The studio had been confronted with the choice of self-applying the X or releasing the picture unrated, Roger Ebert reported. Quotation ("metaphor"), Hinson, "Bestial Brew: 'The Cook,' Serving Up Squalor," *WP*, April 7, 1990, C1. Quotation ("clearly"), Heffner, "Pre-Oral History Memorandum for 1990," p. 66; see also ibid., 68–9, Box 2, RDH-COHC-BL. David Denby quoted ("raves") in ibid., 66. Quotation ("grisly"), Farber, "Movies: Why Do Critics Love These Repellent Movies?" *LAT*, March 17, 1991, Calendar sec., p. 5.

exchanges between those who thought it exemplified brilliant filmmaking and those who thought it too gruesome to watch. Because it lacked an R rating, *Henry* played in relatively few theaters.[8]

Of the three films, *Tie Me Up! Tie Me Down!* brought Heffner the severest criticism. That it opened about the same time as Arnold Schwarzenegger's science fiction movie *Total Recall* (1990) led to renewed charges that the ratings were biased against sex but not against violence. Despite its mean-spirited jokes about freaks and violence, which included a scene in which a man's eyeballs pop out of his head, *Total Recall* was R-rated. *Tie Me Up! Tie Me Down!*, in contrast, dealt mostly with sex, and to a lesser degree, profanity and substance abuse.[9] In Spanish with English subtitles, the movie starred Victoria Abril, who portrays a drug-addicted actress with a background in pornography. In the film, she is kidnapped by a former psychiatric patient (played by Antonio Banderas), who ties her up in the hope that she will fall in love with him, and she does. Several scenes caught the attention of the rating board. In one scene, the actress masturbates in the bathtub. In another, Abril and Banderas make love (under a picture of the Last Supper) in an intense and realistic manner. Twice women were shown urinating, and viewers saw Banderas' character trying to buy illicit drugs, including heroin, for his prisoner.

When it met on March 23, 1990, CARA voted unanimously to give the movie an X rating. Heffner, who had not been involved in the first vote, thought the picture probably deserved an R when he saw it, but when Miramax appealed, he had no difficulty defending the X. He believed the appeal was disingenuous and that the studio was merely exploiting the X for publicity (as he also thought it had done for *The Cook*). Before the appeal, Miramax held a party at which tiny souvenirs with an X on them were handed out, no doubt meant to recall Abril's bathtub scene. In Heffner's opinion, many members of the press willingly participated in this publicity scheme, portraying the rating board as "puritanical" about sex but soft on violence. As the *Los Angeles Times* reported, *Tie Me Up!*

---

[8] Ebert acknowledged that many viewers found *Henry* "too violent and disgusting to be endured," but he praised the picture because it dealt "honestly with its subject matter." Note quotations ("violent," "honestly"), Ebert's review of *Henry: Portrait of a Serial Killer*, Sept. 14, 1990 (www.suntimes.com/ebert/ebertser.html).

[9] Earlier Pedro Almodóvar gained praise for his film *Women on the Verge of a Nervous Breakdown* (1988), which had been nominated for an Academy Award for Best Foreign Film. See Barricklow, "Almodóvar Appeals X Rating on Latest Film," UPI release, April 24, 1990.

got an X for "one explicit but arguably non-arousing sex scene...while the extremely violent...*Total Recall,* replete with human mutilations, was graded R."[10]

Civil rights attorney William Kunstler represented Miramax at the appeal on April 24. Heffner found his presentation "terrible, totally unprepared." The Appeals Board split evenly, six to six, far short of the votes needed to change the rating. When Miramax released the film unrated on May 4, it played in twenty-five cities and in fewer than a hundred theaters.[11]

The rating controversies and legal challenges created by *The Cook, Henry,* and *Tie Me Up!* presented filmmakers with an opportunity to vent their frustration with Heffner and the system. Critics accused Heffner of brandishing the X "like a sword of Damocles," and used words like "imperious," "arrogant," and "duplicitous." "He's a bully," said producer Robert Radnitz, who had disagreed with Heffner over the rating for *A Hero Ain't Nothin' But a Sandwich* (1978) about a black teenager's struggle with drugs in the ghetto (the film eventually received a PG). Wes Craven, who directed horror films, including *The Hills Have Eyes* (1977), *A Nightmare on Elm Street* (1985), *Deadly Friend* (1986), and *Shocker* (1989), charged that Heffner had problems with movies that depicted "a certain level of rage," and that he simply refused to "allow a certain kind of view to be expressed, period." William Friedkin revisited his experience with *Cruising.* "He saw the picture himself four or five times. He flew in from New York just to see it. He made the decision, not the board. The board was more on the fence."[12] Eastwood, who had

---

[10] Quotation ("non-arousing"), S. Mitchell, "The X Rating Gets Its Day in Court," *LAT,* June 21, 1990, 1F. See also Granville, "Judge Asked to Overturn Film Rating System," *LAT,* June 22, 1990, F10; and Heffner, "Pre-Oral History Memorandum for 1990," p. 74, Box 2, RDH-COHC-BL.

[11] Heffner came to like William Kunstler, and later, not long before the attorney's death, had him as a guest on *The Open Mind.* Quotation ("terrible"), Heffner, "Pre-Oral History Memorandum for 1990," p. 76, Box 2, RDH-COHC-BL. See also ibid., pp. 69–75, 80, Box 2; Heffner, *Reminiscences,* vol. 9, pp. 1624–5, Box 5, RDH-COHC-BL; Collins, "Judge to Rule in July on X Rating for 'Tie Me Up!,'" *NYT,* June 22, 1990, C4; and UPI release, "Judge Adds a P.S. to X-Rated Film Ruling," *Bergen County Record* (NJ), July 22, 1990, E03.

[12] Quotations ("imperious," "duplicitous"), S. Mitchell, "The X Rating Gets Its Day in Court," F1. Alan Parker quoted ("arrogant"), ibid. Robert Radnitz quoted ("bully"), ibid. Wes Craven quoted ("rage," "period"), ibid. William Friedkin quoted ("fence"), ibid. See also Heffner, *Reminiscences,* vol. 8, p. 1421, Box 5, RDH-COHC-BL.

run-ins with Heffner on several films including *The Outlaw Josie Wales* (1976), *Honkytonk Man* (1982), *Sudden Impact* (1983), and *Pale Rider* (1985), weighed in, as did director Alan Parker, who accused Heffner of misleading him during the making of *Angel Heart* (1987).[13]

In such disputes, Heffner often could not be certain of how much support he had in the MPAA. He suspected that Valenti and the studios sometimes worked behind the scenes to undermine CARA. Valenti had lobbied for a more lenient rating for Craven's *Deadly Friend* when it had first been given an X, although Heffner convinced Warner Bros. to make enough changes in the film for its rating to be changed to R. The strong sexuality in Parker's *Angel Heart* had initially led the rating board to give the movie an X. Enough editing was done to move the film to an R, but at the same time, Heffner believed that the Tri-Star publicity campaign had done a "hatchet job" on CARA and that the MPAA's public relations people had been in on the smear.[14]

Along with the criticism of Heffner came a rising chorus denouncing the entire rating system and calling for change. A *Washington Post* writer said the X given to *The Cook* made Greenaway and Miramax seem heroic. Novelist and screenwriter Jesse Hill Ford called for abandoning the ratings altogether. The studios easily outwitted the rating board, he concluded. By charging censorship they could gain a good deal of free publicity for films that few people would ever see, or want to see. It was time to depend on responsible media, churches, and word-of-mouth to inform parents, Ford said. Radnitz also called for eliminating the rating system.[15] At the same time that Ford and Radnitz urged ending classification, other people called for adding a new rating category. The National Society of Film Critics urged adopting an "A" rating for adults only. Ebert and fellow film critic Gene Siskel used their nationally syndicated television program and their newspaper columns to endorse an "A" category.[16]

---

[13] For *Sudden Impact,* see Heffner, "Pre-Oral History Memorandum for 1983," p. 42, also 43–4, Box 2, RDH-COHC-BL. See also Heffner, *Reminiscences,* vol. 1, p. 97, Box 5, ibid. For *Pale Rider* and other films, see Heffner, "Pre-Oral History Memorandum for 1985," p. 7, Box 2, ibid. For *Angel Heart,* which starred Mickey Rourke and Lisa Bonet, see S. Mitchell, "The X Rating Gets Its Day in Court," F1.

[14] Quotation ("hatchet"), Heffner, *Reminiscences,* vol. 8, p. 1426, Box 5, RDH-COHC-BL. See also ibid., vol. 7, pp. 1313–18, Box 5, ibid.

[15] See Hinson, "Bestial Brew," C1; Ford, "Abolish Film Ratings; Trust the Moviegoers," *USA Today,* May 2, 1990, A10; and Radnitz, "Counterpunch: It's Time to Eliminate the Present Movie Rating System," *LAT,* July 23, 1990, F5.

[16] See Ebert's review of *The Cook, the Thief, His Wife and Her Lover* (wysiwyg:// 142//http://www.suntimes.com/ebert/ebert_reviews/1990/01/thecook.html). See also S.

Valenti remained unimpressed, and in early May 1990 defended the status quo in a *Washington Post* guest editorial. Calls for reform sounded "like the mating call of a randy rhino," he said, and he speculated that attacks on the rating system had been inspired by the work of a few "public relations wizards." He had seen no indication that parents were unhappy with the system. To add a new category would make matters too complicated. It would require CARA members to distinguish between "an 'artistic' portrayal of aberrational behavior...and a 'nonartistic' one. Alas, that is a task for divinely inspired miracle workers, not rating board members." Two weeks later, Valenti defended the system when he appeared on Siskel and Ebert's television program.[17]

For quite some time, Heffner had favored adding a category between R and X, but he objected to the A classification recommended by Ebert and others. He was unhappy with Ebert who, he felt, had misrepresented CARA's work in the past, especially in the controversy over *Cruising*. He thought that Ebert misunderstood the purpose of the ratings, or at least was unsympathetic to the system's goals. To adopt the A would change the nature of CARA's work because it would ask the board to make a judgment between "'good' not-for children" films and "'bad' not-for-children" pictures, the former presumably getting an A, the latter an X. He also suspected that Ebert had ulterior motives because, in June 1990, an application had been submitted to re-rate Russ Meyer's *Beyond the Valley of the Dolls* (1970), a movie that Ebert had helped to write. The film, one of the first exploitation pictures made by a major studio (20th Century Fox), became a cult hit. Containing nudity, promiscuous sex, casual drug use, lesbianism, stereotypes of gay males, and several grisly murders, including a decapitation, it originally received an X from CARA (before Heffner's time). When it was later re-rated, it again received an X. Rating the Meyer-Ebert movie A would presumably move it into the category of "'good' not-for-children films." After watching Valenti on the Siskel and Ebert program, Heffner urged him to create a new category immediately – not the evaluative kind that Ebert had been recommending,

Mitchell, "The X Rating Gets Its Day in Court," F1. Kunstler also advocated a rating between R and X to designate movies with strong sexuality but "in which sex is not used for sex's sake, but for the story's sake." Kunstler quoted ("sex") in Yarrow, "Almodóvar Film's X Rating Is Challenged in Lawsuit," *NYT,* May 24, 1990, C14.
[17] Quotation ("mating," "members"), Valenti, "Art, Smut and Movie Ratings," *WP,* May 6, 1990, B7. See also Braxton, "Morning Report: TV & Video," *LAT,* May 21, 1990, F2.

but a rating that would replace the X and simply be designated "NC" for No Children.[18]

Meanwhile, Maljack Productions and Miramax Films (together with Almodóvar) filed suits challenging the X ratings given to *Henry: Portrait of a Serial Killer* and to *Tie Me Up! Tie Me Down!* These were the first suits contesting the constitutionality of the MPAA's ratings since 1970, when producer-director Joseph Strick had sued the MPAA and Paramount challenging the X rating given to his adaption of Henry Miller's *Tropic of Cancer*.[19] Filmmakers watched these cases closely, as two other soon-to-be-released movies, Martin Scorsese's *Goodfellas* (1990) and David Lynch's *Wild at Heart* (1990), were also expected to test the classification system. The U.S. District Court for the District of Columbia dismissed the Maljack suit in October without much fanfare, but the Miramax case resulted in considerable publicity, most of it bad for the MPAA.[20]

The *Tie Me Up!* suit, filed in the New York State Supreme Court, was heard by Judge Charles E. Ramos on June 7. Kunstler argued that the X rating had been "arbitrary, capricious and unreasonable," that the system had become a "private preserve" favoring American-made movies and was prejudiced against foreign pictures and independent producers. The sex scenes in *Tie Me Up!* he contended, were no worse than those shown in several R-rated films made by larger studios: *The Postman Always Rings*

---

[18] The NC would be consistent with the other ratings and reemphasize that the rating system was "simply and purely age-specific and box-office-admission-policy-specific," Heffner said. Quotation ("simply"), Heffner to Valenti, May 22, 1990, doc. [90-1], with Heffner, "Pre-Oral History Memorandum for 1990," Box 2, RDH-COHC-BL. See also Heffner to Valenti, Nov. 11, 1981; and Heffner to Valenti, March 11, 1987, ibid. Quotation ("'good'"), Heffner, "Pre-Oral History Memorandum for 1990," p. 44; see also ibid., p. 43, Box 2, ibid. See also Heffner, *Reminiscences* (Editing Copy), vol. 8, pp. 1422–5, Box 5, ibid.; Hunt, "Home Tech/Video: New Releases from the 'Valley' of the Clunkers," *LAT,* May 21, 1993, F24; and Klawans, "It's One Long Dirty Joke But Hey, Man, It's a Classic," *NYT,* Nov. 17, 2002, sec. 2, p. 13.

[19] Joseph Strick argued the X rating violated Sherman antitrust laws. See Weiler, "Producer with 'X' Sues Over Rating," *NYT,* March 10, 1970, p. 51.

[20] On May 14, 1990, Maljack Productions filed suit in federal court in Washington, DC. The suit involving *Tie Me Up! Tie Me Down!* came a few days later. See Yarrow, "Almodóvar Film's X Rating Is Challenged in Lawsuit," *NYT,* C14. See also *Maljack Productions, Inc., vs. Motion Picture Association of America,* 1990 U.S. Dist. LEXIS 13284 (Oct. 3, 1990) (Civil Action No. 90–1121). Maljack appealed the dismissal. See *Maljack Productions, Inc. vs. Motion Picture Association of America,* 311 U.S. App. D.C. 224; 52 F. 3d 373; 1995 U.S. App. LEXIS 9675 (April 28, 1995) (No. 93-7244). This case reversed the district court's order that dismissed the original complaint and remanded the case for additional proceedings.

Twice (1981), *Body Heat* (1981), *9½ Weeks* (1986), *Blue Velvet* (1986), *Fatal Attraction* (1987), *No Way Out* (1987), *The Accused* (1988), and *Lethal Weapon 2* (1989).[21]

The MPAA found Ramos's ruling troubling. Although he upheld the X rating and agreed that Miramax had brought the suit, in part, to gain publicity, he questioned the system's integrity. The ratings amounted to "censorship from within the industry," and they failed to shield children from inappropriate images. "The industry that profits from scenes of mass murder, dismemberment and the portrayal of war as noble and glamorous apparently has no interest in the opinions of professionals, only the opinions of its consumers," the judge concluded. He criticized the lack of medical and psychiatric professionals to advise CARA. The MPAA's more lenient approach toward violence was inexcusable, and he urged the industry either to revise the system or to abandon it. Ramos did not rule out future legal challenges. "My hands were tied," he remarked after releasing the opinion, "but I left open the door . . . for a case to be made of discrimination against foreign film makers, or against certain types of film makers."[22]

In the reactions to the case, some saw problems with the judge's suggestion to bring psychiatrists and other professionals into the rating process. It would change the nature of the system, said Charles Champlin of the *Los Angeles Times,* and would result in "a nightmare of intrusion in the creative process that would dwarf any of the present cries that the ratings constitute censorship." Valenti issued an even sourer assessment. Almost everything Ramos had said was "absurdly wrong," he argued. "The system is for parental responsibility," and the "judge completely overlooked that."[23]

---

[21] Floyd Abrams, who represented the MPAA, argued that Miramax sought to create and impose a state-controlled rating system, something that would have violated New York law and the First Amendment. Quotation ("arbitrary"), Yarrow, "Almodóvar Film's X Rating Is Challenged," C14. Kunstler quoted ("preserve") in S. Mitchell, "The X Rating Gets Its Day in Court," F1.

[22] Charles E. Ramos quoted ("industry," "consumers") in Collins, "Judge Upholds X Rating For Almodóvar Film," *NYT,* July 20, 1990, C12. Ramos's opinion quoted ("censorship") in Kasindorf, "Judge's 'X' Ruling Rated an 'F,'" *Newsday,* July 21, 1990, 6. Ramos quoted ("hands," "makers") in ibid. See also UPI release, "Judge Adds A.P.S. to X-Rated Film Ruling," E03.

[23] Quotation ("dwarf"), Champlin, "Critics at Large: MPAA Ratings: A Crisis of Confidence, a System in Disarray," *LAT,* July 24, 1990, F3. Valenti quoted ("absurdly") in Kasindorf, "Judge's 'X' Ruling Rated an 'F,'" 6. Valenti quoted ("system," "overlooked") in Fox, "Rating System Faces Challenges on Two Fronts," *LAT,* July 21, 1990, F1. See also Collins, "Judge to Rule in July on X Rating for 'Tie Me Up!'," C4.

The suits filed on behalf of *Tie Me Up!* and *Henry* encouraged others to challenge the system and led to speculation that the ratings might "be sued out of existence." In early July, Omega Entertainment announced that it would file a $15 million suit to challenge the X given to its movie *In the Cold of the Night* (1990). Nico Mastorakis, who had produced and directed the film, described the movie as a psychological thriller and claimed that it had been denied an R because of a "three-minute non-explicit love scene." Mastorakis planned to finance a seven-person independent rating panel made up of well-known film critics. "It is our duty to remove the ax from the hands of the executioner," he said.[24]

Also in July, a number of well-known directors – Sydney Pollack, Francis Ford Coppola, Ron Howard, Spike Lee, Barry Levinson, John Sayles, Rob Reiner, and others – signed a petition in the form of an open letter to Valenti. It charged that "the taint of an X rating clearly results in massive and arbitrary corporate censorship" because "an X-rated or unrated film is denied exhibition in thousands of cinemas worldwide." It called for the creation of an "A" or "M" category to warn of "strong adult themes or images, and that minors are not to view them."[25]

Although delivered to Valenti shortly after Ramos's ruling, the petition had been circulated earlier by a small New York distributor, Silverlight Entertainment, which was promoting Wayne Wang's movie *Life Is Cheap... But Toilet Paper Is Expensive* (1990). Set in Hong Kong, the film tells the story of a crime boss and reputedly had scenes showing coprophilia and defecation. Mark Lipsky, Silverlight's president, claimed that several parts of the film would have to be cut or altered in order to avoid an X rating. These included a scene showing a nude pregnant woman in a magazine photograph, a scene with scatological humor, and scenes of a recurring nightmare in which a person's arms are being ripped off. Lipsky argued that the movie was no more violent than the R-rated films *Total Recall* or *Die Hard 2* (in which more than two hundred deaths occurred).[26]

---

[24] Quotation ("sued"), Champlin, "Critics at Large," F3. Nico Mastorakis quoted ("three-minute," "executioner") in J. Mathews, "Top Directors Join New Drive to Overhaul X," *LAT*, July 5, 1990, F7.

[25] "An Open Letter to Jack Valenti...," quoted ("taint," "minors") in "Hollywood Film Makers Protest Rating System," *NYT*, July 21, 1990, A14.

[26] Lipsky believed that if the rating system was to be changed, the pressure had to come from the major MPAA studios rather than from the independent producers. See J. Mathews, "Top Directors Join New Drive to Overhaul X," F7; and Hall, "Occasional," *WP*, Aug. 10, 1990, C2.

Silverlight released *Life Is Cheap* in late August with a self-imposed "A" rating accompanied with an explanation that, while the film had a serious purpose, some of its scenes might be inappropriate for children. The *New York Times,* which normally did not run ads for X- or self-rated films, accepted advertising for the movie. Silverlight's strategy was repeated by another distributor, Shapiro-Glickenhaus, for an X-rated movie entitled *Frankenhooker,* (1990) about a mad scientist who attempts to restore life to his dead fiancée. Shapiro-Glickenhaus had lost two appeals and preferred to use the self-imposed A rather than release the film unrated or with an X. By late July, *Frankenhooker* was being shown mostly in art theaters and to midnight audiences in Los Angeles and in perhaps twenty other cities.[27]

Exhibitors were also starting to take matters into their own hands. In Cleveland, the owner of the independent Colony Theatre, which seated more than thirteen hundred people, announced that he was dropping CARA's ratings. Henceforth, he would rate movies "F" for family fare, "L" for profanity, "A" for adult subject matter, "V" for violence, and "X" for sex.[28]

HENRY AND JUNE

By late July 1990, speculation was rife that the system might not survive unless it replaced the X with another classification that would alert theater owners to films that might bring legal action if shown to those under seventeen. Despite Valenti's public disavowals that no change was needed, privately he feared more lawsuits and wished to defuse criticism.[29] He, and a majority of the major studio chiefs, now leaned toward creating a new rating category, possibly called "RR." But he encountered opposition from at least two studio executives and from exhibitors. One studio head, Joe Roth of 20th Century Fox, opposed jettisoning the X, because he

---

[27] Rohter, "A 'No Children' Category to Replace the 'X' Rating," *NYT,* Sept. 27, 1990, A1; and Kasindorf, "Future of X-Rating Debated," *Newsday,* Aug. 9, 1990, 7 (Nassau and Suffolk Edition); Fox, "Valenti Agrees to Talk to Critics of Movie Ratings," *LAT,* July 26, 1990, F7. For the *New York Times* accepting A ratings, see Hall, "Occasional," C2; and Fox, "Jack Valenti Says Change Possible for Film Ratings," *LAT,* Aug. 10, 1990, F1.

[28] See Wilson, "Outtakes: Ahead of His Time?" *LAT,* Aug. 5, 1990, Calendar sec., 23.

[29] Valenti defended the system in *USA Today,* saying that responsible parents were its bedrock and that there was no need to inject psychiatrists or government officials into the rating process. Valenti, "Movie Rating System Is Working Fine [Guest Columnist]," *USA Today,* July 26, 1990. See also Champlin, "Critics at Large," F3; and Mathews, "Oct. 3 Marks the Spot for Movie Showdown," *LAT,* Sept. 15, 1990, F1.

believed that its association with pornography, and the economic losses that association guaranteed, remained the best way to keep recalcitrant moviemakers in line. Filmmakers who aggressively challenged convention would consider the NC-17 a weaker deterrent than an X, in his opinion. The theater owners argued that having to check identifications at adults-only movies would create bottlenecks at entrances. Moreover, a new rating would make them, not parents or CARA, primarily responsible for the system's integrity.[30]

Although dismayed that he had not been able to obtain an agreement for a new rating category, Valenti moved forward. In early August, he met in Hollywood with directors and writers, some of whom had signed the petition asking for a new rating category; afterward he reportedly said that "nothing lasts, everything is subject to change." But he also warned that an A rating might cause the system to collapse, because if CARA started evaluating, or grading, adult pictures, it could reopen the movie industry to state and municipal legislation. "If people don't believe that could happen," he said, "look at the furor over the National Endowment for the Arts," which was then under attack by conservatives in Congress and elsewhere for its funding of Robert Mapplethorpe's work.[31]

With pressure for change building, Wasserman's Universal Studios went forward with plans to make *Henry and June,* a film about the ménage à trois of writer Henry Miller (played by Fred Ward), his wife June (Uma Thurman), and the diarist Anaïs Nin (Maria de Medeiros). The story, based on Nin's diary, included nudity, profanity, and both heterosexual and lesbian love scenes, and critics considered it more graphic than *Tie Me Up! Tie Me Down!* Would CARA hold *Henry and June* to the same standard as *Tie Me Up!* and would the MPAA uphold the standard when Universal appealed?[32]

CARA reviewed the movie in early June and gave it an X. Heffner told director Philip Kaufman, who earlier had directed such films as *The*

---

[30] See Heffner, *Reminiscences,* vol. 8, pp. 1598–9; and vol. 9, p. 1603, Box 5, RDH-COHC-BL; Champlin, "Critics at Large," F3; and Mathews, "Oct. 3 Marks the Spot for Movie Showdown," F1.

[31] Valenti quoted ("nothing") in Fox, "Jack Valenti Says Change Possible for Film Ratings," *LAT,* Aug. 10, 1990, F1. Valenti quoted ("people," "Arts") in C. Hall, "Directors, MPAA Chief Meet on Film Ratings," *WP,* Aug. 10, 1990, C2. See also Heffner, *Reminiscences,* vol. 9, p. 1602, Box 5, RDH-COHC-BL; and Fox, "Valenti Agrees to Talk to Critics of Movie Ratings," *LAT,* July 26, 1990, F7.

[32] See Mathews, "Oct. 3 Marks the Spot for Movie Showdown," F1.

Right Stuff (1983) and *The Unbearable Lightness of Being* (1988), to release *Henry and June* as an X, because to make the necessary cuts to earn the R would "eviscerate" what he considered to be "an absolutely beautiful, splendid film." When the rating board watched the final version of *Henry and June* about three months later, it still adhered to the X because of several sex scenes. CARA was not trying to brand the movie pornographic, Heffner tried to explain. "But we believe most parents would consider this out of bounds for children. All we're saying with an X rating is that this is an adult film."[33]

Henry and June (Fig. 13) premiered at the Venice Film Festival on September 14, and then was released throughout the rest of Europe. But as of early September, with the ratings controversy over the film continuing, no American release was scheduled.[34]

Clearly Universal and its parent company, Music Corporation of America (which controlled the Cineplex Odeon theater chain), were unlikely to settle for an X rating. At the time, about half of American theaters would not play X-rated movies, and television would not take advertising for them, no matter how critically acclaimed they might be.[35] Kaufman's contract with Universal gave him the right to make the final cuts on the film, but only if it qualified for an R. As Universal president Tom Pollock explained, the studio would not release an X-rated film. He felt that he had little choice but to challenge the rating. The appeal, scheduled for October 3, promised to be nasty.

As battle lines were drawn, defenders of the movie associated it with the long struggle for literary freedom. The studio turned to Alan Dershowitz for advice. Kaufman argued that the movie was not unlike Henry Miller's novel, *Tropic of Cancer*, which had been available in Europe for almost thirty years before being allowed to be published in the United States in 1964. Even then, it faced litigation in several states until the U.S. Supreme Court said the work was not obscene. "In a way, our film is about the struggle for freedom from censorship," he said. "So it's ironic that the first people to see the movie were a board of censors." Pollock said that "Henry Miller stood for freedom of expression and waged a life-long battle against literacy [*sic*] censorship." It was therefore appropriate that *Henry and*

[33] Heffner quoted ("eviscerate") by Philip Kaufman in Farber, "A Major Studio Plans to Test the Rating System," *NYT*, Sept. 4, 1990, C14. Heffner quoted ("absolutely," "adult film") by Farber in ibid.
[34] Ibid.
[35] Ibid.; and Maslin, "Is NC-17 an X in a Clean Raincoat?" *NYT*, Oct. 21, 1990, sec. 2, p.1.

FIGURE 13. Maria de Medeiros, Henry Ward, and Uma Thurman in Universal's *Henry and June* (1990). The film was about the ménage à trois of writer Henry Miller (played by Ward), his wife, June (Thurman), and was based on the diary of Anaïs Nin (played by de Medeiros). It was the first movie to receive an NC-17 rating. Photograph courtesy of the Wisconsin Center for Film and Theater Research.

June be "remembered as a work that was pivotal in bringing about a change in the way adult-themed motion pictures are made available to the public."[36]

Before the appeal of *Henry and June*'s X rating took place, the MPAA and National Association of Theater Owners announced on September 26 that the X category would be dropped in favor of the NC-17 rating (no children under seventeen allowed). The expectation – or at least the hope – was that the new rating would remove the stigma of pornography from serious adult pictures. Valenti was not so certain. "I expect criticism to continue," he speculated. "I do know, however, that what I'm doing is in the long-range best interests of an enduring and useful ratings system."[37]

[36] Philip Kaufman quoted ("way," "censors") in Farber, "A Major Studio Plans to Test the Rating System," C14. Tom Pollock quoted ("Miller," "public") in "Universal Pictures to Release 'Henry & June' as First Film with NC-17 Rating," *PR Newswire*, Sept. 26, 1990. See also Rohter, "A 'No Children' Category to Replace the 'X' Rating," *NYT*, Sept. 27, 1990, A1; and De Grazia and Newman, *Banned Films*, 107–10.

[37] Valenti quoted ("expect," "system") in Hinson, "Film Industry Revises Rating System," *WP*, Sept. 27, 1990, A1.

With the NC-17 rating came progress on providing the public with information about why ratings had been given. Henceforth, R-rated movies would carry short explanations about why they had been restricted. Two years later (July 1992), the industry began offering explanatory statements for the PG and PG-13. It was all part of a trend, said NATO's president William F. Kartozian, "to make ourselves more user-friendly."[38]

For those at Universal, the announcement of the new rating category came at an opportune time. Kaufman applauded it as "a fresh, bold step." Pollock immediately pushed to have *Henry and June* given an NC-17, which he thought would be "a rating with honor, rather than...dishonor." But Heffner, in an attempt to keep Wasserman's name from being associated with the new category, suggested that Pollock wait to allow another movie to be the first to receive the NC-17. When Pollock refused and *Henry and June* was released in the United States on October 5, it became the first film to carry the NC-17 rating. From that point on, according to Heffner, the rating "literally" became "known around town as Lew Wasserman's rating."[39] Valenti denied that Wasserman or Universal had influenced the decision to reform the ratings. Russell Schwartz of Miramax Films, who praised the new category, was nevertheless more skeptical about why the NC-17 had been adopted. It was meant to avoid an awkward situation: "The ratings appeal for 'Henry and June' was scheduled for October 3...and the release for October 5. I think the timing of these changes speaks for itself."[40]

GATEKEEPING

The dispute over replacing the X rating involved a struggle for power. Protestant and Catholic leaders preferred the X because of the stigma it carried. It served as a barrier that kept a certain level of explicit sexuality and violence out of the mainstream. They saw its abandonment as

---

[38] William F. Kartozian quoted ("user-friendly") in Fox, "Ratings to Give Parents More Data," *LAT,* July 29, 1992, F1. See also Hinson, "Film Industry Revises Rating System," A1. For an explanation of each category, see also "NC-17, R or PG-13? How the MPAA Votes," *CST,* Jan. 23, 1994, Show sec., p. 4.

[39] Philip Kaufman quoted ("bold") and Tom Pollock quoted ("dishonor") in Hinson, "Film Industry Revises Rating System," A1. Quotation ("literally"), Heffner, "Pre-Oral History Memorandum for 1990," 14–15; see also ibid., 28–9, Box 2, RDH-COHC-BL.

[40] Russell Schwartz quoted ("speaks") in Hinson, "Film Industry Revises Rating System," A1.

an effort to legitimize material previously off-limits. Studio executives, including Roth, also saw the X as a gate that kept undesirable filmmakers at bay. Some observers believed that the adoption of NC-17 involved a subtle shift that gave directors advantage at the expense of the producers. Directors such as Paul Verhoeven and Oliver Stone became hot properties in Hollywood.[41] It quickly became apparent, though, that the NC-17 would carry much the same baggage as had the X. Opponents of the new rating mounted protests and threatened boycotts. The NC-17 soon became a disreputable brand in some quarters. Studios drafted contracts that would not accept an NC-17 rating, and some video chains would not stock movies so rated.

The adoption of the NC-17 hardly stopped studios from exploiting the ratings for publicity, as was evident in the marketing of *Basic Instinct* (1992), starring Michael Douglas and Sharon Stone. Douglas plays a policeman who enters into an affair with a murder suspect, played by Stone. Stone's character is a wealthy bisexual mystery writer who had written a novel describing an ice-pick murder very similar to a real murder that had been committed. Joe Eszterhas wrote the screenplay and Carolo Pictures, which had produced *Terminator 2* (1991), reportedly purchased the script from him for $3 million. Tri-Star Pictures, part of the Sony Corporation, distributed the film. Paul Verhoeven, a Dutch moviemaker, directed *Basic Instinct*. He had made such violent and successful futuristic thrillers as *Robocop* (1987) and *Total Recall*, and was well aware of how the ratings game was played. (CARA originally voted to give *Robocop* an X for violence, but then, after much haggling with MGM and over Heffner's objections, changed the rating to R after revisions were made.)[42]

The makers of *Basic Instinct* generated tremendous publicity for the movie before it ever appeared in theaters by capitalizing on several themes: accusations of gay and lesbian stereotyping, Stone's nudity, reportedly steamy sex scenes and the cutting of almost a minute of footage involving Douglas and Stone, and charges that CARA had mishandled the ratings. Heffner believed that these were manufactured controversies and that the press was again a willing co-conspirator. "The American press can't be

---

[41] See remarks by Heffner and Charles Champlin in Heffner, *Reminiscences*, vol. 9, pp. 1602–4, Box 5, RDH-COHC-BL.

[42] Easton, "Eszterhas vs. Verhoeven," *LAT*, Aug. 23, 1990, F1. See also Weinraub, "Violent Melodrama of a Sizzling Movie Brings Rating Battle," *NYT*, Jan. 30, 1992, C15; and Heffner, *Reminiscences*, vol. 8, pp. 1480–1, Box 5, RDH-COHC-BL.

bought," he would later say, "but it can be sold...bills of goods." At some level, reporters had "a sense of the essential dishonesty of the whole proceeding in Hollywood," in his opinion.[43]

And so the buildup began. In late August 1990, the *Los Angeles Times* reported that Eszterhas and producer Irwin Winkler had quit the film (although Eszterhas would keep his $3 million fee) in a disagreement with Verhoeven because the director wanted to turn the movie into a "sexually explicit thriller," adding a lesbian lovemaking scene and frontal nudity. Douglas, who was reported to have been paid more than $10 million up front with guarantees that might raise the total to $15 million, agreed with Verhoeven's changes and indicated that he might replace Winkler as producer. An article appeared in a well-known trade publication about how Hollywood images fueled gay and lesbian bashing. During the making of *Basic Instinct*, gay groups organized street protests in San Francisco in order to disrupt filming, and a leader of the Gay and Lesbian Alliance against Defamation in Los Angeles denounced the movie for branding lesbians as man haters.[44]

Then there were the sex scenes. One of the most talked about involved Stone crossing and uncrossing her legs in front of police during an interrogation. Stone was said to have expressed surprise that the camera would zoom in for a revealing shot. Verhoeven, though, set the record straight in an interview in the *Miami Herald*. "Now wait just a moment!" he said. "She says she didn't know?! She knew I was going to do that. Absolutely! She gave me her panties as a present before I shot the scene! She's just upset because it is more clear and less dark than she thought."[45] Publicity also promised unusually explicit lovemaking scenes between Douglas and Stone, and between Douglas and actress Jeanne Tripplehorn. Richard Corliss of *Time* magazine called *Basic Instinct* a "cop-and-copulation thriller," with a climactic scene "drenched in violence." It had, he said, "courted scandal" from the start. The *New York Times* reported in early 1992 that studio executives who had previewed the film considered it "the steamiest movie of the year." Rarely had a picture, "especially one

---

[43] Quotations ("American," "Hollywood"), Heffner, *Reminiscences,* vol. 2, pp. 263–4, Box 5, RDH-COHC-BL.

[44] Joe Eszterhas quoted ("explicit") in Easton, "Eszterhas vs. Verhoeven," F1. See also Heffner, "Pre-Oral History Memorandum for 1992," p. 21, Box 2, RDH-COHC-BL; and Weinraub, "Violent Melodrama," C15.

[45] Paul Verhoeven quoted ("Now," "thought") in Murphy, "Director: Don't Take *Instinct* the Wrong Way," *Miami Herald,* March 22, 1992, I 5.

that so few people have seen, stirred such intense discussion, rumor and uneasiness and rung so many alarms." The movie seemed "a guaranteed blockbuster."[46]

Yet, despite the massive buildup, it appeared as though *Basic Instinct* might be headed for financial trouble. It seemed clear that if Verhoeven and Douglas carried through on their plans, the film would get an NC-17, a rating that would be financially disastrous for Carolo Pictures, and perhaps for Douglas too. The Carolo Corporation reportedly teetered "on the edge of collapse," and *Basic Instinct* would be "either a lifeline from drowning or a lead weight that will sink the company." Douglas was also thought to have a heavy financial stake in it. Valenti let Heffner know that the actor had his "last $14 million" in the picture.[47]

There remained the publicity bonanza to be gained from exploiting the movie's likely rating. Verhoeven, whose contract obligated him to deliver no worse than an R-rated film to Tri-Star, of course had every intention of making the necessary changes to obtain that rating. But much hyperbole surrounded the changes that were made, and the film, or at least parts of it, was shown to the ratings board more than a dozen times before CARA awarded the R. Verhoeven trimmed a brutal ice-pick attack during an explicit sex scene and cut about forty-seven seconds from a lovemaking scene between Douglas and Stone. In his public appearances to promote the movie, Douglas made the most of the cuts. He appeared on the *Tonight Show with Jay Leno* to suggest how much could happen in those forty-plus seconds. Ebert contributed to the buzz with a tongue-in-cheek piece from the Cannes Film Festival in May saying that he had seen the forty-five seconds cut from the Douglas-Stone love scene. The R-rated movie opened March 20, 1992, in about 1,000 to 1,200 American theaters. A more sexually explicit, unrated version of the movie was released abroad. The forty-plus seconds that had been cut were restored to some videotape editions in 1993, and both the R-rated and unrated versions were available for rental.[48]

[46] Quotation ("cop-and-," "scandal"), Corliss, "What Ever Became of NC-17?" *Time* 139 (Jan. 27, 1992), 64. Unnamed film executives quoted ("steamiest," "blockbuster") in Weinraub, "Violent Melodrama," C15. See also Heffner, *Reminiscences*, vol. 1, p. 113, Box 5, RDH-COHC-BL.

[47] Quotations ("collapse," "lifeline"), Weinraub, "Violent Melodrama," C15. Valenti quoted ("last") in Heffner, *Reminiscences*, vol. 1, p. 115, Box 5, RDH-COHC-BL.

[48] See Grimes, "Reviewing the NC-17 Film Rating: Clear Guide or an X by a New Name?" *NYT,* Nov. 30, 1992, C11; Ebert, "Satisfying the Most Basic of Instincts: Curiosity," *CST,* May 8, 1992, sec. 2, p. 33; and Welkos, "Director Trims 'Basic Instinct' to Get R Rating," *LAT,* Feb. 11, 1992, F1.

Other studios played the NC-17 card to advertise their movies. When Disney executives realized that *Color of Night* (1994) – which is about a psychiatrist (played by Bruce Willis) who encounters death threats after taking over a therapy group from a murdered associate – might not meet expectations, they publicized Willis's full frontal nudity in the film. "It was Disney's plan all along to use the erotic elements to attract an audience," admitted Richard Rush, the picture's director. "There was a tacit conspiracy between the press and the public relations department to exploit the NC-17." But little doubt existed that an R-rated film would be delivered to the theaters. "Most of the papers suggested I was fighting for an NC-17, which is wrong," Rush said. "I had signed a contract to deliver an R-rated film." The scenes of Willis that had been cut for theaters were reinserted for the NC-17 version released on video.[49]

Releasing multiple versions of a movie on video was common practice. The producers of *Whore* (1991) used this strategy. The film, directed by Ken Russell and starring Theresa Russell (no relation), was about the life of a prostitute. Ken Russell had clashed with CARA over another movie about a prostitute called *Crimes of Passion* (1984). Trimark Pictures, which distributed *Whore*, challenged the film's NC-17 rating, arguing that another recent film that glamorized the life of a prostitute, *Pretty Woman* (1990), had been rated R. *Whore*'s marketers said that their movie should be seen by young people because it was offered "as a lesson in the realities of street life."[50] Heffner pointed out that *Whore* differed from *Pretty Woman,* and that it had been given the NC-17 because it was "chock full of graphic violence" and intense sensuality and profanity.[51] That said, Heffner did not apparently consider that *Pretty Woman* and its beautiful star, Julia Roberts, might have done far more than *Whore* to glamorize the life of prostitution. After its unsuccessful appeal, Trimark released an R-rated version of the film in October 1991, but it had only a brief run in theaters. Vidmark Entertainment, eager to capitalize on the publicity, released the movie on home video in early 1992, sooner than the normal six-month delay between theatrical appearance and video debut. Moreover, Vidmark released the picture in four video versions: the NC-17, an R-rated version, an unrated director's cut that added two minutes of film not seen in theaters, and a variant with a new title. Fearing that

[49] Richard Rush quoted ("Disney's," "conspiracy," "R-rated") in Brodie, "NC-17 Threat Highly Rated by Marketers," *CST,* Sept. 6, 1994, sec. 2, p. 27.
[50] Quotation ("lesson"), Fox, "Movie on Prostitution Still Gets an NC-17 Rating," *LAT,* Sept. 9, 1991, F2.
[51] Richard Heffner quoted ("chock"), ibid.

supermarkets might not carry a movie called *Whore,* the R-rated cassette was also sold under the title *If You Can't Say It, Just See It.* Vidmark shipped about ninety thousand copies of *Whore* to video stores, and in late January 1992 it was the studio's second most popular release. The unrated version accounted for about 65 percent of the order and the NC-17 copy another 15 percent.[52]

There were several other well-known movies for which the NC-17 rating was at issue during the early 1990s. Peter Greenaway's *Prospero's Books* (1991) and Louis Malle's *Damage* (1993) originally received an NC-17 before being edited to an R.[53] Other movies that were reedited to avoid the NC-17 included *The Lover* (1992), directed by Jean-Jacques Annaud, and *Body of Evidence* (1993), a vehicle for Madonna and Willem Dafoe, and one that billboards proclaimed to be "the erotic thriller of the year."[54] Some moviemakers chose to retain the NC-17 rating, as was the case for Abel Ferrara's *Bad Lieutenant* (1993) and Fine Line Features' *Wide Sargasso Sea* (1993), a film based on Jean Rhys's novel. For the latter two movies, both an R-rated and an unrated version could be rented on videocassette in addition to the NC-17 version.[55]

One of Heffner's last NC-17 controversies involved director Oliver Stone and his film *Natural Born Killers* (1994). By this time, Stone had achieved notoriety as a talented filmmaker. No stranger to cinematic violence, he had been the writer for Universal's *Scarface.* He had also gained a reputation as an interpreter of the American past, having directed pictures about Vietnam that included *Platoon* (1986), starring Dafoe and Tom Berenger; *Born on the Fourth of July* (1989), starring Tom Cruise; and *Heaven and Earth* (1993), a true story about the ordeal of a Vietnamese woman who survived the French and American invasions and later came to the United States after marrying a violent soldier. In addition, Stone had directed *Salvador* (1986), which starred James Wood and was based on journalist Richard Boyle's experiences in El Salvador during the early 1980s; and *Wall Street* (1987), about corporate greed, starring

[52] See Hunt, "Ken Russell's Movie Available in Four Versions," *LAT,* Jan. 31, 1992, F25.

[53] See Gray, "The Movie Ratings Code: Grade it C for Confusing," *CST,* Jan. 23, 1994, Show sec., p. 1; Mathews, "NC-17: A Commentary on Controversies Past and Future," *LAT,* Sept. 22, 1991, Calendar sec., p. 19; and Heffner, "Pre-Oral History Memorandum for 1992," pp. 78–9, 81–2; also ibid. 69–85, Box 2, RDH-COHC-BL.

[54] Quotation ("thriller"), Fox, "R Vs. NC-17 – What's the Difference?" *LAT,* Jan. 18, 1993, F1. See also Grimes, "Reviewing the NC-17 Film Rating," C11.

[55] See Willman, "Off-Centerpiece: Abel Ferrara: Lights! Camera! Anguish!" *LAT,* Jan. 3, 1993, Calendar sec., p. 24.

Michael Douglas. Stone's most controversial interpretations of history came in his films *JFK* (1991), starring Kevin Costner, about the assassination of President John F. Kennedy, and *Nixon* (1995), starring Anthony Hopkins.

Heffner admired Stone's filmmaking ability, but when it came to history, as noted, he thought the director was dangerously irresponsible in the way he mixed fact and fiction. *JFK* had suggested a grand conspiracy behind the assassination, and the manner in which Stone interwove actual newsreel footage with staged scenes made it difficult for knowledgeable observers to trust his account. Creating an illusion of reality in this manner was not original to Stone. Propagandists have long practiced this technique.[56]

Valenti, who drew on the past in his own public pronouncements and understood that leaders often embellish history to make a point, was upset with Stone's insinuation that Lyndon B. Johnson had been connected to the plot to kill Kennedy. Valenti admired Reagan's storytelling, for example, and thought that he had redefined the politician's role; no longer was it "enough to know. Now one must present one's self interestingly." But when biographers and moviemakers such as Stone presented Johnson in a negative way, he reacted strongly. After the first volume of Robert Caro's biography of Johnson appeared, Valenti worked vigorously behind the scenes to discredit the work, according to Heffner, and then moderated a public tribute to LBJ. Even more objectionable to Valenti than Caro's book was Stone's movie. Where thousands may have read Caro's book, millions saw *JFK*. Valenti obtained an advance copy of the script and, with the help of his public relations department, worked privately and quietly to discredit Stone's thesis.[57]

The manipulation of history upon such a large canvas as cinema was troubling to Heffner – as it should be to any citizen – but of more

---

[56] During World War II, for example, Ronald Reagan had been involved with an Army Air Corps project that created a make-believe aerial view of Tokyo on a sound stage in California. When film clips from this set were mixed with actual footage shot from planes, even the generals were unaware that they were watching a fictional account of bombing raids over Japan. Reagan, *Where's the Rest of Me?* 118–20; and Vaughn, *Ronald Reagan in Hollywood*, 114.

[57] Quotation ("interestingly"), Valenti, "In Today's Politics, a Seasoned Ham Brings Home the Bacon," *LAT*, Jan. 19, 1989, sec. 2, p. 7. See also Heffner, "Pre-Oral History Memorandum for 1992," pp. 59–62, Box 2, RDH-COHC-BL. See also Conconi, "Personalities," *WP*, March 30, 1990, B3. Valenti continued to defend Johnson after the appearance of Caro's second volume, *Master of the Senate* (2002). See Sperling, "Remembering LBJ, the Masterful Schemer," *Christian Science Monitor*, March 4, 2002, 9.

immediate concern in 1994 were the violence and overall content of *Natural Born Killers*. The Warner Bros. movie, which starred Woody Harrelson, Juliette Lewis, Robert Downey, Jr., and Tommy Lee Jones, purported to explore the relationship between media violence and celebrity. Harrelson and Lewis play a low-life couple who commit several brutal murders and in the process achieve fame in the tabloids. In one scene, Jones, who plays a prison warden, is decapitated and his severed head is displayed on a spike. In another, Downey, who portrays a tabloid reporter, is able to see through the hole in the palm of his hand after being shot by Harrelson's character.

The marketing strategy for *Natural Born Killers* exploited the film's violence and the fact that it had originally been rated NC-17. Stone adopted a variety of styles for effect, using black-and-white, color, video, slow motion, Super -8, and 16-mm animations. The movie, billed as a satire, "had its own rules," the director said. It targeted eighteen-to-twenty-four-year-old-males who "had grown up on a diet of tabloid news, video games, and MTV." One goal was to use the underground and alternative media to help create "cult" status for the film by the time it was released. Promoters also tried to connect the story in *Natural Born Killers* to recent real-life media circuses: the Menendez brothers' trial for murdering their parents; the Tonya Harding ice-skating scandal; the Rodney King beating by Los Angeles police; and, most sensationally, O. J. Simpson's arrest for the murder of his ex-wife. Stone insisted on inserting snippets from media coverage of these events into his movie.[58] *Time,* which was owned by the same conglomerate that held Warner Bros. (Time Warner, Inc.), ran an article misleadingly headlined "Murder Gets an R; Bad Language Gets NC-17," in which readers learned that Stone was eager to explain "about the 150 shots he had to remove or trim" in order to achieve an R rating. The article assured readers that the scene with Jones's severed head would be reinserted in a director's cut.[59]

Stone complained that Heffner was unreasonable. He asserted that violence was "salvational in the American epic," and that "the law of survival, the natural law," was being "perverted by the politically correct

---

[58] Quotation ("rules"), [Stone], "Stone Responds: On Seven Films," in Toplin, ed., *Oliver Stone's USA,* 243. Quotations, Hamsher, *Killer Instinct,* 210 ("cult"), 211 ("diet"); see also ibid., 215, 217. See also Ansen, "Raw Carnage or Revelation? The Overkilling Fields," *Newsweek,* Aug. 29, 1994, 54; and Lippert, "Bear Trap: Coke's Cuddly Mascots Are Fair Game for Oliver Stone's 'Killers,'" (critique), *Adweek,* Sept. 5, 1994.

[59] Quotation ("150"), "Murder Gets an R; Bad Language Gets NC-17," *Time,* 144 (Aug. 29, 1994), 68; and Brodie, "NC-17 Threat Highly Rated by Marketers," 27.

PG... 'family entertainment.'"[60] For his part, Heffner thought the director was hypocritical. When Heffner once complimented Stone on *Heaven and Earth,* Stone had told him that the picture had made little money and that he was on the verge of being rejected for future films by the major studios. Henceforth, Stone was reported to have said, his movies would be different. Heffner also suspected that someone in the MPAA – possibly Barbara Dixon, who handled publicity for Valenti – was trying to undercut him by telling Stone that he, Heffner, would be removed from CARA because he had been "influenced by the far right" and had become too conservative.[61]

In the end, Stone's contract with Warner Bros. required an R rating, so he made at least five revisions to *Natural Born Killers* for CARA and cut five minutes from the original picture. He and the others who worked on the movie believed that the changes "completely destroyed the whole pace and rhythm of the film." Infuriated by the "intense hypocrisy" of the rating procedure, they considered CARA "a de facto censorship board." An NC-17 version of the movie was released on video, although Stone claimed that the unedited, long version of the movie remained locked in a Warner Bros. vault and had been seen by only a handful of people.[62]

Critics gave *Natural Born Killers* mixed reviews. Ebert gave it his highest rating, and Stanley Kauffmann, writing for the *New Republic,* called it a "paradigm... of the ills and the imbalances in American life." *Rolling Stone,* though, called it a "surreal splatterfest," and a historian of violence compared Stone to a baseball batter who had just "beaned some kids in the cheap seats" with a hard line drive. Perhaps a *Los Angeles Times* movie critic said it best when he observed that the film revealed "the danger of satire becoming the object of its own scorn."[63]

---

[60] Quotations ("salvational," "perverted"), [Stone], "Stone Responds: On Seven Films," 248.

[61] Quotations ("influenced"), Heffner, *Reminiscences,* vol. 10, p. 1829; see also pp. 1903–4, 1942, Box 5, RDH-COHC-BL. Also Heffner, interview (phone) with author, Aug. 27, 2002.

[62] Quotations, Hamsher, *Killer Instinct,* 216 ("de facto"), 217 ("hypocrisy," "destroyed"). See also [Stone], "Stone Responds: On Seven Films," 247–8.

[63] Quotation ("paradigm"), "Stanley Kauffmann on Film," *New Republic Online,* July 12, 1999 (http://www.tnr.com/archive/0799/071299/kauffmann071299.html). Quotation ("surreal"), "Natural Born Killers [review]," *Rolling Stone* (online), Sept. 8, 1994 (http://www.rollingstone.com/mv_reviews/review.asp?mid=73132&afl=imdb). Quotation ("beaned"), Courtwright, "Way Cooler Than Manson: *Natural Born Killers,*" in Toplin, ed., *Oliver Stone's USA,* 201. Quotation ("scorn"), Charles Champlin in Heffner, *Reminiscences,* vol. 10, p. 1904, Box 5, RDH-COHC-BL. See also Ebert,

Despite the producer's claim that the film "exhorted no one to violence," a number of reports of copy-cat crime sprees that involved kidnapping and murder followed the showing of *Natural Born Killers*. Press accounts linked these actions to the movie. Novelist John Grisham, whose friend had been killed in one of the rampages in Mississippi, became involved in a suit against the makers of the film.[64]

Battles over NC-17 also sometimes involved new editions of older films. In 1969, *The Wild Bunch* was originally rated R after Sam Peckinpah reportedly cut six minutes to avoid being given an X. Some viewers who previewed the movie's original version had walked out because of the violence. Warner Bros. planned a twenty-fifth anniversary restored version of *The Wild Bunch* to be shown in theaters in 1994 and timed it to coincide with the release of a new laser-disc version. The question of re-rating the new version came up shortly before Heffner retired. Heffner suspected that Warner Bros. intended to use the deleted violent scenes, and, given that the rating board was now more sensitive to violence than it had been in 1969, it seemed likely that CARA would give the new version an NC-17. The matter stewed until after Heffner retired. Under Heffner's successor, Richard Mosk, CARA initially rated the new edition of *The Wild Bunch* NC-17, but studio executives pressed Valenti, who pushed for a more lenient rating. CARA, after being assured that the new director's cut would be the same as the original film, reissued the R.[65]

Many film critics and moviemakers were dissatisfied with the NC-17 rating and believed that the system remained inconsistent, providing no clear distinction between the R and the new rating category. The NC-17 had merely taken movies out of the "forbidden zone" and placed them in "limbo," said one reviewer. Malle found the rating process for *Damage* frustrating. "We never knew exactly what their problem was," he said of CARA. (The episode also took its toll on Heffner, who was hospitalized for hypertension.)[66] For another reviewer, the ratings had become the tail that wagged the dog, and the NC-17 only guaranteed that a movie would be

"Natural Born Killers" (review), *Chicago Sun-Times* (online), Aug. 26, 1994 (http://www.suntimes.com/ebert_reviews/1994/08/937174.html).

[64] Quotation ("exhorted"), Hamsher, *Killer Instinct*, 211. On copy-cat crimes, see Courtwright, "Way Cooler Than Manson: *Natural Born Killers*," 191–5.

[65] See Galbraith, "Taming *The Wild Bunch* with NC-17 Rating," *CST*, March 21, 1993, Show sec., p. 2. See also Greene, "Censors Ambush *Wild Bunch*," *CST*, Oct. 2, 1994, Show sec., p. 2; Heffner, "Pre-Oral History Memoradum for 1993," pp. 17–23, Box 2, RDH-COHC-BL; and Heffner, "Pre-Oral History Memorandum for 1994," p. 20, Box 2, ibid.; and Heffner, *Reminiscences*, vol. 1, pp. 44–7, Box 5, ibid.

[66] Quotations ("zone," "limbo"), Corliss, "Taking the Hex out of X," *Time* 136 (Oct. 8, 1990), 70. Louis Malle quoted ("problem") in Gray, "The Movie Ratings Code: Grade it

marginalized. Stephen Deutsch, who produced *Body of Evidence,* called the ratings experience "Kafkaesque."[67]

There were attempts to breathe new life into the rating as a category for serious adult films. One of the few NC-17 releases to come from a major studio following Universal's *Henry and June* was MGM/UA's *Showgirls* (1995). The product of screenwriter Eszterhas and director Verhoeven, it told the story of a young stripper in a Las Vegas casino and included considerable nudity, violence, and profanity. Eszterhas encouraged young teenage girls to ignore the NC-17 and sneak into the picture. "What I want to say to teenagers under 17 is, don't let anyone stop you from seeing this movie," the *Cleveland Plain Dealer* reported him saying. "Do whatever you've got to do to see it. Use your fake ID's." The story, he said, had a lesson to teach about how success is not worth it if it involves corrupting your soul.[68] The movie, which reputedly cost $40 million and was the most expensive NC-17 movie made up to that time, had been backed by the French company Chargeurs. It had an unusually large opening in the United States, being shown in about thirteen hundred theaters in September 1995, the largest number up to that time for an NC-17 film. The figure would have been higher if two theater chains in the South, Carmike Cinemas and Cinemark USA, had not refused to show it. The movie brought in $8 million its first weekend, although its box office dropped off sharply thereafter, more the result of bad word-of-mouth publicity than because of the rating. The wide release of *Showgirls* led to speculation that the movie would reinvigorate the NC-17 rating, but in Los Angeles and elsewhere fears that it would encourage a flood of similar movies led to calls to ban NC-17 movies altogether.[69]

The NC-17 rating quickly became stigmatized, as had the X. The threat of boycotts and other economic intimidation that restricted mainstream outlets for X-rated pictures also limited showings for NC-17 movies. In

---

C for Confusing," *CST,* Show sec., 1. See also Heffner, "Pre-Oral History Memorandum for 1992," pp. 78–9, 81–2; also ibid., 69–85, Box 2, RDH-COHC-BL.

[67] Stephen Deutsch quoted ("Kafkaesque") in Fox, "R vs. NC-17 – What's the Difference?" F1. (Deutsch pointed to the PG-13 given to Tim Burton's *Batman Returns* [1992] as evidence that CARA still graded sex more severely than violence.) See also Gray, "The Movie Ratings Code, *CST,* Show sec., 1.

[68] Joe Eszterhas quoted ("teenagers") in "Eszterhas Urges Teenagers to Sneak into *Showgirls,*" *Cleveland Plain Dealer,* Sept. 15, 1995, E8.

[69] See Bowman, "City May Ask Theaters Not to Screen NC-17 Films," *LAT,* Sept. 30, 1995, 1B. See also Puig, "*Showgirls* and NC-17: Grin and Bare It," *LAT,* Sept. 16, 1995, F1; and Puig, "*Showgirls* May Help Give NC-17 Releases a Leg Up," *LAT,* Oct. 10, 1995, F1.

Dedham, Massachusetts, officials forced a theater to drop *Henry and June* by threatening the owner with the loss of his license. Nationwide, the movie appeared in only about 307 theaters and grossed a relatively weak $11.6 million. The distribution of *Henry and June* was typical of most NC-17 films. During the first half of the 1990s, a studio could anticipate that an NC-17 picture would appear in only about 300 to 500 theaters, which meant that, in order to make a profit, the film would usually have to be made for $3 million or less. It made little sense for major studios to invest large sums in NC-17 films. The new rating saddled movies with the same disadvantages as had the X: contracts routinely continued to require moviemakers to produce entertainment with nothing stronger than an R rating; shopping malls had lease arrangements that banned NC-17 films from the lucrative multiplexes; many newspapers, radio, and TV stations would not take ads.[70] Nor was it possible to exploit video fully. In January 1991, the nation's biggest retailer of videos, Blockbuster, announced that it would not carry movies designated for adults only (the chain later considered unrated movies on a case-by-case basis). By the end of 1992, K-Mart and Wal-Mart had also refused to handle NC-17 films. These two outlets plus Blockbuster accounted for more than half of the videocassette sales in the United States.[71]

After an initial flurry of NC-17 films, their numbers dropped sharply. While twenty pictures received the NC-17 in 1990, and another twenty-one the following year, fewer than ten movies a year received the rating for the remainder of the decade. During the first eleven months of 1993, only 4 out of 556 rated movies had been NC-17, and none had been

[70] See Weinraub, "Violent Melodrama of a Sizzling Movie Brings Rating Battle," C15; Ziehm, "Counterpunch: The NC-17 Movie Rating Gets an X from Director," *LAT*, May 20, 1991, F3; and Grimes, "Reviewing the NC-17 Film Rating," p. C11. See also Mathews, "Movies: Off-Centerpiece: NC-17: A Commentary on Controversies Past and Future," *LAT*, Sept. 22, 1991, 19; Gray, "The Movie Ratings Code: Grade it C for Confusing," *CST*, Show sec., 1.

[71] Blockbuster Video grew rapidly during the early 1990s and altered the dynamics of the video rental business. Between early 1991 and mid-1993, its outlets expanded from 1,600 to 3,000. The chain put many local video rental stores out of business. Many of these smaller concerns had carried NC-17 and X-rated films, and as they disappeared from the scene, speciality shops that offered adult rental entertainment moved in to fill the vacuum. For Blockbuster, see Fox, "Blockbuster Video Rates NC-17 Films Unsuitable for All," *LAT*, Jan. 14, 1991, F1; Nichols, "Home Video," *NYT*, Dec. 3, 1992, C20; and Clemmons and Puzzanghera, "How a Ban Changed All," *Newsday*, July 7, 1993 (Nassau and Suffolk Edition), p. 7. See also Grimes, "Reviewing the NC-17 Film Rating," *NYT*, Nov. 30, 1992, C11; Gray, "The Movie Ratings Code," 1; and Heffner, *Reminiscences*, vol. 8, p. 1577, Box 5, RDH-COHC-BL.

a major studio release. By 1994, the NC-17 had become known as the industry's "scarlet letter." *Showgirls* – made by a large studio and widely shown – was an anomaly, one of but four films so rated to appear in theaters in 1995. During the next four years, only 15 of 2,731 motion pictures rated for theaters carried the NC-17.[72]

---

[72] Quotation ("scarlet"), Gray, "The Movie Ratings Code," 1. The number of NC-17 films are as follows: 1990 – 20 (3.5% of 572 rated); 1991 – 21 (3.4% of 614 rated); 1992 – 8 (1.3% of 621 rated); 1993 – 4 (0.6% of 608 rated); 1994 – 4 (0.6% of 635 rated); 1995 – 4 (0.6% of 697 rated); 1996 – 3 (0.4% of 715 rated); 1997 – 5 (0.7% 676 rated); 1998 – 5 (0.8% of 663 rated); 1999 – 2 (0.3% of 677 rated). Statistics are from the CARA's *Annual Reports*, 1969–1981, RDHPP.

9

Television

Television adopted a classification plan in 1997 that was modeled after the motion picture industry's rating system. Civic and parent groups, major medical and scientific organizations, and powerful politicians all pushed hard for a television rating system, and Jack Valenti had little choice but to acquiesce. Concerned groups of people argued that some kind of regulation was long overdue, because people were now watching far more movies on TV than in theaters and the number of television programs saturated with violence and sex was rapidly expanding – subscribers to cable and satellite systems now had access to several hundred channels. Creating a television rating system acceptable to most people was not easy. Valenti opposed it, and from the outset there were skeptics who said that the plan that was eventually enacted was inadequate. Only after the federal government threatened to intervene did a ratings process come into existence.

Interestingly, even though the Hollywood film classification scheme served as the model for the television classification system, the TV plan emerged during a time of considerable dissatisfaction with the movie rating system and the nature of entertainment. Criticism of the movie ratings, which persisted through the 1990s, came from both those who thought the system did too little and those who felt it did too much. Religious leaders condemned the decision to create the NC-17 category. So unhappy were some Roman Catholics that Cardinal Roger M. Mahony of Los Angeles floated a proposal to create a new production code for both Hollywood and television. A more formidable challenge to the industry came from researchers, public health advocates, and parents who thought the system was ineffectual. They continued to argue that entertainment violence and explicit sexuality had harmful social effects, which made a rating system for television programming essential. The changing of the guard at the Classification and Rating Administration in 1994 upon Richard Heffner's resignation also brought a wave of criticism and calls for reform from people who thought the system was too harsh. Movie producers and marketers chafed under the restriction of the ratings. Civil libertarians let it be known that they considered CARA to be repressive, and some of them urged abolishing the ratings altogether.

By this time, even Heffner had become a critic of the system he had once headed. He had moved away from his earlier absolutist position on the First Amendment. He worried that the ratings had become outdated. At the very least, the system needed serious reforms. He was one of a few people who took an interest in how other countries classified entertainment and he came to have a greater appreciation for how ratings were handled abroad. There might even be, he thought, a few ideas there that could improve the American system.

Valenti resisted these criticisms and calls for change. He and Lew Wasserman easily sidetracked Cardinal Mahony's plan for a new code, which never gained wide support. He remained unpersuaded by the research of people who argued that violence in mass media might have harmful effects. "We've been unable to define what is too much violence, any more than the Supreme Court has been able to define, to this hour, what is pornography," he said in late 1993. "The definition of violence is gauzy and very shadowy. It's almost like trying to pick up mercury with a fork." Valenti denounced moviemakers, distributors, and the trade papers for their attacks on the ratings and claimed that they were using the system as a "marketing punching bag, trashing it to gain free publicity." He warned those who wanted to abandon the rating system altogether that state and local censors would move in to fill the vacuum. He dismissed Heffner as a "limousine liberal" and replaced him at CARA with a lawyer named Richard Mosk, who let it be known that he was not inclined to make major changes.[1]

The TV rating system that was reluctantly adopted in 1997 retained some of the flaws found in the Hollywood system and faced difficulties of a greater scale. The sheer volume of material to be rated was staggering.

[1] Valenti quoted ("define") in Arar, "Movie-Ratings Boss Says System Works," *Cleveland Plain Dealer*, L3. Quotation ("punching"), Valenti, "The Nation: Why Assault after Assault Can't Kill the Rating System," *LAT*, Nov. 20, 1994, 2. Valenti quoted ("limousine"), Heffner, *Reminiscences*, vol. 8, Box 5, pp. 1408, RDH-COHC-BL.

The Classification and Rating Administration might have to rate two or three movies daily. But how would the new system classify two thousand hours of television programming each day? And who would do the rating? Valenti, who chaired the television industry group that came up with the TV rating system, thought the job would be overwhelming.

Technology figured prominently in the plan for television ratings. Cable, satellites, VCRs, video games, DVDs, computers, and the Internet had all helped change the nature of TV entertainment. Heffner had been speculating since the early 1980s that new media made the Hollywood rating system obsolete, and they certainly ensured that the plan proposed by Cardinal Mahony would have been unworkable. In 1997, though, technology was invoked to help implement the TV rating system: the V-chip, a filtering technology that by law all manufacturers were required to embed in new television sets.

PROPOSING A NEW CODE

In deciding to create the NC-17 category for the movie rating system, Valenti had made a number of complicated calculations that balanced the interests of filmmakers, studio executives, and theater owners. He had weighed the advice of advertising and public relations specialists, who warned of potential bad publicity that might come from tinkering with the ratings, against the possibility that lawsuits challenging CARA's decisions might drain the classification system. But one constituency he had largely ignored in his considerations was the religious community, which reacted strongly to the news of the NC-17 classification.[2]

Conservative Christians were cynical about the rating system. They had had reservations about the PG-13 rating from its inception. Although Valenti had consulted their leaders assiduously while creating the original system in 1968, they believed that he had largely excluded them from the decision making in 1984 that led to the creation of the PG-13 category. James Wall of the National Council of Churches gave only a limited endorsement to PG-13. Like Heffner, he wanted the new rating to be a restricted category – children under thirteen would be required to be accompanied by a parent or guardian. The United States Catholic Conference (USCC) was more critical still. The bishops denounced the PG-13 as a move to open previously restricted movies to teenagers and called it a "transparent ploy to exploit the young for crass commercial purposes."

---

[2] Heffner, *Reminiscences*, vol. 9, p. 1602, Box 5, RDH-COHC-BL.

The ratings, they believed, were "not used so much to guide parents as a way to sell movies." Their attacks on the ratings continued during the campaign against pornography during the 1980s. It was not surprising, therefore, that conservative Christians would see NC-17 as just a new way to bring pornography into mainstream theaters.[3]

The USCC protested the lack of involvement by religious and public interest groups. The Reverend Edward J. O'Donnell told Valenti in October 1990 that the NC-17 rating was an "ill-advised and . . . ill-fated action" that damaged the rating system's credibility and made government intervention more likely. NC-17 was merely another way to spell X, he said, and it was "clearly an attempt to create an impression of 'artistic' legitimacy for movies that resort to explicit sex, sadistic violence and indecent language, in order to get them into general theatrical release."[4]

Valenti defended the change. The NC-17 merely renamed the X to return the rating to its original intent, which had not been to signal pornography but to identify "adults only" films, he explained. Unlike the X, the NC-17 had been copyrighted and could not be self-applied by pornographers. The addition of short explanations for why R ratings had been given would also aid parents. A poll had shown that 75 percent of parents with children under thirteen found the rating system useful, he told O'Donnell.[5]

Opponents of adult films were generally unimpressed by polls, or by other justifications for the new rating for that matter, and campaigns started almost at once to press theater owners into refusing to show NC-17 films. Roman Catholic leaders also wanted stronger regulation. The *Los Angeles Times* reported in early 1992 that Cardinal Mahony (he had been elevated to that position in June 1991) planned to endorse a new code of morality to govern motion pictures and television. "In an age of rape, date-rape, sexual harassment, child molestation, sex addiction, serial killings, AIDS and venereal disease epidemics, Hollywood simply must stop glorifying evil," the Cardinal said. The line separating unvarnished pornography from modern movies and TV programs had all but disappeared, he claimed, and moviemakers should no longer be allowed

---

[3] Quotation ("parents"), Gaughan, testimony, *U.S. Senate Hearings,* Oct. 24, 1985, 130. Quotation ("transparent"), quoted in Gaughan, statement, ibid., 145. See also Wall, statement, ibid., 149.

[4] Quotation ("ill-advised," "release"), Edward J. O'Donnell to Valenti, Oct. 4, 1990, Document [90-6], with Heffner, "RDH Pre-Oral History Memorandum for 1990," Box 2, RDH-COHC-BL. O'Donnell chaired the USCC's Committee on Communications.

[5] Valenti to Your Excellency, Oct. 10, 1990, doc. [90-6], with ibid.

to "hide behind a misplaced cry for 'freedom of expression.'" Mahony
believed that cinema and television contributed to the destruction of "our
social fabric," yet he stopped short of recommending that the new code
be mandatory.[6]

The idea of returning entertainment to the principles of the Production
Code had been brewing for some time. After the Meese Commission's
Final Report, Mahony appointed Santa Barbara businessman Dennis Jarrard to lead a Commission on Obscenity and Pornography that spear-
headed the Los Angeles archdiocese's antipornography efforts. The commission recommended stronger obscenity laws.[7] Jarrard, seeing a huge
challenge, moved ahead aggressively. "We're under no illusions about
how difficult our job is," he said. "We're up against a multibillion-dollar
industry."[8]

In early 1991, Jarrard called for a new code based on the Ten Commandments. It was needed, he said, because modern entertainment contributed to the rampant spread of venereal disease and AIDS, and because
mainstream films degraded women with profanity and nudity. The new
code would update the Hays-Breen formula, making it similar to the version of the Production Code that had been revised in 1956. Its man-
agement would be independent of the entertainment industry, and it
would end "discrimination against the people who believe in time-tested

---

6 Cardinal Roger M. Mahony quoted ("age," "evil") in Welkos, "Mahony to Propose New
   Code for Films, TV," *LAT,* Jan. 29, 1992, B1. Mahony quoted ("fabric," "'expression'")
   in Wallace, "Mahony Urges Film Industry to Accept Code," *LAT,* Feb. 2, 1992, A1.
   In early February, Mahony spoke at a public forum on pornography, First Amendment
   rights and a family film code. See also Heffner, *Reminiscences,* vol. 9, pp. 1738–9, Box 5,
   RDH-COHC-BL.
7 The fifteen-person commission included nuns, priests, educators, lawyers, and psychologists. It planned to join forces with such national organizations as Morality in Media,
   Citizens through Decency in Law, and the National Religious Alliance against Pornography. See "Archdiocese Demands Stronger Anti-Porn Laws and Prosecution," *LAT,* March
   15, 1987, A32.
8 Dennis Jarrard, quoted ("illusions," "multibillion-") in ibid. When serial killer Ted Bundy
   told James Dobson in 1989 that sexually violent pornography had influenced him, his
   remarks confirmed for Jarrard "what we've known all along – that so many mass murderers were addicted to pornography." Bundy's interview and its appropriation by Jarrard,
   Dobson, and others brought protests from researchers who debated how much weight
   to give to Bundy's remarks; he was, as one biographer described him, a "chameleon"
   who "gave back what the listener wanted." Edward Donnerstein argued that Bundy's
   motivations were more complex than his interview indicated and speculated that, even
   had Bundy never encountered pornography, he still most likely would have committed
   murder. Jarrard quoted ("murderers") in Scott and Dart, "Bundy's Tape Fuels Dispute on
   Porn, Antisocial Behavior," *LAT,* Jan. 30, 1989, A1. Ann Rule quoted ("chameleon") in
   ibid. For Donnerstein and other researchers' views, see ibid.

Judeo-Christian values of human dignity and human rights." The original Production Code had been grounded in Judeo-Christianity, and under it, things had been much healthier, Jarrard said. "I don't believe you saw the blood and gore. You didn't see a lot of people in bed." Hollywood could not be trusted to regulate itself, Jarrard argued. "The industry loves to administer their own codes and you can see the result of it. We have an enormous public safety and public health and morality problem in the country."[9]

The proposed new code owed a good deal to Ted Baehr, who headed the Christian Film and Television Commission in Atlanta. Baehr's organization published *Movieguide*, which rated films not only with regard to sex, violence, and language, but also for homosexuality, lesbianism, Satanism, and Marxism. Baehr encouraged Christians to produce motion pictures that reflected their beliefs. Like the old Production Code, Baehr's streamlined version connected entertainment to the Ten Commandments, emphasized the sanctity of human life, and opposed cruelty to animals. It forbade showing law officers being killed by criminals, life stories of gangsters, depictions of prostitution, prolonged or passionate kissing, "sex perversion or any inference of it," nudity, and dances that revealed breast movement. If this new code was followed to the letter, the *Los Angeles Times* reported, it "would probably prevent the production of most films now showing in theaters."[10]

The cardinal's association with Jarrard and Baehr and his apparent receptivity to a new code surprised those Catholics who considered him rather "liberal" within the context of the Church and also alarmed Hollywood and opponents of censorship. Valenti called the proposed document an "anachronism." The best way to reject a movie was simply not to buy a ticket, he declared. The ACLU took out ads in *Daily Variety* to denounce the plan. "Images of the Inquisition were practically invoked," the *Los Angeles Times* wrote. The issue became entangled in the 1992 presidential campaign and the national debate over family values.[11]

[9] Quotation ("time-tested"), Jarrard, "Clean Entertainment," *LAT*, Feb. 16, 1991, F12. Jarrard quoted ("country") in Welkos, "Mahony to Propose New Code for Films, TV," *LAT*, Jan. 29, 1992, B1. See also Jarrard, "Cardinal Lets Hollywood Off the Hook," *LAT*, Oct. 9, 1992, B7.

[10] Quotations ("perversion," "theaters"), Wallace, "Mahony Urges Film Industry to Accept Code," *LAT*, Feb. 2, 1992, A1. For an account of Christian cinema during the late 1990s and early 2000s, see Spencer, "Lights! Camera! Rapture!" *The New Yorker*, Sept. 10, 2001, 105–9.

[11] Quotation ("liberal"), Charles Champlin, in Heffner, *Reminiscences*, vol. 9, p. 1740, Box 5, RDH-COHC-BL. Valenti quoted ("anachronism") in Wallace, "Mahony Urges

By October, Mahony was backpedaling. In a pastoral letter to entertainment leaders, the cardinal rejected censorship and urged instead the
importance of adding "human values" to motion pictures and television
programs. In place of a new code, he now called on filmmakers to think
about the impact of their work and to consider moral guidelines in treat-
ing family life, sexuality, work, violence, and authority. He urged that
women be treated with the same dignity as men, that religion be shown
as important, and that creativity be coupled with morality.[12]

Why did the cardinal back away from his earlier position? Between
January and October, Mahony met with Valenti as well as with leaders
of the Writers Guild of America and the Directors Guild of America. He
also consulted with his friend, Wasserman, who had donated $1 million to
the archdiocese's Education Foundation in 1990. Their thinking, Mahony
acknowledged, was "very, very crucial" as he had composed his letter.[13]

Outraged, Jarrard accused Mahony of selling out, after which the cardinal dismissed him from the commission. But Jarrard was not finished.
"As a father of three daughters," he wrote in an op-ed piece for the *Los
Angeles Times*, "I am saddened that the Cardinal seems to worry more
about what is acceptable to Hollywood than about what the Catholic
Church teaches about movies and television." The Church's position from
the time of Pope Pius XI through that of John Paul II had been consistent
about endorsing a sound moral code, he said. Mahony's capitulation was
an especially bitter disappointment for Jarrard because it came after the
cardinal had consulted with Valenti and Wasserman, the movie mogul
whose studio had made the "blasphemous" *Last Temptation of Christ*.[14]

Pleased that Mahony had rejected the idea of censorship, Valenti
praised the cardinal for his "wise and thoughtful" decision to leave entertainment content up to "the individual creative consciences of each producer, director and writer.... That's where it should be." There was no

Film Industry to Accept Code," A1. Quotation ("Inquisition"), "Culture Watch; Cardinal
Rules," *LAT*, Oct. 2, 1992, B6. See also Medved, *Hollywood vs. America*, 322–3; and
Stammer and Fox, "Mahony Urges 'Human Values' in Films, TV," *LAT*, Oct. 1, 1992,
A1.

12 Quotation ("human"), Stammer and Fox, "Mahony Urges 'Human Values' in Films,
TV," A1. Mahony's letter marked the fifth anniversary of Pope John Paul II's 1987 visit
to Los Angeles.

13 Mahony quoted ("crucial") in ibid., A1.

14 Quotation ("father," "television," "blasphemous"), Jarrard, "Cardinal Lets Hollywood
Off the Hook," 7B. The Los Angeles County's Commission on Obscenity and Pornography was disbanded in February 2001 by the Board of Supervisors. See Manzano, "Supervisors Disband Pornography Panel," *LAT*, Feb. 21, 2001, B5.

other solution. "Who would draw the line on such questions of how far to go? Who would be the guardians? And who guards the guardians?" Valenti asked.[15] Privately, Heffner had to acknowledge, and perhaps even admire, the considerable political clout that Valenti and Wasserman wielded. Mahony had retreated, he believed, "under the influence of his connections with the industry."[16]

Even if Cardinal Mahony's support of a new production code had not wavered in 1992, it would not have been possible to turn the clock back – certainly not to the 1930s, or even to the 1950s. Too much had changed. The widespread availability and sophistication of communication technologies alone had made Mahony's plan highly unfeasible.

CONTINUING CRITICISM OF MEDIA VIOLENCE AND SEX

Reputable organizations in the medical and scientific communities also assailed entertainment and the rating system. The American Psychological Association (APA) concluded in 1993 that mass media exposed virtually all American children to high levels of violence, and that there could be "absolutely no doubt" that people who watched a great deal of this violence demonstrated "increased acceptance of aggressive attitudes and increased aggressive behavior."[17] The American Academy of Pediatrics (AAP) estimated in 1995 that the average person, by the time he or she reached age seventy, would have devoted seven to ten years looking at television. What would they see in addition to sex? Profanity had become widespread, even in the prime time hours of 8 p.m. to 10 p.m., the AAP found. The average young person would probably have seen 200,000 acts of violence and 40,000 murders on television alone by the time he or she reached age eighteen. (Such figures were thought to be even higher – 300,000 and 60,000 respectively – for African Americans, who watched more television than did whites.) These calculations did not count what was seen in movie theaters and video games. They confirmed earlier studies that revealed that on a typical broadcast day, network and cable TV might show upwards of two thousand acts of violence, less than one-tenth of which were judged to be criminal within the context of the

---

[15] Valenti quoted ("wise," "guardians") in Stammer and Fox, "Mahony Urges 'Human Values' in Films, TV," A1.
[16] Quotation ("connections"), Heffner, "Pre-Oral History Memorandum for 1992," p. 55, Box 2, RDH-COHC-BL.
[17] Quotations ("absolutely," "behavior"), *National Television Violence Study: Scientific Papers, 1994–1995,* I-5; see also ibid., I-3–I-5.

programming. Such media violence contributed "to the unwholesome social environment in which we live, the frequency with which violence is used to resolve conflict, and the passivity with which violence is perceived," the AAP concluded.[18] Although violence in mass media was not the only cause for violent behavior, it was "the single most easily remediable contributing factor."[19]

The American Psychological Association and the AAP were not alone in their assessments. The American Medical Association (AMA) told a U.S. Senate committee investigating television ratings essentially the same thing in 1997. It was well established, the AMA said, that media violence "may lead to real life violence. Science has proven this link time and time again."[20] The association called the rating system "fundamentally flawed," and recommended including child development experts in CARA, greater sensitivity to the complexities of preteen development, and more detail on why ratings were given. Along the same lines, Mothers Offended by Media asked the MPAA to create a new "PS" category for preschool children, a proposal that had support from other child advocacy organizations.[21]

The Surgeon General's Advisory Committee on Television and Behavior, the National Institute of Mental Health, National Academy of Science, and Centers for Disease Control and Prevention were among the other organizations to comment on the connection between mass media and violence. "While recognizing the complexity in determining the causes of violent behavior, all of these groups have concluded that the mass media bear some responsibility for contributing to real world violence," a national study concluded in 1997. "Viewing media violence is not the only, nor even the most important, contributor to violent behavior." Nor did every violent act shown affect every child or adult who saw it. But "children's exposure to violence in the mass media, particularly at young ages, can have lifelong consequences," this study found. There was "clear evidence that exposure to media violence" contributes significantly to the problems of violence in society in at least three ways. First, it increases

---

[18] Quotation ("unwholesome"), American Academy of Pediatrics (AAP), statement, *U.S. Senate Hearings,* Feb. 27, 1997, 343. See also ibid., 344. The estimate of 2,000 acts of violence shown in a typical broadcast day was made by the nonprofit Center for Media and Public Affairs, Washington, DC. For this and other studies, see Barry, "Screen Violence and America's Children," 37–43.

[19] Quotation ("remediable"), Shelov et al. (AAP, Committee on Communications), "Media Violence," 949. See also Courtwright, *Violent Land,* 249.

[20] Quotation ("link"), American Medical Association (AMA), statement, *U.S. Senate Hearings,* Feb. 27, 1997, 335; see also ibid., 334–41.

[21] AMA quoted ("flawed"), Federman, *Media Ratings,* 7; also see ibid., 5–8.

aggression toward others because some people imitate what they have learned by watching. Second, it desensitizes people, or makes them more callous, to violence toward others. Finally, it elevates people's fear of becoming a victim. These conclusions were "based on careful and critical readings in the social science research collected over the last 40 years."[22] Three years after this study, in July 2000, the AMA, APA, AAP, and the American Academy of Child and Adolescent Psychiatry joined to point out that several hundred studies then existed that pointed "overwhelmingly to a causal connection between media violence and aggressive behavior in some children."[23]

The endorsement of these conclusions by so many professional organizations amounted to a formidable indictment of media violence. Commentators who rejected these findings found themselves having to argue that all these organizations had been misled. Yet some critics attempted to make this case. It was highly unlikely that any of them made "a thorough review of the research," asserted Jonathan Freedman, and thus they were "guilty of the worst kind of irresponsible behaviour."[24] What typically happened, he said, was that the organizations depended on committees, which in turn were dominated by "one or two 'experts'" who had "built their reputations on the harmful effects of television violence" and who were little more than "true believers."[25]

While such critics as Freedman claimed that the "experts" had exaggerated the link between media violence and real-world problems, other commentators continued to emphasize the limitations of social science research. People concerned about civil liberties were justifiably worried

---

[22] Scholars of American violence observed during the mid-1990s that the United States ranked "first among all developed countries in the world in homicides per capita," and that the "pervasiveness of violence is staggering, particularly involving children and adolescents." In 1993, the American Psychological Association provided statistics that showed that a child was arrested for a violent crime every five minutes in America; that every three hours a child died from gun-related violence; that each day, more than 100,000 children took guns to school; and that a child living in Chicago was fifteen times more likely to be murdered than one living in Northern Ireland. Text and note quotations, Center for Communication and Social Policy, *National Television Violence Study: Volume 1*, 8 ("complexity," "Viewing," "clear," "40 years," "first"), 10 ("children's exposure"); see also ibid., 11.

[23] Quotation ("causal"), Joint Statement on the Impact of Entertainment Violence on Children, Congressional Public Health Summit, July 26, 2000, http://www.aacap.org/press releases/2000/0726.htm). See also Anderson and Bushman, "The Effects of Media Violence on Society," 1.

[24] Quotations ("thorough," "guilty"), Freedman, *Media Violence and Its Effect on Aggression,* 9.

[25] Quotations ("experts," "reputations," "believers"), Freedman, "Viewing Television Violence Does Not Make People More Aggressive," 835.

that lawmakers would appropriate media-effects research to justify repressive legislation. The emotional responses people have to art and other messages that come through the mass media are highly varied, concluded Marjorie Heins, who defended the idea that violent entertainment might actually have a therapeutic effect. "Just as imitation sometimes occurs, so does catharsis."[26]

It is reasonable to ask at what point and at what level the entertainment industry joined this debate and to what extent it mounted a campaign to refute the studies linking media violence to antisocial behavior. After all, this issue was just another chapter in a long-running battle between Hollywood and researchers that harked back at least as far as the 1930s, when Will Hays had used the work of philosopher Mortimer Adler and the movie industry's formidable publicity resources to discredit the Payne Fund Studies. What role the industry's financing, advertising, and public relations have played in framing considerations of media violence in the post-1968 era is a question of major importance. Freedman acknowledged support from the MPAA in writing his 2002 book *Media Violence and Its Effect on Aggression,* although he maintained that the movie industry approached him after his views were well known, and that the support in no way influenced his conclusions.[27] Even if we take Freedman at his word, we need to know the answers to several key questions. To what extent has the MPAA (and other entertainment industry interests) supported researchers, and how might that support have influenced their thinking about the effects of mass media? To what degree has entertainment advertising and public relations been enlisted to discredit unfavorable research? Because most studio and MPAA records from this period are not available to scholars, it is impossible to determine with certainty the answers to these important questions.

Heffner believed that movies and television contributed to real violence (and, as seen, to such sexually related problems as AIDS as well), and he considered the industry's handling of this issue to be hypocritical.[28] With regard to violence, entertainment industry leaders often argued

---

[26] For research studies that found little or no effect of television violence upon real-world violence, see Fowles, *Case* for *Television Violence,* 47–9. For a defense of catharsis theory and a critique of media effects research relating to violence, see Heins, *Not in Front of the Children,* 228–53. Quotation ("imitation"), ibid., 253.

[27] Indeed, Freedman had made similar arguments in 1994 about media effects research, in Freedman, "Viewing Television Violence Does Not Make People More Aggressive," 833–55.

[28] See Chapter 5.

that the media should be placed near the bottom of a long list of factors that cause violent behavior – for example, they ranked unemployment, poverty, and poor family environment higher. Heffner believed the media should be given greater weight. Media violence was "not a root cause, by any means," he believed, but movies and TV shows demonstrated how one could be violent, and, for the underprivileged who lacked stable homes, good jobs, and education, such images were tremendously significant.[29]

Moviemakers seemed little concerned about research revealing that their work might have harmful effects. Studios often tailored pictures to audiences that liked violence (and sex). Heffner once became privy to the screening report for an audience recruited to watch the movie *Above the Law* (1988), an action film starring Steven Seagal, who played an undercover Chicago policeman and Vietnam veteran expert in martial arts investigating illicit CIA activity. Warner Bros. recruited moviegoers between the ages of fifteen and thirty for the screening – the age group usually most receptive to violent movies, but certainly a different demographic from the parents for whom CARA rated films. Other studios held similar screenings, Heffner was convinced; and if they showed that a movie was popular, the screening results were used to leverage CARA into issuing more lenient ratings.[30]

During the late 1990s, marketing violence went beyond in-house screenings, as a Federal Trade Commission (FTC) report revealed. Such studios as MGM/United Artists, Columbia Tri-Star, and Disney frequently targeted children, some as young as ten, for violent, adult-oriented movies, music, and electronic video games, the FTC discovered. These studios used advertising, comic books, and cartoon programs to reach the children. Both President Bill Clinton and Vice President Al Gore threatened to support strong regulatory legislation unless such advertising stopped.[31]

---

[29] Quotations ("root"), Heffner, *Reminiscences*, vol. 7, pp. 1356–7, Box 5, RDH-COHC-BL. See also ibid., vol. 10, p. 1925, Box 5.

[30] Heffner, *Reminiscences*, vol. 8, pp.1477–8, Box 5, RDH-COHC-BL.

[31] The Federal Trade Commission found that 80 percent of forty-four R-rated motion pictures they studied between 1995 and 1999 were marketed for children under seventeen. (Seventy percent of the video games that had mature ratings were aimed at those under seventeen.) See "Marketing Violent Entertainment to Children: Self-Regulation and Industry Practices in the Motion Picture, Music Recording, and Electronic Game Industries: A Report of the Federal Trade Commission," Sept. 11, 2000; see http://www.ftc.gov/opa/2000/09/youthviol.htm (accessed Nov. 27, 2002). See also Rosenbaum, "Protecting Children, Tempting Pandora," *NYT*, June 27, 2001, E1; Shiver, Jr., "Hollywood Sells Kids on Violence, FTC Says," *LAT*, Sept. 11, 2000, A1; Allen and

One should note parenthetically the importance of video games, which by the early 1990s had become important ancillary products in marketing mainstream Hollywood movies. During the decade they also became important in their own right. By 1996, twice as much money was spent on video games as on motion pictures. In the United States, video game revenue totaled $10 billion, and worldwide, more than $18 billion. By 2002, Americans spent more time playing video games than watching DVDs or videos. In the United States, the industry was expanding at a rate of 20 percent annually, and globally the video game industry earned $28 billion. Increasingly, video games became more realistic and, like motion pictures, exploited violence and sex. Some researchers speculated that the effects of long-term use of violent video games were not unlike those produced by viewing violent movies and TV programs. One analysis of the literature in this still relatively new area concluded that the research showed that "violent video games increase aggressive behavior in children and young adults." Reacting to pressure from Congress, the U.S. Interactive Digital Software Association, the major trade association in the field, created in 1994 the Entertainment Software Rating Board (ESRB), which provided ratings and content descriptions.[32]

Both video games and movies were popular worldwide, and foreign markets no doubt contributed to the level of violence in American-made entertainment. Audiences abroad seemed to have a large appetite for this

Nakashima, "Clinton, Gore Hit Hollywood Marketing," *WP,* Sept. 12, 2000, A1; and Federal Trade Commission, "Excerpts from the Report on Violence," *NYT,* Sept. 12, 2000, A24.

[32] The maker of each game submitted a tape and questionnaire to a rating board made up of "three independent, trained raters" of varied backgrounds who had "no ties to the interactive entertainment industry." Text quotation ("violent"), Anderson and Bushman, "Effects of Violent Video Games on Aggressive Behavior, Aggressive Cognition, Aggressive Affect, Physiological Arousal, and Prosocial Behavior," 353. Note quotations ("three," "industry"), Media Awareness Network, "Entertainment Software Rating Board (ESRB)" (2002) see http://www.media-awareness.ca/eng/indus/games/esrb.htm (accessed Dec. 16, 2002). See also Bushman and Cantor, "Media Ratings for Violence and Sex"; Klinkenborg, "Living under the Virtual Volcano of Video Games This Holiday Season," *NYT,* Dec. 16, 2002, A30; "Ratings for Video Games," *NYT,* Jan. 4, 1994, p. D11; Rowan, "Games Are Getting Dirtier," *The Times* (London), Oct. 22, 2002, Features sec., p. 16; Dee, "Playing Mogul," *NYT Magazine,* Dec. 21, 2003, p. 36; and Federman et al., *Social Effects of Electronic Interactive Games,* i, iv, 1. The last work provides an annotated bibliography of research about video games' effects. Research on the possible link between violent video games and aggressive behavior was relatively sparse as late as 1996. Most studies on the topic up to that time had been conducted during the 1980s; see ibid., iii–iv, xi–xii, 126–34. For the connection between video games and movie marketing, see Wasko, *Hollywood in the Information Age,* 209–10.

kind of entertainment. To what extent studios increased levels of violence to appeal to this market, what effect such violent movies, video games, and TV programs might have on other societies, and how such entertainment may influence perceptions of America elsewhere in the world are all questions of considerable significance that deserve greater attention from scholars.[33]

Just how interested the public was in media-effects research was uncertain, but by the mid-1990s many people in the United States and elsewhere believed that there was some link, if only indirect, between a popular culture saturated in sex and violence and a real world of permissiveness and violent crime. A *New York Times* survey revealed that three-fourths of Americans polled held movies, television, and other mass media at least partly responsible for increasing teen sexual activity and violence. "It's the way they talk and the way they view life in general," said one mother of two teenage sons. "They say 'I'm going to kill you' like it's O.K. They don't understand that you kill someone, that's it, they're gone." Other surveys indicated that Americans were more worried about violence in mass media than they were about sex or profanity, and that similar concerns were also common in such industrialized nations as the United Kingdom, Spain, Canada, France, Italy, and Germany. Yet the American movie rating system was perceived as being out of step with these sentiments and more lenient toward violent entertainment than were its counterpart rating agencies in other countries.[34]

EXIT HEFFNER

When Heffner left CARA at the end of June 1994, he was almost sixty-nine and felt that he had been forced out. His relationship with Valenti had been fragile for years. Tensions were high between him and Barbara Dixon, who handled the MPAA's public relations, and between him and Bethlyn Hand, Valenti's former secretary, who became director of the Advertising Code and administrative vice president of the MPAA on the West Coast. Relations with Valenti deteriorated further when Heffner opposed Kathy Heller, Valenti's choice to be the new head of CARA.

---

[33] One attempt to explore this topic globally is Carlsson and von Feilitzen, eds., *Children and Media Violence.*
[34] Mother quoted ("talk"), Kolbert, "Americans Despair of Popular Culture," *NYT,* Aug. 20, 1995, sec. 2, p. 1. See also Federman, *Media Ratings,* 32–3; Kahn, "Censorship Reshaped by Violence," *Boston Globe,* Jan. 2, 1994, 1; and Holson, "Studios Are Killing (Bloodily but Carefully) for an R Rating," *NYT,* Oct. 21, 2003, B1, B5.

FIGURE 14. Richard D. Heffner, courtesy of *The Open Mind*. Photo by Gerald Bloch.

Heller, who was already on the rating board, had been a lobbyist for the movie industry, and Heffner argued that her first loyalty would be to moviemakers, not to parents. He apparently managed to derail her appointment.[35]

---

[35] See Heffner, *Reminiscences*, vol. 1, p. 104, Box 5, RDH-COHC-BL; Heffner, "Pre-Oral History Memorandum for 1990," 16, Box 2, ibid.; Heffner, "Pre-Oral History

Richard Mosk, who eventually replaced Heffner, was a fifty-five-year-old Los Angeles attorney and son of a California supreme court justice who specialized in arbitration law. He had been a member of the Warren Commission that investigated John F. Kennedy's assassination, and was on the Iran–U.S. Claims Tribunal following the hostage crisis during the Jimmy Carter administration and the Christopher Commission that investigated the Los Angeles police department after the beating of Rodney G. King. "He has a lawyerly mind, is skillful in mediation, gracious and courteous," said Valenti when he announced Mosk's appointment. "That's important when dealing with some of these hysterical people in our business." As a parent, Mosk said, the rating system had worked for him, and he considered it preferable to government controls. He seemed unlikely to challenge the system. "Anything can be improved, but I don't foresee any revolutionary changes," he explained. "It's not my style. I'm not a rabble-rouser." In responding to CARA's critics, he indicated that he would not reveal board members' names and that he believed that filmmakers and the public already received sufficient information about why ratings were given. "If it ain't broke, don't break it," he said.[36]

Mosk did, however, bring a different approach to CARA. Heffner had believed in looking at a film as a whole, and even if it violated formal rules about language or drug use, if the movie in its totality clearly called out to parents not to be harshly rated, he had been inclined to be lenient. That concept was difficult to grasp even for some rating board members, Heffner admitted, and apparently for Mosk, too, who was more inclined to follow the rules, say, on language even though the movie's overall tone might not be offensive. He also looked at the appeals process differently. Whereas Heffner had hoped the Appeals Board would be yet another layer of ratings, another opportunity for a panel to provide a barometer of what parents might think about a film, Mosk saw the board as having a straightforward task of deciding whether CARA had made a mistake. If the answer was yes, then the rating should be overturned.[37]

Memorandum for 1992," 103; see also ibid., 103–9, ibid.; Heffner, "Pre-Oral History Memorandum for 1993," 68–78, ibid.; and Heffner, "Pre-Oral History Memorandum for 1994," 5–11, Box 2, ibid.

[36] Valenti quoted ("lawyerly," "hysterical") in Galbraith, "His Job: G, PG, PG-13, R and NC-17," *Newsday*, July 21, 1994, sec. 2, p. B02. Richard Mosk quoted ("improved," "ain't") in Eller, "Ratings 'Ain't Broke,' Board Chair Says," *LAT*, Aug. 4, 1994, F1. On Mosk, see also Dutka, "Film Ratings Board Picks Mosk as Its New Leader," *LAT*, June 29, 1994, F1.

[37] See Heffner, "Pre-Oral History Memorandum for 1990," 7, Box 2, RDH-COHC-BL; and Heffner, *Reminiscences*, vol. 1, pp. 119–20, Box 5, ibid.

Mosk's appointment came as attacks on the rating system continued. New Line Cinema's marketing president, Mitch Goldman, said the system favored the large MPAA member companies and had become as outdated as the 1930 Production Code. Samuel Goldwyn, Jr., labeled it inadequate for a "multi-cultural society." Both *Time* and *Entertainment Weekly* carried critical articles. Criticism of the system also came from civil libertarians. The ACLU dubbed the rating system a "Star Chamber" under Heffner and urged eliminating its "chilling influence." If the system continued, at the very least it should identify rating board members, explain their qualifications, give filmmakers more detailed reasons for ratings, and allow them to interact directly with CARA.[38]

By this time Heffner had separated himself from the ACLU, but he had become a critic too. His disillusionment had been growing for several years. When he talked to the British Board of Film Censors in London in 1982, he had done so at Valenti's insistence and there embraced "voluntarism in a mass-media, free-market, free speech driven society." All the while, he admitted, he was "beginning to have my doubts about it!" He later predicted that the public would not long tolerate "unbridled freedom" now that cable, satellites, and videocassettes had unleashed an avalanche of "essentially valueless" information and allowed "extreme obscenity" to invade homes. Interactive video games and other virtual-reality media that portrayed sex and violence with an intense realism unimaginable only a few years earlier made matters even worse. And then, of course, there was the Internet. Attempts to rate all this material had become "woefully inadequate."[39]

The system had failed in several ways, in Heffner's opinion. First, it no longer protected children. It had been created when most people went to theaters to watch movies; the box office had been the gatekeeper for the young and a barometer of public support. Because the new media now easily bypassed the box office and went "directly to children," the idea that "anything goes" just so long as it is rated was no longer

---

[38] Samuel Goldwyn, Jr., quoted ("multi-cultural") in Dutka, "Film Ratings Board Picks Mosk as Its New Leader," F1. Quotations ("Star," "chilling"), Ripston and Parachini, "Counterpunch: MPAA's Big Chance to Change," *LAT*, July 18, 1994, F3. See also "Murder Gets an R; Bad Language Gets NC-17," *Time*, 144 (Aug. 29, 1994), 68; and Svetkey, "Sex, Violence and Movie Ratings," *Entertainment Weekly*, Nov. 25, 1994, 28.

[39] Quotations ("voluntarism," "doubts," "unbridled"), Heffner, "Pre-Oral History Memorandum for 1982," pp. 4–5, Box 1, RDH-COHC-BL. Quotation ("extreme"), Heffner, "Here Come the Video Censors," *NYT*, May 1, 1994, Sec. 4, p. 17. Quotation ("valueless"), film critic Charles Champlin speaking to Heffner in Heffner, *Reminiscences*, vol. 10, p. 1902; see also ibid., 1897–8, Box 5, RDH-COHC-BL.

appropriate.[40] "I don't think ratings, given the fact that it's not theatrical exhibition movies anymore, but it is television movies and cable movies and home video games – all of this stuff pouring into our homes – I don't think the concept of ratings, which was so appropriate for theatrical exhibition movies, is going to work," he said.[41] Second, he doubted that most parents used the ratings. The system depended on their engagement, but most modern-day parents were too busy, "encumbered as they are by the pleasure principle" and burdened by the work needed to maintain a standard of living. And parents themselves were apparently dubious about the system's value. One survey revealed that a large majority of them believed that the ratings did nothing to prevent children from watching adult-oriented motion pictures.[42] Third, self-regulation had failed because it lacked "selfless leadership at the very top." Voluntarism, Valenti had said in 1969, required entertainment makers "to temper freedom with responsibility." But in his rating bouts with George C. Scott, Arthur Krim, Jerry Weintraub, Steven Spielberg, Brian De Palma, Lew Wasserman, Robert Radnitz, Wes Craven, Clint Eastwood, Michael Douglas, and the others, it was obvious to Heffner that self-interest trumped self-restraint.[43] The run-in with Krim over *Rollerball* had been especially enlightening. He admired Krim, but even his actions suggested that leadership and restraint were "*absent when you're functioning within an extreme kind of competitive economy and society as we are*" (Heffner's emphasis). That someone as high-minded as "Krim could have demanded a PG for this film [was] the clearest sign of that for me."[44]

And then there was Valenti, who led the industry and set the tone. Although he was a brilliant lobbyist for the Hollywood chieftains – he had "real political genius," Heffner admitted – rarely was he an advocate

[40] Quotations ("directly," "anything"), Heffner, *Reminiscences*, vol. 1, p. 166, RDH-COHC-BL. See also ibid., vol. 10, pp. 1897–8; also 1902, Box 5, ibid.

[41] Quotation ("think"), ibid., vol. 1, p. 168, Box 5, RDH-BL-COHC. See also Heffner, "Here Come the Video Censors."

[42] Quotation ("encumbered"), Heffner, *Reminiscences*, vol. 10, p. 1847, Box 5, RDH-COHC-BL. For survey, see Kolbert, "Americans Despair of Popular Culture," *NYT*, Aug. 20, 1995, sec. 2, p. 1. See also Kahn, "Censorship Reshaped by Violence," *Boston Globe*, Jan. 2, 1994, 1.

[43] Quotation ("selfless"), Heffner, "Pre-Oral History Memorandum for 1980," p. 3, Box 1, RDH-COHC-BL. Valenti quoted ("temper") in "Motion Picture Association of America: 1968 – A Year of New Developments," *1969 Film Daily Year Book of Motion Pictures*, 617. See also Heffner, "Pre-Oral History Memorandum for 1983," 28, Box 2, RDH-COHC-BL.

[44] Quotations ("*absent*," "sign") (emphasis in original text), Heffner, "Pre-Oral History Memorandum for 1980," p. 2, Box 1, RDH-COHC-BL. See also ibid., p. 3.

for the public good when the interests of rich and powerful executives were at stake. Heffner contrasted the Hollywood he knew under Valenti with the world he had known during his early days in television. In Valenti's Hollywood, "they want what they want when they want it," he explained. During the 1950s and 1960s, people in commercial television "felt the restraint, real or imagined, philosophical or psychological or whatever," because they were in "a regulated industry, and so it couldn't just be that you got what you wanted when you wanted it, because there was the sense of responsibility to the public *that was going to be enforced,* or at least looked after by a government agency." In that earlier era, television people had been schooled in a "culture of responsibility," and in addition, they were licensed and lived "in fear of having the license taken away."[45]

Finally, the appeals process needed major reform. It was little more than "window dressing" for the industry, Heffner concluded. In the end, he favored an appeals panel that would be a "blue ribbon organization, literally not connected by the links of profit" to the entertainment producers. It would have the power to impose stiff penalties, including "elimination from the field." The penalty could not be just "a slap on the wrist," or "just a million bucks, when these people are making $50 million on every video they send out. It has to be effective."[46]

Parenthetically, it should be noted that Heffner was not alone in his criticism of the appeals process. Film critic Jack Mathews suggested an appeals board made up of parents from different parts of the country linked by satellite television conferences. "Showing the movie simultaneously to viewers in the West, Southwest, East and North, in both rural and urban areas, could be done easily . . . , and their decisions would certainly be more relevant than the partisan political decisions now being made," Mathews contended.[47]

When he began at CARA in 1974, Heffner was enthusiastic about voluntarism and considered himself to be a "very, very, very absolutist, free-speech person."[48] As a New Dealer, he believed that regulation was

[45] Quotations ("genius," "culture," "fear"), Heffner, *Reminiscences,* vol. 7, p. 1398, Box 5, RDH-COHC-BL. Quotations ("want," "restraint," *"enforced"* [emphasis in original]), Heffner, "Pre-Oral History Memorandum for 1983," p. 28, Box 2, ibid.

[46] Quotation ("window dressing"), Heffner, *Reminiscences,* vol. 1, p. 162, Box 5, RDH-COHC-BL. See also ibid., 163–4. Quotations ("blue," "elimination," "slap," "effective"), ibid., vol. 7, p. 1281, Box 5, ibid.

[47] Quotation ("simultaneously"), Mathews, "Fanfare; On the Movies," *Newsday,* May 8, 1994, p. 4.

[48] Quotation ("absolutist"), Heffner, *Reminiscences,* vol. 1, p. 161, Box 5, RDH-COHC-BL.

needed for goods and services but not ideas. If movies were censored, "there would soon be censorship of speech in areas that really reflected political speech," he feared. "I wasn't that much concerned with the dollars involved," he said, "but I realized that if there were to be censorship in Hollywood, there would be censorship in my classroom, ultimately, in terms of my writing for my children, in terms of the way they were to be brought up in the future."[49]

After two decades of rating movies, he concluded that "in any society in which the major values are material, there's no way out other than regulation."[50] Heffner could no longer "find room in Mill's sacred precinct of 'opinion' for entertainment-for-profit – for media whose purpose is not to inform" but to make money. Entertainment-for-profit should not be confused with the kinds of expression that Mill wrote about, he said, nor be protected "as if privileged." He rejected the "whole unthinking acceptance of limitless First Amendment protection" for moviemakers.[51] Regulation was justified when the public was consuming what looked like ideas but were in reality only "entertainment and diversion and some kind of narcotizing influence that contemporary media know how to manipulate." And so he concluded that something stronger than the "namby-pamby, totally voluntary system" was required, something that had "real sanctions, real harshness, real authority." First Amendment advocates needed to find a formula, one acceptable to American courts, that would "put a burden upon the purveyor, the seller, the communicator, just as in product liability laws... protected the consumer." Had Jefferson been alive he would have agreed, Heffner thought.[52]

[49] Quotations ("censorship," "dollars," "future"), Heffner, *Reminiscences,* vol. 1, p. 42, Box 5, RDH-COHC-BL.

[50] Quotation ("society"), ibid., vol. 10, pp. 1890, Box 5, ibid.

[51] Quotations ("sacred," "privileged"), Heffner, "Pre-Oral History Memorandum for 1982," 6–7, Box 1, RDH-COHC-BL. Quotation ("unthinking"), Champlin speaking to Heffner in Heffner, *Reminiscences,* vol. 10, p. 1898; see also ibid., 1895, Box 5, RDH-COHC-BL.

[52] This goal could not be achieved without a government agency run on the basis of public service by those who were "most concerned with our children's education." Society needed to find some way to shield not only thirteen-year-olds but even immature twenty-year-olds from such movies as *Natural Born Killers.* Text quotations ("narcotizing," "burden," "consumer"), Heffner, *Reminiscences,* vol. 10, p. 1900; see also ibid., 1901, Box 5, RDH-COHC-BL. Text quotations ("namby-pamby," "sanctions"), Heffner, "Pre-Oral History Memorandum for 1992," 49, Box 2, ibid. Note quotation ("education"), Heffner, *Reminiscences,* vol. 8, p. 1475, Box 5, ibid. For Jefferson, see ibid., vol. 10, p. 1895.

LOOKING ABROAD

As criticism of the United States rating system swelled, a few people looked abroad to see if there they might find a better way of handling classification. Americans have usually been little inclined to look in this direction for guidance, perhaps because they so dominated mass communication during the twentieth century. A survey of thirty-one countries taken in 1996 found that the United States was one of only three nations in which the rating system was totally independent of the government (Japan and Spain were the others). In the vast majority of nations with classification systems, government appointees played a part in the rating process. The role played by entertainment industry representatives varied from country to country. Switzerland and Spain specifically excluded them. Argentina, France, Germany, and Luxembourg required members of the media industries to be part of the ratings procedure. The entertainment industry sometimes had only minority representation. Germany, for example, had 180 people, each selected for three-year terms, involved in rating films. Of this pool, more than three-fourths were from public organizations such as churches and youth groups; only about forty members of the pool were chosen by the motion picture industry. Usually seven individuals from the pool were used to classify any given film. Germany was one of three nations that required religious leaders to be among the raters (Argentina and Mauritius were the others). Only a minority of countries included representation from diverse professions among raters. Three countries mandated psychologists (France, Luxembourg, and Sweden); three had journalists and critics (Argentina, Luxembourg, and Mauritius); and four required educators (Argentina, Israel, Luxembourg, Mauritius). In Sweden, the law dictated that two of the six members of the National Board of Film Censors be behavioral scientists (the government appointed all of the board's members). Only in the United States was being a parent one of the criteria for rating board membership. Indeed, it was the sole qualification.[53]

The British, Australian, and New Zealand systems rated movies and videos on the basis of their potential harmfulness. The British Board of Film Classification (BBFC), a nonprofit, independent, nongovernmental organization, had regulated movies for local authorities since 1912. Originally known as the British Board of Film Censorship, it had been created to circumvent local censors, not unlike its American counterpart, the

---

[53] Federman, *Media Ratings*, 40–2, 75, 81.

MPPDA. In Great Britain, local authorities retained the authority to over-turn the BBFC's decisions. With the passage of the Video Recordings Act in 1984, the Home Secretary designated the BBFC to classify videos for sale or rent using a new standard that judged their appropriateness for home viewing.[54] The British rating system made distinctions among children aged twelve, fifteen, and eighteen. To watch some movies, children under twelve needed to be accompanied by an adult, and some videos could not be bought or rented by those under twelve. Heffner rejected the British system in 1982, but by the time he retired he was more sympathetic to its effort to make intelligent decisions about potentially harmful effects.[55] As he described the system: "The British say, 'What do those wogs out there know? We're going to rate films, classify films, censor films, in terms of what we more highly educated, much more sophisticated, much more psychologically in-tune persons are going to say is good or is not good for our children.'"[56]

Both Australia and New Zealand had an Office of Film and Litera-ture Classification. There the government appointed the raters, and board members tended to be swayed by ratings that had been given by the BBFC. The Australian Film Censorship Board, a government agency empow-ered by customs legislation, rated movies and videos. The law required it to protect children from anything considered harmful. During the mid-1990s, Heffner thought this system had a rationality and reasonableness that CARA lacked. Like the British, the Australians were not especially concerned about what parents thought. Where Heffner picked people "as average as possible," the Australians (like the British) sought rating board members who were well educated, even elitist, and who used their own judgment about what was appropriate for children. When Heffner observed the Australian system, he found members engaged in an "incred-ibly high level of discussion, on aesthetic grounds, on critical grounds, on psychological grounds" – the very issues that CARA "had avoided

[54] See British Board of Film Classification (BBFC) Web site: http://www.bbfc.co.uk/; and Federman, *Media Ratings*, 24–5, 27, 41. For an argument that the American rating system should take into account research on child development and based on the potential harmfulness of films and videos, see Linz, Wilson, Donnerstein, "Sexual Violence in the Mass Media," 152; and Wilson, Linz, Randall, "Applying Social Science Research to Film Ratings," 443–68.

[55] See Heffner, *Reminiscences*, vol. 1, p. 169, Box 5, RDH-COHC-BL. See also ibid., vol. 8, p. 1557. For British rating categories, see official BBFC Web site: http://www.bbfc.co.uk/ (accessed Nov. 18, 2003).

[56] Quotation ("wogs"), Heffner, *Reminiscences*, vol. 1, p. 169, Box 5, RDH-COHC-BL. See also ibid., vol. 8, p. 1557.

like the plague." In New Zealand, the Office of Classification had a staff of thirty people who regulated material "likely to be harmful, or injurious to the public good." A chief censor and a deputy chief censor administered the system.[57]

To anyone considering the American system of rating movies and television programs, this international context offered much of interest. Some things about the foreign rating systems gave many Americans pause, and with good reason. Allocating a large role for the government in ratings, as is the case in many countries, runs counter to a strong tradition of self-regulation in the United States. Most Americans during the mid-1990s preferred to strengthen that tradition rather than to rely on federal, state, and local government. Other aspects of these systems were more attractive. Deemphasizing the role of industry representatives in the rating process, as several other nations had done, would surely have increased the system's credibility. For classification to serve the public first rather than industry interests, ultimate control of ratings should not rest with those who have created the entertainment. Many social scientists, health professionals, and child advocates approved of the greater weight given abroad to the views of experts. For them, bringing psychologists, educators, clergy, historians, and behavioral scientists into the ratings and involving fewer industry representatives would have brought major improvements to the American system. To bring experts into the initial phase of the ratings was controversial (many believed it would change the nature of classification), but to engage such experts in the appeals process was likely to have a positive influence. Their involvement at this stage

---

[57] Text quotations Heffner, *Reminiscences*, vol. 7, pp. 1334 ("average"), 1335 ("incredibly," "plague"); see also ibid., 1331, 1337, 1341, Box 5, RDH-COHC-BL; and Federman, *Media Ratings*, 62–3. The Australian Film Censorship Board had no more than twelve members, all appointed by the governor-general to three- to six-year terms. John Dickey headed this system during the mid-1990s. The Australian system was less concerned with majority rule than the American system. Usually only two or three people examined each movie, although for a controversial film the entire board might become involved and outside advice solicited from psychologists and religious leaders. The system also maintained thorough records about why each rating had been given. For Australia, see Office of Film and Literature Classification Web site: http://www.oflc.gov.au.

In New Zealand, the Classification Office and the position of Chief Censor had been created by the Films, Videos, and Publications Classification Act of 1993. Bill Hastings was appointed Chief Censor of Film and Literature in 1999. The act defined what was thought to be harmful, and it established an office to deal with people who made, distributed, or showed restricted material. Text quotation ("harmful"), from Office of Film and Literature Classification Web site: http://www.censorship.govt.nz/censorship.html. Both the Australian and the New Zealand systems were formerly known as Office of Film and Literature Censorship.

would likely give an additional level of ratings to supplement CARA's work. Judgments at the appeals level would probably then be perceived to be more in the public's interest than was the case when the industry dominated appeals decisions.

THE V-CHIP AND TELEVISION RATINGS

As critics excoriated violent entertainment and underscored weaknesses in the American method of classifying movies and videos, public attention turned toward television. Some people hoped that the very technology which had helped to create the problems of modern entertainment might be used to alleviate some of those problems. To that end, the Federal Telecommunications Act (FTA), passed in February 1996, mandated that by 1998 all new televisions with screens thirteen inches or larger had to have a V-chip, a device that, when placed in a set, allowed its owner to block violent or sexually explicit programs as well as profanity and suggestive dialogue. Although the date was later moved forward to January 1, 2000, by the Federal Communication Commission (FCC), the innovation seemed to be a technological panacea.[58]

The V-chip was one of several filtering technologies available to consumers that allowed them to block specific types of TV programming. The device was invented by Tim Collings, a professor at Simon Fraser University in British Columbia, Canada. After the murder of fourteen women at the University of Montreal on December 6, 1989, by a gunman who had collected violent videos, Collings vowed to do something. The V-chip was the result. "I think we're influenced very heavily by the images and the ideas that reach our minds," he said.[59]

In order to enable this technology, a rating system for television had to be in place so that the chip could be calibrated. The FTA therefore instructed the FCC to make recommendations for a ratings system if the television industry did not voluntarily established guidelines acceptable to the FCC by February 1997. As so often in the past, legislation and the threat of government intervention galvanized entertainment industry

---

[58] See Federal Communications Commission, Consumer and Governmental Affairs Bureau, "The V-Chip: Putting Restrictions on What Your Children Watch, Even When You're Not There" (March 16, 2005), http://www.fcc.gov/cgb/consumerfacts/vchip.html (accessed Nov. 25, 2002).

[59] Tim Collings quoted ("heavily") in Monaghan, "Controlling TV Access," *Chronicle of Higher Education*, Nov. 21, 1997, A9. See also Federman, *Media Ratings*, 43–52. For Internet blocking technologies, see ibid., 52–61.

leaders into action. Led by Valenti, they set out a rating plan known as the TV Parental Guidelines that called for age-based symbols and a two-tier system – one for children, one for adults. The symbols were similar to those used in the MPAA ratings: TV-G (general audience), TV-PG (parental guidance advised), TV-PG-14 (likely inappropriate for those under fourteen), TV-MA (for mature audiences), TV-Y (for children of all ages), and TV-Y7 (for children over seven).[60]

Many critics considered the TV Parental Guidelines inadequate because they failed to give information about program content. Age-based labels alone, they said, would not satisfy the "Parental Choice" section of the FTA that had been designed to give parents more control over programming. Critics vented their dissatisfaction in late February 1997, when the U.S. Senate Committee on Commerce, Science, and Transportation, chaired by Senator John McCain (R-AZ), held hearings on the proposed television ratings. The committee heard the president of the National PTA say that unless there were changes in industry policy, she was prepared to recommend that Congress "go far beyond the V-chip venturing into far more restrictive quagmires of safe harbor resolutions." Children's advocacy groups overwhelmingly recommended a rating system that would give content information, and such groups as the AAP and the AMA spelled out the dangers of violence in mass media, noted above.[61]

Valenti at first resisted content categories. The Canadians had tried this approach, he said, but abandoned it because it was too complicated. It was likely to encounter even greater problems in the United States, where panels would have a massive volume of TV programming to classify each day, far beyond anything CARA had faced. "The minute you get into V-2 or V-3 or V-4 or S-2 or L-4, when you have 300 or 400 people assigning these labels, it's going to be difficult to find consistency," he said. *TV Guide,* newspapers, and others who printed television schedules would find it difficult to accommodate extended ratings in their grids. Viewers would find an expanded system too complex, and it would make programming remote control devices too difficult. "Calculus is easier," he said.[62]

---

[60] Mifflin, "Industry Leaders Unveil Technique for Ratings of TV," *NYT,* Dec. 2, 1996, A1, also A12; and Rosenberg, "Year in Review 1997," *LAT,* Dec. 21, 1997, 6 (Calendar).

[61] Quotation ("quagmires"), Joan Dystra, statement, *U.S. Senate Hearings,* Feb. 27, 1997, 50. See also Cantor, "Ratings for Program Content," *AAAPSS* 557 (May 1998): 54–69.

[62] Valenti quoted ("minute") in Mifflin, "TV Industry Vows Fight to Protect New Ratings Plan," *NYT,* Dec. 13, 1996, A1; see also A19. Quotation ("calculus"), Valenti, "Critics Maul TV Rating System, Ignore Its Virtues of Simplicity," *The Capital Times* (Madison,

There were also other objections to content ratings. Cynics believed that Valenti had neglected to mention that adding such descriptors as V (violence), S (sex), and L (language) might scare off potential viewers and advertisers. People who considered ratings a form of censorship opposed adding yet another layer of classification, but in so doing, they opened themselves to attack. "Naysayers," wrote one reporter, "seem to be saying . . . that expanding information equals suppression, a bit of logic that remains murky."[63]

Strong support existed in both political parties for a content-based rating system and for the V-chip. Vice President Gore took a leading role in promoting both, and President Clinton said, "We're handing the TV remote control back to America's parents."[64] Senator Robert Dole (R-KS), who had attacked Hollywood and TV entertainment during his 1996 presidential campaign, endorsed these measures. Some members of Congress wanted to go even further in regulating television. Senators Joseph Lieberman (D-CT) and Sam Brownback (R-KS) proposed legislation to require networks to reinstitute early in the evening a family hour free of violence, sex, and suggestive dialogue. "The industry's system is like putting a sign in front of shark-infested waters saying, 'Be careful when swimming,'" said Lieberman. "Television . . . has become a destructive force in our culture – I wish I could wave a magic wand and get rid of some of the junk on TV today." Lieberman later proposed a bill, cosponsored by Senator Hillary Rodham Clinton (D-NY), that relied on the authority of the Federal Trade Commission to regulate misleading advertising. Under the bill, studios that marketed movies, TV programs, or recordings carrying an adult-oriented rating to children would be fined. Valenti predicted that if this kind of bill became law, MPAA companies would probably abandon the voluntary rating system in order to avoid paying large fines.[65]

With politicians and advocacy groups continuing to exert pressure for a ratings system, the White House unveiled a compromise in July 1997 that

---

WI), Jan. 8, 1997, A11. See also Valenti, "The Simpler the Better," *USA Today*, Dec. 20, 1996, A22; and Valenti, statement, *U.S. Senate Hearings*, Feb. 27, 1997, 95–108.

[63] Quotation ("murky"), Rosenberg, "Year in Review 1997; TV's New Ratings; L for Lack of Interest," 6 (Calendar).

[64] President Bill Clinton quoted ("handing") in Bloomberg Business News, "Broadcasters Give Clinton Ratings Plan TV Rating System," *Omaha World-Herald*, March 1, 1996, 13 (News).

[65] Joseph Lieberman quoted ("shark-infested") in J. Hall, "Senators Push Content-Based TV Ratings," *LAT*, Feb. 28, 1997, A4. See also J. Hall, "FCC Chairman Backs Bill on TV Content," *LAT*, July 17, 1997, A17; and Rosenbaum, "Protecting Children, Tempting Pandora," *NYT*, June 27, 2001, E1.

went into effect the following October. All the major networks, except NBC, agreed to amend the TV Parental Guidelines by adding content symbols to the age-based labels. FV was added TV-Y7 to indicate fantasy violence. V was added to the PG, PG-14, and MA categories to indicate "moderate," "intense," and "graphic" violence, respectively. S added to these age-based symbols indicated "some sexual situations," "intense sexual situations," and "explicit sexual activity," respectively. L warned of "infrequent coarse language," "strong coarse language," and "crude indecent language," respectively. A "D" was added to the PG and PG-14 categories to indicate "some suggestive dialogue" and "intensely suggestive dialogue," respectively.[66] Vice President Gore hailed the compromise as "a major step forward." It "will change the relationship between American families and their TV sets," predicted Representative Ed Markey (D-MA), the man who had sponsored the law requiring the V-chip.[67]

Although these changes mollified some critics, concerns remained. Parent advocates contended that age guidelines actually attracted children to restricted entertainment.[68] They also complained that the compromise would mask some content. A program might receive a TV-14-V for violence, but that rating would not indicate the presence of other elements that might be objectionable to parents, such as suggestive dialogue. Finally, critics argued that the entertainment industry's use of euphemisms such as D (dialogue) and FV (fantasy violence) had been devised merely to avoid using such terms as "sex" and "violence," which surely would frighten advertisers.[69]

---

[66] See TV Parental Guidelines, "The TV Parental Guidelines: Frequently Asked Questions": http://www.tvguidelines.org/ratings.asp (accessed March 17, 2005).

[67] Al Gore quoted ("major") in "TV Ratings," *Tampa Tribune,* July 11, 1997, 6 (Nation/World Section). Ed Markey quoted ("change") in J. Hall, "TV Industry Reportedly OKs New Ratings," *LAT,* July 10, 1997, A1. See also Mifflin, "Groups Strike Agreement to Add TV Rating Specifics," *NYT,* July 10, 1997, A12.

[68] In some cases the ratings appeared to attract young people to the more violent and sexually oriented programs. One study found that the MPAA ratings strongly influenced children's interest in motion pictures. When parents were involved in helping children, especially those between the ages of five and nine to decide what would be watched, decisions tended to avoid movies with advisories and moved toward selecting films with PG and G ratings. But boys between ten and fourteen years of age were most attracted to PG-13 and R movies. The study concluded that "children who reported higher levels of aggression-related behaviors were more apt to choose programs with advisories." Note quotation ("aggression-related"), Cantor, Harrison, and Krcmar, "Ratings and Advisories for Television Programming," in *National Television Violence Study: Executive Summary, 1994–1995,* 44; see also ibid., 41–7.

[69] See Cantor, "Ratings for Program Content," 54–69.

The TV rating system had a more glaring problem, however. Under it, networks and distributors rated their own shows. Putting the new rating system into effect was a task of daunting magnitude for the television industry, to be sure. Valenti estimated that the two thousand hours of programming to be classified each day was the equivalent of one thousand motion pictures. A monitoring board oversaw rating appeals in an effort to ensure that the TV Parental Guidelines were applied fairly and consistently. The TV rating system favored entertainment producers even more strongly than did the motion picture rating system. In the latter case, at least parents unconnected to Hollywood initially applied the ratings. The TV Parental Guidelines Monitoring Board was weighted heavily in favor of the television industry's interests. The board had twenty-four members, a half-dozen each from the TV and cable industries, six representing those who produced the programs, and "five non-industry members from the advocacy community" who were chosen by the chair. To Heffner, this rating and appeals structure went against everything he had learned in two decades in Hollywood. He thought it unlikely that people heavily invested in a program would voluntarily put the public interest ahead of their own.[70]

If the TV ratings were less than perfect, the V-chip hardly proved to be the cure-all its supporters had hoped. It appeared to have little impact on how consumers watched television. "We're very supportive of it, but there's very little real media information about it," said the president of the National PTA in late 1999. "There's a huge percentage of the population that's unaware that it's even available, and unless a family's in the market for a new TV, it's not on their radar." With Hollywood leaders and many TV producers unenthusiastic about a technology that prevented people from watching shows, the V-chip received relatively little advertising or publicity and became "the runt of the litter for the television business, ignored and overlooked." By July 2001, about 40 percent of American families had at least one TV set with a V-chip, but one survey suggested that even though parents remained worried about the levels of violence

---

[70] Quotation ("non-industry"), Federal Communications Commission (FCC), Consumer and Governmental Affairs Bureau, "The V-Chip: Putting Restrictions on What Your Children Watch, Even When You're Not There: The Rating System" (http://www.fcc.gov/cgb/consumerfacts/vchip.html). See also Valenti, "TV Ratings Are Easy, Efficient," *Cleveland Plain Dealer*, Feb. 26, 1997, B11; Heffner, *Reminiscences*, vol. 7, pp. 1245, 1398, Box 5, RDH-COHC-BL; Heffner, Interview with author, Aug. 16, 2002; and "TV Parental Guidelines: About the TV Ratings and V-Chip" (http://www.tvguidelines.org/) (accessed March 17, 2005).

and sex on television, only about 7 percent of them used this technology. More than one-fifth of set owners did not even know they had the
chip.[71]

[71] Ginny Markell quoted ("supportive," "radar"), in Greenman, "The V-Chip Arrives with
a Thud," *NYT,* Nov. 4, 1999, D1. Quotation ("runt"), Barnhart, "'V' Is for Virtually
Ignored," *Wisconsin State Journal* (Madison), April 28, 2000, D1. See also Rutenberg,
"Few Parents Use the V-Chip, a Survey Shows," *NYT,* July 25, 2001, B1, B7. Heffner
predicted that the V-chip would lose money and fail to protect the public interest. Heffner,
Reminiscences, vol. 7, p. 1247, Box 5, RDH-COHC-BL.

IO

The Digital Future

By the last decade of the twentieth century, cinema and related forms of mass entertainment had outpaced efforts to regulate them. During the 1970s and 1980s, such analog media as cable television and videocassettes carried uncensored movies and other entertainment directly into homes and led some people to question the relevance of Hollywood's rating system. The rating system, it should be noted, actually touched only a fraction of what was being produced, because videotape, video cameras, camcorders, and other similar innovations increased the number of people who could create moving images. Regulation became more complicated, and efforts at control, either through codes of conduct, legislation and prosecution, boycotts, or technological remedies, met with only limited success, or no success at all.

The difficulties involved in regulating media increased exponentially with the arrival of digital communication technologies. Digital communication, which encoded information into a series of 1s and 0s and transmitted it electronically, challenged established standards in almost every realm – information storage and retrieval, journalism, publishing, law, warfare, and many other areas.[1] Cinema was, and is, no exception. "Being digital," wrote one of its enthusiastic proponents, "creates the potential

---

[1] There is a rapidly growing literature on the impact of digital communication. See, for example, Katsh, *Law in a Digital World* and *The Electronic Media and the Transformation of the Law;* Mitchell, *The Reconfigured Eye;* Rochlin, *Trapped in the Net;* Thornburgh and Lin, *Youth, Pornography and the Internet;* and two works by the National Research Council, *The Digital Dilemma,* and *LC21: A Digital Strategy for the Library of Congress.* See also Vaughn, ed., *New Communication Technologies: Their History and Social Influence: An Annotated Bibliography* (2003).

for new content to originate from a whole new combination of sources." "Creatively," said another commentator, "it means a whole new set of possibilities."² Digital transmissions made it possible to develop powerful linkages between personal computers, telephones, the Internet, televisions, videos and DVDs, and video games. As Hollywood feature films were becoming extraordinarily expensive to make, a new wave of digital cameras, projectors, and digital editing software was becoming easily affordable to a wider range of people, many of whom had grown up with electronic wizardry. Digital media opened new avenues for creativity and for distributing moving images that threatened the existing social and economic structure of entertainment.³

Moviemakers witnessed a transformation of historic proportions. George Lucas, an innovator in this area, likened digital moviemaking to the transition from silent to sound films during the 1920s, or to the change from black-and-white to color movies, and suggested that it was even more significant. Film was a "nineteenth-century invention," he said, and the "century of film has passed. We are in the digital age now, and trying to hold on to an old-fashioned technology that's cumbersome and expensive."⁴ Film editor Walter Murch compared the arrival of digital cinema to the change in painting that occurred during the fifteenth century when oil on canvas superseded an older technique of using pigments on fresco. Still others saw a shift in power. Movie producing appeared to be entering a "largely unknown period when the economics of film making and the very foundations of the power structures that have governed the business for almost a century are more fluid than at any time in its history," commented one observer.⁵ German moviemaker Wim Wenders thought historical analogies were inadequate. The digital revolution was on the threshold of "reconstructing cinema from scratch.... The entire landscape of film is about to be shaken up completely," he said. "The past will no longer be its future." Creating motion pictures will not "be based on what we know now or what we've learned

² Quotation ("digital"), Negroponte, *Being Digital*, 19. Quotation ("possibilities"), Roston, "Filmmaking without Film," *Premiere* (American ed.), 15 (Nov. 2001), 49:
³ Lyman, "Film's Digital Potential Has Hollywood on Edge," *NYT*, Dec. 20, 1999, C41; and Marriott, "If Only DeMille Had Owned a Desktop," *NYT*, Jan. 7, 1999, E1.
⁴ George Lucas quoted ("invention") in Sabin, "The Movies' Digital Future Is in Sight and It Works," *NYT*, Nov. 26, 2000, sec. 2, p. 1.
⁵ Quotation ("unknown"), Lyman, "Film's Digital Potential Has Hollywood on Edge," C41. See also George Lucas, in Lyman, "A Monument to the Filmless Future," *NYT*, March 1, 2001, p. B10; and Murch, "The Future: A Digital Cinema of the Mind? Could Be," *NYT*, May 2, 1999, 35 (Arts and Leisure).

from the past."[6] Another perceptive student of new media argued that rapidly developing interfaces between humans and computers offer "radical new possibilities for art and communication" that will lead to "a new cultural metalanguage, something that will be at least as significant as the printed word and cinema."[7]

DIGITIZATION

The ability to transmit images digitally owes much to the exploration of space during the 1950s and 1960s. NASA used digital imaging techniques in 1964 to enhance pictures of the moon's surface taken by the Ranger 7 spacecraft. Scientists refined the technology during the 1970s and 1980s and applied it to many areas – from satellites improving infrared scans of the earth from space to microscopes producing images of molecules and atoms. This new technology made possible far more sophisticated surveillance cameras, and the military found multiple uses for it in weaponry.[8] Digital transmissions first came into the mass market during the early 1980s in the form of the compact disc (CD) and by way of the telephone-line modem, which often used optical fiber. Other applications of digital transmission included the Internet, a network connecting computers worldwide that appeared first during the late 1970s and early 1980s, and began to grow at a geometric rate during the late 1980s and 1990s; high-definition TV (HDTV); and the digital versatile disc (DVD), a more sophisticated version of the CD that can store digitized video. Another important application of digital transmission was moviemaking. Digital moviemaking can be done without film or videotape and permits the moviemaker to bypass normal channels of distribution.

Early on, the technology for capturing and processing information digitally was expensive and difficult to use. That soon changed. During the late 1980s and early 1990s, small, relatively inexpensive still-video cameras appeared that could transfer high-quality images directly to discs, thus making silver-based film unnecessary. Just as video cameras had earlier superseded 8-mm and 16-mm home movie cameras, digital systems now provided an alternative to videotape. Digital camera

[6] Quotations ("reconstructing," "past"), Wim Wenders interview in Roman, *Digital Babylon*, 36.
[7] Quotations, Manovich, *Language of New Media*, 93 ("metalanguage"), 94 ("radical").
[8] See "How Technology from the Moon Will Advance Photography on Earth," *AC*, 48 (Jan. 1967), 49–50; and Mitchell, *Reconfigured Eye*, 11–13.

systems also expunged the boundaries between photography and computer graphics. The work of processing images became progressively easier and better with such improvements in personal computers as increased processing power, memory, storage and graphic display capabilities, and with the arrival of affordable digital copying technology such as laser scanners. Sophisticated image-processing software gave even amateurs the ability to generate results that once only scientists and other professionals with access to expensive laboratory equipment had been able to produce.[9]

Digitization also meant that in the not-too-distant future, as the entertainment and information worlds moved from analog to digital communication, the movies would continue to converge with other media – television, video games, music, radio, books, newspapers, magazines, telephones, and the World Wide Web – and could be accessed from any place, at any time, on TV sets, personal computers, and automobile dashboards, with eyeglasses and wristwatches – even, some predicted, with retinal implants. It seemed certain that these media would become more sophisticated in their capacities both to capture and mimic real-life experiences and to create imagery unrelated to the real world.[10]

Some of its proponents believed that digital technology would make moviemaking more democratic, by giving individual artists greater power to realize their visions in the content of their pictures and by amplifying "voices from the margins" of society. It would also give moviemakers "a much wider range of subject matter," Lucas predicted.[11] Such speculations recall the arrival of offset printing during the 1960s, which made possible inexpensive newspaper publishing and a more diverse journalism than previously, although proponents of digital cinema foresaw results on a grander scale. Traditional moviemaking was "so heterogeneous, with so many technologies woven together in a complex and expensive fabric, that it is almost by definition impossible for a single person to control," said Murch. "By contrast, digital techniques naturally tend to integrate with each other because of their mathematical commonality; thus they

---

[9] Mitchell, *Reconfigured Eye*, 17–20.
[10] Fischetti, "The Future of Digital Entertainment," *Scientific American*, 283, no. 5 (Nov. 2000), 47–9; and Forman and Saint John, "Creating Convergence," ibid., 50–56. For an informative introduction to digital communication, see Lebow, *Information Highways and Byways*, 149–290; and Lebow, *Understanding Digital Transmission and Recording*.
[11] Quotation ("voices"), Dixon, *Second Century of Cinema*, 1. See also ibid., 1–57. Quotation ("wider"; George Lucas, interview by Benjamin Bergery), "Digital Cinema, by George," *AC*, 82 (Sept. 2001), 73.

come under easier control by a single person." More than ever before, digital technology allowed "a single vision to work itself out," Murch explained, "and that carries a particular danger because you need fewer collaborators."[12]

Where previously only large studios could afford to make and distribute motion pictures and television programs, now inexpensive digital cameras and computer editing software made it possible for one person to do these things for only a few thousand dollars. The new technology gave independent moviemakers the "freedom of novelists to be spontaneous, to improvise, to strike out in new directions and to start over," said a financial backer of digital moviemaking.[13] "Movie making was previously one of the most expensive art forms," commented the *Scientific American* in 2000. "Unlike a poet or a painter, a film maker needed substantial financial resources and expensive equipment. Now, for the first time, independent film makers can afford to own the means of both production and postproduction."[14] Now a writer could "write anything he wants," producer Rick McCallum explained. "A director is only limited by his imagination."[15] "The idea of a movie studio is changing as we watch," said Rodger Raderman, an executive who founded a company that distributed digital movies through the Internet. "What is a studio? If you think of it as a place where movies are developed, produced, marketed and distributed, then we are very close to having a technology where one person can do that all by himself. Each person can be his own studio."[16]

There are many advantages to digital moviemaking. Digital cameras can be run on the set for a much greater percentage of the time than was the case with film cameras. On low-budget films, the ratio between film recorded and that which was actually used was about 3:1. On a digital set,

---

[12] Quotations ("heterogeneous," "person"), Murch, "The Future: A Digital Cinema of the Mind?" 35. Quotation ("single"), Murch, in Ondaatje, *The Conversations*, 214.

[13] Quotation ("spontaneous"), Broderick, "Moviemaking in Transition," *Scientific American* 283, no. 5 (Nov. 2000), 63. See also Fischetti, "The Future of Digital Entertainment," ibid., 48–9; Lyman, "Film's Digital Potential Has Hollywood on Edge," C41; and Marriott, "If Only DeMille Had Owned a Desktop," E1.

[14] Quotation ("Movie making,") Broderick, "Moviemaking in Transition," 62.

[15] Quotations ("write," "imagination"), Rick McCallum interviewed in "Digital Lucasfilm," *Digital Cinema Magazine* (2001), 34 (reprinted in Bob Zahn and Brian McKernan, "Report from the Ranch: Star Wars Episode II," at http://216.130.185.100/artman/publish/printer_58.shtml) (accessed March 17, 2005).

[16] Rodger [sic] Raderman quoted ("idea," "studio") in Lyman, "Film's Digital Potential Has Hollywood on Edge," C41.

the ratio might be 50:1, which means that the director can better capture spontaneous moments, reshoot scenes, or take scenes from rehearsals. Experimentation is thus much easier – a director can try many different versions of a scene.[17]

Digital movies promise huge savings. They allow for more streamlined crews. Equipment is generally cheaper, and lighting requirements are less elaborate than for film or videotape, and there are no costs for developing film or making prints. Studios typically used to spend $1,500 to $2,000 to duplicate one 35-mm print of a first-run motion picture and then had to ship it to and from a theater. For a single movie, several thousand copies of a feature film might be created for an opening week using upwards of 50 million feet of film. Digital cameras do not need film, but store images on computer disks or digital tape. Instead of having to transport 35-mm prints to movie houses, digital movies can be sent to theaters by way of relatively inexpensive, light-weight electronic tapes or disks, and increasingly they are delivered by fiber optic cables or beamed in by satellite. If a motion picture is unpopular, this process allows theaters to change programs quickly. Digital movies can also easily be played in different languages (e.g., English or Spanish) and over highly sophisticated sound systems.

Digital movie projection offers better picture quality. The process, which uses hundreds of thousands of tiny mirrors, rivals high-definition television in clarity. Traditional motion pictures required threading celluloid through a mechanical projector. Digital movies have eliminated this step and, with it, the projection flaws associated with wear and tear on prints and old or poorly operated equipment.[18]

Digital technology has also vastly improved special effects. It has freed special-effects creators from the slow and expensive process of working first with raw film, then videotape, and then back to film. Digital cameras also make it easier to take advantage of scenes in the real world. Shooting can be done almost inconspicuously, and a fictional story can be set against a nonfictional backdrop more easily than with film cameras. During the 1990s, it became common to combine the images from digital cameras with computer-generated digital effects in order to let "directors

[17] Broderick, "Moviemaking in Transition," 66–7.
[18] See Lyman, "A Monument to the Filmless Future," B1, B10; Sabin, "Taking Film Out of Films," *NYT*, Sept. 5, 1999, 12 (Arts and Leisure); Mathews, "Cinema's Digital Divide," *WSJ*, March 28, 2002, B1; Murch, "The Future: A Digital Cinema of the Mind?" 1; Sterngold, "A Preview of Coming Attractions," *NYT*, Feb. 22, 1999, C2; and Marriott, "Digital Projectors Use Flashes of Light to Paint a Movie," *NYT*, May 27, 1999, D7.

capture any vision." In traditional film, images were "frozen on celluloid," but digital cinema allows moviemakers to change the context of scenes, insert new camera movements, enhance performers' acting, "transfer the location from Red Square to Times Square, speed up time, slow it down and generally do whatever schedule and budget allow to get the desired images up there on the screen." As Lucas explained, "where I can go is unlimited."[19]

Digital technology points to a future where computer-generated virtual reality could become increasingly indistinguishable from real-life experience. Digitally created images can be subjected to "infinite manipulation," one observer remarked; "its reality is a function of complex algorithms stored in computer memory rather than a necessary mechanical resemblance to a referent." As a result, "unreal images have never before seemed so real."[20] Digital technology therefore has greatly increased the possibilities for creating real or fictitious images of violence and horror, and for fabricating false or misleading images of the past (fabrications that are much more difficult to detect or refute than those created by analog media). Digital technology can provide new ways of presenting sexuality, and can challenge laws that in the past attempted to regulate the narrow areas on which there was still consensus, such as child pornography. The Child Pornography Prevention Act of 1996 tried to address the problems posed by digital communication and the Internet, declaring that even soft-core pornography involving children is damaging and could have long-lasting harmful effects on the young. Given that the technical quality of digital simulations had advanced rapidly, Congress banned simulated child pornography – that is, computer-generated images depicting sex with children in which no real children were involved – on the ground that these virtual depictions could have such harmful consequences as enticing children into real pornographic situations and feeding the sexual proclivities of pedophiles.[21]

How difficult is it to censor or regulate digital transmissions? It is worth noting that where many proponents of the technology saw a bright new

---

[19] Quotations ("directors," "frozen," "transfer"), Lyman, "A Monument to the Filmless Future," B10; see also ibid., B1. Quotation ("unlimited"; Lucas interview), "Digital Cinema, By George," 72. See also Broderick, "Moviemaking in Transition," 66–7; Sabin, "Taking Film Out of Films," 12; Mathews, "Cinema's Digital Divide," B1.

[20] Quotations, Prince, "True Lies: Perceptual Realism, Digital Images, and Film Theory," *Film Quarterly* 49 (Spring 1996): 3 ("manipulation," "referent"), 8 ("unreal") (from Web site: http://communication.ucsd.edu/tlg/123/prince.html).

[21] Liptak, "When Is a Fake Too Real?" *NYT*, Jan. 28, 2001, 3 (Week in Review).

future for moviemaking, critics of film morality saw powerful new tools for censorship, of which the V-chip was only one possibility. With digital television, wrote one observer, electronic bits of information "may be the control data for a knob that allows you to change X-rated to R-rated to PG-rated (or the reverse). Today's TV sets let you control brightness, volume, channel. Tomorrow's will allow you to vary sex, violence, and political leaning."[22]

Digital movie projection promises to tighten studio control over when and where pictures can be shown. An analog film print, once distributed to theaters, could be easily duplicated; it was also difficult to determine how often and to whom it was shown. Digital movies give the distributor the power to control projection from a central location. It gives studios an exact accounting of where and how often their pictures are shown. Moreover, the movie can be encrypted in such a way that only projectors with the right code can show it. Certainly anyone wanting to censor digital movies would consider the point of transmission to be an important target.[23]

The Digital Versatile Disc (sometimes known as the Digital Video Disc or simply the DVD), which by the beginning of the twenty-first century seemed destined to supersede the videocassette, offered similar possibilities for censorship. DVDs are cheaper to produce than videocassettes, have superior picture quality, and consumers are more likely to purchase them than cassettes. Some enthusiasts believed this technology would reshape "the way we experience culture."[24] The electronic bits that make up digital movies can be manipulated, and a market has emerged for sanitized versions of movies on DVD. For example, censors gave actress Kate Winslet a digital corset to wear in some of her nude scenes in *Titanic,* the smash hit of 1997, and they toned down the gruesome re-creations

---

[22] Quotation ("control"), Negroponte, *Being Digital,* 49.

[23] See, for example, the comments of cinematographer John Bailey in Roman, *Digital Babylon,* 120–1. See also Harmon, "Studios Using Digital Armor to Fight Piracy," *NYT,* Jan. 5, 2003, A1, A21.

[24] Quotation ("culture"), "The DVD Comes of Age," *NYT,* Aug. 17, 2003, sec. 2, p. 1. See also E. Mitchell, "Everyone's a Film Geek Now," *NYT,* sec. 2, p. 1; Lyman, "Revolt in the Den," *NYT,* Aug. 26, 2002, A1, A13. Consumers spent more money on DVDs in 2001 than they did for VHS cassettes, although cassette rentals still surpassed DVDs. The price of DVD players dropped substantially as Chinese manufacturers began to compete with Japanese companies. Manufacturing a DVD could be done for less than half the cost of making a videocassette. Picture quality was superior, and consumers were more likely to purchase DVDs than cassettes. An added advantage of DVDs was that they could be played on computers and video-game systems, not simply on television. Yet copying programs on cassettes remained easier and cheaper than on the newer technology. How the DVD might influence amateur and low-budget moviemaking remained to be seen.

of combat during the D-Day assault at Normandy during World War II in *Saving Private Ryan* (1998). Companies in Utah and Colorado not only have offered edited rentals but have provided software that can be downloaded to home computers, laptops, and DVD players that can be connected to television sets, allowing customers to watch more than thirty different versions of some movies. Other companies have provided filters for TVs and DVD players. Moviemakers have complained that this censorship violates the federal law that forbids changing a creative work and then reselling it with the original title and the artist's name.[25]

On the whole, though, digital communication has created far more problems for censors than it has solved. The fact that technology has continued to change rapidly complicates the work of gatekeepers who seek to control transmissions at their source.[26] The DVD has added a new dimension to sexually explicit movies by making them interactive. Companies specializing in hologram technology hope soon to offer three-dimensional pornographic images. "Men will love it," said one porn provider. "They'll sit in front of their giant-screen TV, turn off the lights and the only thing lit will be the girl."[27] The Internet, which provides an outlet for digital moviemakers, is another complication for censors. Whatever the difficulties television and movies have posed for regulation, they pale in comparison to those presented by the World Wide Web. Using the Internet, a digital moviemaker can send a movie directly into a home, bypassing theaters, cable and satellite providers, and rental stores. The Internet offers largely unfettered and anonymous access to an incredibly varied array of entertainment, including pornography. By the end of the twentieth century, there were perhaps four hundred thousand pornographic web sites, three-quarters of which originated from outside the United States. Many offered movies.[28]

---

[25] Lyman, "Hollywood Balks at High-Tech Sanitizers," *NYT*, Sept. 19, 2002, B1, B5. Clean-Flicks, a company based in Utah, had a chain of rental shops that offered more than a hundred sanitized movies in 2002. Other American companies providing screening filters included MovieMask, ClearPlay, and Family Shield Technologies.

[26] Sterngold, "A Preview of Coming Attractions," C2. See also Lyman, "Film's Digital Potential Has Hollywood on Edge," C41.

[27] Quotation ("Men"), "Joone," quoted in Kennedy, "The Fantasy of Interactive Porn Becomes a Reality," *NYT*, Aug. 17, 2003, sec. 2, p. 7. About 65 percent of pornographic movies sold are on DVDs (ibid.). Money from home video made up about 58 percent of Hollywood's revenue in 2002, more than double box-office income. DVD sales were the largest and most rapidly growing part of home video revenue. Action-oriented movies appeared most popular among DVD users. See Kirkpatrick, "Action-Hungry DVD Fans Sway Hollywood," *NYT*, Aug. 17, 2003, A1, A15.

[28] See Thornburgh and Lin, *Youth, Pornography and the Internet*, 4.

In 1996, Congress passed the Communications Decency Act (CDA), which was part of the Telecommunications Act and had two provisions aimed to protect children under eighteen from certain types of communications sent on the Internet. One provision of the act made it a crime to transmit knowingly "obscene or indecent" materials to minors. The other provision would have made it illegal to use a computer service deliberately to send to those under eighteen messages depicting or describing "sexual or excretory activities or organs" in a "patently offensive manner," as judged by "contemporary community standards." The U.S. Supreme Court declared these provisions unconstitutional, in part because they amounted to an abridgment of free speech protected under the First Amendment. The scope of the CDA was too broad, the Court said, and such terms as "indecent" and "patently offensive" were so ambiguous as to "silence speakers whose messages would be entitled to constitutional protections."[29] Even had this legislation remained in place, though, regulating materials that originate from outside the United States and are conveyed through a medium that passes so easily through national boundaries is difficult. As with television, blocking or filtering technologies exist that give parents a small measure of control. But whether such remedies prove effective, and whether they can be required for such public institutions as libraries, remains contested. Censoring large parts of the Internet is not impossible. One need only turn to such countries as China and Saudi Arabia for examples. But when it is done, it severely damages freedom.[30]

At the end of the twentieth century, digital cinema was still in an embryonic stage, and predictions that it would replace 35-mm and other traditional filmmaking seemed premature. As late as 2002 there were still only about two dozen American theaters where one could watch a movie projected digitally. Part of the problem hindering the growth of digital cinema is the expense of converting theaters to the new technology. It could cost between $150,000 and $200,000 to outfit one theater screen (there were about 34,000 screens in the United States in 1999), and the question of who will pay for this new equipment is at the center of the problem. During the late 1920s, when studios owned large theater chains, the cost of converting theaters to sound usually ran between $8,000 to $15,000 per theater and was borne by the studio. That expense, combined with

[29] Quotations ("obscene," "protections"), *Reno v. ACLU,* 521 U.S. 844, June 26, 1997.
[30] See Kahn, "China Has World's Tightest Internet Censorship," *NYT,* Dec. 4, 2002, A15. For Internet censorship abroad, see Zittrain and Edelman, "Documentation of Internet Filtering Worldwide": ⟨http://cyber.law.harvard.edu/filtering/⟩ (accessed March 17, 2005).

the Great Depression, contributed in no small way to Hollywood's acceptance of the Production Code. But by the twenty-first century, the studios had long been divested of their theater chains, and theater owners now have to bear the costs of conversion, even though it is the studios that will realize the greatest savings by converting to digital cinema. Because digital technology continues to change at a rapid pace, large theater chains have resisted investing in high-priced digital equipment, fearing that, in the absence of firm guidelines, they will be forced to spend even more for expensive upgrades in the future.[31] And as for the studios, they worry, with good reason, about piracy. Although in theory it may be difficult to pirate an encoded movie, with the right code – or with a digital camera at a movie screening – duplication is relatively easy. Despite the safeguards that encryption provides, estimates indicate that by 2003 the industry had lost $3.5 billion (U.S. billion) a year to illegally copied motion pictures. Analysts believe that as many as a half-million copies of pirated movies were swapped each day over the Internet. For these reasons, it appears likely that 35-mm movies will continue to thrive, even if digital cinema is the wave of the future.[32]

THE FUTURE

Given (*a*) the capability of new communication technologies to transform society; (*b*) the tremendous popularity of cinema and the fact that it touches so many aspects of our lives; (*c*) the great influence of related media such as television and the Internet; and (*d*) the extraordinary power of advertising and public relations to shape perceptions, it has never been more important than now for scholars to study the historical significance of new media, for citizens to be involved in the major issues that involve entertainment, and for institutions concerned with education and ethics to teach media literacy. Media literacy requires more than learning about the scientific and technical aspects of cinema or any other medium. It means

---

[31] Mathews, "Cinema's Digital Divide," B1. See also Lyman, "New Digital Cameras Poised to Jolt World of Filmmaking," *NYT*, Nov. 19, 1999, C5.

[32] On illegal copying, see Weinraub, "The Man Who Unites the Moguls," *NYT*, Oct. 27, 2003, B1; Sterngold, "A Preview of Coming Attractions," *NYT*, Feb. 22, 1999, C2; and Holson, "Studios Moving to Block Piracy of Films Online," *NYT*, Sept. 25, 2003, A1, C6. See also Bailey, "Film or Digital? Don't Fight. Coexist," *NYT*, Feb. 18, 2001, 9 (Arts and Leisure).

Hollywood, it should be noted, has often resisted new technologies. High-definition television is one recent example. The use of color and 16-mm film are earlier examples. See Winston, "HDTV in Hollywood: Lights, Cameras, Inaction," 123–37; and Winston, *Technologies of Seeing*.

understanding how stories and images are created. It means being able to distinguish between real-world issues and the worlds created by entertainment, propaganda, advertising, and other forms of publicity. Liberal arts and moral education remain essential to creating this kind of informed citizenry. This learning experience must be separated from the lucrative marketing forces that have been allowed to permeate modern education as well as most mass media.

Media literacy involves understanding the possible effects mass communication may have. During the past century and a half, new communication technologies have entered our lives at an accelerating rate. We should pay close attention to their possible long-term significance. Both the Production Code of 1930 and the rating system adopted in 1968 assumed that the youngest members of our society need protection from some types of material conveyed through mass media. That assumption remains widely held today, but what materials the young should be protected from and if, in fact, it is still possible to shield the young from them remain complex and urgent questions.

Although we need greater understanding of new media, we also need to scrutinize more carefully the power of advertising and public relations. Advertising and public relations messages are often produced and disseminated behind the scenes. The motives of the creators of these messages are rarely revealed, yet these "hidden persuaders" have been powerful influences in framing how we consider such fundamental issues as sexuality, violence, the First Amendment, religion, history, and many others. Efforts to reform cinema and other media are likely to continue to face obstacles created by the entertainment industry's formidable publicity resources. This is not a new problem. Will Hays established a public relations network during the 1920s and 1930s that effectively absorbed criticism of the movie industry and discredited its critics. To understand the system, one must enter the murky terrain of media manipulation and image creation, a world difficult for scholars to penetrate. Until we have better histories of the industry's public relations and advertising, our understanding of cinema's place in America and throughout the world will be inadequate. Given the lack of primary materials available for the post-Hays era, it has been easy for Valenti and other entertainment promoters to argue that any conclusions drawn about the marketing strategies of filmmakers can only be subjective.[33]

---

[33] See Valenti paraphrased in Shiver, Jr., "Hollywood Sells Kids on Violence, FTC Says," *LAT,* Sept. 11, 2000, A1.

The ability of advertising and public relations to influence perception is especially important in considering what effects media may have. A distinction must be drawn between *perception* and *reality*. What people *perceive* to be the effects of violence and sex in the media, and what the *actual* effects are, constitute two separate questions. Public perceptions may not necessarily correspond to reality but can nonetheless be powerful factors in political calculations. One senses, for example, that during Heffner's early years at CARA, he was most concerned about public perceptions of certain kinds of movies, fearing that they might provoke reactions that would lead to censorship. This worry did not disappear from his thinking, and by the end of his career he still considered it likely that an alliance between Christian conservatives who opposed the depiction of sex in the media and liberals who objected to the prevalence of violence in the media might become strong enough to pass legislation.[34] But over his years with CARA, Heffner became ever more concerned about the actual effects that sexually explicit and violent films might have. It is difficult to find a similar change in Valenti's position. His leadership of the MPAA has consistently focused on how best to alter public perceptions about cinema's impact rather than on what the reality of that impact may be. In a world where publicity and imagery reign supreme, even the best scholarship will be at a severe disadvantage, at least in the short term. Research on media effects is not easily explained to nonspecialists. Part of the fault has been and is attributable to researchers who have too little appreciation for narrative and for linking their work to larger issues of interest to citizens. This failure has led critics to contend that media-effects research amounts to little more than an "academic Tower of Babel." Then, too, the best work often does not lend itself to simplistic interpretation. As one student of the field observes: "If I had to summarize the standing of effects research today, it would be that both the 'strong effects' and 'weak effects' camps are right! Put another way, media effects are contingent on a host of variables. Get those predictors in the right configuration and you will get very strong effects. If predictors are not aligned properly, there will be very weak effects." A comprehensive, clearly written history of media-effects research would contribute greatly to the public debate over violence and sexuality in modern communication.[35]

---

[34] See Heffner, *Reminiscences,* vol. 1, p. 43, Box 5, RDH-COHC-BL.
[35] Quotation ("Babel"), Trend, "Merchants of Death," 292. Quotation ("summarize"), Sharon Dunwoody to author, Nov. 3, 2002. At the time, Dunwoody was director of the School of Journalism and Mass Communication, University of Wisconsin, Madison.

Better journalism would also help to clarify this issue. Press coverage of issues related to sexuality and violence in mass media has too often been superficial or misleading. One analysis concluded that a half-century of news reporting on the connection between media violence and aggression had left the American public "confused." As scientific research showing a link between media violence and aggression grew stronger, the trajectory of most press accounts actually reported that this linkage had grown weaker.[36] A new (or perhaps old) journalism that is independent of the influence of entertainment and advertising, and one that will make the public interest its primary priority, is therefore an essential element in developing media literacy. The alliance of journalism with advertising and public relations – a union that, unfortunately, is now deeply embedded in the curricula of many universities – has blurred the line between hard news and the pseudo-events created by the world of entertainment. If the press has often been a willing accomplice in marketing violent and sexually provocative entertainment, as this book maintains, why then should we have confidence in its ability to report fully and accurately on what research may show about the effects of sex and violence in mass media, or about how cinema and television interpret the meaning of freedom, politics, history, religion, or the many other areas where mass media touch humanity? Since the time of Will Hays, entertainment has so saturated the news media and other communication outlets that it is now virtually impossible to engage the public in sustained and rational dialogue over how moving pictures may influence our understanding of profoundly important issues. Media literacy requires better journalism. The very idea of serving the "public good" needs to be reinvigorated, not only in journalism, but more broadly in American society.

Another element vital to serving the public interest is greater public access to information. Although in the interest of freedom of expression the government should be involved in regulation as little as possible, there is one area in which its greater involvement would be healthy. It should mandate that the entertainment industries retain their historical records and, after a prescribed time, open them to independent scholars. Why should institutions that wield such great influence be exempt from this requirement? Even the federal government is required to open its historical documents to the public after an appropriate time.

---

[36] Quotation ("confused"), Bushman and Anderson, "Media Violence and the American Public," 477; see also ibid., 477–89.

The availability of historical documents will improve our understanding of past efforts to regulate mass entertainment, another requirement of media literacy. Throughout the twentieth century, the technology of cinema demonstrated its ability to overwhelm the people and groups who attempted to control it. Heffner lived and worked primarily in a predigital world, as did his counterpart from an earlier era, Joseph Breen. Although Heffner's Jeffersonian liberalism and anything-goes-as-long-as-it-is-properly-rated approach to movies differed sharply from Breen's Catholic conservatism and eagerness to censor film scripts, both Heffner and Breen concluded that the world of cinema had little commitment to the values they held most important, and that it exploited those values with impunity. Similarly, communication technologies frustrated attempts to control pornography during the late 1980s. Boycotts and aggressive prosecutions during the Reagan and first Bush administrations had only limited success. Economic pressures were effective in convincing mainstream studios and theaters to all but abandon NC-17 films. But the overall availability of sexually explicit and violent materials made possible by VCRs, cable, satellite, computers, and the Internet increased dramatically. In this media environment, Cardinal Mahony's plan for a new production code stood little chance for long-term success. Legislation often fared no better. The Communication Decency Act, designed to limit pornography on the Internet, failed to find a formula that safeguarded basic constitutional freedoms.

At the beginning of the twenty-first century Americans face a dilemma. A tremendously lucrative and powerful entertainment complex encompassing many media has been created. Throughout the previous century this complex demonstrated scant regard for values that could not be put to the service of image, power, wealth, or sex. The technologies that made this complex possible have continued to evolve at an accelerating rate, so even greater changes appear probable in the future. We are not yet able to see the full scope of what these changes will bring, but if the past is prologue, then at the very least they promise a future where any system of regulation will be severely tested. It is not nearly enough simply to leave control of all aspects of these media in the hands of those who own them.

Archives

California

Simi Valley, Ronald Reagan Presidential Library
   WHORM Subject Files

District of Columbia

Washington, Library of Congress, Motion Picture and Television Reading Room
   Motion Picture Association of America Rating Sheets
Washington, National Archives I
   RG 46: U.S. Senate Committee on Commerce Papers (1968), Sen 90A-E6, Box
   53
   RG 59: Department of State Decimal File, 1945–9, Boxes 4452, 5924, 6659

Indiana

Bloomington, Indiana University, Kinsey Institute Archives
   Kinsey Institute Library Film and Video Collection
   Photography Collection

Maine

Skowhegan, Margaret Chase Smith Library, The Northwood Institute
   Margaret Chase Smith Papers

Maryland

College Park, National Archives II
   RG 60: Records of the Attorney General's Commission on Pornography
   RG 444: Office of Technology Assessment Records, Technology Assessment
   Advisory Council Meeting Files (1978)

New York

New York, Columbia University, Butler Library, Columbia Oral History Collection
Papers of Richard D. Heffner
New York, Museum of Television and Radio
The Open Mind [taped guest interviews]
New York
Papers of Richard D. Heffner, Private Collection: Classification and Rating
Administration *Annual Reports* (1969–99)

Texas

Austin, Lyndon Baines Johnson Library
Oral History Collection

Utah

Provo, Brigham Young University, Harold B. Lee Library, Special Collections and
Manuscripts
Records of the National Association of Theater Owners (NATO)

Wisconsin

Madison, Wisconsin Historical Society
Merle Curti Papers
Otto Preminger Papers, 1948–72
United Artists Collection Addition, 1950–80

Government Hearings and Publications

Note: This list is arranged chronologically.

"Juvenile Delinquency (Television Programs)." U.S. Congress. Senate. Committee on the Judiciary. *Hearings, Subcommittee to Investigate Juvenile Delinquency.* 84th Cong., 1 session, S. Res. 62, June 5, Oct. 19–20, 1954, and April 6–7, 1955. Washington, DC: Government Printing Office, 1955. Cited as *U.S. Senate Hearings (TV), 1954–55.*

"Juvenile Delinquency (Motion Pictures)." U.S. Congress. Senate. Committee on the Judiciary. *Hearings, Subcommittee to Investigate Juvenile Delinquency.* 84th Cong., 1 sess., S. Res. 62, June 15–18, 1955. Washington, DC: Government Printing Office, 1955. Cited as *U.S. Senate Hearings (movies), 1955.*

"The Committee on Film Classification." U.S. Congress. Senate. Committee on Commerce. *Hearings.* 90th Cong., S. Res. 9, June 11, 1968. Washington, DC: Government Printing Office, 1968. Cited as *U.S. Senate Hearings, 1968.*

Baker, Robert K., and Sandra J. Ball. *Mass Media and Violence. Volume IX. A Report to the National Commission on the Causes and Prevention of Violence.* Washington, DC: Government Printing Office, 1969.

Commission on Obscenity and Pornography. *The Report of the Commission on Obscenity and Pornography.* Washington, DC: Government Printing Office, 1970. Cited as *RCOP.*

The Report of the Commission on Obscenity and Pornography: Volume I: Preliminary Studies. Washington, DC: Government Printing Office, 1971. Cited as *TRCOP: Vol. I.*

The Report of the Commission on Obscenity and Pornography: Volume II: Legal Analysis. Washington, DC: Government Printing Office, 1971. Cited as *TRCOP: Vol. II.*

The Report of the Commission on Obscenity and Pornography: Volume III: The Marketplace The Industry. Washington, DC: Government Printing Office, 1971. Cited as *TRCOP: Vol. III.*

The Report of the Commission on Obscenity and Pornography: Volume IV: The Marketplace Empirical Studies. Washington, DC: Government Printing Office, 1971. Cited as *TRCOP: Vol. IV.*

The Report of the Commission on Obscenity and Pornography: Volume V: Societal Control Mechanisms. Washington, DC: Government Printing Office, (1971). Cited as *TRCOP: Vol. V.*

The Report of the Commission on Obscenity and Pornography: Volume VI: National Survey. Washington, DC: Government Printing Office, (1971). Cited as *TRCOP: Vol. VI.*

The Report of the Commission on Obscenity and Pornography: Volume VII: Erotica and Antisocial Behavior. Washington, DC: Government Printing Office, (1971). Cited as *TRCOP: Vol. VII.*

The Report of the Commission on Obscenity and Pornography: Volume VIII: Erotica and Social Behavior. Washington, DC: Government Printing Office, (1971). Cited as *TRCOP, Vol. VIII.*

The Report of the Commission on Obscenity and Pornography: Volume IX: The Consumer and the Community. Washington, DC: Government Printing Office, (1971). Cited as *TRCOP, Vol. IX.*

Comstock, George A., Eli A. Rubinstein, and John P. Murray, eds. *Television and Social Behavior Reports and Papers. Volume IV, Television in Day-to-Day Life Patterns of Use: A Technical Report to the Surgeon General's Scientific Advisory Committee on Television and Social Behavior.* Rockville, MD: National Institute of Mental Health, (1972). Cited as *TSBRP: Vol. IV.*

Comstock, George A., Eli A. Rubinstein, and John P. Murray, eds. *Television and Social Behavior Reports and Papers. Volume V, Television's Effects Further Explorations: A Technical Report to the Surgeon General's Scientific Advisory Committee on Television and Social Behavior.* Rockville, MD: National Institute of Mental Health, (1972). Cited as *TSBRP: Vol. V.*

"Movie Ratings and the Independent Producer." U.S. Congress. House. Committee on Small Business. *Hearings before Subcommittee on Special Small Business Problems.* 95th Cong., 1st sess., March 24, April 14, May 12, June 15, July 21, 1977. Washington, DC: Government Printing Office, 1977. Cited as *U.S. House Hearings, 1977.*

Royal Commission on Violence (Ontario, Canada). *Report of The Royal Commission on Violence in the Communications Industry: Volume I: Approaches, Conclusions and Recommendations.* Toronto: Queen's Printer for Ontario, (1977).

Office of Technology Assessment. *Computer-Based National Information Systems Technology and Public Policy Issues.* (Washington, D.C.): OTA/Government Printing Office, 1981.

"Copyright Infringements (Audio and Video Recorders)." U.S. Congress. Senate. Committee on the Judiciary. *Hearings.* 97th Cong., 1st and 2d sessions on S. 1758, Nov. 30, 1981 and April 21, 1982. Washington, DC: Government Printing Office, 1982. Cited as *U.S. Senate Hearings, 1981–82.*

"Home Recording of Copyrighted Works." U.S. Congress. House. Committee on the Judiciary. *Hearings before the Subcommittee on Courts, Civil Liberties, and the Administration of Justice.* 97th Cong., 2d sess., on H.R. 4783,

H.R. 4794, H.R. 4808, H.R. 5250, H.R., 5488, and H.R. 5705, April 12–14, June 24, Aug. 11, Sept. 22–23, 1982. Washington, DC: Government Printing Office, 1983. Cited as *U.S. House Hearings, 1982*.

Pearl, David, Lorraine Bouthilet, and Joyce Lazar, eds. *Television and Behavior: Ten Years of Scientific Progress and Implications for the Eighties. Volume I: Summary Report*. Rockville, MD: National Institute of Mental Health, 1982.

Television and Behavior: Ten Years of Scientific Progress and Implications for the Eighties. Volume II: Technical Reviews. Rockville, MD: National Institute of Mental Health, 1982.

"Public Hearings on Ordinances to Add Pornography as Discrimination against Women." Session I, Minneapolis, MN, Dec. 12, 1983, Box 69, Records of the Attorney General's Commission on Pornography, RG 60 (Justice Dept. Records), NARA 2, College Park, MD. Cited as *Minneapolis Hearings, 1983*.

"Role of the Feature Film Industry in a National Effort to Diminish Drug Use among Young People." U.S. Congress. Senate. Committee on Governmental Affairs. *Hearings before Permanent Subcommittee on Investigations*, 99th Cong., 1st sess., Oct. 24, 1985. Washington, DC: Government Printing Office, 1985. Cited as *U.S. Senate Hearings, 1985*.

Hearings before the Attorney General's Commission on Pornography, 1985–86. Records of the Attorney General's Commission on Pornography, RG 60 (Justice Dept. Records), NARA II, College Park, MD. Cited as *Meese Commission Hearings, 1985–86*.

Attorney General's Commission on Pornography. *Final Report of the Attorney General's Commission on Pornography*. Nashville, TN: Rutledge Hill Press, 1986. Cited as *Final Report, 1986*.

Office of Technology Assessment. *New Developments in Biotechnology Background Paper Public Perceptions of Biotechnology*. Vol. 2. Washington, DC: Congress of the United States, Office of Technology Assessment, 1987.

United States Department of Justice. *Beyond the Pornography Commission: The Federal Response*. Washington, DC: Government Printing Office, 1988.

"Television Ratings System." U.S. Congress. Senate. Committee on Commerce, Science, and Transportation. *Hearings*. 105th Cong., 1st sess., Feb. 27, 1997. Washington, DC: Government Printing Office, 1997. Cited as *U.S. Senate Hearings, 1997*.

Federal Trade Commission. *Marketing Violent Entertainment to Children: Self-Regulation and Industry Practices in the Motion Picture, Music Recording, and Electronic Game Industries: A Report of the Federal Trade Commission*. Washington, DC: Federal Trade Commission, 2000.

"Marketing Violent Entertainment to Children: Self-Regulation and Industry Practices in the Motion Picture, Music Recording, and Electronic Game Industries." U.S. Congress, House, Committee on Energy and Commerce. *Hearings before the Subcommittee on Telecommunications and the Internet*, July 20, 2001 (http//www.ftc.gov/os/2001/07/violencetest.htm).

Motion Pictures

Above the Law. 1988. Directed by Andrew Davis. Warner Bros. Distribution / Warner Home Video / Canal Plus Group TV.

The Accused. 1988. Directed by Jonathan Kaplan. Paramount Pictures.

Agnes of God. 1985. Directed by Norman Jewison. Columbia Pictures.

Airplane! 1980. Directed by Jim Abrahams, David Zucker, and Jerry Zucker. Paramount.

Alfie. 1966. Directed by Lewis Gilbert. Paramount.

Alice's Restaurant. 1969. Directed by Arthur Penn. United Artists.

All the President's Men. 1976. Directed by Alan J. Pakula. Warner Bros.

American Gigolo. 1980. Directed by Paul Schrader. Paramount.

Andy Warhol's Frankenstein. 1974. Directed by Paul Morrissey. Brayanston Pictures.

Angel Heart. 1987. Directed by Alan Parker. Tri-Star Pictures.

Arthur. 1981. Directed by Steve Gordon. Orion Pictures.

Atlantic City. 1981. Directed by Louis Malle. Dennis Heroux, Cine Neighbor, Selta Films.

The Baby Maker. 1970. Directed by James Bridges. National General Pictures.

Back to the Future. 1985. Directed by Robert Zemeckis. Universal/Universal Studios Home Video.

Bad Lieutenant. 1992. Directed by Abel Ferrara. Aries Films.

Bad Timing: A Sensual Obsession. 1980. Directed by Nicholas Roeg. A Recorded Picture Company Production World Northal.

Barry Lyndon. 1975. Directed by Stanley Kubrick. Warner Bros.

Basic Instinct. 1992. Directed by Paul Verhoeven. Carolo Pictures / Le Studio Canal Plus / Basic Inst. Inc. – Tri-Star Pictures.

Batman Returns. 1992. Directed by Tim Burton. Warner Bros.

Behind the Green Door. 1973. Directed by Jim Mitchell and Art Mitchell. Mitchell Bros. Film Group.

Being There. 1979. Directed by Hal Ashby. Warner Studios, Lorimar Productions, Andrew Braunsberg Productions.

The Bells of St. Mary's. 1945. Directed by Leo McCarey.

Ben-Hur. 1959. Directed by William Wyler. MGM.

Beyond the Valley of the Dolls. 1970. Directed by Russ Meyer. 20th Century Fox/ Baker & Taylor Video.

The Big Chill. 1983. Directed by Lawrence Kasdan. Columbia Tri-Star.

Bird. 1988. Directed by Clint Eastwood. Malpaso Productions.

Birds Do It, Bees Do It. 1974. Columbia Pictures.

The Birth of a Nation. 1915. Directed by D. W. Griffith. Epoch.

Blade Runner. 1982. Directed by Ridley Scott. Warner Bros.

Blue Velvet. 1986. Directed by David Lynch. De Laurentiis Entertainment Group.

The Blues Brothers. 1980. Directed by John Landis. Universal.

Body Double. 1984. Directed by Brian De Palma. Columbia Pictures.

Body Heat. 1981. Directed by Lawrence Kasdan. Ladd Company/ Warner Bros.

Body of Evidence. 1993. Directed by Uli Edel. MGM.

Bonnie and Clyde. 1967. Directed by Arthur Penn. Warner Bros./Seven Arts/ Tatira/Hiller.

Born on the Fourth of July. 1989. Directed by Oliver Stone. Fourth of July / Universal.

Bound for Glory. 1976. United Artists.

Boxcar Bertha. 1972. Directed by Martin Scorsese. American International Pictures.

Boys' Town. 1938. Directed by Norman Taurog. MGM.

A Bridge Too Far. 1977. Great Britain. Directed by Richard Attenborough. United Artists.

Brother Sun, Sister Moon. 1973. Italy; Great Britain. Directed by Franco Zeffirelli. Euro International Films/ Vic Film/ Paramount.

Caddyshack. 1980. Directed by Harold Ramis. Warner Bros.

Cagney and Lacy. 1984–5. Orion Pictures Corp.

Caligula. 1980. Directed by Tinto Brass, Bob Guccione, and Franco Rossellini.

Cape Fear. 1962. Directed by J. Lee Thompson. Melville-Talbot / Universal.

Cape Fear. 1991. Directed by Martin Scorsese. Universal / Cape Fear Inc. / Amblin Entertainment / Cappa Films / Tribeca Productions.

Carnal Knowledge. 1971. Directed by Mike Nichols. AVCO Embassy Pictures/ Mike Nichols Productions/ Columbia Tri-Star Home Video.

Chinatown. 1974. Directed by Roman Polanski. Paramount.

The Chosen. 1981. Directed by Jeremy Paul Kagan. Trimark/ 20th Century Fox Home Entertainment.

A Clockwork Orange. 1971. Directed by Stanley Kubrick. Warner Bros./Polaris.

Close Encounters of the Third Kind. 1977. Directed by Steven Spielberg. Columbia.

The Color of Night. 1994. Directed by Richard Rush. Buena Vista, Hollywood Pictures, Cinergi Productions, Color of Night Productions.

The Cook, the Thief, His Wife and Her Lover. 1990. Directed by Peter Greenaway. Miramax Films / Allarts Cook / Erato Films, Great Britain.

Crimes and Misdemeanors. 1989. Directed by Woody Allen.

Crimes of Passion. 1984. Directed by Ken Russell. New World Pictures.

Cruising. 1980. Directed by William Friedkin. Lorimar/ United Artists.

Damage. 1992. Directed by Louis Malle. New Line Cinema.
Dawn of the Dead. 1979. Directed by George A. Romero. United Film.
Days of Heaven. 1978. Directed by Terrence Malick. Paramount.
Deadly Friend. 1986. Directed by Wes Craven. Warner Bros./ Pan Arts – Layton.
Death Wish. 1974. Directed by Michael Winner. DeLaurentiis / Paramount.
Deep Throat. 1972. Directed by Jerry Gerard [Gerard Damiano]. Aquarius.
Desert Hearts. 1986. Directed by Donna Deitch. Samuel Goldwyn Company; British Film Institute.
Desperate Lives. 1982. Directed by Robert Lewis. Lorimar Productions.
The Devil in Miss Jones. 1973. Directed by Gerard Damiano. VCA.
Die Hard. 1988. Directed by John McTiernan. Gordon – Silver / 20th Century Fox.
Die Hard 2. 1990. Directed by Renny Harlin. 20th Century Fox.
The Dirty Dozen. 1967. Directed by Robert Aldrich. MGM.
Dressed to Kill. 1980. Directed by Brian De Palma. Samuel Z. Arkoff / Filmways.
E. T. – The Extra-Terrestrial. 1982. Directed by Steven Spielberg. Universal.
Easy Rider. 1969. Directed by Dennis Hopper. Pando-Raybert/ Columbia.
Emmanuelle. 1974. Columbia Pictures Corp./Europe.
The Empire Strikes Back. 1980. Directed by Irvin Kershner. 20th Century Fox.
Enemies, a Love Story. 1989. Directed by Paul Mazursky. 20th Century Fox/ Morgan Creek Productions.
The Entity. 1982. Directed by Sydney J. Furie. Belleport Investors/ 20th Century Fox.
The Exorcist. 1973. Directed by William Friedkin. Warner Bros.
Facts of Life. 1985. Embassy Communications.
Fame PSA. 1984. MGM/UA.
Fatal Attraction. 1987. Directed by Adrian Lyne. Paramount.
The Fighting 69th. 1940. Directed by William Keighley. Warner Bros.
A Fish Called Wanda. 1988. Directed by Charles Crichton. MGM.
For God and Country. 1944. U.S. Army Air Corps.
Fort Apache – The Bronx. 1981. Directed by Daniel Petrie. 20th Century Fox.
Four Seasons. 1981. Directed by Alan Alda. Universal.
Frankenhooker. 1990. Directed by Frank Henenlotter. Shapiro-Glickenhaus.
French Connection. 1971. Directed by William Friedkin. 20th Century Fox.
Friday the 13th. 1980. Directed by Sean S. Cunningham. Paramount.
Friday the 13th: Part II. 1981. Directed by Steve Miner. Paramount.
The Front. 1976. Directed by Martin Ritt. Columbia Pictures.
The Getaway. 1972. Directed by Sam Peckinpah.
The Girl on a Motorcycle. 1968. Warner Bros. – Seven Arts.
The Godfather, Part III. 1990. Directed by Francis Ford Coppola. Paramount.
Godspell. 1973. Directed by David Greene. Columbia Pictures.
Going My Way. 1944. Directed by Leo McCarey. Paramount.
Goodfellas. 1990. Directed by Martin Scorsese. Warner Bros.
The Graduate. 1967. Directed by Mike Nichols. United Artists/Embassy.
The Greatest Story Ever Told. 1965. Directed by George Stevens. United Artists/ George Stevens.
Gremlins PSA. 1984. Directed by Joe Dante. Warner Bros.

Hail Mary (Je Vous Salue Marie). 1985. France. Directed by Jean-Luc Godard. Gaumont.

Halloween. 1978. Directed by John Carpenter. Falcon / Compass.

The Handmaid's Tale. 1990. Directed by Volker Schloendorff. Cinecom Pictures, Master Partners, Cinetudes Film Productions.

Hannah and Her Sisters. 1986. Directed by Woody Allen. Orion Pictures.

Hard Country. 1981. Directed by David Greene.

Hardware. 1990. Directed by Richard Stanley. Palace Productions and Millimeter Films.

Heaven and Earth. 1993. Directed by Oliver Stone. New Regency Films/ Warner Bros./Studio Canal Plus/ Alcor Films/ Heaven and Earth Change Places, Inc. / TAE, Inc.

Heaven Help Us. 1985. Directed by Michael Dinner. Tri-Star Pictures.

Henry and June. 1990. Directed by Philip Kaufman. Universal/ Walrus and Associates.

Henry: Portrait of a Serial Killer. 1990. Directed by John McNaughton. Maljack Productions/ Greycat Films.

A Hero Ain't Nothin' But a Sandwich. 1977. Directed by Ralph Nelson. New World.

The Hills Have Eyes. 1978. Directed by Wes Craven. Blood Relations / Vanguard.

Honky Tonk Freeway. 1981. Directed by John Schlesinger. EMI Productions/ Univ-AFD.

Honkytonk Man. 1982. Directed by Clint Eastwood. Warner Bros.

I Spit on Your Grave (a.k.a. *Day of the Woman*). 1978, 1981. Directed by Meir Zarchi. Cinemagic Pictures.

If You Can't Say It, Just See It. 1991. Directed by Ken Russell. Trimark / Lion's Gate Home Entertainment.

In the Cold of the Night. 1990. Directed by Nico Mastorakis. Omega Entertainment.

Indiana Jones and the Temple of Doom. 1984. Directed by Steven Spielberg. Paramount Pictures.

Inserts. 1976. Directed by John Byrum. CBS/ Fox Video.

Jaws. 1975. Directed by Steven Spielberg. Universal.

The Jay Leno Show. 1990s.

Jesus Christ Superstar. 1973. Directed by Norman Jewison. Universal Pictures.

Jesus of Nazareth. 1977. Directed by Franco Zeffirelli. ATV, Ltd./ RAI.

JFK. 1991. Directed by Oliver Stone. Camelot Productions/ Warner Bros.

The Johnny Carson Show. 1960s–1970s.

King of Kings. 1927. Directed by Cecil B. DeMille. Cecil B. DeMille/ Pathé.

King of New York. 1990. Directed by Abel Ferrara. Medusa/ Seven Arts Pictures.

Lady Chatterley's Lover. 1957. Kingsley International, France/Gilbert Cohn-Seat.

Last Summer. 1969. Directed by Frank Perry. Alsid-Francis/ Allied Artists.

Last Tango in Paris. 1973. Directed by Bernardo Bertolucci. United Artists, United Artists/Italy.

The Last Temptation of Christ. 1988. Directed by Martin Scorsese. Universal – Cineplex Odeon / Universal.

The Last Tycoon. 1976. Directed by Elia Kazan. Paramount.

Lethal Weapon II. 1989. Directed by Richard Donner. Warner Bros.

Life Is Cheap ... but Toilet Paper Is Expensive. 1990. Directed by Wayne Wang. Silverlight Entertainment / Forever Profits Investments.

The Lover (L'Amant). 1992. Directed by Jean-Jacques Annaud.

M*A*S*H. 1970. Directed by Robert Altman. Aspen/ 20th Century Fox.

Making Love. 1982. Directed by Arthur Hiller. Indie Productions/ 20th Century Fox.

Manhattan. 1979. Directed by Woody Allen. United Artists.

The Marathon Man. 1976. Directed by John Schlesinger. Paramount.

Men of Boys' Town. 1941. Directed by Norman Taurog. MGM.

Midnight Cowboy. 1969. Directed by John Schlesinger. United Artists.

Midnight Express. 1978. Directed by Alan Parker. Columbia Pictures.

The Miracle. 1948. Directed by Roberto Rossellini. Joseph Burstyn.

Misery. 1990. Directed by Rob Reiner. Castle Rock Entertainment/ Nelson Entertainment.

The Mission. 1986. Directed by Roland Joffe. Golderest Films/ Kingsmere.

Modern Problems. 1981. Directed by Ken Shapiro. 20th Century Fox.

Mommie Dearest. 1981. Directed by Frank Perry. Paramount.

Monsignor. 1982. Directed by Frank Perry. 20th Century Fox.

Monty Python's Life of Brian (a.k.a. *Life of Brian*). 1979. Directed by Terry Jones. Warner Bros. – Orion, Great Britain.

Moonraker. 1979. Directed by Lewis Gilbert. MGM.

Mother Teresa. 1987. Directed by Ann Petrie and Jeanette Petrie. Today Home Entertainment.

Mr. T. PSA. 1984. Warner Bros.

My Beautiful Laundrette. 1985. Directed by Stephen Frears. Orion Pictures.

My Dinner with André. 1981. Directed by Louis Malle. Saga Productions/ New Yorker Films.

My Left Foot. 1989. Directed by Jim Sheridan. Miramax Films/ Granada Film Productions.

Myra Breckinridge. 1970. Directed by Michael Sarne. 20th Century Fox.

Nashville. 1975. Directed by Robert Altman. ABC/Paramount.

Nasty Habits. 1976. Great Britain. Directed by Michael Lindsay-Hogg. Bowden/ Brut.

National Lampoon's Animal House. 1978. Directed by John Landis. Universal Pictures.

National Lampoon's Class Reunion. 1982. Directed by Michael Miller. 20th Century Fox/ ABC.

Natural Born Killers. 1994. Directed by Oliver Stone. New Regency Pictures/ Warner Bros.

A New Leaf. 1971. Directed by Elaine May. Paramount/ Howard W. Koch – Hillard Elkins.

Night of the Living Dead (a.k.a. *Night of the Flesh Eaters*). 1968. Directed by George A. Romero. Image Ten / Continental.

A Nightmare on Elm Street. 1985. Directed by Wes Craven. New Line Cinema/ Media Home Entertainment/ Image Associates/ Condor Productions.

Nijinsky. 1980. Directed by Herbert Ross. Paramount.

9 1/2 Weeks. 1986. Directed by Adrian Lyne. MGM/Home Entertainment.

Nine to Five. 1980. Directed by Colin Higgins. 20th Century Fox / Independent Film Corp.

Nixon. 1995. Directed by Oliver Stone. Cinerg: Productions / Illusion Entertainment Group / Hollywood Pictures – Buena Vista.

No Way Out. 1987. Directed by Roger Donaldson. Orion Pictures.

Oh God! 1977. Directed by Carl Reiner. Warner Bros.

The Outlaw Josie Wales. 1976. Directed by Clint Eastwood. Malpaso / Warner Bros.

Pale Rider. 1985. Directed by Clint Eastwood. Malpaso / Warner Bros.

Panic in Needle Park. 1971. Directed by Jerry Schatzberg. Dunne – Didion – Dunne/20th Century Fox.

The Passover Plot. 1976. Israel. Directed by Michael Campus. Atlas.

Pawnbroker. 1965. Directed by Sidney Lumet. Landau – Unger – Pawnbroker.

Personal Best. 1982. Directed by Robert Towne. Geffen/Warner Bros.

Platoon. 1986. Directed by Oliver Stone. Hemdal Films/ Arnold Kopelson.

Police Academy III: Back in Training. 1986. Directed by Jerry Paris. Warner Bros.

Poltergeist. 1982. Directed by Tobe Hooper. MGM/United Artists.

Popeye. 1980. Directed by Robert Altman. Paramount.

The Postman Always Rings Twice. 1981. Directed by Bob Rafelson. Northstar International / Paramount.

Pretty Baby. 1978. Directed by Louis Malle. Paramount.

Pretty Woman. 1990. Directed by Garry Marshall. Touchstone Pictures.

Private Benjamin. 1980. Directed by Howard Zieff. Warner Bros.

Prospero's Books. 1991. Directed by Peter Greenaway. 20th Century Fox International/Miramax Films.

Psycho. 1960. Directed by Alfred Hitchcock. Paramount.

Radio Days. 1987. Directed by Woody Allen. Orion Pictures.

Raiders of the Lost Ark. 1981. Directed by Steven Spielberg. Lucasfilm Productions/Paramount.

Rambo: First Blood II. 1985. Directed by George Pan Cosmatos. Tri-Star Pictures.

The Rapture. 1991. Directed by Michael Tolkin. New Line Home Entertainment/ Columbia Tri-Star Home Video.

Reds. 1981. Directed by Warren Beatty. Paramount.

Return of the Jedi. 1983. Directed by Richard Marquand. Lucasfilm Productions/ 20th Century Fox.

Revenge of the Nerds. 1984. Directed by Jeff Kanew. 20th Century Fox.

The Right Stuff. 1983. Directed by Philip Kaufman. Ladd/ Warner Bros.

Risky Business. 1983. Directed by Paul Brickman. Geffen/ Warner Bros.

The Robe. 1953. Directed by Henry Koster. 20th Century Fox.

Robocop. 1987. Directed by Paul Verhoeven. MGM.

Rocky. 1976. Directed by John G. Avildsen. United Artists.

Rollerball. 1975. Directed by Norman Jewison. MGM / United Artists.

The Rose. 1979. Directed by Mark Rydell. 20th Century Fox.

Salem's Lot. 1979. Directed by Tobe Hooper. Warner Bros.

Salvador. 1986. Directed by Oliver Stone. Hemdale, Great Britain.

Saturday Night Fever. 1977. Directed by John Badham. Paramount.
Saturday Night Live. 1970s.
The Savage Is Loose. 1974. Directed by George C. Scott. Campbell – Devon.
The Saving of Young Anderson. 1914. Reliance.
Scalawag. 1973. Yugoslavia. Directed by Kirk Douglas. Inex-Oceania-Byrna/Paramount.
Scandal. 1989. Directed by Michael Caton-Jones. Miramax.
Scarface. 1983. Directed by Brian De Palma. Universal.
The Seven Samurai. 1954. Directed by Akira Kurosawa. Criterion Collection (DVD, 1998).
Sex, Lies, and Videotape. 1989. Directed by Steven Soderbergh. Miramax Films/ Outlaw Productions.
Shampoo. 1975. Directed by Hal Ashby. Columbia Pictures.
She's Gotta Have It. 1986. Directed by Spike Lee. Island Pictures/ Spike Lee.
The Shining. 1980. Directed by Stanley Kubrick. Warner Bros.
Shocker. 1989. Directed by Wes Craven. Alive Films/ Mark Huffam.
Showgirls. 1995. Directed by Paul Verhoeven. MGM/United Artists.
Silver Bullet. 1985. Directed by Daniel Attias. Paramount.
Sin with a Stranger. 1968. Paramount, Paramount (French-Italian).
Sixteen Candles. 1984. Directed by John Hughes. Universal.
Snuff. 1973. Directed by Michael Findlay and Roberta Findlay. Monarch Releasing Corporation.
Soldier Blue. 1970. Directed by Ralph Nelson. Avco Embassy.
Star Wars. 1977. Directed by George Lucas. 20th Century Fox.
Still Smokin'. 1983. Directed by Thomas Chong. Paramount.
The Street Fighter. 1974. Directed by Shigehiro Ozawa. New Line Cinema.
The Stunt Man. 1980. Directed by Richard Rush. 20th Century Fox.
The Sugarland Express. 1974. Directed by Steven Spielberg. Universal.
Superman. 1978. Directed by Richard Donner. Warner Bros.
Superman II. 1980. Directed by Richard Lester. Warner Bros.
Swept Away (a.k.a. *Swept Away by an Unusual Destiny in the Blue Sea in August*). 1975. Directed by Lina Wertmuller. Medusa (Italy).
T. J. Hooker: Blood Sport. 1986. Directed by Vincent McEveety. Columbia Pictures.
Taxi Driver. 1976. Directed by Martin Scorsese. Bill / Phillips / Columbia Pictures.
Teen Wolf. 1985. Directed by Rod Daniel. Wolfkill Productions/ Paramount Home Video.
The Ten Commandments. 1956. Directed by Cecil DeMille. Paramount.
Terms of Endearment. 1983. Directed by Harold Michelson. Paramount.
Texas Chainsaw Massacre. 1974. Directed by Tobe Hooper. Vortex – Henkel – Hooper/ Bryanston.
Tie Me Up! Tie Me Down! 1990. Directed by Pedro Almodóvar. Miramax Films / El Deseo.
Titanic. 1997. Directed by James Cameron. 20th Century Fox/Paramount.
The Toolbox Murders. 1978. Directed by Dennis Donnelly. Cal-Am.
Total Recall. 1990. Directed by Peter Verhoeven. Carolco Pictures.
Tron. 1982. Directed by Steven Lisberger. Buena Vista (Walt Disney).

Tropic of Cancer. 1970. Directed by Joseph Strick. Paramount Pictures / Paramount Home Video.

True Confessions. 1981. Directed by Ulu Grosbard. United Artists.

2001: A Space Odyssey. 1968. Directed by Stanley Kubrick. MGM/Stanley Kubrick.

The Unbearable Lightness of Being. 1988. Directed by Philip Kaufman. Orion Pictures/ Saul Zaentz Company.

Up In Smoke. 1978. Directed by Lou Adler. Paramount.

Wall Street. 1987. Directed by Oliver Stone. 20th Century Fox.

When the Screaming Stops. 1974. Directed by Amando de Ossorio.

Who's Afraid of Virginia Woolf? 1966. Directed by Mike Nichols. Warner Bros.

Whore (a.k.a. *If You Can't Say It, Just See It*). 1991. Directed by Ken Russell. Trimark/ Lion's Gate Home Entertainment.

Wide Sargasso Sea. 1993. Directed by John Duigan. New Line Home Entertainment/Laughing Kookaburra Productions.

Wild at Heart. 1990. Directed by David Lynch. Polygram/ Propaganda Films.

The Wild Bunch. 1969. Directed by Sam Peckinpah. Warner Bros. / Seven Arts.

Windows. 1980. Directed by Gordon Willis. United Artists.

The Winning Team. 1952. Directed by Lewis Seiler. Warner Bros.

Wolfen. 1981. Directed by Michael Wadleigh. Orion Pictures/ Warner Bros.

Women on the Verge of a Nervous Breakdown. 1988. Directed by Pedro Almodóvar. El Deseo/Laurenfilm/Orion Home Video.

Zorba the Greek. 1963. Directed by Michael Cacoyannis. 20th Century Fox/ Cacoyannis–Rochley/ International Classics.

Bibliography

Adler, Mortimer J. *Art and Prudence: A Study in Practical Philosophy*. New York: Longmans, Green and Co., 1937.

AFA: American Family Association of New York. http://www.AFANY.org (accessed March 29, 2005).

Allen, Mike, and Ellen Nakashima. "Clinton, Gore Hit Hollywood Marketing; Ads Aimed at Kids Could Spur Rules, Industry Is Told." *Washington Post*, Sept. 12, 2000, A1.

American Academy of Child and Adolescent Psychiatry et al. "Joint Statement on the Impact of Entertainment Violence on Children – Congressional Public Health Summit (July 26, 2000)." http://www.aacap.org/press_releases/2000/0726.htm (accessed Feb. 2, 2003).

American Academy of Pediatrics (AAP). "Statement, . . . on the Television Ratings System." *U.S. Senate Hearings*, 1997, 342–45.

American Civil Liberties Union. *Rating Systems Sponsored by the Communications Industries, Policy no. 18*, Document 88-14A. In Richard D. Heffner, "Pre-Oral History Memo for 1988," Box 4, RDH-COHC-BL.

American Medical Association (AMA). "Statement, . . . RE Ratings System for Violence on Television," *U.S. Senate Hearings*, 1997, 334–41.

American Psychiatric Association (APA). "Statement on the Television Parental Guidelines System," *U.S. Senate Hearings*, 1997, 240–4.

Anderson, Craig A., and Brad J. Bushman. "The Effects of Media Violence on Society." *Science* 30 (2002): 1–2.

Anderson, Craig A., and Brad J. Bushman. "Effects of Violent Video Games on Aggressive Behavior, Aggressive Cognition, Aggressive Affect, Physiological Arousal, and Prosocial Behavior: A Meta-Analytic Review of the Scientific Literature." *Psychological Science* 12, no. 5 (2001): 353–9.

Anderson, Patrick. "Born Hero-Worshiper Who Serves His Hero." *New York Times Magazine*, 1966, 28–9, 64, 66, 71–2.

Anderson, Patrick. *The President's Men: White House Assistants of Franklin D. Roosevelt, Harry S. Truman, Dwight D. Eisenhower, John F. Kennedy* and Lyndon B. Johnson. Garden City, NY: Doubleday & Company, 1968.

Ansen, David. "Raw Carnage or Revelation? The Overkilling Fields." *Newsweek,* Aug. 29, 1994, 54.

Arar, Yardena. "Movie-Ratings Boss Says System Works." *Cleveland Plain Dealer,* Nov. 25, 1993, L3.

"Archdiocese Demands Stronger Anti-Porn Laws and Prosecution." *Los Angeles Times,* March 15, 1987, A32.

Atkinson, Terry. "Home Tech: Quiet Release of Controversial 'Last Temptation of Christ.'" *Los Angeles Times,* June 30, 1989, sec. 6 (Calendar), p. 25.

Austin, Charles. "Bishops in Plea against Smut." *New York Times,* May 25, 1983, A19.

Bach, Steven. *Final Cut: Dreams and Disaster in the Making of Heaven's Gate.* New York: William Morrow and Company, 1985.

Bailey, John. "Film or Digital? Don't Fight. Coexist." *New York Times,* Feb. 18, 2001, sec. 2 (Arts and Leisure), 9, 20.

Barish, Jonas. *The Antitheatrical Prejudice.* Berkeley: University of California Press, 1981.

Barnhart, Aaron. "'V' Is for Virtually Ignored: In a Software Age, the Hard-Wired V-Chip Hasn't Caught On." *Wisconsin State Journal* (Madison), April 28, 2000, D1, D3.

Barricklow, Denis. "Almodovar Appeals X Rating on Latest Film." UPI Release, April 24, 1990.

Barry, David S. "Screen Violence and America's Children." *Spectrum* 66, no. 3(1993): 37–43.

Barry, Kathleen. *Female Sexual Slavery.* Englewood Cliffs, NJ: Prentice-Hall, 1979.

Bates, James, and Jube Shiver, Jr. "Film Industry Gets New Top Lobbyist." *Los Angeles Times,* July 2, 2004, A1.

Baughman, James L. *Television's Guardians: The FCC and the Politics of Programming, 1958–1967.* Knoxville: University of Tennessee Press, 1985.

Becker, Judith, and Ellen Levine. "Statement of Dr. Judith Becker and Ellen Levine." *Final Report* (1986), 540–6.

Becker, Judith, Ellen Levine, and Deanne Tilton-Durfee, "Statement of Judith Becker, Ellen Levine and Deanne Tilton-Durfee." *Final Report* (1986), 540.

"Bennett Urges Entertainment Industry to Join War on Drugs." *St. Petersburg Times,* Oct. 24, 1989, A3.

Bennetts, Leslie. "Conservatives Join on Social Concerns." *New York Times,* July 30, 1980, A1.

Bergery, Benjamin. "Framing the Future." *American Cinematographer* 82, no. 9(2001): 76–83.

Berinstein, Paula. *Statistical Handbook on Technology.* Phoenix, AZ: Oryx Press, 1999.

Berkowitz, Leonard, ed. *Advances in Experimental Social Psychology.* Vol. 15. New York: Academic Press, 1982.

Aggression: A Social Psychological Analysis. New York: McGraw-Hill Book Company, 1962.

Berkowitz, Leonard. Interview, *New York Times*, June 20, 1982.

Berns, Walter. "On Pornography: I – Pornography vs. Democracy: The Case for Censorship." *Public Interest* 22 (Winter 1971), 3–24.

Bickel, Alexander, Stanley Kauffmann, Wilson Carey McWilliams, and Marshal Cohen. On Pornography: II – Dissenting and Concurring Opinion. *Public Interest* 22 (1971), 25–44.

Bien, P. A. "A Note on the Author and His Use of Language." In Nikos Kazantzakis, *The Last Temptation of Christ*, trans. P. A. Bien, 497–506. New York: Simon & Schuster/Touchstone Books, 1960.

"Biographical Sketch: Dan Glickman, Secretary of Agriculture." http://www.usda.gov/agencies/gallery/glickman.htm (accessed July 5, 2004).

Bishop, Katherine. "Justice Dept. Team Leading Broad Effort on Obscenity." *New York Times*, Aug. 22, 1987, A6.

Black, Gregory D. *The Catholic Crusade against the Movies, 1940–1975*. New York: Cambridge University Press, 1997.

Blau, Eleanor. "A Good Time to Ask: What Do We Mean By 'Liberty'?" *New York Times*, June 22, 1986, 26.

Blodgett, Nancy. "Porno Blacklist? Magazines Fight Meese Panel." *ABA Journal* 72 (1986): 28.

Bloomberg Business News. "Broadcasters Give Clinton Ratings Plan TV Rating System." *Omaha World-Herald*, March 1, 1996, News sec., col. 13.

Blumenthal, Ralph. "Porno chic." *New York Times Magazine*, 1978, 28, 30, 32–4.

Boddy, William. "Senator Dodd Goes to Hollywood: Investigating Video Violence. " In *The Revolution Wasn't Televised: Sixties Television and Social Conflict*, ed. Lynn Spigel and Michael Curtin, 161–83. New York and London: Routledge, 1997.

Boliek, Brooks. "Glickman Relishes New Role." *The Reporter* (Hollywood Reporter), July 2, 2004. Online.

Bonniwell, Bernard L. "The Social Control of Pornography and Sexual Behavior." *Annals of the American Academy of Political and Social Science* 397 (1971): 97–104.

Boorstin, Daniel J. *The Image: A Guide to Pseudo-Events in America*, 25th Anniversary Edition. New York: Atheneum, 1961.

Bowman, Lisa M. "City May Ask Theaters Not to Screen NC-17 Films." *Los Angeles Times*, Sept. 30, 1995, B1.

Boyer, Paul S. *Purity in Print: Book Censorship in America from the Gilded Age to the Computer Age*. 2nd ed. Madison: University of Wisconsin Press, 2002.

Braxton, Greg. "200 Christians Protest Universal's Depiction of Jesus." *Los Angeles Times*, July 17, 1988, sec. 2 (Metro), p. 4.

"Morning Report: TV & Video." *Los Angeles Times*, May 21, 1990, F2.

Briggs, Kenneth A. "Evangelicals Debate Their Role in Battling Secularism." *New York Times*, January 27, 1981, A12.

Brigman, William E. "Politics and the Pornography Wars." *Wide Angle* 19, no. 3 (1997): 149–70.

"British Board of Film Classification." http://www.bbfc.co.uk (accessed March 17, 2005).

Brittan, David. "Being There: The Promise of Multimedia Communications." *Technology Review* 95, no. 4 (1992): 42.

Brode, Douglas. *The Films of Steven Spielberg.* New York: Citadel Press, 1995.

Broderick, Peter. "Moviemaking in Transition: Digital Video Cameras and Editing Equipment Are Transforming the Way Movies Are Made – and Even *Which* Movies Get Made." *Scientific American* 283, no. 5 (2000), 61–3, 66–9.

Brodie, John. "NC-17 Threat Highly Rated by Marketers." *Chicago Sun-Times,* Sept. 6, 1994, sec. 2, p. 27.

Broeske, Pat H. "Outtakes: Missing Link." *Los Angeles Times,* Sept. 18, 1988. Calendar sec., 19.

Bronstein, Carolyn. "Porn Tours: The Rise and Fall of the American Feminist Anti-Pornography Movement." Ph.D. diss., University of Wisconsin, 2001.

Brosnan, John. *Movie Magic: The Story of Special Effects in the Cinema.* London: MacDonald and Jane's St. Giles House, 1974.

Brownstein, Ronald. *The Power and the Glitter: The Hollywood–Washington Connection.* New York: Pantheon Books, 1990.

Brozan, Nadine. "Chronicle [Richard Heffner, 71, and *Open Mind*]." *New York Times,* Aug. 5, 1996, B8.

Bruck, Connie. "The Personal Touch." *The New Yorker,* Aug. 13, 2001, 42–54, 56–9.

Bruck, Connie. *When Hollywood Had a King: The Reign of Law Wasserman, Who Leveraged Talent into Power and Influence.* New York: Random House, 2003.

Buckley, Tom. "Oh! Copenhagen." *New York Times Magazine,* Feb. 8, 1970, 32–46.

"Bush Lashes Hollywood's Lax Attitude toward Drugs." *Toronto Star,* March 23, 1989.

Bushman, B. J., and J. Cantor. "Media Ratings for Violence and Sex: Implications for Policy Makers and Parents." *American Psychologist* 58, no. 2 (February 2003): 130–41.

Bushman, Brad J., and Craig A. Anderson. "Media Violence and the American Public: Scientific Facts versus Media Misinformation." *American Psychologist* 56, no. 6/7 (2001): 477–89.

Byerly, Greg, and Rich Rubin. *Pornography: The Conflict over Sexually Explicit Materials in the United States: An Annotated Bibliography.* New York and London: Garland Publishing, 1980.

"Canadian Rating and Classification Systems." http://www.media-awareness. ca/english/resousces/ratings_classification_system/film_classification/canada_ film_classification.cfm (accessed March 17, 2005).

Canby, Vincent. "Czar of the Movie Business." *New York Times Magazine,* April 23, 1967, 38–9, 42, 44, 47, 49, 52, 57, 59.

"Films Exploiting Interest in Sex and Violence Find Growing Audience Here." *New York Times,* Jan. 24, 1968, C38.

"For Better or Worse, Film Industry Begins Ratings." *New York Times,* Nov. 1, 1968.

"What Are We to Think of 'Deep Throat'?" *New York Times,* Jan. 21, 1973, sec. 2, pp. 1, 33.

Cantor, Joanne. "Statement." "Television Ratings System." *U.S. Senate Hearings,* 1997, 159–63.

Cantor, Joanne, and Marina Krcmar. "Ratings and Advisories Implications for the New Rating System for Television [June 28–29, 1996]." *U.S. Senate Hearings,* 1997, 164–205.

Cantor, Joanne, Kristen Harrison, and Marina Krcmar. "Ratings and Advisories for Television Programming: University of Wisconsin, Madison Study." In *National Television Violence Study: Executive Summary, 1994–1995,* 41–7. Studio City, CA: Mediascope, Inc. [1996].

Cantor, Joanne. Book review of Jonathan Freedman's *Media Violence and Its Effect on Aggression.* In *Journalism and Mass Communication Quarterly* 80 (Summer 2003): 468.

"'I'll Never Have a Clown in My House!' – Why Movie Horror Lives On." *Poetics Today: International Journal for Theory and Analysis of Literature and Communication* 25, no. 2 (2004): 283–304.

"Mommy, I'm Scared": How TV and Movies Frighten Children and What We Can Do to Protect Them. New York: Harcourt Brace & Company, 1998.

"Ratings for Program Content: The Role of Research Findings." *Annals of the American Academy of Political and Social Science* 557 (1998): 54–69.

Cantor, Joanne. Interview with author, Madison, WI, 2003.

Carlen, Claudia. *The Papal Encyclicals, 1903–1939.* Raleigh, NC: McGrath Publishing Company, a Consortium Book, 1981.

The Papal Encyclicals, 1939–1958. Raleigh, NC: McGrath Publishing Company, a Consortium Book, 1981.

The Papal Encyclicals, 1958–1981. Raleigh, NC: McGrath Publishing Company, a Consortium Book, 1981.

Humanae Vitae. Encyclical of Pope Paul VI on the Regulation of Birth, July 25, 1968, 223–36.

Dives in Misericordia. Encyclical of Pope John Paul II on the Mercy of God, Nov. 30, 1980, 287.

Carlsson, Ulla, and Cecilia von Feilitzen, eds. *Children and Media Violence: Yearbook from the UNESCO International Clearinghouse on Children and Violence on the Screen.* Göteborg, Sweden: UNESCO International Clearinghouse on Children and Violence on the Screen, 1998.

Center for Communication and Social Policy, University of California, Santa Barbara ed. *National Television Violence Study: 1.* Thousand Oaks, CA: Sage Publications, 1997.

National Television Violence Study: 2. Thousand Oaks, CA: Sage Publications, 1998.

National Television Violence Study: 3. Thousand Oaks, CA: Sage Publications, 1998.

Champlin, Charles. "Critic at Large: Lasting Imprint of 'Last Temptation.'" *Los Angeles Times,* Aug. 16, 1988, sec. 6 (Calendar), p. 1.

"Critics at Large: MPAA Ratings: A Crisis of Confidence, a System in Disarray." *Los Angeles Times,* July 24, 1990, F3.

"Critics at Large: Scorsese in the Wake of 'Temptation.'" *Los Angeles Times,* Jan. 19, 1989, sec. 6 (Calendar), p. 1.

"Small Screen Takes on the Big Issues – Again; Show-Biz Star Makers Dazzled by a Luminary from Another Galaxy." *Los Angeles Times*, Sept. 17, 1987, sec. 6 (Calendar), p. 1.

"What Will H. Hays Begat: Fifty Years since His Code Rule Hollywood." *American Film* 6, no. 1 (1980): 42–6, 86, 88.

Chandler, Russell. "25,000 Gather at Universal to Protest Film." *Los Angeles Times*, Aug. 12, 1988, sec. 1, p. 1.

"Protests Aided 'Temptation,' Foes Concede." *Los Angeles Times*, Aug. 14, 1988, sec. 2 (Metro), p. 1.

Changas, Estelle, and Stephen Farber. "Insiders Rate Film Code Board as 'Unreformed.'" *Los Angeles Times*, Aug. 8, 1971, Calendar sec., pp. 1, 22–5.

"Charity's Report Backs Allegations That Priest Engaged in Misconduct." *Los Angeles Times*, Aug. 5, 1990 (Metro), B3.

"Child Pornography Law Enacted." *New York Times*, May 22, 1984, A20.

City of Renton v. Playtime Theatres, Inc. 475 U.S. 41 (1986).

Classification and Rating Administration. *Annual Reports (1969–1999)*. RDHPP.

Clemmons, C. J., and Jim Puzzanghera. "How a Ban Changed All." *Newsday*, July 7, 1993 (Nassau and Suffolk edition), 7.

"Clerics Say President Vows a Major Drive to Curb Smut." *New York Times*, Nov. 15, 1986, sec. 1, p. 9. A9.

Cline, Victor B., ed. *Where Do You Draw the Line? An Exploration into Media Violence, Pornography, and Censorship*. Provo, UT: Brigham Young University Press, 1974.

Clines, Francis X. "Reagan Sees U.S. Regaining 'Moral Bearings.'" *New York Times*, March 7, 1984, A1.

Cockburn, Alexander. "Violence Has Become the Pornography of the '80s." *Wall Street Journal*, June 19, 1986, sec. 1, p. 31.

Coe, Richard L. "Senator Smith vs. Violence in Films." *Washington Post*, Feb. 4, 1968.

Cohen, Richard. "Pornography: The 'Causal Link'" (Op-Ed). *Washington Post*, June 3, 1986, A19.

Collier, Everett D. *Oral History Interview of Everett D. Collier* (interviewed by Michael L. Gillette). Oral History Collection, Lyndon Baines Johnson Library, Austin, TX, 1975.

Collins, Glenn. "Guidance or Censorship? New Debate on Rating Films." *New York Times*, April 9, 1990, C11.

"Judge to Rule in July on X Rating for 'Tie Me Up!'" *New York Times*, June 22, 1990, C4.

"Judge Upholds X Rating for Almodovar Film." *New York Times*, July 20, 1990, C12.

Commission on Obscenity and Pornography. "The Effects of Explicit Sexual Materials" *Report of The Commission on Obscenity and Pornography*, 23–7. Washington, DC: U.S. Government Printing Office, 1970.

"The Volume of Traffic and Patterns of Distribution of Sexually Oriented Materials." *Report of the Commission on Obscenity and Pornography*, 7–21. Washington, DC: Government Printing Office, 1970.

Conconi, Chuck. "Personalities." *Washington Post*, March 30, 1990, B3.

Connors, Joanna. "Real Erotica More Than Skin Deep; Many Hollywood Movies Fail to Flesh Out Spiritual, Truly Human Side of Sex. *Cleveland Plain Dealer,* Jan. 24, 1993, H1.

Cook, David A. *Lost Illusions: American Cinema in the Shadow of Watergate and Vietnam, 1970–1979.* New York: Charles Scribner's Sons, 2000.

Cook, James. "The X-Rated Economy." *Forbes* 122, no. 6 (1978), 81–8, 92.

Cook, T. D., D. A. Kendzierski, and S. V. Thomas. "The Implicit Assumptions of Television Research: An Analysis of the 1982 NIMH Report on Television and Behavior." *Public Opinion Quarterly* 47 (1983): 161–201.

Copp, David, and Susan Wendell, eds. *Pornography and Censorship.* New York: Prometheus Books, 1983.

Corliss, Richard. "He Lost It at the Movies." *Time* 139 (1992), 64.

"Taking the Hex out of X." *Time* 136 (Oct. 8, 1990), 70.

"What Ever Became of NC-17?" *Time* 139 (Jan. 27, 1992), 64.

Corry, John. "'Open Mind' Speaks of Ideas." *New York Times,* April 26, 1987, sec. 2.

Costello, Thomas J. "Testimony on Behalf of the National Conference of Catholic Bishops, Department of Communication." *U.S. Senate Hearings,* 1997, 287–90.

"Court Upholds Porn Film Law." *Pittsburgh Post-Gazette,* Sept. 21, 1994, A6.

Court, J. H. "Pornography and Sex Crimes – Re-Evaluation in Light of Recent Trends around the World." *International Journal of Criminology and Penology* 5 (1977): 129–57.

Court, John. "Testimony." *Meese Commission Hearings,* Sept.12, 1985, Box 2, Records of the Attorney General's Commission on Pornography, RG 60, NARA 2.

Courtwright, David T. *Violent Land: Single Men and Social Disorder from the Frontier to the Inner City.* Cambridge, MA: Harvard University Press, 1996.

"Way Cooler Than Manson: Natural Born Killers." *Oliver Stone's USA: Film, History, and Controversy,* ed. Robert Brent Toplin, 188–201. Lawrence: University Press of Kansas, 2000.

"Culture Watch; Cardinal Rules." *Los Angeles Times,* Oct. 2, 1992. B6.

Cusack, Diane D. "Statement of Diane D. Cusack." *Final Report* (1986), 486–7.

Cutlip, Scott M. *The Unseen Power: Public Relations, a History.* Hillsdale, NJ: Lawrence Erlbaum Associates, 1994.

Dallek, Robert. *Flawed Giant: Lyndon Johnson and His Times, 1961–1973.* New York: Oxford University Press, 1998.

"Dan Glickman To Succeed Jack Valenti as Head of MPAA; Valenti Resigns after 38-Year Tenure." Motion Picture Association of America Press Release, July 1, 2004.

Dart, John. "Age-Old Problem: Portrayals of Christ Tempt Controversy." *Los Angeles Times,* July 30, 1988, sec. 1, p. 1.

"Church Declares 'Last Temptation' Morally Offensive." *Los Angeles Times,* Aug. 10, 1988, sec. 2 (Metro), p. 3.

"Church Likely to Condemn 'Temptation,' Mahony Says." *Los Angeles Times,* July 20, 1988, sec. 2 (Metro), p. 3.

"Evangelist Offers to Buy All Copies of Christ Movie." *Los Angeles Times*, July 16, 1988, sec. 2 (Metro), p. 3.

"'Last Temptation' Views Still Coming In; Boycott of 'E.T.' among Religious Reactions to Controversial Movie." *Los Angeles Times*, Aug. 27, 1988. sec. 2 (Metro), p. 6.

"Some Clerics See No Evil in 'Temptation.'" *Los Angeles Times*, July 14, 1988, sec. 6 (Calendar), p. 1.

"'Temptation' May Lead to Examination and Renewal of Faith." *Los Angeles Times*, Aug. 13, 1988, sec. 2 (Metro), p. 6.

"'Temptation,' with a New Cover, Due at Bookstores, Publisher Says." *Los Angeles Times*, Aug. 19, 1988, sec. 6 (Calendar), p. 6.

Dart, John, and Russell Chandler. "Full Theaters, Protests Greet 'Temptation.'" *Los Angeles Times*, Aug. 13, 1988, sec. 1, pp. 1ff.

Davenport, Gorianna. "Your Own Virtual Storyworld: True Interactive Entertainment Will Arise Once Engineers and Artists Create Virtual Realities That Can Unfold Improvisationally." *Scientific American* 283, no. 5 (2000), 79–82.

Davies, Lawrence E. "Reagan Promises to Rid Campuses of 'Anarchists.'" *New York Times*, Jan. 8, 1969, 36.

De Grazia, Edward. *Girls Lean Back Everywhere: The Law of Obscenity and the Assault on Genius*. New York: Random House, 1992.

De Grazia, Edward, and Roger K. Newman. *Banned Films: Movies, Censors and the First Amendment*. New York: R. R. Bowker Company, 1982.

Dee, Jonathan. "Playing Mogul." *New York Times Magazine*, Dec. 21, 2003, 36–41, 52–3, 66–8.

"Defeated by Pornography" (editorial). *New York Times*, June 2, 1986, A2.

Deibel, Mary. "Court Supports Laws to Prevent Porn Using Kids." *Denver Rocky Mountain News*, June 27, 1995, A21.

Detenber, Benjamin H., Robert F. Simons, and Jason E. Reiss. "The Emotional Significance of Color in Television Presentations." *Media Psychology* 2 (2000): 331–55.

Detenber, B. H., and S. P. Winch. "The Impact of Color on Emotional Responses to Newspaper Photography." *Visual Communication Quarterly* 8, no. 3 (2001): 4–14.

Dietz, Park Elliott. "Statement of Park Elliott Dietz...." *Final Report* (1986), 487–92.

Dietz, P. E., B. Harry, and R. R. Hazelwood. "Detective Magazines: Pornography for the Sexual Sadists?" *Journal of Forensic Science* 31 (1986): 197–211.

"Directors Approve Voluntary Classification at Scottsdale Meeting." *National Association of Theatre Owners, Inc., Newsletter* 3 (1968): 1–2.

Dixon, Wheeler Winston. *The Second Century of Cinema: The Past and Future of the Moving Image*. Albany: State University of New York Press, 2000.

Dobson, James C. *Dare to Discipline*. Wheaton, IL: Tyndale House Publishers, [1970].

Hide or Seek. Old Tappan, NJ: Revell, 1979.

"Personal Comments by Commissioner James Dobson." *Final Report* (1986), 504–9.

Docherty, James. "Testimony." *Meese Commission Hearings,* Oct. 16, 1985, Box 3, Records of the Attorney General's Commission on Pornography, RG 60, NARA 2.

Donnerstein, Edward. "Testimony." *Meese Commission Hearings,* Sept. 11, 1985, Box 2, Records of the Attorney General's Commission on Pornography, RG 60, NARA 2.

"[Testimony]: Public Hearings on Ordinances to Add Pornography as Discrimination against Women." *Minneapolis Hearings,* Session I, Dec. 12, 1983, Box 69, Records of the Attorney General's Commission on Pornography, RG 60, NARA 2.

Donnerstein, Edward, Daniel Linz, and Steven Penrod. *The Question of Pornography: Research Findings and Policy Implications.* New York: The Free Press, 1987.

Dougherty, Philip H. "Hill & Knowlton to Buy Gray, the Lobbyists." *New York Times,* June 4, 1986, D1.

Downs, Donald Alexander. *The New Politics of Pornography.* Chicago: University of Chicago Press, 1989.

Dunwoody, Sharon. Interview with author, Nov. 3, 2002, Madison, WI.

Dutka, Elaine. "Film Ratings Board Picks Mosk as Its Leader." *Los Angeles Times,* June 29, 1994, F1.

"The DVD Comes of Age." *New York Times,* Aug. 17, 2003, sec. 2, pp. 1–26.

Dworkin, Andrea. *Pornography: Men Possessing Women.* New York: Perigee Books, 1981.

Dykstra, Joan. "Statement of Joan Dykstra, President, National Parent-Teacher Association." *U.S. Senate Hearings,* 1997, 50–4.

Easton, Nina J. "Eszterhas vs. Verhoeven." *Los Angeles Times,* Aug. 23, 1990, F1.

"'Last Temptation' Draws Mostly Sold-Out Houses." *Los Angeles Times,* Aug. 15, 1988, sec. 6 (Calendar), p. 1.

"Slow Release Strategy Pays Big Dividends." *Los Angeles Times,* Aug. 16, 1988, sec. 6 (Calendar), col. 1.

"Studio Fires Back in Defense of 'Temptation.'" *Los Angeles Times,* July 22, 1988, sec. 2 (Metro), p. 1.

Ebert, Roger. "Movie Reviews." http://www.suntimes.com/ebert/ebertser.html (accessed March 17, 2005).

"Satisfying the Most Basic of Instincts: Curiosity." *Chicago Sun-Times,* May 8, 1992, sec. 2, p. 33.

"Edwards Cinemas Chain Won't Run 'Last Temptation.'" *Los Angeles Times,* Aug. 7, 1988, p. 8.

Egan, Timothy. "Technology Sent Wall Street into Market for Pornography." *New York Times,* Oct. 23, 2000, A20.

Eller, Claudia. "Ratings 'Ain't Broke,' Board Chair Says.'" *Los Angeles Times,* Aug. 4, 1994, F1.

"Eszterhas Urges Teenagers to Sneak into *Showgirls.*" *Cleveland Plain Dealer,* Sept. 15, 1995, E8.

Eszterhas, Joe. *Hollywood Animal: A Memoir.* New York: Alfred A. Knopf, 2004.

"Hollywood's Responsibility for Smoking Deaths." *New York Times*, Aug. 9, 2002, A17.

Eysenck, Hans J., and D. K. B. Nias. *Sex, Violence and the Media*. London: Maurice Temple Smith, 1978.

Fabrikant, Geraldine. "Attack of the Disruptive Disc; Sales of DVD's Are Challenging the Business of Renting Movies." *New York Times*, April 16, 2001, C1, C5.

Farber, Stephen. "A Major Studio Plans to Test the Rating System." *New York Times*, Sept. 4, 1990, C14.

"Movies: Why Do Critics Love These Repellent Movies? Point: Moviegoers Looking for Guidance Are Becoming Alienated by Reviewers, Penchant for Grotesque Violence." *Los Angeles Times*, March 17, 1991, Calendar sec., 5.

"Testimony." *U.S. House Hearings*, 1977, 78–90.

The Movie Rating Game. Washington, DC: Public Affairs Press, 1972.

Federal Communications Commission v. Home Box Office. 434 U.S. 988 (1977).

Federal Communications Commission v. Midwest Video Corp. 440 U.S. 689 (1979).

Federal Communications Commission. Consumer and Governmental Affairs Bureau. "The V-Chip: Putting Restrictions on What Your Children Watch, Even When You're Not There." http://www.fcc.gov/cgb/consumerfacts/vchip.html (accessed March 17, 2005).

Federal Communications Commission. "V-Chip: Viewing Television Responsibly." http://www.fcc.gov/vchip/ (accessed March 17, 2005).

Federal Trade Commission. "Excerpts from the Violence Report." *New York Times*, Sept. 12, 2000, A24.

Federal Trade Commission. FTC Releases Report on the Marketing of Violent Entertainment to Children (Sept. 11, 2000). http://www.ftc.gov/opa/2000/09/youthviol.htm) (accessed March 17, 2005).

Federman, Joel (with the assistance of Stephanie Carbone and Linda Evans). *Media Ratings: Design, Use and Consequences*. Studio City, CA: Mediascope, Inc., 1996.

Federman, Joel, Stephanie Carbone, Helen Chen, and William Munn comps. and eds. *Social Effects of Electronic Interactive Games: An Annotated Bibliography*. Studio City, CA: Mediascope, Inc., 1996.

Film Daily Yearbook (a.k.a. *Film Daily Yearbook of Motion Pictures*). New York: The Film Daily, 1968, 1969.

Finch, Christopher. *Special Effects: Creating Movie Magic*. New York: Abbeville Press, 1984.

Fischetti, Mark. "The Future of Digital Entertainment. *Scientific American* 283, no. 5 (November 2000), 47–9.

Ford, Jesse Hill. "Abolish Film Ratings; Trust the Moviegoers." *USA Today*, May 2, 1990, A10.

Ford, Luke. *A History of X: 100 Years of Sex in Film*. New York: Prometheus Books, 1999.

Forman, Peter, and Robert W. Saint John. "Creating Convergence." *Scientific American* 283, no. 5 (2000), 50–6.

Forshey, Gerald E. *American Religious and Biblical Spectaculars.* Westport, CT: Praeger, 1992.

Fowles, Jib. *The Case* For *Television Violence.* Thousand Oaks, CA: Sage Publications, 1999.

Fox, David J. "Blockbuster Video Rates NC-17 Films Unsuitable for All." *Los Angeles Times,* Jan. 14, 1991. (Calendar), F1.

"Jack Valenti Says Change Possible for Film Ratings." *Los Angeles Times,* Aug. 10, 1990. (Calendar), col. F1.

"Movie on Prostitution Still Gets an NC-17 Rating." *Los Angeles Times,* Sept. 9, 1991, F2.

"R Vs. NC-17 – What's the Difference?: Filmmakers, Exhibitors Are Bewildered by Inconsistent Ratings." *Los Angeles Times,* Jan. 18, 1993, F1.

"Rating System Faces Challenges on Two Fronts." *Los Angeles Times,* July 21, 1990, F1.

"Ratings to Give Parents More Data." *Los Angeles Times,* July 29, 1992, F1.

"Valenti Agrees to Talk to Critics of Movie Ratings." *Los Angeles Times,* July 26, 1990, F7.

Frank, Richard H. "Media/Entertainment White House Conference for a Drug Free America, Post Conferees Meeting Version, May 1988." In *Reminiscences of Richard D. Heffner,* Exhibit 88-11, Box 4, RDH-COHC-BL.

Freedman, Jonathan L. *Media Violence and Its Effect on Aggression: Assessing the Scientific Evidence.* Toronto: University of Toronto Press, 2002.

"Viewing Television Violence Does Not Make People More Aggressive." *Hofstra Law Review* 22 (Summer 1994): 833–55.

Friedman, David. "The Fat Cat of Porn; Al Goldstein Claims He's Misunderstood: 'I've created this character the Fred Flintstone of Flesh, and that's all they know.'" *Newsday,* Sept. 4, 1990, sec. 2, p. 8.

Gabler, Neal. *Life the Movie: How Entertainment Conquered Reality.* New York: Alfred A. Knopf, 1998.

Galbraith, Jane. "His Job: G, PG, PG-13, R and NC-17." *Newsday,* July 21, 1994, B02.

"Taming *The Wild Bunch* with NC-17 Rating." *Chicago Sun-Times,* March 21, 1993, Show sec., p. 2.

Gambardello, Joseph A. "Ministry Barred for Ritter." *Newsday,* March 30, 1990, News sec., p. 8.

Gaughan, Norbert F. "Statement." *U.S. Senate Hearings,* Oct. 24, 1985, 141–7.

"Testimony." *U.S. Senate Hearings,* Oct. 24, 1985, 129–40.

Gilmore, Donald H. "Preface." In *Illustrated Presidential Report of the Commission on Obscenity and Pornography,* ed. Earl Kemp, 8–9. San Diego, CA: Greenleaf Classics, 1970.

Goldman, Eric F. *The Tragedy of Lyndon Johnson.* New York: Alfred A. Knopf, 1969.

Goldman, Marvin. "Statement." *U.S. Senate Hearings,* 1985, 126–8.

"Testimony." *U.S. Senate Hearings,* 1985, 122–5.

Goldstein, Tom. "Obscenity Law: Standards Vary." *New York Times,* Feb. 10, 1977, p. 20.

Gomery, Douglas. *Shared Pleasures: A History of Movie Presentation in the United States*. Madison: University of Wisconsin Press, 1992.

Goodell, Jeffrey. "What Hill & Knowlton Can Do for You (And What It Couldn't Do for Itself)." *New York Times*, Sept. 9, 1990, sec. 6 (Magazine Desk), p. 44.

Goodman, Walter. "Battle on Pornography Spurred by New Tactics." *New York Times*, July 3, 1984, A8.

"Liberty Panel Ponders Wherefores of Freedom." *New York Times*, July 7, 1986, B4.

"Liberty Weekend/The People: Liberty Conferees Debate Judges' Role." *New York Times*, July 6, 1986, A18.

Gould, Jay. "TV Violence Held Unharmful to Youth." *New York Times*, Jan. 11, 1972, 1, 75.

Granville, Kari. "Judge Asked to Overturn Film Rating System: Lawsuit: He Takes the Request under Advisement. He'll also Rule Whether 'Tie Me Up!' Was Rated Fairly." *Los Angeles Times*, June 22, 1990, F10.

Gray, Timothy M. "The Movie Ratings Code: Grade It C for Confusing." *Chicago Sun-Times*, Jan. 23, 1994, Show sec., p. 1.

Green, Thomas Hill. *Lectures on the Principles of Political Obligation*. Ann Arbor: University of Michigan Press, 1967.

Greenberg, Bradley S. "Televised Violence: Further Explorations (Overview)." *In Television and Social Behavior: Reports and Papers. Volume IV: Television in Day-to-Day Life: Patterns of Use: A Technical Report to the Surgeon General's Scientific Advisory Committee on Television and Social Behavior,* ed. George A. Comstock, Eli A. Rubinstein, and John P. Murray. National Institute of Mental Health, Rockville, MD. [1972].

Greene, Jay. "Censors Ambush *Wild Bunch.*" *Chicago Sun-Times*, Oct. 2, 1994, Show sec., p. 2.

Greenfield, Jeff. "'The Open Mind': A Talk Show with Real Talk." *Los Angeles Times*, April 24, 1978.

Greenman, Catherine. "The V-Chip Arrives with a Thud: Program-Blocking Device Is in TV's, But Few Consumers Are Aware of It." *New York Times*, Nov. 4, 1999, D1, D8.

Griffin, Susan. *Pornography and Silence: Culture's Revenge against Nature*. New York: Harper & Row, 1981.

Grimes, William. "Reviewing the NC-17 Film Rating: Clear Guide or an X by a New Name?" *New York Times*, Nov. 30, 1992, C11.

Haberman, Clyde. "Vatican Condemns Kung Fu Films and Sex on TV." *New York Times*, May 17, 1989, A3.

Hall, Carla. "Directors, MPAA Chief Meet on Film Ratings." *Washington Post*, Aug. 10, 1990, C2.

"Occasional." *Washington Post*, Aug. 10, 1990, C2.

Hall, Jane. "FCC Chairman Backs Bill on TV Content." *Los Angeles Times*, July 17, 1997, A17.

"Senators Push Content-Based TV Ratings...." *Los Angeles Times*, Feb. 28, 1997, A4.

"TV Industry Reportedly OKs New Ratings." *Los Angeles Times*, July 10, 1997, A1.

Hamilton, Denise. "Church Leaders to Urge Boycott of 'Temptation.'" *Los Angeles Times*, Oct. 20, 1988, sec. 9 (Ventura County), p. 1.

Hamilton, Dorothy. "Hollywood's Silent Partner: A History of the Motion Picture Association of America Movie Rating System." Ph.D. diss. University of Kansas, 1999.

Hamsher, Jane. *Killer Instinct: How Two Young Producers Took on Hollywood and Made the Most Controversial Film of the Decade*. New York: Broadway Books, 1997.

Harmon, Amy. "Studios Using Digital Armor to Fight Piracy." *New York Times*, Jan. 5, 2003, A1, A21.

Harrington, Richard. "The Capitol Hill Rock War: Emotions Run High as Musicians Confront Parents' Groups at Hearing." *Washington Post*, Sept. 20, 1985, B1.

"Is It Cleaner in the Country?" *Washington Post*, Oct. 16, 1985, B7.

Hawkins, Robert. Interview with author, Madison, WI. Nov. 3, 2002.

Hedlund, Kristen. "Valenti Opposes Plan for Drug Use Rating for Films." *Los Angeles Times*, Oct. 25, 1985, 8.

"Heffner to Study TV's Impact on Americans' Attitudes about Environment." *New York Times*, March 23, 1971, 75.

Heffner, Elaine. *Mothering: The Emotional Experience of Motherhood After Freud and Feminism*. Garden City, NY: Doubleday & Company, 1978.

Heffner, Richard D. "ALA Conference: Caution: This Program Is Rated X." *Newsletter on Intellectual Freedom* 34 (1985): 176–8.

Alexis de Tocqueville, Democracy in America: Specially Edited and Abridged for the Modern Reader. New York: Penguin Books, 1956.

A Conversational History of Modern America. ed. Marc Jaffe. New York: Carroll & Graf Publishers, 2003.

"Democracy in a Hurry" (book review). *Saturday Review* 48 (1965), 64–5.

"Design for Learning." *Saturday Review* 42 (1959), 17–19, 47–53.

A Documentary History of the United States: An Expanded Edition. New York: New American Library (1952), 1965. 7th ed. 2002.

"Freedom and Responsibility in Mass Communications." Address delivered in London, March 22, 1982. RDHPP.

"A Gadget Cure" (book review). *Saturday Review* 41 (1958), 38–9.

"Guidance to Parents, Not Profits, Governs Movie Rating System." *Los Angeles Times*, July 2, 1990.

"Here Come the Video Censors" (editorial). *New York Times*, May 1, 1994, sec. 4, p. 17.

Interview with author Bear Mountain, NY, Aug. 13, 1999.

Interview with author Bear Mountain, NY, Aug. 10, 2000.

Interview with author New York, Aug. 16, 2002.

Jefferson Revisited. Address delivered in Toronto, 1984. RDHPP.

"Last Gasp of the Gutenbergs" (editorial). *Los Angeles Times*, Feb. 19, 1992, B11.

"'Narrowcasting' and the Threat to Morals." *New York Times*, Aug. 17, 1980, sec. 2 (Arts and Leisure), p. 29.

The Open Mind (tape interviews). Museum of Television and Radio, New York.

Reminiscences of Richard D. Heffner (oral history). 20 vols. Columbia Oral History Collection, Butler Library, Columbia University, New York.

Richard Heffner Associates. *Network Television's Business-Related Content,* 1974. RDHPP and University of California, Los Angeles.

Richard Heffner Associates. *Network Television's Environmental Content,* 1972. RDHPP and University of California, Los Angeles.

Richard Heffner Associates. ["Report and Proposal: Concerning the Identification of Entertainment Television's Aging-Related Content"] 1973. RDHPP and University of California, Los Angeles.

"A Television Rating System Won't Hurt Anyone" (editorial). *New York Times,* Dec. 19, 1996, A28.

"Testimony." *U.S Senate Hearings,* 1985, 117–22.

"Testimony." *U.S. House Hearings,* 1977, 195–210.

"TV as Teacher: Of Adults, Too." *New York Times Magazine,* Aug. 17, 1958, 19, 74.

"What G, PG, R and X Really Mean." *TV Guide,* Oct. 4–10, 1980, 38–40, 42, 44, 46.

Heffner, Richard D., and Charles Champlin. "The Case of the Missing Rating" (editorial). *Los Angeles Times,* Dec. 16, 1996.

Heidenry, John. *What Wild Ecstasy: The Rise and Fall of the Sexual Revolution.* New York: Simon & Schuster, 1997.

Heins, Marjorie. *Not in Front of the Children: 'Indecency,' Censorship, and the Innocence of Youth.* New York: Hill and Wang, 2001.

Hentoff, Nat. "The Justice Department's Tainted Fruit: Harassing Those Engaged in Lawful Activity Is Not a Proper Function of Government." *Washington Post,* July 25, 1992, A21.

"Highlights of Lab History." *American Cinematographer* 50, no. 1 (1969), 104–5, 167, 174–6.

"Highlights of Opinion Research Corporation 1970 Survey on Code and Rating System." [1970]. Box 5, Mss 1446, NATOR-BYU.

Hinson, Hal. "Bestial Brew: 'The Cook,' Serving Up Squalor." *Washington Post,* April 7, 1990, C1.

"Film Industry Revises Rating System; Controversial X Movie Category Abandoned to Avoid 'Stigma.'" *Washington Post,* Sept. 27, 1990, A1.

Hobsbawm, E. J. "Revolution Is Puritan." In *The New Eroticism: Theories, Vogues and Canons,* ed. Philip Nobile, 36–40. New York: Random House, 1970.

Hoffman, David. "Reagan Hears Pleas to Battle Pornography." *Washington Post,* March 29, 1983, A5.

"Hollywood: The First 100 Days." *Time* 88, no. 10 (1966), 38.

"Hollywood Film Makers Protest Rating System." *New York Times,* July 21, 1990, sec. 1, p. 14.

Holson, Laura M. "Studios Are Killing (Bloodily But Carefully) for an R Rating." *New York Times,* Oct. 21, 2003, B1, B5.

"Studios Moving to Block Piracy of Films Online." *New York Times*, Sept. 25, 2003, A1, C6.

Home Box Office, Inc., et al. v. Federal Communications Commission. 190 U.S. app. D.C. 351 (1978).

"How Technology from the Moon Will Advance Photography on Earth." *American Cinematographer* 48, no. 1 (1967), 48–50.

Howard, James L., Clifford B. Reifler, and Myron B. Liptzin. "Effects of Exposure to Pornography." *Technical Report of the Commission on Obscenity and Pornography*, 8: 97–132. Washington, DC: U.S. Government Printing Office, 1970.

Howe, Robert F. "U.S. Accused of 'Censorship by Intimidation' in Pornography Cases." *Washington Post*, March 26, 1990, A4.

Hozic, Aida A. *Hollyworld: Space, Power, and Fantasy in the American Economy*. Ithaca and London: Cornell University Press, 2001.

Hubner, John. *Bottom Feeders: From Free Love to Hard Core: The Rise and Fall of Counterculture Heroes Jim and Artie Mitchell*. New York: Doubleday, 1992.

Hudson, Henry E. "Statement of Henry E. Hudson, Chairman." *Final Report* (1986), 484–6.

Hughes, Douglas A., ed. *Perspectives on Pornography*. New York: St. Martin's Press, 1970.

Hunnings, Neville March. *Film Censors and the Law*. London: George Allen & Unwin, 1967.

Hunt, Alan. *Governing Morals: A Social History of Moral Regulation*. Cambridge: Cambridge University Press, 1999.

Hunt, Dennis. "Fundamentalists Urge 'E.T.' Video Boycott; Pre-Orders Set Record." *Los Angeles Times*, Sept. 16, 1988, sec. 6 (Calendar), p. 4.

"Home Tech/Video: New Releases from the 'Valley' of Clunkers." *Los Angeles Times*, May 21, 1993, sec. F (Calendar), p. 24.

"Ken Russell's Movie Available in Four Versions." *Los Angeles Times*, Jan. 31, 1992, F25.

"'Temptation' Video to Rekindle Fundamentalist Ire?" *Los Angeles Times*, June 2, 1989, sec. 6 (Calendar), p. 13.

Hunter, James Davison. *Culture Wars: The Struggle to Define America*. New York: Basic Books, 1991.

Hyer, Marjorie. "Evangelical Broadcasters Define Role in Politics." *Washington Post*, Feb. 4, 1984, B6.

Interstate Circuit, Inc., v. Dallas. 390 U.S. 676 (1968).

Jacobellis v. Ohio. 378 U.S. 184 (1964).

Jacobs, Jody. "A Special Award for Nancy Reagan." *Los Angeles Times*, Aug. 15, 1985, sec. 5 (View), col. 4.

Janet Reno, Attorney General of the United States et al. v. American Civil Liberties Union, et al. 1997 521 U.S. 844 (1997) // 117 S. Ct. 2329; 138 L. Ed. 2d 874; 1997 U.S. LEXIS 4037; 65 U.S.L.W. 4715; 25 Media L. Rep. 1833; 97 Cal.Daily Op. Service 4998; 97 Daily Journal DAR 8133; 11 Fla. L. Weekly Fed. S 211: U.S.

"Japanese Urged to Control Video Cassette Tape Piracy." *Journal of Commerce*, 1987 (Foreign Trade Section), A4.

Jarrard, Dennis. "Cardinal Lets Hollywood Off the Hook." *Los Angeles Times*, Oct. 9, 1992 (Metro), B7.

"Clean Entertainment." *Los Angeles Times*, Feb. 16, 1991 (Calendar), F12.

Jenkins v. Georgia. 418 U.S. 153 (1974).

John Paul II, Pope. Address to Communication Industry Executives, Los Angeles, Sept. 15, 1987 (excerpts). *New York Times*, Sept. 16, 1987, A24.

Encyclical Letter *Evangelium Vitae* Addressed by the Supreme Pontiff John Paul II to the Bishops, Priests, and Deacons, Men and Women Religious, Lay Faithful, and All People of Good Will on the Value and Inviolability of Human Life, March 25, 1995. In *The Encyclicals of John Paul II*, ed. and intro. J. Michael Miller, 792–892. Huntington, IN: Our Sunday Visitor, Inc., 1996.

Encyclical Letter *Redemptoris Missio* of the Supreme Pontiff John Paul II on the Permanent Validity of the Church's Missionary Mandate [Dec. 7, 1990]. In *The Encyclicals of John Paul II*, ed. and intro. J. Michael Miller, 525–7. Huntington, IN: Our Sunday Visitor, Inc., 1996.

Encyclical Letter *Sollicitudo Rei Socialis* of the Supreme Pontiff John Paul II for the Twentieth Anniversary of *Populorum Progressio*, Dec. 30, 1987 [publ. Feb. 19, 1988]. In *The Encyclicals of John Paul II*, ed. and intro. J. Michael Miller, 443. Huntington, IN: Our Sunday Visitor, Inc., 1996.

Johnson, Weldon T., Lenore R. Kupperstein, W. Cody Wilson, et al. "The Impact of Erotica: Report of the Effects Panel to the Commission on Obscenity and Pornography." *Report of the Commission on Obscenity and Pornography*, 139–263. Washington, DC: U.S. Government Printing Office, 1970.

Jonas, Gerald. "The Man Who Gave an 'X' Rating to Violence." *New York Times*, May 11, 1975, sec. 2, pp. 1, 13.

Joseph Burstyn, Inc. v. Wilson. 343 U.S. 495 (1952).

Joseph, Burton. "Presentation." *Meese Commission Hearings*, July 24–5, 1985, Box 70, Records of the Attorney General's Commission on Pornography, RG 60, NARA 2.

Jowett, Garth. *Film: The Democratic Art*. Boston: Little, Brown and Company, 1976.

"Judge Adds a P.S. to X-Rated Film Ruling." *Bergen [NJ] County Record*, July 22, 1990, E03.

Kahn, Joseph P. "Censorship Reshaped by Violence." *Boston Globe*, Jan. 1, 1994, p. 1.

"China Has World's Tightest Internet Censorship, Study Finds." *New York Times*, Dec. 4, 2002, A15.

Kandell, Jonathan. "Lew Wasserman, 89, Is Dead, Last of the Hollywood Moguls." *New York Times*, June 4, 2002, A1, A19.

Kasindorf, Martin. "Future of X-Rating Debated." *Newsday*, Aug. 9, 1990 (Nassau and Suffolk Edition), 7.

"Judge's 'X' Ruling Rated an 'F.'" *Newsday*, July 21, 1990, 6.

Katsh, M. Ethan. *The Electronic Media and the Transformation of the Law*. New York: Oxford University Press, 1989.
  Law in a Digital World. New York: Oxford University Press, 1995.
Kaufman, Michael T. "PG Man Hangs up That Hat." *New York Times*, June 8, 1994 (Metro), B3.
Kauffmann, Stanley. "Review, *Natural Born Killers*." http://www.tnr.com/archive/0799/071299/kauffmann071299.html (accessed July 12, 1999).
Kearns, Doris. *Lyndon Johnson and the American Dream*. New York: Harper & Row, 1976.
Keating, Charles H., Jr. "The Report That Shocked the Nation." *Reader's Digest*, January 1971, 37–41.
Kelley, Daryl. "Meese Outlines New War on Pornography." *Los Angeles Times*, Feb. 11, 1987, sec. 1, p. 1.
Kelley, Jack. "Hollywood Plans Starring Role in Drug War." *USA Today*, June 23, 1989, A1.
Kemp, Earl, ed. *Illustrated Presidential Report of the Commission on Obscenity and Pornography*. San Diego, CA: Greenleaf Classics, 1970.
Kendrick, Walter. *The Secret Museum: Pornography in Modern Culture*. New York: Penguin Books, 1987.
Kennedy, Dana. "The Fantasy of Interactive Porn Becomes a Reality." *New York Times*, Aug. 17, 2003, sec. 2, p. 7.
Kinsey, Alfred C., Wardell B. Pomeroy, Clyde E. Martin, and Paul H. Gebhard. *Sexual Behavior in the Human Female*. Philadelphia: Saunders, 1953.
Kirkpatrick, David D. "Action-Hungry DVD Fans Sway Hollywood." *New York Times*, Aug. 17, 2003, A1, A15.
Klawans, Stuart. "It's One Long Dirty Joke But Hey, Man, It's a Classic." *New York Times*, Nov. 17, 2002, sec. 2 (Arts and Leisure), p. 13.
Kleiman, Dena. "Films to Get Stricter Ratings." *New York Times*, April 9, 1986, C18.
Klinkenborg, Verlyn. "Living under the Virtual Volcano of Video Games This Holiday Season." *New York Times*, Dec. 16, 2002, A30.
Kolbert, Elizabeth. "Americans Despair of Popular Culture." *New York Times*, Aug. 20, 1995, sec. 2 (Arts and Leisure), p. 1.
Krattenmaker, Thomas G., and Marjorie L. Esterow. "Censoring Indecent Cable Programs: The New Morality Meets the New Media." *Fordham Law Review* 51, no. 4 (1983): 606–36.
Krim, Arthur. *Oral History Interview of Arthur Krim: I, II, IV*. Oral History Collection, Lyndon Baines Johnson Library, 1987. http://www.lbjlib.utexas.edu/johnson/archives.hom/oralhistory.hom.
Kristof, Nicholas D. "X-Rated Industry in a Slump." *New York Times*, Oct. 5, 1986, sec. 3 (Financial), p. 1.
Kristol, Irving. "Pornography, Obscenity and the Case for Censorship." *New York Times Magazine*, March 28, 1971, 24–5, 112–15.
Kurtz, Howard. "Pornography Panel's Objectivity Disputed; Critics Call Meese Commission Overzealous." *Washington Post*, Oct. 15, 1985, A4.

Kutschinsky, Berl. "The Effect of Easy Availability of Pornography on the Incidence of Sex Crimes: The Danish Experience." *Journal of Social Issues* 29 (1973): 163–81.

Landsbaum, Mark. "Bishop, Schuller Join Voices Urging 'Temptation' Boycott." *Los Angeles Times*, Aug. 10, 1988, sec. 2 (Metro), p. 1.

Lane, Frederick S. III. *Obscene Profits: The Entrepreneurs of Pornography in the Cyber Age*. New York and London: Routledge, 2000.

Larrabee, Don. "Violence in Movies: Sen. Smith's Crusade." *"MST,"* June 23, 1968, D-7. (Clipping MCSP-NISM.)

Lebow, Irwin. *Information Highways and Byways: From the Telegraph to the 21st Century*. New York: IEEE Press, 1995.

——— *Understanding Digital Transmission and Recording*. New York: IEEE Press, 1998.

Lederer, Laura, ed. *Take Back the Night: Women on Pornography*. New York: Morrow, 1980.

Leff, Leonard J., and Jerold L. Simmons. *The Dame in the Kimono: Hollywood, Censorship, and the Production Code from the 1920s to the 1960s*. New York: Grove Weidenfeld, 1990.

Lewis, Jon. *Hollywood v. Hard Core: How the Struggle over Censorship Saved the Modern Film Industry*. New York: New York University Press, 2000.

Lewis, Peter H. "Business Technology: Advances in Film; Low-Budget Movies Get a High Gloss." *New York Times*, Feb. 11, 1987, D6.

"Librarians in Court, Again" (editorial). *Washington Post*, Feb. 26, 1991, A20.

Liebert, Robert M., and Joyce Sprafkin. *The Early Window: Effects of Television on Children and Youth*. New York: Pergamon Press, 1988.

Linz, Daniel, Barbara Wilson, and Edward Donnerstein. "Sexual Violence in the Mass Media: Legal Solutions, Warnings, and Mitigation through Education." *Journal of Social Issues* 48, no. 1 (Spring 1992): 145–71.

Lippert, Barbara. "Bear Trap: Coke's Cuddly Mascots Are Fair Game for Oliver Stone's 'Killers'" (critique). *Adweek*, Sept. 5, 1994.

Liptak, Adam. "Is Litigation the Best Way to Tame New Technology?" *New York Times*, Sept. 2, 2000, B9.

——— "When Is a Fake Too Real? It's Virtually Uncertain." *New York Times*, Jan. 28, 2001, sec. 4 (Week in Review), p. 3.

"The Little Man Who's Always There." *Time* 83, no. 14 (April 3, 1964), 25–6.

"Local News in Brief: City Panel Won't Try to Close Bondage Club." *Los Angeles Times*, Jan. 16, 1992, B2.

Lord, Daniel A. *Played By Ear: The Autobiography of Daniel A. Lord, S.J.* Chicago: Loyola University Press, 1955.

"A Loyal Lieutenant Views LBJ." *Newsweek* 66 (July 12, 1965), 16–17.

Lubell, Peter D. "Digital Cinema Is for Reel: Digital Projection Works, But It's Not at a Theater Near You – Yet." *Scientific American* 283, no. 5 (Nov. 2000), 70–1.

Lucas, George. Interview by Benjamin Bergery, edited by Rachael K. Bosley). In "Digital Cinema, By George." *American Cinematographer* 82, no. 9 (September 2001): 66–75.

Lyle, Jack. [1972]. "Television in Daily Life: Patterns of Use Overview." *Television and Social Behavior: Reports and Papers. Volume IV: Television in Day-to-Day Life: Patterns of Use: A Technical Report to the Surgeon General's Scientific Advisory Committee on Television and Social Behavior.* ed. Eli A. Rubinstein, George A. Comstock, and John P. Murray, eds., 1–32. Rockville, MD: National Institute of Mental Health, [1972].

Lyman, Rick. "Film's Digital Potential Has Hollywood on Edge." *New York Times,* Dec. 20, 1999, C41.

"Hollywood Balks at High-Tech Sanitizers: Some Video Customers Want Tamer Films, and Entrepreneurs Rush to Comply." *New York Times,* Sept. 20, 2002, B1, B5.

"Hollywood Writing Its Script for Senate Hearings Sequel." *New York Times,* Sept. 24, 2000, A26.

"A Monument to the Filmless Future." *New York Times,* March 1, 2001, B1, B10.

"New Digital Cameras Poised to Jolt World of Filmmaking." *New York Times,* Nov. 19, 1999, A1, C5.

"Revolt in the Den: DVD Has the VCR Headed to the Attic." *New York Times,* Aug. 26, 2002, A1, A13.

Lynes, Russell. "Channel 13 in Biz." *Harper's Magazine* 225 (Sept. 1962), 26, 28–9.

Lynn, Barry W. *Polluting the Censorship Debate: A Summary and Critique of the Final Report of the Attorney General's Commission on Pornography.* [Washington, DC]: American Civil Liberties Union, 1986.

Lyons, Charles. *The New Censors: Movies and the Culture Wars.* Philadelphia: Temple University Press, 1997.

Maguire, Charles M. *Oral History Interviews with Charles M. Maguire: I, II, III* (interviewed by Dorothy Pierce McSweeny). Oral History Collection, Lyndon Baines Johnson Library, Austin, TX, 1969.

Malamuth, Neil M., and Ed Donnerstein. "The Effects of Aggressive-Pornographic Mass Media Stimuli." In *Advances in Experimental Social Psychology,* ed. Leonard Berkowitz 15: 104–30. New York: Academic Press, 1982.

Malamuth, Neil. "Testimony." *Meese Commission Hearings,* Sept. 11, 1985, Box 2, Records of the Attorney General's Commission on Pornography, RG 60, NARA 2.

Maljack Productions, Inc. v. Motion Picture Association of America. 1990, LEXIS 13284 (Civil Action No. 90-1121). 1990 U.S. Dist. LEXIS 13284 (Oct. 3, 1990) (Civil Action No. 90-1121) // 311 U.S. App. D.C. 224; 52 F. 3d 373; 1995 U.S. App. LEXIS 9675 (April 28, 1995) (No. 93-7244).

Maljack Productions, Inc. v. Motion Picture Association of America. LEXIS 9675. 311 U.S. App. D.C. 224; 52 F. 3d 373; 1995 U.S. App.

Manovich, Lev. *The Language of New Media.* Cambridge, MA: MIT Press, 2001.

Manzano, Roberto J. "Supervisors Disband Pornography Panel." *Los Angeles Times,* Feb. 21, 2001, B5.

Maraniss, David, and Loren Jenkins. "Pope Asks Entertainers, Media to Be Forces for 'Great Good.'" *Washington Post,* Sept. 16, 1987, A8.

Marlow, Eugene, and Eugene Secunda. *Shifting Time and Space: The Story of Videotape*. Westport, CT: Praeger, 1991.

Marriott, Michel. "Digital Projectors Use Flashes of Light to Paint a Movie." *New York Times*, May 27, 1999, D7.

"If Only DeMille Had Owned a Desktop; New Low-Cost Camera and Software Put Filmmaking within Reach of Digital Auteurs." *New York Times*, Jan. 7, 1999, E1, E5.

Maslin, Janet. "Is NC-17 an X in a Clean Raincoat?" *New York Times*, Oct. 21, 1990, sec. 2 (Arts and Leisure), p. 1.

Mathews, Anna Wilde. "Cinema's Digital Divide: Who Will Pay for Next Wave of Theater Technology? 'Star Wars' Forces the Issue." *Wall Street Journal*, March 28, 2002, B1, B3.

Mathews, Jack. "Fanfare; On the Movies: The Politics of PG, PG-13, R and NC-17." *Newsday*, May 8, 1994, 4.

"NC-17: A Commentary on Controversies Past and Future." *Los Angeles Times*, Sept. 22, 1991 (Calendar), p. 19.

"Oct. 3 Marks the Spot for Movie Showdown." *Los Angeles Times*, Sept. 15, 1990, F1.

"Top Directors Join New Drive to Overhaul X." *Los Angeles Times*, July 5, 1990, F7.

"'Mature' Films % Jump in 1968." *Hollywood Reporter*, July 2, 1968.

McDaniel, Ann. "A Salvo in the Porn War." *Newsweek*, July 21, 1986, 18.

McDougal, Dennis. *The Last Mogul: Lew Wasserman, MCA, and the Hidden History of Hollywood*. New York: Crown Publishers, 1998.

McDowell, Edwin. "Some Say Meese Report Rates an 'X.'" *New York Times*, Oct. 21, 1986, C13.

McGee, Jim. "U.S. Crusade against Pornography Tests the Limits of Fairness." *Washington Post*, Jan. 11, 1993, A1.

"U.S. Reviews Reagan-Bush Obscenity Tactic; Justice Department May End Multiple Prosecutions of Pornographers." *Washington Post*, Nov. 24, 1993, A1.

McKay, H. B., and D. J. Dolff. "The Impact of Pornography: A Decade of Literature." 1984. Folder 22, Box 70, RG 60, RAGCP-NARA 2.

McLeod, Jack. E-mail to author, Aug. 30, 2004.

McLuhan, Marshall. *Understanding Media: The Extensions of Man*. New York: McGraw-Hill, 1964.

McManus, Michael J. "Introduction." In United States Attorney General's Commission on Pornography, *Final Report of the Attorney General's Commission on Pornography*, ix–l. Nashville, TN: Rutledge Hill Press, 1986.

McPherson, Harry. *Oral History Interview of Harry McPherson: II, III* (interviewed by T. H. Baker). Oral History Collection, Lyndon Baines Johnson Library, Austin, TX, 1968. http://www.lbjlib.utexas.edu/johnson/archives.hom/oralhistory.hom.

Mead, Margaret. "Can We Protect Children from Pornography." *Redbook* 138 (March 1972), 74–80.

Media Awareness Network. "Entertainment Software Rating Board (ESRB)." http://www.media-awareness.ca/eng/indus/games/esrb.htm (accessed Dec. 16, 2002).

Medved, Michael. *Hollywood vs. America: Popular Culture and the War on Traditional Values*. New York: HarperCollins Publishers, 1992.

Mehren, Elizabeth. "A Tiny Firm Will Publish Meese Commission Report." *Los Angeles Times*, Aug. 15, 1986, sec. 5 (View), p. 1.

Memoirs v. Massachusetts [A Book Named "John Cleland's Memoirs of a Woman of Pleasure" et al. v. Attorney General of Massachusetts] (*Memoirs v. Massachusetts*) 383 U.S. 413 (1966).

Merzer, Martin. "Self-Appointed Censors on Crusade." *Houston Chronicle*, Oct. 5, 1986.

Michelson, Peter. *Aesthetics of Pornography*. [New York]: Herder and Herder, 1971.

Mifflin, Lawrie. "Groups Strike Agreement to Add TV Rating Specifics." *New York Times*, July 10, 1997, A12.

"Industry Leaders Unveil Technique for Ratings of TV; Critics Are Unmollified; Some Popular Programs Might Be Labeled 'Over 14,' but Defining News Is Issue." *New York Times*, Dec. 2, 1996, A1, A12.

"TV Industry Vows Fight to Protect New Ratings Plan." *New York Times*, Dec. 13, 1996, A1.

Mill, John Stuart. *On Liberty*. Boston: Ticknor and Fields, 1863.

Miller v. California 413 U.S. 15 (1973).

Miller, Frank. *Censored Hollywood: Sex, Sin and Violence on Screen*. Atlanta: Turner Publishing, 1994.

Miller, J. Michael, ed. and intro. *The Encyclicals of John Paul II*. Huntington, IN: Our Sunday Visitor, 1996.

Encyclical letter *Sollicitudo Rei Socialis* of the Supreme Pontiff John Paul II for the Twentieth Anniversary of *Populorum Progressio*, Dec. 30, 1987 (publ. Feb. 19, 1988), 443.

Encyclical letter *Redemptoris Missio* of the Supreme Pontiff John Paul II on the Permanent Validity of the Church's Missionary Mandate (Dec. 7, 1990), 525–27.

Encyclical letter *Centesimum Annus*. Addressed by the Supreme Pontiff John Paul II to His Venerable Brothers in the Episcopate, the Priests and Deacons, Families of Men and Women Religious, All the Christian Faithful, and to All Men and Women of Good Will on the Hundredth Anniversary of *Rerum Novarum*, May 1991, 631.

Encyclical letter *Evangelium Vitae*. Addressed by the Supreme Pontiff John Paul II to the Bishops, Priests, and Deacons, Men and Women Religious, Lay Faithful, and All People of Good Will on the Value and Inviolability of Human Life, March 25, 1995, 792–892.

Milton, John. *Areopagitica*. Ed. Edward Arber. Winsminster: A. Constable, 1899.

Mitchell, Elvis. "Everyone's a Film Geek Now." *New York Times*, Aug. 17, 2003, sec. 2 (Arts & Leisure), pp. 1, 15.

Mitchell, Sean. "The X Rating Gets Its Day in Court." *Los Angeles Times*, June 21, 1990, F1, F6–F8.

Mitchell, William J. *The Reconfigured Eye: Visual Truth in the Postphotographic Era*. Cambridge, MA: MIT Press, 1994.

Molotsky, Irvin. "Hearing on Rock Lyrics." *New York Times*, Sept. 20, 1985, C8.

Monaghan, Peter. "Controlling TV Access: The Scientist Behind the V-Chip." *Chronicle of Higher Education*, Nov. 21, 1997, A9.

Money, J., and R. Athanasiou. "Pornography – Review and Bibliographic Annotations." *American Journal of Obstetrics and Gynecology* 115 (1973): 130–46.

Monroe, Eason. "Introduction." In *Illustrated Presidential Report of the Commission on Obscenity and Pornography*, ed. Earl Kemp, 7–8. San Diego, CA: Greenleaf Classics, 1970.

Moos, Rudolf H. "The Effects of Pornography: A Review of the Findings of the Obscenity and Pornography Commission." *Comments on Contemporary Psychiatry* 1 (1972): 123–31.

"Morning Report: Movies." *Los Angeles Times*, July 13, 1987, sec. 6 (Calendar), col. 2.

Morris, Madeline (prepared by). "Contemporary Research between 1970 through 1985 Relating to Exposure to Explicit Sexual Material and Aggression or Anti-Social Consequences [1985]." Folder 22, Box 70, RG 60, RAGCP-NARA 2.

Mosher, Donald L. "Psychological Reactions to Pornographic Films." *Technical Report of the Commission on Obscenity and Pornography: Volume VIII: Erotica and Social Behavior*, 255–312. Washington, DC: U.S. Government Printing Office, 1971.

"Sex Callousness toward Women." *Technical Report of the Commission on Obscenity and Pornography: Volume VIII: Erotica and Social Behavior*, 313–25. Washington, DC: U.S. Government Printing Office, 1971.

Mosher, Donald L., and Harvey Katz. "Pornographic Films, Male Verbal Aggression against Women, and Guilt." *Technical Report of the Commission on Obscenity and Pornography: Volume VIII: Erotica and Social Behavior*, 8: 357–79. Washington, DC: U.S. Government Printing Office, 1971.

Motion Picture Association of America. *The Green Sheet*, 1933–68.

"The Motion Picture Code and Rating Program: A System of Self Regulation." *The 1969 Film Daily Year Book of Motion Pictures*. New York: Film and Television Daily, 1969, 625–30.

"Official Code Objectives." In Stephen Farber, *Movie Rating Game*, 112–15. (Washington, DC: Public Affairs Press, 1972).

Rating Sheets. MPTRR-LC.

A Year in Review. New York, June 1968.

MPAA Worldwide Market Research. *US Economic Review.* http://www.mpaa. org./useconomicreview/ (accessed Jan. 9, 2004).

"MPAA's Jack Valenti: Parlayer of Power." *Broadcasting* 87, no. 12 (1974), 57.

Muller, Eddie, and Daniel Faris. *Grindhouse: The Forbidden World of 'Adults Only' Cinema*. New York: St. Martin's Griffin, 1996.

Murch, Walter. "The Future: A Digital Cinema of the Mind? Could Be." *New York Times*, May 2, 1999, Arts and Leisure sec., pp. 1, 35.

"Murder Gets an R; Bad Language Gets NC-17." *Time* 144 (Aug. 29, 1994), 68.

Murphy, Ryan. "Director: Don't Take *Instinct* the Wrong Way." *Miami Herald*, March 22, 1992 (Arts), I1, I5.

Myers, Nat C. "The Story of 8mm Cartridges." *American Cinematographer* 50, no. 12 (1969), 1178–9, 1225–7.

"The Nation." *Los Angeles Times*, Oct. 26, 1986, sec. 1, p. 2.

National Association of Theatre Owners, Inc. "Directors Approve Voluntary Classification at Scottsdale Meeting." *Newsletter* 3, no. 6 (1968), 1–2.

["National Commission on the Causes and Prevention of Violence"]. *St. Louis Post Dispatch*, A1, A13.

[National Research Council]. *The Digital Dilemma: Intellectual Property in the Information Age*. Washington, DC: National Academy Press, 2000.

National Research Council et al. *LC21: A Digital Strategy for the Library of Congress*. Washington, DC: National Academy Press, 2000.

National Television Violence Study: Scientific Papers, 1994–1995. Studio City, CA: Mediascope, Inc, c. 1996.

"NC-17, R or PG-13? How the MPAA Votes." *Chicago Sun-Times*, Jan. 23, 1994, Show sec., p. 4.

Negroponte, Nicholas. *Being Digital*. New York: Alfred A. Knopf, 1995.

Nichols, Peter M. "Home Video." *New York Times*, Dec. 3, 1992, C20.

Nobile, Philip. "Body and Soul." *Village Voice* 35, no. 5 (Jan. 30, 1990), 25.

Nobile, Philip. *The New Eroticism: Theories, Vogues and Canons*. New York: Random House, 1970.

Nobile, Philip, and Eric Nadler. *United States of America vs. Sex: How the Meese Commission Lied about Pornography*. New York: Minotaur Press, Ltd., a Penthouse International Company, 1986.

Norris, Clive, and Gary Armstrong. *Maximum Surveillance Society: The Rise of CCTV as Social Control*. New York: Berg, 1999.

Numungwun, Aaron Foisi. *Video Recording Technology: Its Impact on Media and Home Entertainment*. Hillsdale, NJ: Lawrence Erlbaum Associates, 1989.

O'Connor, John J. "TV: Returning 'Open Mind' Looks at Presidency." *New York Times*, Dec. 15, 1973, p. 62.

"Of Extra Glands, Giant Agony and the Grey Stone Mountain" (re Jack Valenti). *Time* 86, no. 2 (July 9, 1965), 19–20.

"Office of Film and Literature Classification (Australia)." http://www.oflc.gov.au (accessed March 17, 2005).

"Office of Film and Literature Classification (New Zealand)." http://www.censorship.govt.nz/censorship.html (accessed March 17, 2005).

Ondaatje, Michael. *The Conversations: Walter Murch and the Art of Editing Film*. New York: Alfred A. Knopf, 2002.

O'Shaughnessey, Lynn. "Boycott Aimed at Stores with X-Rated Films." *Los Angeles Times*, July 12, 1987, sec. 1, p. 1.

Orth, Maureen. "The Wiz of Showbiz." *Newsweek*, Dec. 20, 1976, 65–6, 68.

O'Toole, Laurence. *Pornocopia: Porn, Sex, Technology and Desire*. London: Serpent's Tail, 1998.

Oumano, Ellen. *Film Forum: Thirty-Five Top Filmmakers Discuss Their Craft*. New York: St. Martin's Press, 1985.

Paik, Haejung, and George Comstock. "The Effects of Television Violence on Antisocial Behavior: A Meta-Analysis." *Communication Research* 21, no. 4 (1994): 516–46.

Pardes, Herbert. "Foreword." In *Television and Behavior: Ten Years of Scientific Progress and Implications for the Eighties. Volume I: Summary Report* (2 volumes), eds. David Pearl, Lorraine Bouthilet, and Joyce Lazar. Washington, DC: U.S. Government Printing Office, 1982.

Paris Adult Theatre I v. Slaton. 413 U.S. 49 (1973).

Paul VI, Pope. *Humanae Vitae.* Encyclical of Pope Paul VI on the Regulation of Birth, July 25, 1968. In *The Papal Encyclicals, 1958–1981,* ed. Claudia Carlen, 5:223–36. Raleigh, NC: McGrath Publishing Company, 1981.

"Penthouse Fights Moral Majority." *Financial Times* (London), April 21, 1986, 24.

Peters, Robert. "Statement." *Meese Commission Hearings,* Oct. 16, 1985, Box 3, Records of the Attorney General's Commission on Pornography, RG 60, NARA 2.

———. "Testimony." *Meese Commission Hearings,* Oct. 16, 1985, Box 3, Records of the Attorney General's Commission on Pornography, RG 60 (Justice Dept. Records), NARA 2.

Petersen, James R. *The Century of Sex: Playboy's History of the Sexual Revolution: 1900–1999.* New York: Grove Press, 1999.

Pius XII, Pope. *Miranda Prorsus*: Encyclical of Pope Pius XII on the Communications Field: Motion Pictures, Radio, Television, September 8, 1957. In *The Papal Encyclicals, 1939–1958,* ed. Claudia Carlen, 4:347–64. Raleigh, NC: McGrath Publishing Company, 1981.

"The Playboy Philosopher." *Newsweek,* Aug. 4, 1986, 3, 50.

"Playboy Sues Meese, Porn Panel, Cite 'Blacklist.'" *Adweek,* May 26, 1986, Southeast Edition sec. (online ed.).

Plummer, William. "Sex Charges Pit Four Young Men against the Revered Founder of Covenant House." *People's Weekly,* 33 Feb. 26, 1990, 38–40.

"Pornography: Smut City." *The Economist,* Sept. 23, 1989, 28 (p. 58, UK ed.).

Postman, Neil. *Amusing Ourselves to Death: Public Discourse in the Age of Show Business.* New York: Penguin Books, 1986.

Preminger, Otto. Interview with Otto Preminger, September 1958. Popular Arts Project Series, ser. I, vol. 4, pt. 2. Columbia Oral History Collection, Butler Library, Columbia University, New York.

———. *Reminiscences of Otto Preminger* (Sept. 14, 1971). Hollywood Film Industry Oral History Project, Columbia Oral History Collection, Butler Library, Columbia University, New York.

"Presidency: Revolving Door at 1600." *Newsweek* 67 (May 9, 1966), 26–7.

Prince, Stephen. "The Aesthetic of Slow-Motion Violence in the Films of Sam Peckinpah." In *Screening Violence,* ed. and intro. Stephen Prince, 175–201. New Brunswick, NJ: Rutgers University Press, 2000.

———. "Graphic Violence in the Cinema: Origins, Aesthetic Design, and Social Effects." In *Screening Violence,* ed. and intro. Stephen Prince, 1–44. New Brunswick, NJ: Rutgers University Press, 2000.

A New Pot of Gold: Hollywood Under the Electronic Rainbow, 1980–1989. New York: Charles Scribner's Sons, 2000.

Savage Cinema: Sam Peckinpah and the Rise of Ultraviolent Movies. Austin: University of Texas Press, 1998.

ed. and intro. *Screening Violence.* New Brunswick, NJ: Rutgers University Press, 2000d.

"True Lies: Perceptual Realism, Digital Images, and Film Theory." *Film Quarterly* 49, no. 3 (Spring 1996): 27–38.

"Professor at Rutgers New Film-Rating Chief." *New York Times,* July 11, 1974, 24.

Puig, Claudia. "*Showgirls* and NC-17: Grin and Bare It...." *Los Angeles Times,* Sept. 16, 1995 (Calendar), F1.

"*Showgirls* May Help Give NC-17 Releases a Leg Up...." *Los Angeles Times,* Oct. 10, 1995 (Calendar), F1.

Pule, Amy. "Board to Seek Closure of Club Chateau." *Los Angeles Times,* Dec. 11, 1991 (Metro), B3.

Putnam, Robert D. *Bowling Alone: The Collapse and Revival of American Community.* New York: Simon & Schuster, 2000.

Radnitz, Robert. "Counterpunch: It's Time to Eliminate the Present Movie Rating System." *Los Angeles Times,* July 23, 1990, F5.

Raines, Howell. "Reagan Calls New Movies Too Risqué." *New York Times,* Jan. 28, 1982, B8.

Randall, Richard S. "Censorship." In *The Miracle to Deep Throat: The American Film Industry,* rev. ed., ed. Tino Balio, 510–36. Madison: University of Wisconsin Press, 1976.

Censorship of the Movies: The Social and Political Control of a Mass Medium. Madison: University of Wisconsin Press, 1968.

"Classification by the Motion Picture Industry." *Technical Report of The Commission on Obscenity and Pornography. Volume V: Societal Control Mechanisms,* 219–92. Washington, DC: U.S. Government Printing Office, [1971].

Freedom and Taboo: Pornography and the Politics of a Self Divided. Berkeley: University of California Press, 1989.

"Ratings for Video Games." *New York Times,* Jan. 4, 1994, D11.

"Reagan Signs Two Laws to Combat Pornography." *New York Times,* June 27, 1969, 42.

Reagan, Ronald, with Richard G. Hubler. *Where's the Rest of Me?* New York: Duell, Sloan and Pearce, 1965.

Reagan, Ronald. "Excerpts from President's Address." *New York Times,* March 7, 1984, A20.

"Religion Briefs: Billy Graham Says He Will Not See 'Last Temptation,' Calls It Sacrilegious." *Los Angeles Times,* Sept. 17, 1988, sec. 2 (Metro), p. 7.

"Revised Code – Approved Pix Up First 6 Months of 68." *Variety,* July 2, 1968.

Rich, Frank. "Naked Capitalists." *New York Times Magazine,* May 20, 2001, 51-6, 80, 82, 92.

Richter, Paul. "Thrifty Drug to Quit Selling Adult Magazines: Publishers Say U.S. Panel May Have Sparked Recent Decisions by Retailers." *Los Angeles Times,* May 2, 1986, sec. 4 (Business), p. 1.

Ripston, Ramona, and Allan Parachini. "Counterpunch: MPAA's Big Chance to
    Change." *Los Angeles Times*, July 18, 1994, F3.
"Ritter Probe Ends." *Christian Century* 107 (May 9, 1990), 487.
"Ritter Resigns." *Christian Century* 107 (March 14, 1990), 273.
Ritter, Bruce. "Nonviolent Sexually Explicit Material and Sexual Violence." *Final
    Report* (1986), 523–34.
    "Pornography and Privacy," *Final Report* (1986), 518–23.
    "Statement of Father Bruce Ritter." *Final Report* (1986), 509–17.
Roberts, Charles. *LBJ's Inner Circle*. New York: Delacorte Press, 1965.
Roberts, Donald F., Lisa Henriksen, and Peter G. Christenson. "Substance
    Use in Popular Movies and Music." http://www.mediacampaign.org/
    publications/movies/movie_partI.html (accessed 2005).
Rochlin, Gene I. *Trapped in the Net: The Unanticipated Consequences of Com-
    puterization*. Princeton, NJ: Princeton University Press, 1997.
Rohter, Larry. "A 'No Children' Category to Replace the 'X' Rating." *New York
    Times*, Sept. 27, 1990, A1.
[*Rolling Stone*] (online). "Review, *Natural Born Killers*." http://www.rollingstone.
    com/mv_reviews/review.asp?mid=73132&afl=imdb (Sept. 8, 1994).
Roman, Shari. *Digital Babylon: Hollywood, Indiewood and Dogme 95*. Holly-
    wood, CA: IFILM Publishing, 2001.
Rosen, Jeffrey. *The Unwanted Gaze: The Destruction of Privacy in America*. New
    York: Random House, 2000.
Rosenbaum, David E. "Protecting Children, Tempting Pandora." *New York
    Times*, June 27, 2001, E1.
Rosenberg, Howard. "Year in Review 1997; TV's New Ratings; L for Lack of
    Interest...." *Los Angeles Times*, Dec. 21, 1997, Calendar sec., col. 6.
Rosenstiel, Thomas B., and Stephen Braun. "Entertainment: Media Leaders'
    Power Cited." *Los Angeles Times*, Sept. 16, 1987, p. 1.
Rosten, Tom. "Filmmaking without Film." *Premiere* (American Edition) 15
    (November 2001), 48–51.
Roth v. United States. 354 U.S. 476 (1957).
Rowan, David. "Games Are Getting Dirtier." *The Times* (London), Oct. 22, 2002,
    Features sec., p. 16.
Rowland, Willand D., Jr. *The Politics of Violence: Policy Uses of Communications
    Research*. Beverly Hills, CA: Sage Publications, 1983.
Rutenberg, Jim. "Few Parents Use the V-Chip, a Survey Shows." *New York Times*,
    July 25, 2001, B1, B7.
Sabin, Rob. "The Movies' Digital Future Is in Sight and It Works." *New York
    Times*, Nov. 26, 2000 (Arts and Leisure), pp. 1, 22.
    "Taking Film Out of Films." *New York Times*, Sept. 5, 1999 (Arts and Leisure),
    pp. 12, 16.
Salamon, Julie. "Looking Back at the Bonfires, Personal and Professional." *New
    York Times*, June 16, 2002, sec. 2 (Arts and Leisure), p. 28.
    "The Famous and the Witty in a Half-Century of Chats." *New York Times*,
    Nov. 5, 2003, sec. B, col. 8.
Sampson, John J. "Commercial Traffic in Sexually Oriented Materials: In the
    United States (1969–1970)." *Technical Report of The Commission on*

Obscenity and Pornography: Volume III, 3–208. Washington, DC: U.S. Government Printing Office, [1971].

Satchell, Michael. "Does Hollywood Sell Drugs to Kids?" *Parade*, July 21, 1985, 5–7.

Scannell, Nancy. "Arlington's Prosecutor Tapped for U.S. Attorney." *Washington Post*, March 29, 1986, B1.

Schaefer, Dennis, and Larry Salvato. *Masters of Light: Conversations with Contemporary Cinematographers.* Berkeley: University of California Press, 1984.

Schauer, Frederick. "Personal Statement of Commissioner Frederick Schauer." *Final Report* (1986), 534–5.

Schauer, Frederick F. *The Law of Obscenity*. Washington, DC: Bureau of National Affairs, 1976.

Schecter, Harold, and David Everitt. *Film Tricks: Special Effects in the Movies.* New York: Harlin Quist, 1980.

Schlesinger, Arthur M, Jr. "The Velocity of History." *Newsweek* 76 (July 6, 1970), 32–4.

Schmalz, Jeffrey. "Cuomo Sees Peril in Picking Judges on Ideology Basis." *New York Times*, Aug. 12, 1986, A1.

Schultz, Gladys Denny. "What Sex Offenders Say about Pornography." *Reader's Digest*, July 1971, 53–7.

Schumach, Murray. *The Face on the Cutting Room Floor: The Story of Movie and Television Censorship.* New York: Da Capo Press, 1964.

Scot, Jeffry. "Wildmon, NFD Finally Get Some Respect." *Adweek* (Southeast Edition), June 30, 1986.

Scott, Janny, and John Dart. "Bundy's Tape Fuels Dispute on Porn, Antisocial Behavior." *Los Angeles Times*, Jan. 30, 1989, sec. 1, p. 1.

"7-Elevens Drawn Back to 'Playboy' by Vanna Issue." *Adweek*, April 13, 1987, sec. National Newswire.

Seldes, Gilbert. "Incitement to Riot." *Saturday Review* 40 (Oct. 5, 1957), 24.

Sennott, Charles M. *Broken Covenant: The Story of Father Bruce Ritter's Fall from Grace – How Power, Politics, and Sex Rocked the Foundation of the Sprawling Covenant House Charity.* New York: Simon & Schuster, 1992.

"Sex Reports on Priest Called Confirmed; Inquiry: Covenant House Says Probe Found Evidence of Misconduct by Father Ritter, Founder of Shelter for Runaways. He Has Denied Wrongdoing." *Los Angeles Times,* Aug. 4, 1990, A21.

Shannon, William V. "The Death of Time." *New York Times*, July 8, 1971, 35.

Shatner, William. "Testimony." *U.S. Senate Hearings*, 1985, 113–17.

Sheldon, Andrea. "Statement of Andrea Sheldon, Executive Director, Traditional Values Coalition." *U.S. Senate Hearings*, 1997, 257–67.

Shelov, Steven P. et al. American Academy of Pediatrics Committee on Communications. "Children, Adolescents, and Television." *Pediatrics* 96, no. 4 (1995): 786–7.

American Academy of Pediatrics Committee on Communications. "Media Violence." *Pediatrics* 95, no. 6 (1995): 949–51.

Sherwood, Robert. "Will Hays Unhappy Czar of Much-Buffeted Films." *Kalamazoo [MI] Gazette*, [Oct. 6, 1929(?)].

Shiver, Jr., Jube. "Hollywood Sells Kids on Violence, FTC Says; Report: Inquiry Finds Film, Music and Video Industries Actively Market Adult-Themed Material to Children." *Los Angeles Times*, Sept. 11, 2000, A1.

Shurlock, Geoffrey. *Oral History with Geoffrey Shurlock*. Los Angeles, and Beverly Hills, CA: American Film Institute; Center for Advanced Film Studies, 1975.

Siepmann, Charles A. *Television and Education in the United States*. Paris: UNESCO, 1952.

Signorielli, Nancy, and George Gerbner, comps. *Violence and Terror in the Mass Media: An Annotated Bibliography*. Westport, CT: Greenwood Press, 1988.

Simons, G. L. *Pornography without Prejudice: A Reply to Objectors*. London: Abelard-Schuman, 1972.

Sitomer, Curtis J. "Battle Lines Are Drawn over US Pornography Study." *Christian Science Monitor*, July 8, 1986, 3.

Skinner, James M. *The Cross and the Cinema: The Legion of Decency and the National Office for Motion Pictures, 1933–1970*. Westport, CT: Praeger, 1993.

Sklar, Robert. *Movie-Made America: A Social History of American Movies*. New York: Random House, 1975.

Smith, Alvy Ray. "Digital Humans Wait in the Wings: Characters, Scenes and Entire Movies Have Been Crafted Digitally...." *Scientific American* 283, no. 5 (Nov. 2000), 72–8.

Smith, Anthony. *The Shadow in the Cave: The Broadcaster, His Audience, and the State*. Urbana: University of Illinois Press, 1973.

Smith, Margaret Chase. "My One Year War for Better Movies." Margaret Chase Smith Papers, Margaret Chase Smith Library, The Northwood Institute, Skowhegan, ME.

   Radio interview. Margaret Chase Smith Papers, Margaret Chase Smith Library, The Northwood Institute, Skowhegan, ME, 1967.

   "'Sick Movies' – A Menace to Children." *Reader's Digest*, December 1967, 139–42.

   "Statement." *U.S. Senate Hearings, 1968*, 3–6.

Spencer, Scott. "Lights! Camera! Rapture! The Christian Thriller Heads for the Cineplex." *The New Yorker*, Sept. 10, 2001, 105–9.

Sperling, Godfrey. "Remembering LBJ, the Masterful Schemer." *Christian Science Monitor*, March 4, 2002, 9.

Spigel, Lynn, and Michael Curtin, eds. *The Revolution Wasn't Televised: Sixties Television and Social Conflict*. New York and London: Routledge, 1997.

Stafford, Charles. "Pope Reminds the Media to Bear Good, Evil in Mind." *St. Petersburg Times*, Sept. 16, 1987, A1.

Stammer, Larry B., and David J. Fox. "Mahony Urges 'Human Values' in Films, TV." *Los Angeles Times*, Oct. 1, 1992, sec. 1, p. 1.

Statement of Jerry Weintraub and William Friedkin Relative to "Cruising" and Its R Rating [1980?]. Exhibit 80-11, attached to "RDH Pre-Oral History Memorandum to Chuck Champlin for 1980," Box 1, RDH-COHC-BL.

Statement of William Friedkin and Jerry Weintraub Responding to Charges against Them Made by MPAA and the Rating Board Relative to "Cruising" and Its "R" Rating. [1980?]Exhibit 80-12? Attached to "RDH Pre-Oral History Memorandum to Chuck Champlin for 1980," Box 1, RDH-COHC-BL.

Steinem, Gloria. "Pornography – Not Sex But the Obscene Use of Power." *Ms.* 6, no. 2 (Aug. 1977), 1, 43–4.

Sterling, Christopher H., and Timothy R. Haight. *The Mass Media: Aspen Institute Guide to Communication Industry Trends.* New York: Praeger Publishers, 1978.

Sterngold, James. "A Preview of Coming Attractions; Digital Projectors Could Bring Drastic Changes to Movie Industry." *New York Times*, Feb. 22, 1999 (Business Day), C1, C2.

Stone, Lawrence. "Statement of the American Academy of Child and Adolescent Psychiatry." *U.S. Senate Hearings,* 1997, 273–8.

Strauss, Gary. "Glickman Takes Director's Chair at Film Lobbying Group." *USA Today*, July 2, 2004, B1.

[Surgeon General's Report on TV Violence]. *Indianapolis Star*, Sept. 4, 1971, 1.

Suro, Roberto. "The Papal Visit; Pope Preaches Sanctity of Truth in a City of Illusions." *New York Times*, Sept. 16, 1987, A24.

Svetkey, Benjamin. "Sex, Violence and Movie Ratings: Why the System Doesn't Work." *Entertainment Weekly*, Nov. 25, 1994, 28.

Talmadge, Candace, and Betsy Sharkey. "Universal Drops L&H Amid Movie Flap." *Adweek*, Sept. 12, 1988 (Southwest Edition).

Taub, Eric A. "Shooting 'Star Wars,' Bit by Bit." *New York Times*, May 23, 2002, E8.

Tavris, Carol. "The Illogic of Linking Porn and Rape: Meese Commission Overlooks Proper Reasoning in Findings." *Los Angeles Times*, July 7, 1986, sec. 2 (Metro), p. 5.

Tebbel, John. "The Quiet Offset Revolution." *Saturday Review*, Dec. 9, 1961, 60–1.

Television Information Office. "The New Television Pressure Groups: A Perspective on the Drive against Diversity." New York: Television Information Office, [1981], WHORM: Subject Files, Box 24, Ronald Reagan Presidential Library, Simi Valley, CA.

"Tests That Pornography Fails" (editorial). *Christian Science Monitor*, July 10, 1986, 15.

"The TV Parental Guidelines: About the TV Rating and V-Chip." http://www.tvguidelines.org (accessed March 17, 2005).

"The TV Parental Guidelines: Frequently Asked Questions." http://www.tvguidelines.org/ratings.asp (accessed March 17, 2005).

Thiel, Paul. "Gray & Co. Hired to Rebut Meese Panel." *Washington Post*, July 28, 1986, Washington Business sec., p. 5.

Thomas, Christopher. "Spectrum: The White House versus Penthouse." *The Times* (London), July 14, 1986.

Thompson, Bill. *Soft Core: Moral Crusades against Pornography in Britain and America.* London: Cassell, 1994.

Thompson, Tracy. "Part of Child Pornography Law Struck Down." *Washington Post*, May 17, 1989, A19.

Thornburgh, Dick, and Herbert S. Lin, eds. *Youth, Pornography and the Internet.* Washington, DC: National Academy Press, 2002.

Tilton-Durfee, Deanne. "Statement of Deanne Tilton-Durfee." *Final Report* (1986), 536–40.

"A Top Aide's Close-Up of a President Who Never Says 'I'm Tired.'" *U.S. News & World Report* 59, no. 2 (July 12, 1965), 22.

Toffler, Alvin. "Coping with Future Shock." *Playboy* 17, no. 3 (March 1970), 88–90, 96, 174–5.

    "Future Shock." *Playboy* 17, no. 2 (Feb. 1970), 94–8, 202–4, 206, 208.

    The Third Wave. New York : William Morrow and Company, 1980.

Toplin, Robert Brent, ed. *Oliver Stone's USA: Film, History, and Controversy.* Lawrence: University Press of Kansas, 2000.

"Toughened Child Pornography Bill Signed by Reagan." *Los Angeles Times*, Nov. 8, 1986, sec. 2, p. 3.

Trend, David. "Merchants of Death: Media Violence and American Empire." *Harvard Educational Review* 73, no. 3 (Fall 2003): 285–308.

Trento, Susan B. *The Power House: Robert Keith Gray and the Selling of Access and Influence in Washington.* New York: St. Martin's Press, 1992.

Trumpbour, John. *Selling Hollywood to the World: U.S. and European Struggles for Mastery of the Global Film Industry, 1920–1950.* Cambridge: Cambridge University Press, 2002.

Turan, Kenneth, and Stephen F. Zito. *Sinema: American Pornographic Films and the People Who Make Them.* New York: Praeger, 1974.

"TV Ratings." *Tampa Tribune*, July 11, 1997, sec. Nation/World, p. 6.

United States v. Paramount Pictures, Inc. 334 U.S. 131 (1948).

"Universal Pictures to Release "Henry & June" as First Film with NC-17 Rating." *PR Newswire*, Sept. 26, 1990.

"Valenti Exits White House for MPAA Post." *Broadcasting: The Business Weekly of Television and Radio* 70 (1966), 38–9.

[Valenti quoted]. *Washington Post*, Oct. 5, 1968, 29.

"Valenti Seeks VCR Collaboration." *Los Angeles Times*, Jan. 9, 1989, A3.

Valenti, Jack. "Art, Smut and Movie Ratings: We Don't Need a New Category between R and X." *Washington Post*, May 6, 1990, B7.

    "A Badge of Honor." *The 1969 Film Daily Year Book of Motion Pictures*, 78. 51st ed. New York: Film and Television Daily, 1969.

    "The Case for a Six-Year Presidency." *Saturday Review* 51 (Aug. 3, 1968), 13, 32.

    "Critics Maul TV Rating System, Ignore Its Virtues of Simplicity." *The Capital Times* (Madison, WI), Jan. 8, 1997, A11.

    "Film-Making behind the Iron Curtain: The Motion Picture Bridge between East and West." *Saturday Review* 50 (Dec. 23, 1967), 8–9, 39–40.

    "Francis Bacon – The Glory and the Shame." *Saturday Review* 51 (Feb. 17, 1968), 22–3.

    "In Today's Politics, a Seasoned Ham Brings Home the Bacon." *Los Angeles Times*, Jan. 19, 1989, sec. 2 (Op-Ed), p. 7.

"It's Lights, Camera, Politics; The Two Parties Have Merged with Hollywood to Give Audiences (Voters) the Most Favorable Take on Their Stars." *Los Angeles Times*, Sept. 6, 1996, 9.

[Valenti, Jack]. MPAA. "Motion Picture Association of America: 1968– A Year of New Developments." *The 1969 Film Daily Year Book of Motion Pictures*. New York: Film and Television Daily, 1969, 616–25.

"A Movie Czar Prepares to Roll the Credits; Jack Valenti Rates His 38-Year Career in Hollywood as AE – Always Exciting." *Los Angeles Times*, Aug. 2, 2004, B11.

"Movie Rating System Is Working Fine" (guest column). *USA Today*, July 26, 1990, News sec.

"The Nation: Why Assault after Assault Can't Kill Rating System." *Los Angeles Times*, Nov. 20, 1994, 2.

Oral History Interview of Jack Valenti: I (interviewed by T. H. Baker). Oral History Collection, Lyndon Baines Johnson Library, Austin, TX, 1969.

Oral History Interview of Jack Valenti: II, III, IV, V (interviewed by Joe B. Frantz). Oral History Collection, Lyndon Baines Johnson Library, Austin, TX, 1969.

"Perspective on Violence in Films: An Open Letter to Bob Dole Indicting the Industry for the Excesses of a Few Is Like Indicting All Public Servants for the Few Who Break the Public Trust." *Los Angeles Times*, June 6, 1995, B7.

Report on the Worldwide Operation of Our Film Piracy Program, Folder: "Motion Picture Association of America: Rating Sheets." In Motion Picture and Television Reading Room, Library of Congress, Washington, DC.

"The Simpler the Better." *USA Today*, Dec. 20, 1996, A22.

"Statement." *U.S. Senate Hearings*, June 11, 1968, 45–6.

"Statement before the National Commission on the Causes and Prevention of Violence, Dec. 19, 1968." In Stephen Prince, ed., *Screening Violence*, 62–75. New Brunswick, NJ: Rutgers University Press, 2000.

"Statement: The Movie Rating System – How It Began – Its Purpose – How It Works – The Public Reaction." *U.S. House Hearings*, 1977, 19–24.

"Statement: TV Parental Guidelines Helping Parents Monitor the TV Watching of Their Young Children, Simply, Easily, Efficiently." *U.S. Senate Hearings*, 1997, 98–107.

"Statement." *U.S. House Hearings*, April 12, 1982, 17–115.

"Statement." *U.S. Senate Hearings*, April 21, 1982, 461–501.

"Statement." *U.S. Senate Hearings*, 1985, 87–107.

"Statement." *U.S. Senate Hearings*, 1997, 95–108.

"The Television Ratings System Is Simple and User-Friendly; TV: More Complex Categories Would Have Discouraged Parents from Using the Guidelines and Newspapers." *Los Angeles Times*, Jan. 3, 1997, B9.

"Traveling That Sweet Road That Leads to Success." Address to his friends and colleagues at ShoWest, Las Vegas, Nevada, March 6, 2001. (www.mpaa.org/jack/2001_03_06b.htm).

"Testimony." *Meese Commission Hearings*, Oct. 17, 1985, Box 4, Records of the Attorney General's Commission on Pornography, RG 60, NARA 2.

"Testimony." *U.S. House Hearings,* April 12, 1982, 4–16.

"Testimony." *U.S. Senate Hearings,* April 21, 1982, 457–61.

"Testimony." *U.S. House Hearings,* March 24, July 21, 1977, 1–62, 210–23.

"TV Ratings Are Easy, Efficient. *Cleveland Plain Dealer,* Feb. 26, 1997, B11.

A Very Human President. New York: W. W. Norton & Company, 1975.

"Voltaire's Timeless Eminence." *Saturday Review* 50 (March 11, 1967), 27, 138–9.

"Wishful Thinking?" *Columbian* [Vancouver, British Columbia], April 2, 1995, 1.

Vaughn, Stephen. "Morality and Entertainment: The Origins of the Motion Picture Production Code." *Journal of American History* 77, no. 1 (1990): 39–65.

ed. *New Communication Technologies: Their History and Social Influence: An Annotated Bibliography.* Madison: University of Wisconsin Libraries System, 2003.

Ronald Reagan in Hollywood: Movies and Politics. Cambridge: Cambridge University Press, 1994.

"Very Educational." *Newsweek* 61 (April 29, 1963), 86.

"View in Privacy of Home; Women Form Big Market for Hard-Core Porn Tapes." *Los Angeles Times,* Dec. 22, 1985, Metro sec. p. 13.

Vizzard, Jack. *See No Evil: Life Inside a Hollywood Censor.* New York: Simon and Schuster, 1970.

Wall, James M. "Statement." *U.S. Senate Hearings,* 1985, 148-51.

Wallace, Amy. "Mahony Urges Film Industry to Accept Code." *Los Angeles Times,* Feb. 2, 1992, sec. A, col. 1.

Walsh, Frank. *Sin and Censorship: The Catholic Church and the Motion Picture Industry.* New Haven, CT: Yale University Press, 1996.

Wasko, Janet. *Hollywood in the Information Age: Beyond the Silver Screen.* Austin: University of Texas Press, 1994.

Wasserman, Lew. *Oral History Interview of Lew Wasserman: I* (interviewed by Joe B. Frantz). Oral History Collection, Lyndon Baines Johnson Library, 1973. http://www.lbjlib.utexas.edu/johnson/archives.hom/oralhistory.hom/.

Waxman, Sharon. "An Old Washington Hand to Succeed Valenti in Hollywood." *New York Times,* July 2, 2004, C1, C3.

Weare, Eugene [Joseph I. Breen]. "Enter: The 'Hick-Town' Parish." *America* 42 (Oct. 26, 1929), 59–61.

"Have You a Little Bolshevik in Your Home?" *America* 42 (Feb. 8, 1930), 424.

"Laymen on a College Council." *America* 42 (Feb. 22, 1930), 475–6.

Weiler, A. H. "Producer with 'X' Sues over Rating: Strick of 'Tropic of Cancer' Seeks to Ban Classfication." *New York Times,* March 10, 1970, p. 51.

Weinraub, Bernard. "The Man Who Unites the Moguls, Looking Ahead." *New York Times,* Oct. 27, 2003, B1, B6.

"Reagan Predicts Impact of Judicial Appointees." *New York Times,* Aug. 6, 1986, A13.

"Rock Lyrics Irk Reagan." *New York Times,* Oct. 10, 1985, C17.

"Violent Melodrama of a Sizzling Movie Brings Rating Battle." *New York Times,* Jan. 30, 1992, C15.

Weisl, Edwin L. Jr. *Oral History Interviews of Edwin L. Weisl, Jr.: I, II* (interviewed by Joe B. Frantz). Oral History Collection, Lyndon Baines Johnson Library, Austin, TX, 1969.

Welkos, Robert W. "Director Trims 'Basic Instinct' to Get R Rating." *Los Angeles Times*, Feb. 11, 1992 (Calendar), F1.

"Mahony to Propose New Code for Films, TV." *Los Angeles Times*, Jan. 29, 1992, (Metro), B1.

Wertham, Fredric. *Seduction of the Innocent*. New York: Rinehart & Company, 1953.

A Sign for Cain: An Exploration of Human Violence. New York: Macmillan Company, 1966.

"What TV Does to Kids." *Newsweek* 89 (Feb. 21, 1977), 62–3.

Whitman, David. "Are Reagan's New Judges Really Closet Moderates?" *Washington Post*, Aug. 9, 1987, C1.

"Who's Afraid... of Jack Valenti?" *Newsweek* 68 (July 4, 1966), 84–5.

Wicker, Tom. "Johnson's Men: 'Valuable Hunks of Humanity.'" *New York Times Magazine*, May 3, 1964, 11, 104–7.

Wilcox, Brian. "Statement of Brian Wilcox, Director, Center for Children, Families and the Law, University of Nebraska, on Behalf of the American Psychological Association." *U.S. Senate Hearings, 1997*, 268–70.

Wildmon, Don. "That's What Christians Do Now." http://www.alliance4lifemin. org/ThatswhatChristiansdonow.html (accessed March 17, 2005).

Williams, Linda. *Hard Core: Power, Pleasure, and the "Frenzy of the Visible"* Berkeley: University of California Press, 1989.

Willman, Chris. "Off-Centerpiece: Abel Ferrara: Lights! Camera! Anguish!" *Los Angeles Times*, Jan. 3, 1993 (Calendar), p. 24.

Wills, Garry. "Measuring the Impact of Erotica." *Psychology Today*, August 1977, 30–4, 74–6.

Wilson, Barbara, Daniel Linz, and Barbara Randall. "Applying Social Science Research to Film Ratings: A Shift from Offensiveness to Harmful Effects." *Journal of Broadcasting and Electronic Media* 34, no. 4 (1990): 443–68.

Wilson, John M. "Outtakes: Ahead of His Time?" *Los Angeles Times*, Aug. 5, 1990 (Calendar), p. 23.

Winston, Brian. "HDTV in Hollywood: Lights, Camera, Inaction." *Gannet Center Journal* 3, no. 3 (1989): 123–37.

Technologies of Seeing: Photography, Cinematography and Television. London: British Film Institute, 1996.

"X-Rated Motion Pictures: From Restricted Theatres and Drive-ins to the Television Screen?" *Valparaiso University Law Review* 8, no. 1(1973): 107–24.

Yardley, Jonathan. "The Porn Commission's Hidden Agenda." *Washington Post*, July 14, 1986 (Style), C2.

Yarrow, Andrew L. "Almodovar Film's X Rating Is Challenged in Lawsuit." *New York Times*, May 24, 1990, C14.

Young v. American Mini Theatres. 427 U.S. 50 (1976).

Zahn, Bob, and Brian McKerman. "Report from the Ranch: Star wars Episode II." http://216.130.185.100/Artman/publish/printer_58.Shtml. (accessed March 17, 2005).

Zeffirelli, Franco. *Franco Zeffirelli's Jesus: A Spiritual Diary* (Translated from the Italian by Willis J. Egan, S.J.). San Francisco: Harper & Row, 1984.

Ziehm, Howard. "Counterpunch: The NC-17 Movie Rating Gets an X from Director." *Los Angeles Times*, May 20, 1991 (Calendar), F3.

Zillmann, Dolf. *Connections between Sex and Aggression.* Hillsdale, NJ: Lawrence Erlbaum, 1984.

———. "Effects of Prolonged Consumption of Pornography." In *Pornography: Research Advances and Policy Considerations*, ed. Dolf Zillmann and Jennings Bryant, 127–57. Hillsdale, NJ: Lawrence Erlbaum, 1989.

———. "[Testimony]: Effects of Repeated Exposure to Nonviolent Pornography." *Meese Commission Hearings,* Sept. 11, 1985, Box 2, Records of the Attorney General's Commission on Pornography, RG 60, NARA 2.

Zillmann, Dolf, and Jennings Bryant., eds. *Pornography: Research Advances and Policy Considerations.* Hillsdale, NJ: Lawrence Erlbaum, 1989.

Zittrain, Jonathan, and Benjamin Edelman. "Documentation of Internet Filtering Worldwide." http://cyber.law.harvard.edu/filtering (accessed March 17, 2005).

Index